Feminist 1

★ ○ ☽ ★ ○ ☽ ★ ○ ☽

Feminist Fabulation

Space/Postmodern Fiction

By Marleen S. Barr

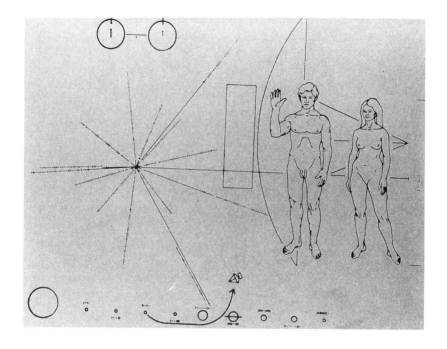

University of Iowa Press   Ψ   Iowa City

University of Iowa Press, Iowa City 52242
Copyright © 1992 by the University of Iowa Press
All rights reserved
Printed in the United States of America

Printed on acid-free paper

96 95 94 93 92 C 5 4 3 2 1

96 95 94 93 92 P 5 4 3 2 1

Library of Congress Cataloging-in-Publication Data
Barr, Marleen S.
    Feminist fabulation: space/postmodern fiction/by
Marleen S. Barr.
        p.   cm.
    Includes bibliographical references and index.
    ISBN 0-87745-376-4, ISBN 0-87745-377-2 (pbk.)
    1. Fiction—Women authors—History and
criticism.   2. Fiction—20th century—History and
criticism.   3. Science fiction—Women authors—
History and criticism.   4. Fantastic fiction—
Women authors—History and criticism.
5. Postmodernism (Literature).   6. Canon
(Literature).   7. Feminism in literature.
8. Feminism and literature.   I. Title.
PN3401.B38   1992   92-20164
809.3'0082—dc20   CIP

Title page: *Pioneer* spacecraft plaque, 1972. National
Aeronautics and Space Administration.

FOR CHERYL HERR,

FABULOUS FRIEND

Contents

★ ○ ❯ ★ ○ ❯ ★ ○ ❯

Acknowledgments

During my 1989–1990 Fulbright year, English or women's studies departments at the following universities invited me to present portions of *Feminist Fabulation*: Ben Gurion University of the Negev, Israel; University of Bologna, Italy; University of Erlangen, Germany; University of Hannover, Germany; the Hebrew University of Jerusalem, Israel; University of Kiel, Germany; University of Innsbruck, Austria; University of Stirling, Scotland; University of Strathclyde, Scotland; University of Southampton, England; University of Utrecht, Holland. I thank the colleagues and students I encountered at these universities for their insightful comments. I appreciate the funding I received from the Fulbright Commission of each country in which I lectured, especially the generous support Ulrich Littmann and Reiner Rohr of the German Fulbright Commission provided.

During my year abroad I was privileged to meet wonderful people: Monica Elbert, Herta Flor, Cornelia and Matthias Knauf, Rosemarie Overstreet, Brigitte Scheer-Schäzler, Brigitte Wenturis, and Sheila Weiss. I thank them all for their friendship and assistance.

While writing *Feminist Fabulation*, I enjoyed the community on my computer screen. I give special thanks to my e-mail cronies: Peter Bauland, Norman N. Holland, Edward James, Eric S. Rabkin, and Darko Suvin. Many a bleary-eyed moment was made better by the sight of the message that new mail had arrived.

In 1991, I was once again able to live near my oldest friends, Carol Braham and Beth Tipperman. I thank them both for encouraging me while I tackled the conclusion of this project. I look forward to the time when Carol's daughter Gail will be able to read this page and to know that "Auntie" Marleen thought of her.

The support I received from Terry Brown, Tony Distler, Minrose Gwin, and Ruth Salvaggio was very important to me.

Mary Russell Curran's copyediting expertise was invaluable. I thank Brooks Landon for the time and attention he devoted to my manuscript.

I am glad that Norris Compton Barr really understands that he is not allowed to push the computer keys. Norris and I appreciate the generosity of my parents, Roslyn and George Barr.

I thank Robert Scholes for "fabulation."

It is a special pleasure to dedicate this book to Cheryl Herr, the most fabulous friend anyone could ever hope to have.

★　○　☽　★　○　☽　★　○　☽

Preface: Having "Nunavit"

Outer space backgrounding planet earth is a recent, familiar view which allows us to see ourselves as we are seen. Yet despite this new vision, we continue to understand and project our world in terms of patriarchal images. Laurie Anderson seems to address this point in the comment she places next to the *Pioneer* spacecraft picture of a woman and a man. Anderson states, "In our country, we send pictures of people speaking our sign language in Outer Space. We are speaking our sign language in these pictures" (Anderson, 7). We are speaking our patriarchal language in this *Pioneer* picture. We are sending patriarchal images into outer space.

According to *Pioneer*'s representation of humanity, males are forward-looking and communicative while females, who are smaller than males, look toward them and do not make communicative gestures. The male appears as the dominant human norm; the female appears as subordinate to the male, the silenced Other.[1] Here is an alternative to *Pioneer*'s patriarchal story:

> A precocious land animal had evolved from one of several similar species, becoming reasonably intelligent. This animal and other larger life forms had only four limbs and there appeared to be two sexes. It had enough intelligence to launch a space vehicle carrying odd information about its planet and a small plaque to show what it looked like, with one of the larger sex making a sign of some sort with an upper limb. The creature was known to have a fear/aggression complex about its own kind, and to be terrified of anything out of its immediate experience. Any contact to be made with extreme caution, if at all. (Palmer, *Watcher*, 9)

This passage from Jane Palmer's *The Watcher*, an example of what I call feminist fabulation, describes a myth which exposes, subverts, and rewrites a patriarchal myth.

Human patriarchs say that men are superior to women; Palmer's aliens, in a different interpretation, say that all humans are dangerous land animals. Yet despite the existence of alternative viewpoints, when we, in Bachelard's words, "cover the universe with drawings we have lived" (Bachelard, 12), we paint pictures of fixed, patriarchal meaning. Bachelard discusses lived pictures in terms of space and imagination: "These drawings need not be exact. They need only to be tonalized on the mode of our inner space. But what a book would have to be written to decide all these problems! Space calls for action, and before action, the imagination is at work" (Bachelard, 12). *Feminist Fabulation: Space/Postmodern Fiction* is written to argue for respecting marginalized feminist fiction which attempts to correct patriarchy's problematic depictions of humanity. *Pioneer*'s representation of women and men exemplifies one such inexact drawing derived from the inner space of the patriarchal mind. I read the *Pioneer* picture and the sexist stories this picture represents as attempts to cover the universe with patriarchal representations and fictions we have, unfortunately, lived.

This book's "action" involves proposing a method to position

feminist imaginative works within the canon of postmodern fiction.[2] I do not wish to imply, however, that the postmodern canon
is an established and monolithic entity. Each of several prominent
theorists of postmodernism has mapped the existence of a postmodern canon; contradictory postmodern canons are still being con-
tested in critical discourse. While the specifics of the canon remain
in doubt, I want to emphasize that any conceivable canon now almost certainly excludes most of the works I champion. To make my
use of the term "postmodern canon" more persuasive, I point to
three studies typical of approaches to postmodern fiction: Linda
Hutcheon's *A Poetics of Postmodernism*, Larry McCaffery's *Postmodern Fiction*, and Brian McHale's *Postmodernist Fiction*.

McCaffery's "Bio-Bibliographical Guide" includes only ten women
writers. Fewer than ten contemporary women writers appear in the
index of McHale's book. Hutcheon, through her discussions of Margaret Atwood, Angela Carter, Maxine Hong Kingston, Toni Morrison, and Alice Walker, devotes much more attention to women than
do McCaffery and McHale. She, however, does not argue that un-
fairly marginalized feminist writers should receive more critical notice. Canon formation rises from precisely this kind of exercise of
pointing to the practices specified or implied in scholarly books.

The blindnesses of studies representing typical approaches to postmodern fiction support my thesis that the postmodern canon has
systematically excluded a wide range of important feminist writing
by dismissing it as genre fiction. Even McHale, who stresses the
connections between postmodernism and science fiction (SF), fails
to extend his valorization of SF to include feminist SF and fantasy.
As I explain throughout this study, postmodern fiction must recognize a new supergenre of women's writing—feminist fabulation—
which includes works now thought of as mainstream, SF, fantasy,
supernatural, and utopian as well as feminist texts men author. Further, critical studies should address the influence and importance of
works of feminist fabulation which have been dismissed as genre
fiction.

I am concerned with how critics represent and define postmodern
fiction and how patriarchal imperatives figure in these representations and definitions. For example, I view the *Pioneer* picture as the

postmodern age's billboard advertising stereotypical gender roles in outer space. It is a patriarchal fiction projecting a representation of ourselves to extraterrestrial aliens via a sign language which tells a story about human females. By launching this picture, patriarchy "tonalized'" (Bachelard, 12) outer space in terms of male inner space, using the patriarchal mode's inexact pictures of women. In *Feminist Fabulation* I address the problematic patriarchal master narratives the *Pioneer* drawing exemplifies. I suggest including space in the postmodern canon for the feminist imagination's rewritten patriarchal master narratives—feminist metafiction about patriarchal fiction. The canon should incorporate the pioneering feminist literary artists who sketch anew "drawings we have lived" (Bachelard, 12) and who reveal that—instead of being indelible, fixed truths— many patriarchal interpretations, drawings, and stories are myths and fictions.

The imaginative works included under the rubric feminist fabulation concern living according to alternative myths and fictions, a change which can be realized by rewriting patriarchal master narratives. *Pioneer* is a vehicle to send patriarchal myths into space; feminist fabulation is a vehicle to view feminist "space fiction" (Doris Lessing's term)—in addition to other categories of fiction written by both women and men—as a means to question and rewrite the patriarchal myths which continue, even during our postmodern era, to be given the status of master narrative. Feminist fabulation enables readers to pioneer spaces beyond patriarchal boundaries.

Feminist Fabulation is sometimes concerned with spaces in outer space. The book reflects my interest in feminist SF's critique of patriarchy and my belief that popular forms can influence cultural constructions. I examine ways in which gender issues invite a reconceptualization of contemporary literature. This reconceptualization opens new canonical space in which to address the constructed nature of patriarchal reality as well as possibilities for new feminist cultural reality. My earlier book, *Alien to Femininity*, focuses on the connections between feminist theory and feminist speculative fiction (SF, fantasy, and utopian literature). *Feminist Fabulation* builds upon these connections to approach a larger, related issue—the relationship between contemporary feminist fiction and the postmodern canon. *Feminist Fabulation* explores this issue in terms of outer space and canonical space.

As I have pointed out in many places, despite feminist speculative fiction's usefulness and importance, it is easy to dismiss this literature as inferior genre fiction justifiably positioned outside literary institutions. I now consider the term "feminist SF" to be obsolete; I situate all feminist speculative fiction within feminist fabulation, which, like Robert Scholes's "structural fabulation," encompasses many literary forms, of which SF is only one. Contemporary feminist writers transform fiction to suit themselves. In addition to works by well-known mainstream feminist novelists, I am thinking of examples of transformed genre fiction, such as Carolyn Heilbrun's feminist detective fiction (written under the pseudonym Amanda Cross), Zoë Fairbairns's feminist business world novel *Closing*, and Doris Piserchia's feminist Western *Star Rider*.[3] These are only a few of the writers who change many varieties of fiction into feminist spaces. Feminist fabulation encompasses these various fictional spaces and seeks to make a space for itself within the postmodern canon. Feminist fabulation calls for a new understanding of postmodern fiction which enables the canon to accommodate feminist difference and emphasizes that the literature which was called feminist SF is an important site of postmodern feminist difference.

My book's subtitle, *Space/Postmodern Fiction*, addresses this needed new understanding and accommodation. "Space" (i.e., expanse, area, or room) refers to location, outer space, and feminist space fiction. "Postmodern fiction" (i.e., the canon and patriarchal myth) relates to excluding feminist fiction from the canon and perpetuating prevalent patriarchal myths about women. The postmodern canon is a masculinist utopia and a "Nowhere" for feminists. Where is the place for feminist fiction within the current understanding of what constitutes canonical postmodern fiction? I think feminist fiction is positioned as a "space between," my subtitle's slash which at once attaches and detaches space from postmodern fiction. I argue that feminist fabulation, rewritten versions of patriarchal fictions (exemplified by the response of Palmer's aliens to *Pioneer*'s depiction of humanity), should be repositioned: the space between should become a space within the canon.

Throughout this study, Scholes's term "fabulation" and the insights Hélène Cixous, Linda Hutcheon, Alice Jardine, and Brian McHale generate inform my arguments about feminist fabulation. According to Cixous, to "admit that writing is precisely working (in) the in-between, inspecting the process of the same and of the other without which nothing can live, undoing the work of death—to admit this is first to want the two, as well as both, the ensemble of the one and the other, not fixed in sequences of struggle and expulsion or some other form of death but infinitely dynamized by an incessant process of exchange from one subject to another" (Cixous, 254). The notion that "writing is precisely working (in) the in-between" addresses feminist fabulation's location in the slash between space and postmodern fiction, the place where marginalized contemporary feminist fiction encounters canonical postmodern nonfeminist fiction. Feminist fabulation allows feminist and masculinist postmodern fiction to function as an ensemble dynamized by exchange rather than as a struggle between the same and the other. Cixous describes a "process of different subjects knowing one another and beginning one another anew only from the living boundaries of the other: a multiple and inexhaustible course with millions of encounters and transformations of the same into the other and into the in-between, from which woman takes her forms (and man, in his turn; but that's his other story)" (Cixous, 254). Encounters and transformations—the infinite possibilities of feminist writing newly ensconced within the canon—are logical alternatives to relegating this writing to outside, marginal status. As Linda Hutcheon explains, the "borders between literary genres have become fluid" (Hutcheon, 9). Cixous's interchanges and Hutcheon's fluid borders enable many contemporary women writers to be moved out of their fixed, noncanonical position. Cixous's and Hutcheon's ideas can be used to free Jardine's woman writer who is "not ultimately as 'important' as the men" from remaining in "her separate chapter with subcategory status—where she has always been" (Jardine, 55).

Jardine discusses "gynesis" in terms of space.[4] She explains that, in relation to various diverse subjects (music, computer sciences, and mathematics, for example), "the collapsing of certain structures into, within, and through new spaces is what is at stake: modernity as a *redefinition of the world"* (Jardine, 72). Feminist fabulation—a new space for certain literary structures (such as contemporary female feminist mainstream fiction, feminist SF, and the work of male feminists)—reflects redefinitions of the patriarchal world. When repositioning these literary structures, feminist fabulation concerns "how to create something different from the same, how to build a structure" (Jardine, 72). Contemporary feminist mainstream works and feminist SF are not the same when understood in terms of the literary space I call feminist fabulation. (I am reminded of a question and answer Fay Weldon places in *Darcy's Utopia*: "Q: But you don't change your nature by changing your name, surely? A: Oh yes, you do" [Weldon, 18].) Jardine also comments that "male philosophers found that those spaces [spaces of the Other] have a certain force that *might be useful to Man if they were to be given a new language"* (Jardine, 73). Feminist fabulation, a feminist literary space of the Other, is useful to feminists.

According to Jardine, new language is at the heart of gynesis: "To give a new language to these other spaces is a project filled with both promise and fear, however, for these spaces have hitherto remained unknown, terrifying, monstrous: they are mad, unconscious, improper, unclean. . . . If philosophy is truly to question those spaces, it must move away from all that has defined them, held them in place: Man, the Subject, History, Meaning. It must offer itself over to them, embrace them. But this is also a dangerous and frightening task" (Jardine, 73). Jardine's ideas are applicable to the relationship between feminist theory and feminist SF. Feminist theory (when it does not ignore feminist SF) very often views feminist SF as an unknown, terrifying, monstrous space and considers it to be mad, improper, unclean.[5] Feminist SF is usually Other to feminist theory. However, as male philosophers find that female spaces are useful to Man in terms of a new language, feminist theorists can find that feminist SF's alternative literary spaces are useful to Woman in terms of providing insights about alternatives to patriarchal social constructions. If feminist theory is truly to question patriarchy, it might move away from the traditional rubric that defines feminist SF—an important aspect of feminist imaginative thought—as subliterary work justifiably ghettoized as a subgenre. Feminist theorists might offer themselves to feminist SF writers. They might embrace these writers as well as the frightening task of letting go of patriarchal reality.

Feminist fabulation facilitates this embrace: it allows feminist theorists to address feminist SF in a manner which connects feminist SF to feminist mainstream fiction and to canonical postmodern fiction. Feminist fabulation revises the present understanding of feminist SF as an unknown monstrous space which is Other to dominant modes of feminist theory and literature. Hence, feminist fabulation involves a simultaneous and doubly inclusive reading practice which connects feminist SF to feminist mainstream fiction as well as feminist mainstream fiction to canonical postmodern fiction. Feminist fabulation is a discourse of this century worthy of a prominent place in institutions such as those held by the teaching of literature and the practice of criticism.

Further, feminist fabulation concerns female writers who create postmodern work relevant to real-world women. It provides a woman-centered alternative to Jardine's description of Woman's relationship to modernity: Woman as catalyst to discourse that male theorists generate, Woman having "very little, if anything, to do with women" (Jardine, 35). Feminist fabulation enables postmodern fiction, in Catharine Stimpson's words, not "to forget actual women—their breath and bone, grit and grandeur—in its [postmodernism's] infatuation with the 'crisis of the subject' and the 'feminine' as a pre-Oedipal discursive mode" (Stimpson, 139).

This concern with real-world women has an impact upon the question and answer Lyotard names in his title "Answering the Question: What Is Postmodernism?" There is now a new question—about women's place within the postmodern canon, about their right to tell their own story and have it be heard—which needs to be answered. Molly Hite poses this question at the start of *The Other Side of the Story: Structures and Strategies of Contemporary Feminist Narrative*. Hite asks, "Why don't women writers produce postmodernist fiction?" (Hite, 1). Her question can be considered in terms of a related question: Why don't feminist theorists address themselves to the many women SF writers who produce postmodernist fiction? Hite answers her own question by mentioning that lists of great English novelists include few women. She explains that only "Virginia Woolf is considered to be a great modernist, and the postmodernist canon is even more rigorously masculinist" (Hite, 12). Hite's own list making is telling. In addition to Jean Rhys, Doris Lessing, Alice Walker, and Margaret Walker (the writers to which she respectively devotes each of her four chapters), Hite mentions nine women writers "whose fictions also belong under the rubric of contemporary feminist narrative: Kathy Acker, Christine Brooke-Rose, Angela Carter, Michelle Cliff, Elizabeth Jolley, Toni Morrison, Grace Paley, Joanna Russ, and Fay Weldon" (Hite, 2). Even though Brooke-Rose, Carter, and Russ write SF, Hite is silent about the relationship between women SF authors and integrating feminist writing within the postmodern canon. In fact, Hite's chapter on Lessing, called "The *Future* in a Different Shape" (italics mine), is devoted to *The Golden Notebook*, not to the Canopus space fiction series Hite cursorily mentions (Hite, 70, 101).

Hite clearly avoids another other side of the story: the relationship between women SF writers, contemporary feminist narrative, and the postmodern canon. Part of feminist fabulation's agenda is to facilitate telling this story, to break the silence with which most feminist critical studies approach women SF writers. Rather than isolating women writers, feminist fabulation connects them to contemporary "dominant modes of fictional experiment" (Hite, 2). It is not pragmatic to position women as the noncanonical, outside Other to "the dominant experimental movement of postmodernism" (Hite, 14). While Hite emphasizes that contemporary feminist narrative is different from the masculinist postmodern canon, I advocate changing our understanding of the postmodern canon to include this difference. One example of this changed understanding appears in chapter 3: I apply McHale's discussion of the differences between the traditional historical novel and the postmodern historical novel to distinguish, in terms of real women's real-world experiences, between the postmodern historical novel and the feminist postmodern historical novel.

McHale's work illuminates my argument for connecting feminist SF to feminist mainstream narrative and placing the two within the postmodern canon. He observes that "science fiction and postmodernist fiction . . . have advanced along parallel literary-historical tracks" (McHale, 62). The same holds true for feminist SF and contemporary mainstream feminist narrative: both question the patriarchal stories which become patriarchal reality. Further, while the "postmodernist fantastic can be seen as a sort of jiu-jitsu that uses representation itself to overthrow representation" (McHale, 75), feminist fabulation uses feminist representation to overthrow patriarchal representation. Within masculinist postmodern fiction, "the characters' failure to be amazed by paranormal happenings serves to heighten *our* amazement" (McHale, 76). Within feminist SF (which could more appropriately be called fantastic feminist fabulation), the characters' failure to be amazed by normal (from the perspective of their particular worlds) utopian or dystopian (from the perspective of our world) conditions for women heightens our amazement at women's condition under patriarchy. However, despite feminist SF's ability to estrange us from patriarchal reality, many feminist critics, when "unmasking the constructed nature of [patriarchal] reality" (McHale, 164), do not turn to feminist SF.

Feminist and canonical postmodernism's parallel tracks mutually traverse resistance to SF. McHale explains it thus:

> Postmodernists have not always been gracious in acknowledging their borrowings from their sister-genre [science fiction], presumably because of the 'low art' stigma that still attaches to science fiction. '*I am not* writing science fiction!' protests the 'author' in Alasdair Gray's *Lanark*, and Raymond Federman seconds this on the opening page of his *The Twofold Vibration*. . . . They protest too much. In fact, both *Lanark* and *The Twofold Vibration* are transparently indebted to science fiction for some of their materials, and many of the motifs dismissed by Federman in fact form a part of his own repertoire, as well as that of other postmodernist writers. (McHale, 65)

Some of the women writers I discuss are not always gracious toward SF. For example, chapter 3 mentions Valerie Miner's statement that she is not writing SF, and chapter 6 includes the comment of Margaret Atwood's protagonist (Joan Foster) to the same effect. Some female authors and their characters protest too much. Some of them are indebted to SF despite the truth of Bonnie Zimmerman's observation that "most fiction by women writers . . . remains committed to realism . . . and even the most experimental of writers remain convinced that language—however variously used—represents something, something real and rational" (Zimmerman, 186). I wish to devote some attention to fiction written by women which is not committed to realism and, hence, does not represent patriarchal reality.

The sections I include within *Feminist Fabulation*—Reclaiming Canonical Space, Redefining Gendered Space, and Reconceiving Narrative Space—focus upon feminist fictions which unmask patriarchal master narratives as mere fictions. To illuminate my intersections between the empowered and the marginalized, my slashing of the distinction between high canonical art and "the 'low art' stigma" (McHale, 65), I turn to paintings and sculptures shown in the Museum of Modern Art's recent exhibit "High & Low Modern Art and Popular Culture."[6] The following art works represent, respectively, each of my seven chapters: René Magritte's *The Treachery of Images (This Is Not a Pipe)*, Claes Oldenburg's *Lipstick Ascending on Caterpillar Tracks*, Pablo Picasso's *The Scallop Shell: Notre Avenir est dans l'air*, Richard Hamilton's *Just What Is It That Makes Today's Homes So Different, So Appealing?*, Constantin Brancusi's *Princess X*, Cy Twombly's *Untitled*, and, finally, serving as a closing frame to this list which began with Magritte, his *The Rape*. These works created by men from different cultures picture my book's feminist concerns.

Chapter 1 (rather than this preface) explains how I arrive at the term "feminist fabulation." This term stems from associating feminist fiction packaged, advertised, and regarded as SF with the treachery of images. I read the literature called feminist SF and, to paraphrase Magritte's title *The Treachery of Images (This Is Not a Pipe)*, I respond by realizing that this literature is not SF.

Chapter 2 links contemporary feminist fabulators to the tradition of women's literature. It reveals the connections between modern mothers (Isak Dinesen, Zora Neale Hurston, and Virginia Woolf) and their postmodern daughters (Mary Caraker, Joanna Russ, and Alice Sheldon, a.k.a. James Tiptree, Jr.). When advocating placing these "monstrous" daughters within the postmodern canon, I evoke juxtaposed images of phallic femininity, mobility, and war. The chapter concerns feminist authors who are threatening and the need to move their visions from outside literary respectability to inside the postmodern canon. The myth about the justifiable marginal status of some literary daughters' texts—a myth perpetuated by those who would believe that Oldenburg's feminine phallic symbol astride a tank, his sculpture *Lipstick Ascending on Caterpillar Tracks*, appropriately represents these texts—can, like a lipstick stain, be erased (with difficulty).

Chapter 3 focuses on flying. After discussing Hilary Masters's portrayal of flying, I turn to feminists Octavia Butler, Carol Hill, Valerie Miner, and Marge Piercy, whose depictions of flight are postmodern (according to a new understanding of the term) and form a continuum ranging from the real to the imaginary, from women World War II pilots to invading extraterrestrials. The chapter concludes by investigating alternatives to patriarchal flying that Susan Daitch, Lisa Goldstein, Erica Jong, Beryl Markham, Jane Palmer, and Kurt Vonnegut envision. I consider what happens to female pilots when, as Picasso's title *The Scallop Shell: Notre Avenir est dans l'air* announces, our future is in the air. Instead of enjoying unrestricted access to air space and flight technology, until very recently, women pilots were grounded by myths about how they should be enclosed within metaphorical, protective scallop shells instead of actual fighter-plane cockpits.[7]

Chapter 4 concerns domestic space. I interpret the way three authors of feminist supernatural fiction—Lynn Abbey, Marion Zimmer Bradley, and Pamela Sargent—challenge patriarchal stories about women's relationships to houses. Then, turning from genre fiction to the canon, I position Charlotte Perkins Gilman as a precursor to contemporary authors Donald Barthelme and Lynne Tillman, who explore the relationship between space, domesticity, and the supernatural. In terms of women, the chapter echoes Richard Hamilton's question, "Just What Is It That Makes Today's Homes So Different, So Appealing?" Hamilton answers his question by using comic book images to exaggerate the impact of consumers' mass-mediated desires upon the domestic environment; the authors I discuss turn to the supernatural to stress that, in relation to women, this impact is more insidious than comical.

Chapter 5 points to literature's inability to imagine a society in which women and men function as equals. After noting the similarities between the failed efforts of Gail Godwin's women and Saul Bellow's men to establish successful heterosexual love relationships, I move from realistic fiction to feminist utopias. I indicate that the feminist utopias Doris Lessing, Pamela Sargent, and Joan Slonczewski imagine are postseparatist visions about attempts to integrate one male into female societies. The chapter shows that within high and low literature created by eminent and relatively unknown writers alike, depicting an egalitarian society both women and men inhabit is still a dream. Perhaps Constantin Brancusi's sculpture *Princess X*, which depicts a juxtaposed dream girl and phallus, represents the dream of a viable female/male space. Brancusi, after all, like the creators of postseparatist feminist SF utopias, "elevated the low in his search for a symbol of androgyny fusing male and female into a single erotic hieroglyph" (Varnedde and Gopnik, 140).

Chapter 6 centers upon female protagonists who transform themselves after hesitating to allow male stories to influence their lives. These protagonists enact impulses to power by conducting self-experiments based upon rewriting patriarchal narratives. I begin by explaining how Tommaso Landolfi's and Philip Roth's stories define women; then I describe female characters (created by Margaret Atwood, Diane Johnson, Marge Piercy, and Christa Wolf) who oppose patriarchal definitions. The chapter concludes with speculation about how changed, unreal writing might transform reality. Cy Twombly's markings and their association with graffiti pictured in *Untitled* seem to address the chapter's concern with moving beyond patriarchal language.

Chapter 7 explains that women replenish literature by offering new female visions of male-centered stories. After positioning Kate Chopin and Elizabeth Stuart Phelps as precursors to contemporary female literary replenishers (such as Elizabeth Scarborough, who, like Chopin and Phelps, rewrites Arthurian legend), I focus upon women's and men's specific methods of retelling myths. After analyzing tales John Barth, Sandi Hall, Thomas Pynchon, and Christa Wolf retell, I explore, in terms of feminist textuality, works written by E. M. Broner, Italo Calvino, and Doris Piserchia. The chapter regards Magritte's *The Rape*, a portrait of Woman reduced to her body, as an exhausted image.

In light of the point that "more arguments exist for a postmodern feminist aesthetic than do examples of one" (Zimmerman, 186), I try to provide such examples throughout my chapters. (Chapter 6, for instance, defines and exemplifies postmodern feminist narrative technique.) The chapters reclaim, redefine, and reconceive postmodern fiction in a manner which facilitates positioning realistic and fantastic feminist narrative within the canon. In other words, *Feminist Fabulation* is about rebuilding the postmodern canon; feminist fabulation metaphorically functions as an extension added to the domicile of canonical postmodern fiction to accommodate a growing family. My efforts to remodel the study, to alter and expand the already constituted stylistic criteria associated with canonical postmodern fiction, can be discussed further by turning from painting and sculpture to architecture.

Simone de Beauvoir describes, in terms of space, the sense of inferiority a little girl feels upon encountering walls and ceilings which enclose her in the male universe:

> It is a strange experience for whoever regards himself as the One to be revealed to himself as otherness, alterity. This is what happens to the little girl when, doing her apprenticeship for life in the world, she grasps what it means to be a woman therein. The sphere to which she belongs is everywhere enclosed, limited, dominated by the male universe: high as she may raise herself, far as she may venture, there will always be a ceiling over her head, walls that will block her way. (de Beauvoir, 297)

The girl learns about the limited space the male universe allots to her. De Beauvoir's male universe resembles Fredric Jameson's description of the Bonaventura hotel.

Both the Bonaventura and the male universe are enclosed, autonomous, and characterized by restricted access. Jameson gives us his analysis:

> The *Bonaventura* aspires to being a total space, a complete world, a kind of miniature city. . . . In this sense, then, ideally

the mini-city of [John] Portman's *Bonaventura* ought not to have entrances at all, since the entryway is always the seam that links the building to the rest of the city that surrounds it: for it does not wish to be a part of the city, but rather its equivalent and replacement or substitute. That is, however, obviously not possible or practical, hence the deliberate downplaying and reduction of the entrance function to its bare minimum. (Jameson, 81)

Many Los Angeles citizens are not welcome to become a part of the Bonaventura's miniature city. People must belong to the proper social class in order to use the downplayed entrances and to function efficiently within the hotel's enclosed, separate world. Class segregation seems also to be behind the design of Portman's New York Marriott Marquis. Placing the registration area floors above a bare, ground-level lobby separates the hotel guests from low-status Broadway pedestrians. Portman's Bonaventura and Marriott, whose inside spaces are enjoyed by an elite group, discard outside space and the diverse social groups located there. His hotels, like de Beauvoir's male universe, exclude the Other.

Jameson points out that recent architectural theory borrows from narrative analysis in other fields, and he sees people's movements through buildings such as the Portman hotels as "virtual narratives or stories, as dynamic paths and narrative paradigms" (Jameson, 82). De Beauvoir's male universe, Portman's hotels, and the postmodern canon all tell the same story of restriction, of lack of universal access to an elite universe. Even the outside Other who, against all odds, does manage to pass through necessary (but unobtrusive) entrances finds it difficult to function effectively within. To my mind, the postmodern canon is analogous to a Portman hotel, and the female feminist fabulator resembles de Beauvoir's venturesome little girl, who, while trying to get through the door to the male canonical universe, finds her movement blocked by walls. *Feminist Fabulation* proposes that reconceptualizing canonical postmodernism according to narrative paradigms pertinent to feminist fiction will enable feminist fabulators to enter the canon via productive dynamic paths rather than blocked doorways and glass ceilings.

This proposal is both optimistic and possible. Although our minds are incapable of mapping "the great global multinational and decentered communicative network in which we find ourselves caught as individual subjects" (Jameson, 84), individual feminist novelists and critics can chart the literary establishment's restrictive networks which name feminist narratives as Other, canonical outsiders. Feminists have found the postmodern canon's unobtrusive doors and they are beginning to venture through them. *Feminist Fabulation* maps this inside space for feminists. As I explain in chapter 1, while Scholes's structural fabulation concerns man's relationship to the system of the universe, feminist fabulation concerns woman's relationship to the system of patriarchy. Patriarchy is much more understandable than the universe; the literary establishment is much more knowable than great, global, multinational communications networks. Feminist fabulators need not be lost in space outside the canon.

Feminist fabulators share much in common with architects whose work differs from Portman's version of the not universally accessible patriarchal universe. He insists upon constructing barriers to separate inside and outside, insiders and outsiders; in contrast, Frank Lloyd Wright's "organic architecture" exemplifies one alternative to the self-contained inside space characterizing both Portman's hotels and the male universe. Wright explains that the "essence of organic building is space, space flowing outward, space flowing inward" (Wright, *Testament*, 232). In addition to this reciprocity between outside and inside space, organic architecture includes the idea that "the reality of the building lies in the space within to be lived in, the feeling that we must not enclose ourselves in an envelope which is the building" (Wright, *House*, 220). Wright's assertion that all "buildings built should serve the liberation of mankind, liberating the lives of *individuals*" (Wright, *Testament*, 24), is in opposition to Portman's hotels, de Beauvoir's metaphors, and a masculinist canon.

Contemporary architects whose work involves interaction between inside and outside exemplify this opposition. For example, the designs of Emilio Ambasz and Steven Holl conform to a major tenet of organic architecture. According to this tenet, a building's beauty "'is emergent from its consonance with nature' [Wright, *Buildings*, 2]. . . . The degree of the relationship of a building to its site and environment determines the degree of its harmony" (Green, 134–135). Unlike Wright, however, Ambasz and Holl create structures which become the landscape.[8] Ambasz's buildings are literally part of the earth; Holl's buildings are connected to their location's cultural and physical characteristics (Wrede, 2). These architects seem to address the potential interaction between feminist fabulation and the postmodern canon, a possible mingling which obscures the distinction between insider and outsider: "Holl speaks of architecture and site as having 'an experimental connection, a metaphysical link, a poetic link.' Ambasz speaks of architecture as 'a mythmaking act'" (Wrede, 3). Such architectural poetic links pertain to feminist fabulation's mythmaking acts, its blueprints for ending distinctions between feminist and patriarchal myths. Ambasz and Holl each design "'mythic retreats,' placed below the earth's surface" (Wrede, 2); feminist fabulators create mythic retreats from patriarchal myths which form reality. These retreats should not be buried. Books, as well as buildings, involve "liberating the lives of *individuals*" (Wright, *Testament*, 24).

   Like the buildings of Ambasz, Holl, and Wright, feminist fabulation is a structure involving harmony between inside and outside (postmodern works situated inside and outside the canon), a space enveloping both the slash between the two and the possibility for real-world change. Wright's liberating walls are positive alternatives to the walls de Beauvoir describes. As Wright explains, "walls are now apparent more as humanized screens. They do define and differentiate, but never confine or obliterate space. . . . A new sense of reality in building construction has arrived" (Wright, *Testament*, 224). *Feminist Fabulation* announces that a new sense of canon construction has arrived which critiques the constructed, patriarchal real world. In terms of *Pioneer*, this announcement stresses that the spacecraft's depiction of humanity is an enclosing wall for women: no matter how far *Pioneer* ventures, the male universe will block women. Not drawn on a humanized screen, the picture etched on *Pioneer*'s wall uses gender differentiation to define Woman as silent Other, to obliterate Woman's communicative potential, and to confine Woman to subordinate space in outer space. The literature which insists that such pictures are inappropriate blueprints for de-

signing the drawings and stories that we live should not be relegated
to an inferior literary space outside the male canonical universe.

A single prestigious location to which feminist and masculinist
postmodern writers have equal access might replace this outside
space. Holl believes that "communal life is encouraged by entrance
and exit through central courtyards" (Filler, 28). Feminist fabulation
and masculinist postmodernism can come together in such a central
communal courtyard, a replacement for the segregating wall which
keeps feminism out of postmodernism. Despite this possibility, Holl
himself must counter critical walls. One critic describes Holl's inspiration as "wholly unencumbered by the practical considerations—
economic, environmental, physical, political and social—that are an
inescapable part of the architectural process in real cities" and dismisses it as "stunning but ultimately superficial exhibitionism"
(Filler, 28). Holl, and feminist fabulators, need not be practical.

Both Holl and his literary counterparts create "an 'anti-world-
view,' a counterreality" which differs from "straight" or "official"
reality (McHale, 168). Their endeavors involve rebuilding the real
in terms of the unreal. Wrede says that Ambasz and Holl, who have
"as yet built relatively little" (Wrede, 2), use architectural stories,
not actual buildings, to communicate many of their ideas: "Both architects focused in their early work on ideal communal projects; often
small and removed from the social mainstream, these include Ambasz's Cooperative of Mexican-American Grapegrowers and Holl's
Autonomous Artisan Houses or his Gymnasium Bridge in the Bronx.
And although unbuilt, posited as ideal communities, these projects
will live on as 'architectural fables,' in Ambasz's words, long after
constructed buildings have crumbled" (Wrede, 2). Holl's proposed
Manhattan high-rise sliver towers reached via underwater passageways[9] and feminist fabulators' utopian visions are metadiscourses
and metafictions, ideas which comment upon language that forms
real-world reality, fictions (fables) about patriarchal fictions. Such
proposals and visions are an "antilanguage" (McHale, 168) which
critiques "the very logical processes through which meaning is produced" (Jardine, 44). This antilanguage stresses that patriarchal language is not a logical communicative process upon which to base
alternative social structures.

The conclusion of Margaret Atwood's *The Handmaid's Tale* makes a similar point about patriarchal language when it describes a possible new social structure and speaks in a feminist antilanguage. Atwood's Maryann Crescent Moon, a scholar of Caucasian anthropology, addresses the International Historical Association Convention held at the University of Denay located in Nunavit (Atwood, 299). "Nunavit" is an antilinguistic, metalinguistic response to the constructed situation in which the Other virtually receives "none of it" (where "it" is defined as what Russ calls "the good things of this world" [Russ, "Recent Feminist Utopias," 77]). Nunavit is a feminist response to a Nowhere for women within the utopias patriarchy makes for a male elite. Feminist should have none of a Nowhere for themselves within postmodern canons. Nunavit exemplifies speaking a feminist language and envisioning an egalitarian utopia. Because feminists are Nowhere within the utopias male theoreticians of the postmodern describe, they literally have nunavit in relation to these utopias.

One such male theoretician, Jean-Joseph Goux, views utopia as "new access to the feminine" (Jardine, 33). Jardine explains that this "(re)union with the feminine is the end point of History— u-topia— here all images have been banned. . . . We might say that what is generally referred to as modernity is precisely the acutely interior, unabashedly incestuous exploration of these new female spaces: the perhaps historically unprecedented exploration of the female, differently maternal body" (Jardine, 33–34). Feminist fabulation mothers the different body of contemporary feminist literature and imagines the end point of patriarchal history as a utopia which ensconces the Other by banning all misogynistic images (such as *Pioneer*'s representation of noncommunicative Woman). *Feminist Fabulation* is a pioneer vehicle built to explore postmodernism in terms of female literary spaces which have something to do with real-world women. I try to enlarge women's space in contemporary fiction by pioneering a location of equal opportunity for feminist mainstream fiction and science fiction and for masculinist postmodern fiction. Feminist fabulation will have nunavit in regard to postmodern theoretical visions which define utopia as a Nowhere for women.

Reclaiming Canonical Space

René Magritte, The Treachery of Images (This Is Not a Pipe), *1928. Los Angeles County Museum of Art, purchased with funds provided by the Mr. and Mrs. William Preston Harrison Collection.*

The Feminist Anglo-American
Critical Empire Strikes Back

*The repressed content, I think, would be, not erotic
impulses, but an impulse to power: a fantasy of
power that would revise the social grammar in which
women are never defined as subjects; a fantasy of
power that disdains a sexual exchange in which
women can participate only as objects of circulation.
The daydreams or fictions of women writers would
then, like those of men, say, 'Nothing can happen to
me!' But the modalities of that invulnerability would
be marked in an essentially different way.*
                        —Nancy K. Miller, "Emphasis Added"

F eminist science fiction[1] flaunts the repressed content of women's serious fiction
by presenting revisionary power fantasies for
women. Its daydreams of female invulnerability posit a revised, nonpatriarchal social grammar and explore essentially different ways to
define invulnerable women. Difference, women's impulse to power—
not science—is at the heart of feminist SF. Hence, even though
women enjoy an influential position within the SF community, I
suggest that most of them are not writing SF. Magritte proclaims
that his picture of a pipe is not a pipe; I believe that the feminist
literature which has been categorized as SF is not SF. "Feminist
SF"—a term I once strongly advocated—has become inadequate and
distorting. It is time to redefine feminist SF, to ensure that this literature's subversive potential is not nullified (and shunned by most
Anglo-American feminist theorists) because of a generic classification connoting literary inferiority.

Students first made the disparate nature of women's and men's notions about SF apparent to me. While female students tended not to enroll in my SF course, the male engineering majors drawn to it vehemently argued that fiction written by such authors as Vonda McIntyre, Joanna Russ, and Pamela Sargent is not SF. My insistence upon a new term for feminist SF writers' work stems from realizing that my students are correct. SF is not feminist; SF is divided into separate women's and men's worlds. Most male SF writers imagine men controlling a universe once dominated by nature; most female SF writers imagine women controlling a world once dominated by men. SF writers of both genders who present new feminist worlds move beyond merely creating woman-oriented versions of a genre which appeals to men, not to women.

William Sims Bainbridge's observation about gender distinctions between SF writers and readers accounts for my students' reactions. Bainbridge states that "women tend to like the traditional hard-science fiction less than men do; and no female author studied writes this variety. . . . the female authors express very different values in their fiction and are urging social activism rather than technical competence" (Bainbridge, 1092). Women tend not to like Heinlein and Asimov, and they fail to associate SF with the visions of feminist writers. Coining the correct descriptive term for feminist SF writers' work, then, is pedagogically as well as theoretically compelling.

Bainbridge signals that establishing this new definition is also a pressing civic responsibility:

> Since the 1950s, science fiction has become a major category of popular culture and one of the most important media for the development and dissemination of radical ideologies. Among the more common topics for fictional exploration are perceived disadvantages of traditional sex roles and possible implications and advantages of novel alternatives. Examination of the new activism of women in science fiction will allow us to see how this field of popular fiction may shape and reflect changing conceptions of the roles available to women in the real world. . . . Women authors have made science fiction a medium for analy-

sis of current sex roles and for advocacy of change. . . . New-Wave science fiction attacks traditional sex roles directly, demanding sweeping cultural change. Women authors' science fiction has become an important medium for public discussion of the disadvantages of contemporary sex roles and consideration of options for the future. (Bainbridge, 1081–1082, 1091–1092)

Since "women authors' science fiction" is a catalyst for social change, feminist literary scholars should surely strive to affect society by introducing these imaginative texts to colleagues, to students, and to the general public. Commitment of this sort opposes isolating the text and the critic from the world, and it marks a path for the feminist critic and the feminist text to begin to change the world.[2]

This chapter describes one method to blaze such a path. In the first section, I insist upon and define a new, more appropriate term to replace feminist SF. While doing so, I look to Robert Scholes, who twenty years ago spoke about the lack of terminology to describe a new literary mode: "Much of the trouble comes from inadequate understanding of this new literary mode I have called fabulation. The trouble is aggravated by the absence of terminology in which to discuss it" (Scholes, *Fabulators*, 13). Now that "fabulation" is a recognized term, I call upon it to quell trouble caused by present-day inadequate understanding of a new feminist literary mode. In the second and third sections, I ask the critical community to accept feminist fabulation as an important contribution to the postmodern literary canon.

Redefining Feminist SF

What is the appropriate name for feminist SF, for literature's new women's worlds? "Science," in the sense of technology, should be replaced by a term which has social connotations and focuses upon new sex roles, not new hardware. One such term, Thomas Kuhn's "paradigm shift," is applicable to women's social roles and to fiction written by feminist SF authors. Kuhn's concept points the way toward coining a new term for feminist SF.

Humanity is, of course, dominated by sexist paradigms, value systems shared by those who advocate perpetuating discourses about how the world should be constructed and controlled by men. Feminists are anomalies who do not fit within prevailing patriarchal systems. Catherine Clément makes this point when she comments that "more than any others, women bizarrely embody this group of anomalies showing the cracks in an overall system" (Cixous and Clément, 7). Feminist SF writers expose these cracks by focusing attention on new theories about how present feminist speculation might eventually become feminist reality.

These writers generate future, feminist scenarios after observing present, obvious phenomena. They see, for example, that women are deprived of political power, that housewives are bored, and that high heels are uncomfortable. They look toward SF to estrange readers from prevailing sexist roles and to reformulate those roles. In other words, feminist SF writers encourage readers to contemplate a paradigm shift regarding human relations. Virginia Allen and Terry Paul, through a discussion of Betty Friedan, link feminist SF to Kuhn's notion of paradigms. Allen and Paul explain that when "Betty Friedan defined 'the problem that has no name' as sexism, she generated a scientific revolution in Kuhn's terms. The problem had been around long before she named it, and many sensitive and observant feminists had grappled with it. But Friedan did for sexual politics what Galileo had done for cosmology: She brought forward so much anomalous data that they could no longer be ignored" (Allen and Paul, 168–169). Feminist SF writers approach the fantastic to generate names for "the problem that has no name." They bring forth a great deal of anomalous data about women which can no longer be ignored.

In Ursula Le Guin's "Daddy's Big Girl," for instance, Jewel Ann is a character who becomes anomalous data. Jewel Ann (like the ponderous protagonist of "Jack and the Bean Stalk") is a giant; she cannot fit within patriarchal social space; she cannot enact feminine gender roles which require women to be small and unobtrusive. She embodies Clément's image of Woman as bizarre anomaly who reveals cracks in an overall system. Jewel Ann can destroy a particular repressive domestic system, the house which imprisons her and her mother: "If she had stretched and pushed and wanted to, she could have pushed out the back wall of that house, pushed it down like the side of a paper box" (Le Guin, 94). Jewel Ann, though, does not want to demolish the house. Instead, she continues to grow in another reality beyond the inhibiting boundaries of patriarchal space and stories. Her situation suggests that reality should be changed to accommodate "giant," expansive women. In the manner of Le Guin, feminist SF writers produce metaparadigmatic literature as they venture outside women's reality and imagine a social revolution directed toward changing patriarchy.

For example, Sheila Finch's *Infinity's Web*, which moves beyond existing sexist paradigms to envision new horizons for women, is a feminist metaparadigmatic novel.[3] Ann, Finch's protagonist, encounters different versions of herself who inhabit alternative realities. Opportunities to confront these differing identity possibilities enrich Ann's daily life. *Infinity's Web* articulates the need for a revised "social grammar" (Miller, "Emphasis Added," 348), a new language, a new nonpatriarchal linguistic perspective: "She [Ann] was aware of the shifting concepts that made up language, the resonance of meanings that could no more translate from tongue to tongue identically than a note played on the violin could duplicate one on a flute. . . . 'It's like linguistic relativity. Once you decide what to see, and what to put a name on, you have a very hard time seeing anything else ever again'" (Finch, *Web*, 212–213). Language's present resonances of meaning sometimes fall short of adequately articulating female experience.[4] After language names—and limits—women's roles, it is difficult to see beyond sexist stereotypes. *Infinity's Web* calls for establishing new feminist paradigms, creating new names for new female possibilities. Finch's novel, which explores women's inner space (instead of the male-controlled domain of outer space), is not science fiction. Rather than emphasizing technology, this novel presents a new feminist behavioral paradigm—women who celebrate their own potential instead of applauding men who send phallic machines into the sky.[5]

Infinity's Web suggests that the patriarchal world is not the only possible reality. The novel points out that sexist societies are artificial environments constructed by patriarchal language which defines sexist as normal. The contrived nature of patriarchal reality, the fiction about women's inferiority and necessarily subordinate status, is best confronted by metafiction which, according to Patricia Waugh, explores "the possible fictionality of the world outside the literary fictional text" (Waugh, *Metafiction*, 2). Waugh explains that "literary fiction (worlds constructed entirely of language) becomes a useful model for learning about the construction of 'reality' itself" (Waugh, 3). Feminist SF writers create metafiction, fiction about patriarchal fiction, to unmask the fictionality of patriarchy. When these authors use language to construct nonsexist fictional worlds, they develop useful models for learning about how patriarchy is constructed. Waugh's definition of metafiction describes their efforts.

According to Waugh, metafiction is "a fictional form that is culturally relevant and comprehensible to contemporary readers. In showing us how literary fiction creates its imaginary worlds, metafiction helps us to understand how the reality we live day by day is similarly constructed, similarly 'written.' . . . Indeed, it could be argued that, far from 'dying,' the novel has reached a mature recognition of its existence as *writing*, which can only ensure its continued viability in and relevance to a contemporary world which is similarly beginning to gain awareness of precisely how its values and practices are constructed and legitimized" (Waugh, 18, 19). Feminist SF metafictionally facilitates an understanding of sexism as a story authored by men who use their power to make women the protagonists of patriarchal fictions. Feminist metafiction is a relevant artistic form for contemporary feminists who are beginning to gain awareness of precisely how patriarchal values are constructed and legitimized.[6]

Marshall Blonsky's comments about signs and reality help to explain how feminist metafiction facilitates rewriting patriarchy's misogynist fictions. Blonsky points out that people's "knowledge of reality, or the real as we like to say, will henceforth be an illusory condition of their comprehension of/captivation by images. . . . the Establishment has been asystematically teaching itself codes which have no responsibility *vis-à-vis* history or the test of the real. . . . The Establishment controls the entire code, [and] the citizen lives with and [becomes] fragmented signs and images, like Humpty Dumpty, unable to ever put himself together again" (Blonsky, 509). Under patriarchy, women conform to the signs (or codes) of femininity. Images of femininity—the Miss America pageant and advertising's degrading depictions of women, for example—are illusory conditions representing real women to their spectators. The patriarchal establishment teaches itself sexist codes and controls the sexist images which are made to represent women's reality. Feminist metafiction suggests ways to change these codes and images by creating feminist signs which put women back together again. When writers such as McIntyre, Russ, and Sargent replace patriarchal signs with feminist signifiers, they announce that Woman is not synonymous with Humpty Dumpty.

SF writers who create feminist metafiction magnify institutionalized—and therefore difficult to view—specific examples of sexism. These writers seem to peer into metaphorical microscopes while playing at being scientists, artful practitioners of soft sciences who expand women's psyche and unearth an archeology of new feminist knowledge. Joy is an important aspect of their enterprise. They refresh embattled feminists by using language artistically to create power fantasies and to play (sometimes vengefully) with patriarchy. Angela Carter creates one of these power fantasies when she describes a four-breasted lesbian fertility goddess cutting off a man's genitals: " 'I am the Great Parricide, I am the Castratrix of the Phallocentric Universe' [says the goddess]. . . . Oh, the dreadful symbolism of that knife! To be castrated with a phallic symbol! . . . She cut off all my genital appendages with a single blow, caught them in her other hand and tossed them to Sophia, who slipped them into the pocket of her shorts" (Carter, *New Eve*, 67, 70–71). Carter seems to rejoice in her creation of vicarious vengefulness which might refresh feminist readers. "The fabulator is important to the extent that he can rejoice and refresh us. . . . Of all narrative forms, fabulation puts the highest premium on art and joy," says Robert Scholes (*Fabulation and Metafiction*, 3). "Feminist metaparadigmatic fiction" and "feminist metafiction" (terms to replace "feminist SF" for power fantasies written for feminists) are components of a wider literary area—feminist fabulation.

Eric S. Rabkin views the fantastic as a supergenre which includes SF, satire, and utopian literature (Rabkin, 147–150). Feminist fabulation, like Rabkin's supergenre, is an umbrella term for describing overlapping genres. The term includes feminist speculative fiction and feminist mainstream works (which may or may not routinely be categorized as postmodern literature) authored by both women and men. (Chapter 5's discussion of Gail Godwin's *The Finishing School* and Saul Bellow's *More Die of Heartbreak* exemplifies feminist fabulation's inclusiveness.) Feminist fabulation, then, is not totalizing, systematic, and contained—characteristics applicable to current discussions about expanding literary canons.

Thinkers such as Foucault, Bernard-Henri Lévy, and Primo Levi—who explain that power is everywhere and cannot be eliminated—provide useful ways to understand feminist fabulation's relationship to the newly enlarged canon. With their ideas in mind, I suggest that although many feminist educators wish to discredit the term "literary canon," the canon, nonetheless, is an organizational system which cannot be abandoned completely.[7] The openness of feminist fabulation limits the canon's ability to focus upon one group of writers at the expense of another group. Feminist fabulation is a canonical system which changes a canonical system. For example, it associates feminist speculative fiction with respected contemporary fiction and, by doing so, expands the definition of the postmodern canon. The chapters which follow at once address connections between noncanonical and canonical texts and posit an expanded definition of literary postmodernism. While doing so, they argue that feminist texts should not be excluded from the postmodern literary canon.

I, of course, claim Scholes's "fabulation" for feminist theory and feminist fiction. Scholes defines fabulation as "fiction that offers us a world clearly and radically discontinuous from the one we know, yet returns to confront that known world in some cognitive way" (Scholes, "Roots of Science Fiction," 47). Feminist fabulation is feminist fiction that offers us a world clearly and radically discontinuous from the patriarchal one we know, yet returns to confront that known patriarchal world in some feminist cognitive way. It provides "cognitive estrangement" (Darko Suvin's term) from the patriarchal world by depicting feminist visions which confront that world. Feminist fabulation is a specifically feminist corollary to Scholes's definition of structural fabulation. Scholes states that "in works of structural fabulation the tradition of speculative fiction is modified by an awareness of the nature of the universe as a system of systems, a structure of structures, and the insights of the past century of science are accepted as fictional points of departure. . . . It is a fictional exploration of human situations made perceptible by the implications of recent science" (Scholes, "Roots," 54–55). He continues: "Man must learn to live within laws that have given him his being but offer him no purpose and promise him no triumph as a species. Man must make his own values, fitting his hopes and fears to a universe which has allowed him a place in its systematic working, but which cares only for the system itself and not for him. Man must create his future himself" (Scholes, "Roots," 55). Structural fabulation addresses man's place within the system of the universe; feminist fabulation addresses woman's place within the system of patriarchy.

Or, in terms of Scholes's language, feminist fabulation modifies the tradition of speculative fiction with an awareness that patriarchy is an arbitrary system which constructs fictions of female inferiority as integral aspects of human culture. Feminist fabulation accepts the insights of this century's waves of feminism as fictional points of departure. It is a fictional exploration of woman's inferior status made perceptible by the implications of recent feminist theory. Woman has been forced to live within patriarchal laws which define her as subhuman, offer her no purpose beyond serving men, and promise her no triumph as a human. Woman must make her own new values, fitting her new objectives to a patriarchal system which gives her a secondary place in its systematic working—and which certainly does not care for her. Woman must create her future herself.

Feminist fabulation addresses issues Cixous raises about women who function as mere shadows to men, about women's exclusion from patriarchal systems. Cixous states, "night to his day—that has forever been the fantasy. Black to his white. Shut out of his system's space, she is the repressed that ensures the system's functioning"

(Cixous and Clément, 67). She seems to address feminist fabulation's role in reclaiming space within literary postmodernism's canonical system. As the next chapter explains, "repressed" female feminist fabulators, who are located outside a literary status system which functions by passing recognition from one male generation to the next, do not shine as brightly as the male structural fabulators Scholes discusses.

Feminist Fabulation addresses the fact that many feminist writers (especially feminists who create the literature Doris Lessing calls space fiction) are shut out of the postmodern literary system's space. I want to reclaim postmodern canonical space for feminists by broadening the definition of postmodern fiction to include the subject matter and structures characterizing contemporary feminist writing. Many feminist authors adhere to an established postmodern literary trait: they rewrite master narratives. More specifically, they rewrite patriarchal master narratives and reveal them to be patriarchal fictions which form the foundation of constructed reality.

If feminist space fiction (one sort of text included under feminist fabulation's aforementioned rubric) is recognized as canonical postmodern fiction, then more Anglo-American feminist theorists can be expected not to shun it. These theorists might be willing to reorient themselves, to redirect some of the reverence they reserve solely for realistic texts.

Reorienting Feminist Literary Theory

Toril Moi faults most major feminist theoretical stances and advocates redirecting feminist theory. She argues that, instead of discrediting the very notion of a canon, feminist critics can establish a canon of women's writing (Moi, 78). I would refocus Moi's criticism of the gynocritical approach to the canon: rather than replacing "the old male text" (Moi, 78) with a new female canon, feminist critics might open themselves to including popular (or despised) nonrealistic literature within a newly expanded postmodern canon which contains both genders. The reluctance of many members of the Anglo-American feminist critical establishment to engage contemporary fantastic works yields theoretical limitation. Moi points to this limitation when discussing humanist feminism in relation to women's realistic and nonrealistic fictional texts: [8]

> It is not accidental that Anglo-American feminist criticism has dealt overwhelmingly with fiction written in the great period of realism between 1750 and 1930, with a notable concentration on the Victorian era. Monique Wittig's *Les guérillères* (1969) is an example of an altogether quite different sort of text. . . . When the text no longer offers an individual grasped as the transcendental origin of language and experience, humanist feminism must lay down its arms. [Nina] Auerbach therefore wistfully hopes for better days in a human-feminist future: "Perhaps once women have proved their strength to themselves, it will be possible to return to the individuality of Meg, Jo, Beth, and Amy, or to the humanly interdependent courtesy of *Cranford*" [Auerbach, 191]. If a nostalgic reversion to *Cranford* or *Little Women* is all this brand of criticism can yearn for, the urgent examination of other, more theoretically informed critical practices must surely be a pressing item on the agenda of Anglo-American feminist critics. (Moi, 79–80)

A nostalgic reversion to *Cranford* and *Little Women* should be accompanied by the hope of constructing Joanna Russ's feminist utopian planet Whileaway ("When It Changed"). Anglo-American feminist criticism might fruitfully examine other, more theoretically informed critical practices while addressing fabulative visions of feminist futures in addition to realistic fiction. Feminist fabulation's depictions of alternative reality are best interpreted by feminist poststructuralist arguments against single, fixed definitions of reality.

Theory is the business of metafiction; feminist fabulation theorizes about feminist futures. This literary form's extrapolative social blueprints are feminist fictions which reflect feminist theory. For example, while Nancy Chodorow theorizes about daughters who mirror mothers, Sydney J. Van Scyoc describes infant girls who develop by literally becoming their mothers (*Star Mother*).[9] Chodorow and Van Scyoc mirror each other. Another example of feminist fabulation's and feminist theory's shared agenda becomes apparent when Moi's discussion of Irigaray is considered in terms of Suzette Haden Elgin's *Native Tongue*. Moi explains that "Irigaray's analysis of femininity is closely bound up with her idea of a specific woman's language which she calls 'le parler femme', or 'womanspeak'. 'Le parler femme' emerges spontaneously when women speak together, but disappears again as soon as men are present" (Moi, 144). *Native Tongue* posits a specifically female language—láadan, or womanspeak—which emerges spontaneously when women speak together and disappears when men are present. Láadan functions as an indispensable step toward the liberation of Elgin's female characters.

Moi's comments about Cixous also pertain to feminist fabulation. Moi explains that "for a reader steeped in the Anglo-American approach to women and writing, Hélène Cixous's work represents a dramatic new departure. . . . marred as much by its lack of reference to recognizable social structures as by its biologism, her work nevertheless constitutes an invigorating, utopian evocation of the imaginative powers of women" (Moi, 126). Feminist fabulation provides a dramatic and needed new departure for Anglo-American feminist critics steeped in a humanist approach to theory. This literature flouts recognizable social structures and constitutes an invigorating utopian evocation of the imaginative powers of women. Reality is patriarchal; realistic texts must mirror the patriarchal myths which form reality. Feminist fabulation, in terms of Moi's description of Cixous's work, is a "passionate presentation of writing as a female essence" (Moi, 126) which can inspire future feminist reality. More Anglo-American feminist literary theorists should redirect a larger portion of their attention from patriarchal reality to feminist daydreams, from the past to the present and future. Cixous would agree; Moi explains that Cixous chastises feminist researchers who turn to the past: "Accusing feminist researchers in the humanities of turning away from the present towards the past, she rejects their efforts as pure 'thematics'. According to Cixous, such feminist critics will inevitably find themselves caught up in the oppressive network of hierarchial binary oppositions propagated by patriarchal ideology" (Moi, 103). Feminist theorists who direct some of their attention to present female writers' visions of feminist futures progress toward ensconcing these futures in the real world.

Cixous titles her section of *The Newly Born Woman* "Sorties: Out and Out: Attacks/Ways Out/Forays." Feminist fabulation can be described as sorties, ways out of patriarchy, out-and-out attacks upon patriarchy, forays into the reality of the future, newly born woman. Cixous, in the manner of feminist fabulators, questions patriarchal definitions of literature and society:

> And if we consult literary history, it is the same story. It all comes back to man—to *his* torment. . . . Now it has become rather urgent to question this solidarity between logocentrism and phallocentrism—bringing to light the fate dealt to woman . . . to threaten the stability of the masculine structure that passed itself off as eternal-natural. . . . What would happen to logocentrism, to the great philosophical systems, to the order of the world in general if the rock upon which they founded this church should crumble? . . .
>
> So all the history, all the stories would be there to retell differently; the future would be incalculable; the historic forces would and will change hands and change body—another thought which is yet unthinkable—will transform the functioning of all society. (Cixous and Clément, 65)

Feminist fabulation articulates woman's torment, brings to light woman's fate, and attempts to threaten the stability of patriarchal structures, the order of the world. It retells and rewrites patriarchal stories, points toward incalculable feminist futures, and thinks the as yet unviable thought of effectively transforming patriarchal society. Reality is made of words; women must nurture their own definitions. Only then will feminist fabulation become empowered reality and patriarchal stories fade as things of the past.

Reinventing the Canon, Reinventing Womanhood

Patriarchy, of course, continues to define feminists and threatening texts (especially SF written by women and men) as second-class. Le Guin calls SF's devaluation "the feminization of science fiction":

> I think science fiction, or speculative fiction, is really an important branch of literature. It allows us to think through dreadful

results. It also, much more important to me, allows us to think of alternatives. . . . But, alas, all is not well in the speculative sphere. . . . Science fiction is called a "genre" and dismissed from the canon of literature. Good science fiction writers, men and women, are pushed aside. Like women, they tend to be conveniently forgotten. And we are losing very good novels by doing that. All science fiction is treated as if it were inherently second-class. You could call it "the feminization of science fiction." (Berkley, 72)

By refusing to perpetuate the feminization of science fiction, the feminist Anglo-American critical empire can strike back. Feminist theorists can elevate to first-class status feminist space fiction, the important literature which names dreadful results of patriarchy and posits feminist alternatives to them. Instead of devoting so much energy to reclaiming the realistic women writers lost in the past (writers steeped in patriarchal definitions of reality), we can also reclaim the fabulative feminist writers "lost" in the present (writers steeped in nonpatriarchal definitions of reality). The feminization of science fiction retards feminist fabulation, keeps it from inspiring readers to create a feminist society. It is in feminist theorists' immediate power to legitimate feminist fabulation, a gesture encouraging the possible eventual wide-ranging legitimation of future feminist acts.

I recognize that many of my colleagues would more readily accept the term "feminist fabulation" than "feminist SF." Their reluctance to approach SF reflects a fundamental fear which thwarts the potential positive interchange between feminist fabulation and women's lives. In short, most Anglo-American feminist critics are afraid to juxtapose feminism with the fantastic. When feminism faces the fantastic, they look away.[10] Linda Leith's review of Mona Knapp's *Doris Lessing* calls attention to this tendency. Leith faults Knapp for reading space fiction inadequately:

Knapp concentrates on describing the "outer space fiction" as matter-of-factly as she can, as if reluctant to make the kind of judgments about the works falling under the heading that liven up her discussions of the realistic works. A more serious, and certainly related, problem with her discussions of the *Canopus* titles is that Knapp is ill at ease with these novels' genre. . . . She considers the question "why this virtuoso of down-to-earth realism should turn to the fantastic at all." . . . [Knapp] writes about the early, realistic Lessing . . . with energy and insight from a feminist and progressive viewpoint. Her comments on Lessing's "outer space fiction," however, are not nearly as valuable, thanks to her evident uneasiness . . . with their genre. Had she understood more about SF . . . she might well have had more perceptive observations about [the *Canopus* novels]. (Leith, 221)

Feminist theorists should feel more comfortable with SF. Feminist theory, after all, is concerned with difference; feminist fabulation is the literature of feminist difference.

A new openness toward feminist fabulation is probably best exemplified by Lessing herself. She is not afraid to break through the barrier separating the mainstream from the fantastic, to let go of man's world. *Memoirs of a Survivor* contains an image pertinent to my wish for Anglo-American feminist critics to act in kind. Near the novel's conclusion, walls dissolve and possibilities expand:

We were in that place which might present us with anything . . . walls broken, falling, growing again. . . . beside Emily was Hugo, and lingering after them Gerald. Emily, yes, but quite beyond herself, transmuted, and in another key, and the yellow beast Hugo fitted her new self: a splendid animal, handsome, all kindly dignity and command. . . . Both walked quickly behind that One who went ahead showing them the way out of this collapsed little world into another order of world altogether. . . . they all followed quickly on after the others as the last walls dissolved. (Lessing, 212–213)

Anglo-American feminist theory might fruitfully shift some emphasis from the age of established patriarchal realism to the place of fabulative feminist potential, a place which might present us with anything. We can allow feminist fabulators to guide us into another order of world altogether. Feminist theorists and feminist fabulators can, together, let go of current reality and penetrate barriers which inhibit creating new reality. As inhabiters of this alternative reality, like Emily's transmuted self, women can move beyond their present selves, can become splendid, dignified selves. Feminists can theorize about dissolving walls which imprison women within a sexist reality they—with few exceptions—have not made. Readers, fiction writers, and theorists can begin to construct new feminist paradigms, viable feminist futures. Reinventing the canon coincides with reinventing womanhood. We can claim that feminist fabulative works (such as Russ's "When It Changed") are important examples of postmodern fiction; we can inhabit Whileaway. The force is with us.

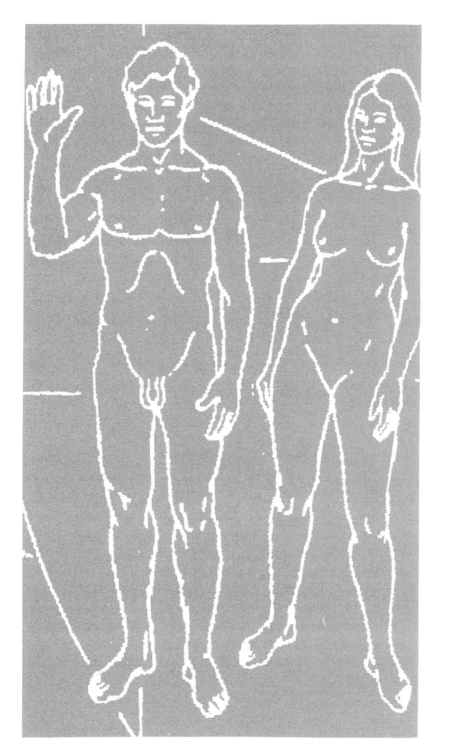

Claes Oldenburg, Lipstick Ascending on Caterpillar Tracks, *1969. Yale University Art Gallery, New Haven, gift of the Colossal Keepsake Corporation.*

Canonizing the Monstrous

"I don't **want** *to see you. I've seen plenty of women,*
I'm sick and weary of seeing them. I want a woman I
don't see."
   "I'm sorry I can't oblige you by being invisible,"
she laughed.

                              —D. H. Lawrence, *Women in Love*

Rupert Birkin wants Ursula Brangwen to be an invisible woman. The critical establishment, in regard to feminist fabulation and its analysis of patriarchy, also wants an invisible woman. Many critics do not want to see alternatives to patriarchal reality. Hence, important feminist imaginative works are ignored, relegated to a generic SF ghetto. With Hélène Cixous's and Jane Gallop's positive definitions of "monstrous" in mind, I argue that feminist fabulation need no longer remain marginalized.[1] Those who define feminist fabulation as women's literature they do not want to see are obliged to consider that (1) "lost" women writers are not always a part of the past and (2) contemporary feminist speculative fiction writers are "lost" postmodernists. I wish to make these writers visible by ensconcing them within the postmodern canon as newly found feminist fabulators.[2]

Feminist fabulation's metafictional commentaries upon patriarchal fictions which become social reality spring from the modern
tradition and deserve a prominent place in the postmodern canonical limelight. This chapter describes a new understanding of the
postmodern canon which asserts, for example, that Joanna Russ's
self-conscious statements about writing are no less important than
Kurt Vonnegut's versions of such statements, that Marion Zimmer
Bradley's retold myth (*The Mists of Avalon*) is no less important
than John Barth's retold myth (*Chimera*), that Octavia Butler should
receive more of the attention black women writers currently enjoy.
Certainly, since *Chimera* and *The Mists of Avalon* are both rewritten myths, it is unfair simultaneously to dismiss Bradley's work as
genre fiction and to laud Barth's work as metafiction. Feminist fabulation is an integral part of literary postmodernism.[3] It is time to
canonize the monstrous.

To begin to overcome feminist fabulation's isolation from the female literary tradition, in this chapter I unearth this literature's connections to Isak Dinesen, Zora Neale Hurston, and Virginia Woolf.
Dinesen, Hurston, and Woolf are modern literary mothers of canonized sons (male postmodernists) and ostracized daughters (feminist fabulators). First I discuss the missing modernist mothers of
metafiction. I suggest that Dinesen should share the parental position Barth attributes to Borges, and I also argue that stories collected
in Dinesen's *Last Tales* and Hurston's *Spunk* are unacknowledged
precursors to the male metafictional enterprise. I then focus upon
the links between modernist mothers and their feminist fabulative
daughters. I assert that Dinesen, Hurston, and Woolf use stereotypical SF tropes (such as the alien encounter story in which the alien
emerges from a technologically sophisticated vehicle), that these
writers engender contemporary feminist SF. References to feminist
SF writers who critique patriarchy—Suzy McKee Charnas, Sally
Gearhart, Sandi Hall, Doris Lessing, Joanna Russ, Jody Scott, and
James Tiptree, Jr.—support these assertions. I turn next to Mary
Caraker's *Seven Worlds*, a novel categorized as genre SF which I
claim is a meta-metafictional commentary upon violent patriarchal
stories. Finally, I apply Donna Haraway's biological understanding
of "regeneration" to feminist fabulation's relationship with feminist

critics. Although some critics may view this chapter's argument for canonizing Dinesen's and Woolf's daughters as being analogous to the invasion vehicle Oldenburg represents as a lipstick astride tank wheels, I see no reason to retreat from my position.

The Missing Modernist Mothers of Metafiction

In "The Literature of Exhaustion," Barth refers to literary inheritance and positions Borges as a father figure. According to Barth, "It is dismaying to see so many of our writers following Dostoevsky or Tolstoy or Balzac, when the question seems to me to be how to succeed not even Joyce and Kafka, but those who *succeeded* Joyce and Kafka [Barth refers to Beckett, Borges, and Nabokov] and are now in the evenings of their own careers" (Barth, 69). How to succeed in literature? Barth answers the question by really trying to act as a son to male writers. He acknowledges his fathers and ignores his mothers. He neglects to mention that metafiction is, in part, derived from female authors who retell patriarchal stories in a manner patriarchy would not sanction. Since (as I explain below) Dinesen's and Borges's short stories share many characteristics, Barth might logically express indebtedness to Dinesen as well as to Borges.

Seeming to anticipate Barth's silence about women writers, Dinesen creates a character who could speak in his place. Her Cardinal Salviati might be addressing Russ's often quoted essay "What Can a Heroine Do? Or Why Women Can't Write" when he explains that a "story . . . has a heroine—a young woman who by the sole virtue of being so becomes the prize of the hero. . . . But by the time when you have no more stories, your young women will be the prize and reward of nobody and nothing" (Dinesen, "The Cardinal's First Tale," 24–25). Russ and the Cardinal explain that heroines function as protagonists of love stories, as prizes for the male heroes.[4] Even though the time for feminist fabulators to desist from challenging patriarchal stories has not yet come, many of these writers who create SF are denied their inheritance from modernism; they receive the prize and reward of nobody and nothing.

While male metafictionists receive their modernist fathers' authoritative name, the influence of modernist mothers upon these metafictionists—as well as upon fabulative daughters—is ignored. Suffering the consequences of anxiety caused by lack of influence, feminist fabulative daughters are unable to claim the name "postmodern" for themselves. In "Copenhagen Season," Dinesen again seems to have in mind her daughters' dilemma regarding their rightful inheritance. The story's discussion of name and inheritance applies to feminist fabulators' status as the canonically dispossessed: "The land went with the name, the big fortunes and the good things of the earth. All were inherited. . . . To be born into the world without any kind of escorting inheritance was an idea so little pleasant as to be almost unseemly. . . . But namelessness was annihilation" (Dinesen, "Copenhagen Season," 252–253). Feminist fabulation's continued lack of association with both the name postmodernism and modernism's inheritance might lead to its annihilation. Literary postmodernism's true parentage can be revealed by uniting fabulative daughters with modernist mothers and by encouraging metafictional sons to acknowledge their mothers as well as their fathers. Such an understanding of the maternal influence upon postmodernism underscores that feminist fabulation—a particular, "monstrous" women's literature—deserves space within the canonical tradition which is rightfully its own. I take an initial step toward claiming this space by explaining why Borges's parental relationship to metafiction should be shared with Dinesen.

Mother Dinesen/Father Borges

Stories collected in Dinesen's *Last Tales* mirror such characteristics of Borges's *ficciones* as the presence of labyrinths, the implications of simultaneously finite and infinite possibilities, and the concern with man-made and natural systems. For example, Angelo Santasilia, the protagonist of Dinesen's "The Cloak," "Night Walk," and "Of Hidden Thoughts and of Heaven," resembles a Borgesian protagonist. Angelo enters a labyrinth when wandering "into a smaller street, and from that into one still narrower" (Dinesen, "Night Walk," 50). The streets Angelo encounters are mazes, seemingly infinite but ultimately finite Borgesian spaces. Like the apparently endless number of books Borges discusses in "The Library of Babel," Dinesen's confusing streets are an ordered, finite system.

One of the potentially multitudinous situations Angelo experiences as he meanders through textual labyrinths echoes Borges's notion that an individual's life extends beyond an individual's lifetime: "'A man is more than one man,' [Angelo] said slowly. 'And the life of a man is more than one life'" (Dinesen, "Of Hidden Thoughts and of Heaven," 62). Angelo's comment is applicable to Borges's "The Circular Ruins," a story about a progression of individuals who are products of other individuals' dreams. The Borgesian idea that all men can be seen as one man is reiterated in Dinesen's "Echoes." One of this story's protagonists, the retired diva Pellegrina Leoni, acquaints herself with an interbred population of a small town: "As she got to know them she saw that they had all of them become alike, their skulls slowly growing narrower and their faces more wooden" (Dinesen, "Echoes," 175). She views all the citizens as one citizen.

Dinesen, in the manner of Borges, describes man-made and natural systems. In "Of Hidden Thoughts and of Heaven," which emphasizes that writing is a constructed system, Angelo mentions "those small instruments that we call words, and by which we have to manage in this life of ours. I was thinking of how, by interchanging two everyday words in an everyday sentence, we alter our world" (Dinesen, "Of Hidden Thoughts and of Heaven," 59). Although systems such as writing provide keys to other constructed systems, people search in vain for keys to the secrets of the divine cosmos. Borges describes this search in "The Babylon Lottery," a story concerned with futile attempts to understand a divine system.

Dinesen parts company with Borges when she adds a female view to pondering human subordination to the divine universe. Her "Tales of Two Old Gentlemen" describes differing female and male approaches to comprehending the effects of the cosmos upon the man-made world. The story explains that men view the deity's relationship to humanity according to oppositions between hierarchies which coincide with a search and investigation model. Here is where the story emphasizes that women interpret this relationship as a love affair in which hierarchy, search, and investigation are inappropriate:

Man, troubled and perplexed about the relation between divinity and humanity, is ever striving to find a foothold in the matter by drawing on his own normal experience. He will view it in the light of relations between tutor and pupil, or of commander and soldier, and he will lose breath . . . in search and investigation. The ladies, whose nature is nearer to the nature of the deity, take no such trouble; they see the relation between the Cosmos and the Creator quite plainly as a love affair. And in a love affair search and investigation is an absurdity, and unseemly. (Dinesen, "Tales of Two Old Gentlemen," 65)

Man's normal experience differs from woman's normal experience. She is not valued by male tutors; she has no foothold in the world of commanders and soldiers; she has no stake in investigating the relationship between the cosmos and the man-made world she has not made. Borges's investigators, after all, are not women. In contrast to his "Tlön, Uqbar, Orbis Tertius," in which a man strives to understand a cosmos governed by strict laws, Dinesen announces that ladies are in the position of the deity. Ladies are creators of life who do not trouble themselves about the key to the universe. Ladies can build a woman's world by turning away from man's world and toward their own embrace with the cosmos. Woman's love affair with a feminist cosmos, her divorce from man's patriarchal world (a world described by Borges's notion of man's place in the divine cosmos—and by Scholes's notion of man's place in the system of the universe), is at the heart of feminist fabulation.

Hurston's Rewritten Tales

As some of Dinesen's tales share characteristics of Borges's *ficciones* and address women's concerns, Hurston's *Spunk* both resembles and differs from Barth's *Chimera*. Hurston rewrites myth from a black and, often, female perspective. "Spunk," for example, retells a white American folktale from a black viewpoint. Spunk Banks, the protagonist, is "a giant of a brown-skinned man [who] . . . ain't skeered of nothin' on God's green footstool—*nothin'*!" (Hurston, "Spunk," 1). He is a black Paul Bunyan, a logger who can subdue his human and supernatural rivals.

"Isis" is another retold tale—and it reflects a specifically female as well as a specifically black perspective. Because Isis's lack of appropriate attire prevents her from attending a carnival, she is analogous to a black Cinderella barred from the prince's ball. Isis lacks a fairy godmother, though: "She realized she couldn't dance at the carnival. Her dress was torn and dirty. She picked a long-stemmed daisy, and placed it behind her ear, but her dress remained torn and dirty just the same" (Hurston, "Isis," 14). In Hurston's retelling of "Cinderella," imagination—rather than fantastic mechanisms such as fairy godmothers or magic flowers—allows Isis to transcend her material limitations. Scarlett O'Hara masks her poverty by altering a curtain; Isis accomplishes this objective by altering a tablecloth: "A crowd of children gathered admiringly about her as she wheeled lightly about . . . with the red and white fringe of the tablecloth—Grandma's new red tablecloth that she wore in lieu of a Spanish shawl—trailing in the dust" (Hurston, "Isis," 15). Isis, a black version of Cinderella and Scarlett, the protagonist of a rewritten myth, explains that "she was really a princess" (Hurston, "Isis," 17). She is really correct.

Pinkie, the female protagonist of "Muttsy," makes a feminist statement by participating in a rewritten fairy tale. This protagonist is a black Sleeping Beauty who differs from the fairy tale character we all know. She refuses to collude with patriarchal silencing and with the intervention of Muttsy (her black Prince Charming): Muttsy "approached the bed and stood for awhile looking down upon her. . . . [He] kissed her lips again [and] . . . removed the largest diamond ring from his hand and slipped it on her engagement finger. . . . 'She's *mine*,' he said triumphantly, 'All mine!'" (Hurston, "Muttsy," 31–32). He views Pinkie as a possession, an inert female body whose thoughts and words are insignificant. She will not cooperate with his wish to own her. This Sleeping Beauty finds her voice. She speaks against sacrificing her individuality in order to receive Prince Charming's kiss: "He ain't goin' to make *me* one of his women—I'll die first! I'm goin' outa this house if I starve, lemme starve!" (Hurston, "Muttsy," 34). Her words oppose the silence of the newly awakened fairy tale Sleeping Beauty. We certainly never imagine the Sleeping Beauty character sounding like Hurston's specifically black and feminist version.

In contrast to Pinkie's protests, Missie May, the protagonist of "The Gilded Six-Bits," welcomes the embrace of her husband, Joe. The couple's environment is a rural, black version of the Garden of Eden: "But there was something happy about the place. . . . A mess of homey flowers planted without a plan but blooming cheerily from their helter-skelter places. The fence and house were whitewashed" (Hurston, "Gilded Six-Bits," 54). Missie May and Joe are cast out of their blissful, domestic garden after she succumbs to the monetary temptation offered by Otis Slemmons, a black man who represents the urban North's demonic corruption. "Gilded Six-Bits" is Hurston's retold Eden story which speaks to the color of metafiction.

Hurston's interchanges between alien individuals and cultures can be understood according to Donna Haraway's description of black women's literature as "cyborg writing." Haraway defines this term as writing about "the power to survive . . . on the basis of seizing the tools to mark the world that marked [black women] as other" (Haraway, 94). Isis, Missie May, and Delia Jones (the protagonist of "Sweat," who is discussed below) survive the world that marks them as Other by seizing and redefining unusual tools. Isis redefines ordinary material as appropriate festive attire; Missie May redefines her sexuality as a means to appropriate Otis Slemmons's money; Delia Jones redefines a rattlesnake as the liberator who eradicates her husband/tormentor. These protagonists transform their identities, their spaces, and their cultural symbols. They accomplish their objectives after forming new "monstrous" wholes from incongruous parts. They speak according to the language of women of color, which Haraway describes as a "chimeric monster, without claim to an original language before violation, that crafts the erotic, competent, potent identities of women of color" (Haraway, 94). Hurston's retold tales are chimeras, black feminist antecedents to Barth's *Chimera*, a black woman's precursor to metafiction. Despite Hurston's achievement, the pages of literary history are blank in regard to her relationship to feminist fabulators and male metafictionists.

Feminist Fabulation Appears on the Blank Page

Dinesen's "The Blank Page" defines a bloodstained bridal sheet as female art, a painting created with body fluid. The stained sheets—

which, in patriarchal terms, attest that the virgin bride conforms to patriarchy's story about suitable female behavior—rephrase patriarchal language. The sheets can be reinterpreted to mean that the virgin, who spends her life as a powerless, sexless blank page, behaves in an improper manner.

Dinesen allows the blank page to serve women's needs. The white sheet, which appears as "snow-white from corner to corner, a blank page" (Dinesen, "The Blank Page," 104), is an empowering blank page symbolizing female potential. The bride who sleeps on the sheet does not fit patriarchal stories; her sheet-as-canvas is blank rather than literally drawn from the patriarchal definition of her blood. This blank sheet becomes an appropriate symbol for new female art forms. Feminist fabulators, for example, stand before blank pages unsullied by patriarchy and fill them as they see fit. These writers are fettered only by the limits of their imaginations.

Feminist fabulators confront the blank pages of female potential, find patriarchal reality too constricting, and create fantastic tales about women's worlds. (They sometimes choose to fill the space of the blank page with space fiction.) Like Dinesen, they allow the word "blank" to assume constructive connotations for women. The feminist fabulator is freed, in Susan Gubar's words, from the "model of the pen-penis on the virgin page," a tradition which "excludes women from the creation of culture" (Gubar, 77). Gubar continues: "Were the female community less sensitive to the significance of these signs [remnants of women's lives], such stained sheets would not be considered art at all. Dinesen implies that woman's use of her own body in the creation of art results in forms of expression devalued or totally invisible to eyes trained by traditional aesthetic standards. She also seems to imply that, within the life of domesticity assigned the royal princess from birth, the body is the only accessible medium for self-expression" (Gubar, 78–79). Many examples of feminist fabulation are hardly considered art at all. Critical eyes trained by traditional aesthetic standards are blind to this literature's importance. The fact that the impulse toward the fantastic, toward SF, forms part of the work of modernist and postmodernist women writers remains unseen.

It is possible to chart the presence of SF in texts authored by Dinesen, Hurston, and Woolf. These writers create a foundation for contemporary feminist speculative fiction; they make space for space fiction. Feminist fabulators' relationship to SF has not been preceded by the blank page of women's silence on the subject.

Modernist Mothers as Precursors to Feminist Science Fiction

Food for Postmodern Thought

Dinesen's "Babette's Feast," an implied feminist utopia,[5] indicates that the fantastic is an appropriate mode for feminist fiction. The story's beginning includes a description of "a Huldre, a female mountain spirit of Norway" (Dinesen, "Babette's Feast," 25–26). Babette is analogous to this spirit in that she is a female alien, a French woman who enters the home of two unmarried sisters residing in the Norwegian town of Berlevaag. The sisters associate her with the marvelous: "They felt that their cook's old carpetbag was made from a magic carpet; at a given moment she might mount it and be carried off, back to Paris" (Dinesen, "Babette's Feast," 38). Babette is a magical alien who soon becomes an integral part of the sisters' familial female community.

Despite the incongruity of a French maid appearing in an austere Norwegian household, Babette adapts to her new environment. The atmosphere which surrounds her becomes welcoming rather than estranging: "The old Brothers and Sisters, who had first looked askance at the foreign woman in their midst, felt a happy change in their little sisters' life, rejoiced at it and benefited by it" (Dinesen, "Babette's Feast," 37). Babette's actions encourage this positive reception. After winning ten thousand francs, instead of choosing to become an image of French elegance supported by a French lottery— an action which would estrange her from her new community— Babette uses the money in a feminist manner. She literally nourishes the community when she creates her feast, a work of art which at once celebrates her substantial talents and serves the needs of the group.

As the ingredients arrive, both Babette and her feast are allied to the world of the fantastic. Robert Langbaum explains that the narrator of "Babette's Feast" alludes to witchcraft when describing Babette's work as she cooks (Langbaum, 251). I would add that the story's imagery also evokes the alien and the monstrous. Here is an example of such imagery:

> Babette, like the bottled demon of the fairy tale, had swelled and grown to such dimensions that her mistresses felt small before her. They now saw the French dinner coming upon them, a thing of incalculable nature and range. . . . In the light of the lamp [a turtle to be cooked for dinner] looked like some greenish-black stone, but when set down on the kitchen floor it suddenly shot out a snake-like head. . . . this thing was monstrous in size and terrible to behold. (Dinesen, "Babette's Feast," 45–46)

Babette becomes a swelled, unearthly demon, a gigantic monster; the dinner is an alien "thing." All the elements of a mediocre SF film are metaphorically present here. The dinner the monstrous Babette prepares could be described on a movie marquee as the attack of the thing that will eventually be eaten in Berlevaag. As an art form, Babette's creation of the alien dinner is akin to the art of feminist fabulation, which produces literature whose alien ingredients are concocted by the female imagination. As the monstrous dinner must be accepted, ingested, and appreciated by the traditional Norwegian community, feminist fabulation is the "monstrous" genre which should be canonized by the traditional academic literary community.

The story implies that, like quilts sewn by American pioneer women, Babette's feast can be viewed as a respected and valued art form. As a master chef, Babette has taken cooking, a part of the domestic female tradition, and manipulated it successfully in the public, masculine world of Parisian gastronomy. Her dual roles as master chef and domestic cook suggest the inappropriateness of evaluating art in terms of gender classifications. Babette, a revolutionary activist, a family cook, and a chef for aristocrats, is not concerned primarily with the moral effect her work may have on any audience. Rather than focusing upon being classified as a chef or a cook, Babette wishes to create as perfect a work as she can. Her skillful execution of both her public and her domestic cooking roles emphasizes that successful, nontraditional artworks (such as pioneers' quilts, Babette's feast, and feminist fabulation) should not be undervalued. Her feast is a transcendent experience, a personal and religious communicative rebirth:

> Of what happened later in the evening nothing definite can here be stated. . . . [The guests] only knew that the rooms had been filled with a heavenly light. . . . Taciturn old people received the gift of tongues; ears that for years had been almost deaf were opened to it. Time itself had merged into eternity. Long after midnight the windows of the house shown like gold, and golden song flowed out into the winter air. (Dinesen, "Babette's Feast," 61)

Babette's dinner coincides with a new manifestation of time, a change in the reflective properties of the window glass, and a merger of metal and art. The feast, then, is an art form initiating a world alien to the one we know, a world which defies natural laws. The event also improves the community's social relationships: "The two old women who had once slandered each other now in their hearts went back a long way, past the evil period in which they had been stuck, to those days of their early girlhood when together they had been preparing for confirmation and hand in hand had filled the roads round Berlevaag with singing" (Dinesen, "Babette's Feast," 61). Like the feast, feminist fabulation presents the possibility of new physical worlds and new mutual social respect. Both the feast and feminist fabulation are particularly female art forms which introduce remade psychic and physical spaces.

The two present fresh possibilities. The story's congregation, for example, enjoys the following experience: "The vain illusions of this earth had dissolved before their eyes like smoke, and they had seen the universe as it really is. They had been given one hour of the millennium. . . . tonight I [General Loewenhielm] have learned . . . that in this world anything is possible" (Dinesen, "Babette's Feast," 62). In feminist fabulative works, vain, patriarchal illusions about women—men's constructions of reality—dissolve; space is cleared for a new female vision of the universe (which might be how the universe really is). "Babette's Feast" establishes a foundation for the eventual appearance of literature depicting women's worlds (such as the stories published in Virginia Kidd's *Millennial Women*). Dinesen prepares a space for the literature that allows women and men to learn that in this world—or in other worlds—anything is possible, reality can be declared a fiction, and women's stories can inspire the construction of a nonpatriarchal society.

It is, of course, difficult to replace patriarchy with feminism. Feminists, like all artists working in noncanonical forms, and feminist art are often misunderstood and unappreciated. Despite this lack of acceptance, however, we must do our best. Langbaum points out that Babette pursues her art in the face of misunderstanding: "She had . . . to do her best even though no one at the dinner—she did not foresee the General's appearance—would understand what she had accomplished" (Langbaum, 254). Babette's artistic accomplishment is comprehended because of the unexpected appearance of a male. Ironically, due to his experience in the alien Parisian culinary world, a powerful male general is the person best equipped to understand Babette's achievement. His presence communicates a positive view of relationships between women and men. The sexes can step out of their respective environments. Babette and General Loewenhielm experience new social worlds. She moves from the excessiveness of Paris to the austerity of Berlevaag; he moves from Berlevaag to Paris. They come together at the table, a particular artistic space where women and men can coexist.

The diners at Babette's table enjoy a "kind of celestial second childhood." They are "bodily as well as spiritually hand in hand" during a time when the "stars have come nearer" (Dinesen, "Babette's Feast," 63). In terms of feminist fabulation, this passage hints that people can attain solidarity when they come nearer to the stars, when they engage with feminist space fiction. The fantastic elements of Dinesen's dinner scene indicate that feminist fabulation is an appropriate space for feminist writers and readers. Literature about stars is not always inferior to mainstream literature about earth's constructed reality.

As the title of the story's twelfth section ("The Great Artist") and Babette herself proclaim, she is in fact a great artist. Her feast validates domestic cooking as an art form and celebrates utopian goals. She indicates that feminist fabulators who use art as she does, to advocate women's utopian concerns, should also be considered great artists, not inhabitants of a female, subgeneric literary ghetto. Patriarchy works against the recognition of women artists, however. Babette's repetition of a remark made by the story's musician (Monsieur Achille Papin) indirectly comments upon this fact: "Through all the world there goes one long cry from the heart of the artist: Give me leave to do my utmost!" (Dinesen, "Babette's Feast," 68). Even though feminist fabulators do their utmost to challenge patriarchy, the politics of interpretation marginalizes their work.

At the conclusion of the story, Babette's body is (like the monoliths in Arthur C. Clarke's *2001: A Space Odyssey*) "a marble monument" (Dinesen, "Babette's Feast," 68), a marker attesting to the location and significance of feminist art. Langbaum states that "as marble monument, Babette symbolizes Achille and art" (Langbaum, 254). Such female art also is an Achilles' heel of patriarchal reality—the patriarchy's vulnerable point, where alternative versions of reality can be expressed. Defining feminist fabulation as an integral part of the postmodern canon and so ending the fiction of its subgeneric status can heighten patriarchy's vulnerability by sparking interest in creating a woman-oriented reality.

The final words of "Babette's Feast" signal the hope of such an occurrence: "Yet this is not the end! . . . In Paradise you [Babette] will be the great artist that God meant you to be! . . . how you will enchant the angels!" (Dinesen, "Babette's Feast," 68). The story is not the end but rather one beginning of respect for female art forms. In paradise, Babette will be recognized as a great artist. She will enchant the angels, who are, for instance, exemplified by the heavenly community of women in Sandi Hall's *The Godmothers*. Langbaum's interpretation of the conclusion of "Babette's Feast" complements my own. He writes, "Now she [Phillipa, one of the sisters] understands what food it is that is symbolized by Babette's food. She understands how art unites heaven and earth" (Langbaum, 254). An appreciation of women's art (symbolized by Babette's feast) can infuse patriarchy with the utopias feminist speculative fiction writers locate in the stars.

Indeed, the stars seem to come nearer to Babette's world. When Babette's guests leave her dinner, stars falling to earth in the form of snow impede them: "In the street the snow was lying so deep that it had become difficult to walk. The guests . . . staggered, sat down abruptly or fell forward . . . and were covered with snow, as if they had indeed had their sins washed white as wool, and in this regained innocent attire were gamboling like little lambs" (Dinesen, "Babette's Feast," 63). This imagery implies that people have a new innocence, a potential for social rebirth. The sisters' father states, "God's paths run across the sea and the snowy mountains, where man's eye sees no track" (Dinesen, "Babette's Feast," 30). The guests cannot make tracks in their own streets. Man's eye, the patriarchal gaze, is stopped in its own tracks. It is time, as feminist fabulation tells us, to emphasize the goddess whose paths run across the sky and the starry galaxies. It is time to try to see the goddess's path, to place feminist tracks in the new space of new reality. "Babette's Feast," collected in *Shadows of Destiny*, is an anecdote about the destiny of respect for feminist art forms and feminist social structures. It is a modernist literary space which anticipates the work of postmodernist feminist fabulators.

Orlando, *Canonized on Canopus?*

Woolf also creates space which prefigures contemporary feminist space fiction. Feminist fabulators (such as Tiptree, who in *Up the Walls of the World* creates the ultimately immortal and androgynous residents of the planet Tyree) retell Woolf's previously told tale of the ageless, androgynous Orlando, a literal transcender of gender. The conclusion of *Orlando*, which describes an unreal setting, marks the beginning of twentieth-century feminist fabulation. Woolf writes, "The moon rose slowly over the weald. Its light raised a phantom castle upon earth. . . . Of wall or substance there was none. All was phantom" (Woolf, 328). When Orlando directs her lover Shelmerdine toward her as he emerges from this moonlit sky, she mentions extraterrestrial spiders and bares her breast to the moon: "'Here! Shel, here!' she cried, baring her breast to the moon (which now showed bright) so that her pearls glowed like the eggs of some vast moon-spider" (Woolf, 328–329). In the manner of the feminist utopians in Sally Miller Gearhart's *The Wanderground*, Orlando eschews patriarchal religions by attempting to merge her female essence (symbolized by her breast) with a goddess (symbolized by the moon). The moon responds by shining bright, signaling a successful communicative link between woman and goddess.

The pearls glowing like the eggs of some vast moon-spider might describe feminist fabulation. Both represent re-creation—not benign accoutrements of femininity. (Further, like black widow spiders and the women who inhabit some separatist feminist utopias, the vast female moon-spider might not welcome the male of her species.) Pearls are beautiful objects constructed in response to sand wounding the oyster's flesh, the encroachment of an alien object into the oyster's space. Feminist fabulation is art created in response to sexism's wounding instances, the encroachment of alien patriarchal ideology into women's space. Orlando's pearls are rather obtrusive: "Her pearls burnt like a phosphorescent flare in the darkness" (Woolf, 329). These burning pearls seem to pertain to feminist fabulation, "monstrous" art which shines like the flare emerging from a launched rocket, women's art created in response to wounds patriarchy inflicts. Feminist fabulation is able to shift women's attention from the earthbound space of patriarchal darkness to the unearthly flare of a new feminist world. Feminist fabulation directs women toward developing nonpatriarchal selves and societies. The phrase the "eggs of some vast moon-spider" brings a specific example of this literature to mind: James Tiptree's "Love Is the Plan, the Plan Is Death," the story of how the eggs of a vast alien spider depend upon eradicating the father's ability to function. (The story describes how a sentient spider plants her eggs in the anesthetized body of her mate.)

SF is further evoked in *Orlando* by Shelmerdine's craft in the sky. This craft does not function in the manner of an ordinary airplane: "The aeroplane rushed out of the clouds and stood over her head. It hovered above her" (Woolf, 329). Airplanes neither stand still in the air nor hover. Although Shelmerdine's "aeroplane" is not literally identical with an extraterrestrial vehicle, it bears an odd likeness to a flying saucer. Orlando, the hailer of this ship, resembles a long-lived alien who, in the manner of Doris Lessing's Canopean agents Ambien II (in *The Sirian Experiments*) and Johor (in *Documents Relating to the Sentimental Agents in the Volyen Empire, The Making of the Representative for Planet 8*, and *Re: Colonised Planet 5, Shikasta*), chronicles earth's changes throughout different centuries. *Orlando* could appropriately function as a text prepared for the Canopean archives; Orlando could appropriately function as an agent sent to earth from Canopus. Woolf is silent about the subject of Orlando's death. *Orlando* stops; Orlando goes on.

Where is Orlando presently? This character who inhabits different bodies might be situated in another fiction. She/he might be Benaroya, a dolphinlike creature from another planet, who becomes Virginia Woolf in Jody Scott's novels, *I, Vampire* and *Passing for Human*. These novels juxtapose fiction and reality through the implication that Benaroya might have written *Orlando*.[6] After all, according to *Passing for Human*, Benaroya is Woolf. The novel describes Benaroya as she dons Woolf's body: "She finally chose a Virginia Woolf body, circa 1903. . . . It had been stored for decades between Marcel Proust and Little Emily. When the body was ready to go, Virginia Woolf cleared her desk. . . . Next Virginia Woolf returned to the United States, doing interviews with anyone and everyone" (Scott, 118). Did Woolf pass for human? Did she walk into the river Ouse, shed her human body, and emerge in her true Benaroya form?

My point is that Woolf, Lessing, and Scott create literature which causes readers to categorize patriarchal reality as fiction that, potentially, can be revised. Feminist fabulation views language as a provider of false security, an illusion of reality which, according to Borges, facilitates people's efforts to inhabit an uncaring, unknowable cosmos. Benaroya's transformation calls into question the immediate decision to classify Virginia Woolf as "human woman." *Orlando* points to this rage for classification when Orlando categorizes the "single wild bird" appearing at the end of the text: " 'It is the goose!' Orlando cried. 'The wild goose' " (Woolf, 329). It does not know or care that we call it a goose. Nor does it consider itself to be wild. It can fly beyond human language systems.

In contrast to the wild goose, the human it born without a penis must become a she, a process which feminizes females, teaches them that they must not become wild, or monstrous. Orlando's transitions and feminist fabulation's sex-role reversals emphasize that women are instructed to stay in a limited space to avoid becoming what Mary Russo calls "female grotesques." As Russo explains, learning that you are a she coincides with learning not to make a spectacle out of yourself: "'She' . . . is making a spectacle out of herself. Making a spectacle out of oneself seemed a specifically feminine danger. . . . For a woman, making a spectacle out of herself had more to do with a kind of inadvertency and loss of boundaries" (Russo, 213). A woman, according to patriarchal definitions, makes a spectacle out of herself when she takes up too much space. *Orlando* and its fabulative descendants unmask the fictionality of such arbitrary prohibitions, the fictionality of becoming a feminine she. These texts proclaim that each she is a fictional shadow of a full human, a shadow of men who are free to make spectacles of themselves.

Orlando begins by insisting that an eventual she is a he: "He—for there could be no doubt of his sex" (Woolf, 13). Woolf's play with "she" and "he" is mirrored in Russ's feminist utopia "When It Changed," a story which begins with gender ambiguity: the narrator who has a wife is not a he. In fact, until men arrive on Russ's women's planet (called Whileaway), there is no need to use the word "he": "He turned *his* head—those words had not been in our language for six hundred years" (Russ, "When It Changed," 2263). Russ is a daughter of Woolf, and progress has been made since her mother's time. (Russ describes herself by saying, "I am indeed a daughter of Woolf. I used to read her in secret in college in my teens. I was ashamed of loving her work because it was so feminine—this was the 50's and nobody knew about her lesbianism either" [Russ, letter to author, March 4, 1991].) Woolf calls for a room of one's own; Russ's space fiction calls for even more room, more space—a planet of one's own.

Woolf's and Russ's fantastic visions underscore that, unlike birds who can fly from the designation "wild goose," real-world women cannot completely escape limitations coinciding with the designation "she." Flights of feminist fantasy, totally effective escape routes from patriarchy, are, to date, available only in feminist fantastic texts. While feminist fabulation's excursions beyond patriarchal boundaries might be canonized on Canopus, they are certainly not canonized on earth.

The terrestrial academic community can fruitfully follow Canopus's hypothetical literary taste. Many postmodern writers designated as "she" are presently labeled as frivolous SF authors, female grotesques, women who make spectacles of themselves, monsters lurking outside the canon. Contrary to these labels, ostracized feminist fabulators, who have up to now claimed the prize and reward of nobody and nothing, can finally declare themselves to be the beneficiaries of modernist mothers.

Alice Walker's "In Search of Our Mothers' Gardens" mentions that black women's experiences are excluded from a particular white modernist mother's text: Woolf's *A Room of One's Own*. Walker discusses Phillis Wheatley by inserting descriptions of Wheatley's experience—"chains, guns, the lash, the ownership of one's body by someone else, submission to alien religion" (Walker, 2377)—within a quotation from *A Room of One's Own*. She applies Woolf's term "contrary instincts" to Wheatley and to "that freest of all black women writers, Zora Hurston" (Walker, 2377). With Walker's expansion of Woolf's text in mind, I supplement my earlier discussion of Hurston's relationship to male metafiction by placing Hurston alongside Dinesen and Woolf. I would like to designate this most free black woman writer as another modernist precursor to the contrary instincts of contemporary feminist fabulators in regard to patriarchy.

Invaders: Aliens in Eatonville, Monsters in Delia's House and Missie May's Garden

Hurston writes stories about intruding aliens and interchanges between alien cultures. Her aliens are black people engaging with white people and black women engaging with black men. Her colliding alien cultures are the black world and the white world, and the differing black worlds of rural Eatonville and urban Harlem. Although Hurston is, of course, recognized as the literary mother of Toni Morrison and Alice Walker, one of her daughters still remains orphaned. I declare Hurston's relationship to black feminist space fiction, to Octavia Butler.

Hurston's stories contain the stuff of genre SF. Isis, for example, experiences an alien encounter when she runs to the woods to escape being beaten by her grandmother. The aliens Isis discovers are white beings (a couple named Helen and Harry) who emerge from a large car, not green beings who emerge from a flying saucer: "The purr of a motor struck her ear and she saw a large, powerful car jolting along the rutty road toward her. . . . She had often dreamed of riding in one of these heavenly chariots but never thought she would, actually" (Hurston, "Isis," 16). The car, which from Isis's perspective seems analogous to a SF spaceship, is the dreamed of heavenly chariot which suddenly appears and becomes accessible.

"Isis" functions in the manner of Tiptree's "The Women Men Don't See." Tiptree is Dinesen's postmodern daughter who inherits Dinesen's female version of Borges's man searching for the key to the universe. In Tiptree's story, Ruth Parsons and her possibly pregnant daughter Althea quietly leave earth, man's constructed social system, and embrace the cosmos. These women, who rendezvous with aliens to venture to an unknown planet, are at odds with the man-made patriarchal system, not with the divinely constructed universe. Ruth and Althea flee this system. They are tired of satisfying Rupert Birkin's desire for women men don't see, tired of being erased by patriarchy's insistence upon invisible women. Feminist fabulation gives female characters the opportunity to oblige both Rupert Birkin and Ursula Brangwen, to be at once visible and invisible. Like Ruth and Althea, feminist fabulation's protagonists become invisible to patriarchy when they inhabit an alternative construction of reality. The patriarchal literary establishment prefers not to see such dangerous female visions and defines them as marginal, invisible.

Because of such purposeful patriarchal blindness, Barth is lauded as a postmodern fabulator while Tiptree is ostracized as a noncanonical SF writer. Further, Tiptree's relationship to Hurston has never been acknowledged. No one has connected Ruth's and Althea's trip to the Mexican jungle, where they implore aliens to help them escape patriarchy, with Isis's trip to the woods. Isis begs aliens from an unknown white world to help her avoid her grandmother's wrath. She plaintively asks the white couple, Helen and Harry, "Do you wanta keep me?" (Hurston, "Isis," 17). (Her reaction to Helen and Harry is too naive to involve racial crosscurrents.) Ruth echoes Isis's childish tone when she addresses aliens from another planet:

"Please take us. We don't mind what your planet is like; we'll learn—we'll learn—we'll do anything! We won't cause any trouble. Please. Oh *Please*" (Tiptree, "Women Men Don't See," 161). Isis is as anxious to enter a large car from the white world as Ruth is to enter a flying saucer from an extraterrestrial world. Both characters look toward aliens to improve their situations.

In "Isis," Hurston exposes white oppression by creating a black character who wishes to join alien white people; in "The Women Men Don't See," Tiptree exposes patriarchy's marginalized, invisible women by creating characters who leave earth literally to become invisible women. Hurston's and Tiptree's characters collude with oppressors to realize their objectives. Althea and Ruth use women's invisibility to demand women's visibility; Isis uses racial difference to seek racial equality. (Similarly, chapter 4 explains that Barthelme uses sexism to unmask sexism.)

In contrast to young Isis, Delia Jones, the protagonist of "Sweat," knows perfectly well that racism makes it possible for white people to be more powerful than black people. She tells Sykes, her black husband and most immediate oppressor, "Ah'm goin' tuh de white folks 'bout *you*" (Hurston, "Sweat," 49). "Sweat" can be read as a feminist dystopia. Delia Jones resembles the "fems," the brutalized women in Suzy McKee Charnas's *Walk to the End of the World*. As men appropriate the space constituting the "Holdfast" in *Walk*, Sykes appropriates the space constituting the house he and Delia share. The house, though, belongs to Delia, who bought it with the money she earned washing clothes. She asserts her right to control the house: "Mah sweat is done paid for this house and Ah reckon Ah kin keep on sweatin' in it" (Hurston, "Sweat," 40). Sykes does not recognize his wife's claim to control the space her labor secures. His failed perception manifests itself when he tries to bar Delia's (and his own) means of support from the house. He says, "Ah done tole you time and again to keep them white folks' clothes outa dis house" (Hurston, "Sweat," 39). Delia is prevented from defining the house her work supports as a woman's space. Sykes's behavior exemplifies the need for specifically feminist spaces, feminist communities. After his demise, Delia is finally able to call her house her own.

The snake is not a menace. Sykes, not the snake, is the story's stock SF monster. Delia behaves in the manner of Isis and the Parsons women, who wish to join invaders whose race (or, in the Parsons's case, species) differs from their own. Delia is rescued by an unexpectedly benign alien—the snake who performs a useful service for her when it causes Sykes to resemble an attacked sentient eye. Delia sees Sykes's "horribly swollen neck and his one open eye shining with hope. A surge of pity too strong to support bore her away from that eye. . . . she knew the cold river was creeping up and up to extinguish that eye which must know by now that she knew" (Hurston, "Sweat," 52–53). She knows that she has been liberated from the venomous patriarchy.

Otis C. Slemmons is the figurative invading snake in Missie May's and Joe's marital garden. Joe's discovery of her adulterous relationship with Slemmons corresponds to an SF alteration of time: "The great belt on the wheel of Time slipped and eternity stood still" (Hurston, "Gilded Six-Bits," 62). Time passes normally again after Missie May ceases to risk her husband's love for a chance to acquire money. She learns to view Slemmons's coin in her husband's pocket as a dangerous alien monster: "In fact the yellow coin in his trousers was like a monster hiding in the cave of his pockets to destroy her" (Hurston, "Gilded Six-Bits," 65). Money becomes monstrous, a gold invader representing white corruption of black culture. Missie May, in the manner of an interplanetary colonizer successfully combating alien intruders, is eventually able to reclaim her Edenic world.

Reading Hurston in terms of SF imagery exemplifies that she, like Dinesen and Woolf, can be positioned as a mother of feminist fabulators. These connections underscore that canonizing the "monstrous" feminist fabulator entails knowing that her female "I" should not be extinguished from women's literary tradition and feminist critical discourse. I now turn from modernist mothers to a particular, extinguished postmodern female "I"—to Mary Caraker and her ostracized genre SF novel *Seven Worlds*.

Exhausting the Literature of Exhaustion: Feminist Meta-metafiction

"Grotesque," "monstrous" feminist fabulators envision new literary spaces which stretch beyond the limits of metafiction. For example, Mary Caraker, a marginalized SF writer, deserves recognition for including this new literary space in *Seven Worlds*. Caraker's protagonist, Space Corps agent Morgan Farraday, following the tradition of Naomi Haldane Mitchison's *Memoirs of a Space Woman*, is a female version of the male interplanetary explorer. While Morgan experiences public adventures on seven worlds, she faces the three private worlds of single, married, and separated women. Caraker's accessible text, which directly addresses female readers' problems, is feminist fabulation's version of Marilyn French's *The Women's Room*.

In addition to engaging a general female audience, Caraker, a former literature graduate student who has taught English, speaks to English teachers. *Seven Worlds* advocates the importance of teaching and takes issue with the lack of respect teachers receive. In the novel's second chapter, "The Vampires Who Loved Beowulf," Morgan's teaching skills are valued, and literature becomes an important item of exchange between the Corps and the alien Rogans: "We need the base here, and they seem to need our stories. Strictly business, that's what it has to be" (Caraker, 44). The Rogans' need for literature transforms Caraker's SF vampire story into an example of feminist meta-metafiction.

Morgan's description of how the Rogans absorb and re-create *Beowulf* pertains to this statement. She explains that

> the Rogans *act out* their epics. They're a degenerated race, and their own history is probably a constant repetition of their songs. . . . They do little but sleep and sing. Add to that—re-create. . . . They're actors. Imitators. Imagine their delight at getting some new material from us. The *Iliad*. The *Odyssey*. Plenty of blood and action there, and I'm sure they performed it all. . . . they feel such an affinity to the *Beowulf*, they can't even wait until it's finished. I read about the murdered thane at my first session. . . . And they've already done that scene—head and all. (Caraker, 50–51)

The Rogans literally retell earth tales, bring fiction about fiction to another fictional level. They act out earth stories before incorporating them within their reality. This merging of fiction and reality causes Rogan reality to become an authored fiction. Hence, *Seven*

Worlds is meta-metafiction, fiction about fiction about reality as fiction.

The exhausted Rogan society re-creates itself in terms of a literature of exhaustion derived from an alien culture's stories. Morgan shows that patriarchy could act in kind: patriarchy could enact the feminist fabulative stories it perceives to be alien.[7] She merely alters the curriculum to coax Rogan behavior toward less violent directions: "I'll end *Beowulf* quickly: an edited version. Then I'll give them something innocuous. *Hiawatha*, maybe—just the pastoral parts. They might even learn to smoke peace-pipes" (Caraker, 52). Although Morgan's shift from *Beowulf* to *Hiawatha* is amusing, her decision has serious implications regarding the effects stories have upon audiences.[8]

Consumers of violent media and games played on computers act according to the Rogan re-creation of *Beowulf*. Rogans chop off one another's heads after reading *Beowulf*. People—using Star Wars technology—chop off other people's heads after being exposed to violent literature, films, and video games. As Haraway explains, "The culture of video games is heavily oriented to individual competition and extraterrestrial warfare. High-tech, gendered imaginations are produced here, imaginations that can contemplate destruction of the planet and a sci-fi escape from its consequences. More than our imaginations is militarized" (Haraway, 88). To counteract the influence of what Haraway calls the "informatics of domination," the transition from "the comfortable old hierarchical dominations to the scary new networks" (Haraway, 80), we need a change in the curriculum. We need a feminist informatics of peace.

As Morgan substitutes *Hiawatha* for *Beowulf*, Americans can substitute Sydney J. Van Scyoc's *Star Mother*, the story of a nurturing interplanetary peace corps cadet, for America's Strategic Defense Initiative—America's *Star Father*—America's story of international antagonism. This chapter advocates behavior-altering changes in the curriculum, movement from texts about violent patriarchal acts (such as works by Hemingway and Mailer) to texts which serve as models for new feminist societies. I cannot resist saying that we can marginalize the war stories stemming from *Beowulf* and emphasize the feminist stories stemming from Virginia Woolf.

If militaristic communications technologies can produce high-tech, gendered imaginations which relish competition and warfare, feminist communicative modes might encourage peace and cooperation. Feminist fabulation is one alternative to video games, one means to produce imaginations directed toward peace. Just as *Hiawatha* encourages the Rogans to smoke peace pipes, feminist fabulation might inspire altruistic rather than militaristic behavior patterns; this literature might defuse the high-tech production of popular culture's masculinist SF myth systems.

Feminist teachers can influence responses to these systems by following Morgan Farraday's example, by redirecting the patriarchal focus of readers' attention. Unfortunately, however, most literary scholars would not choose to introduce students to Morgan Farraday. While the popular marketplace—and the academic scientific community—exalts Star Wars technology, the academic humanities community denigrates feminist fabulation. Most members of English departments would not respect Caraker's text, which, rather than being frivolous, mirrors Haraway's theories about the informatics of domination. This attitude ensures that feminist myths and meanings will continue to fail to structure our imagination and reality. If the feminist academic empire does not strike back, the militaristic informatics of domination will be further strengthened. One alternative is to canonize feminist fabulation and thereby validate a cultural space which opposes popular and high culture infused with patriarchal ideology. Teachers, for instance, can try to convince students that emphasizing ecology (an emphasis exemplified by the kudzu vines growing in the women's spaceships in Tiptree's "Houston, Houston, Do You Read?") is as compelling as imagining zap guns. Teachers can approach students in terms of Morgan's notion that peaceful texts can inspire peaceful behavior. When attempting to fire patriarchy, teachers can try to shoot down violent, misogynist literature and popular culture (such as video games which use war themes). Teachers can try to weaken patriarchy as well as the specter of real war. The failure to attempt to do so is monstrous.

Morgan's changed curriculum shifts a community's behavior from destructive to constructive acts. She single-handedly directs Rogan attention from aggressiveness and domination to an alternative peaceful story. In the manner of Morgan's pedagogical plan, I resort to substitution to discuss modernist mothers' relationship to feminist fabulation and male metafiction: I replace Hurston's poisonous snake with a harmless amphibian—Haraway's regenerated salamander.

Resisting Patriarchal Stories: Amphibian Critic, Regenerated Canon

Feminist fabulation is one example of what Haraway calls the "promising monsters who help redefine the pleasures and politics of embodiment and feminist writing" (Haraway, 98). This literature has the potential to become a "world-changing fiction" (Haraway, 65). However, before feminist fabulation can change the world—or change feminist writing—literary critics must define it as a valuable part of the literary world. This approach entails rethinking definitions of canonical fiction and accepting that "cyborg monsters in feminist science fiction define quite different political possibilities and limits from those proposed by the mundane fiction of Man and Woman" (Haraway, 99). Respecting these different possibilities and limits can lead to establishing political agendas which move beyond the technological informatics of domination.

In short, feminist literary critics can affect the world by applying Haraway's biological understanding of "regeneration" to feminist fabulation—and to themselves. Feminist literary critics are quite analogous to regenerated salamanders:

> For salamanders, regeneration after injury, such as the loss of a limb, involves regrowth of structure and restoration of function with the constant possibility of twinning or other topographical productions at the site of former injury. The regrown limb can be monstrous, duplicated, potent. We have all been injured, profoundly. We require regeneration, not rebirth, and the possibilities of our reconstruction include the utopian dream of the hope for a monstrous world without gender. . . . It [cyborg imagery] means both building and destroying machines, identities, categories, relationships, spaces, stories. (Haraway, 100–101)

Many feminist academicians state that they have been injured by learning to survive in the patriarchal education system. While progressing from graduate student, to assistant professor, to tenured professor, one cannot remain completely unaffected by patriarchal fictions. (I am afraid that a large number of my feminist colleagues believe the fiction of the valueless, subgeneric status of feminist fabulation, for example.) Feminist fabulation, texts severed from the critics' purview which need to be regenerated, is the postmodern canon's lost limb. Feminist fabulation as regrown limb is odd, potent, monstrous. It demands that we embrace monstrous fictions about worlds without gender. Respecting this literature entails ridding ourselves of fictions which marginalize feminist fabulation, creating new spaces for alternative space fiction, and building feminist scholarly communicative machines to nullify patriarchal cyborg machines.

Feminist critics are like salamanders in relation to feminist fabulation as absent canonical component. We are injured monsters who work toward canonizing the monstrous. Monstrous, potent feminist fabulation can spring from the site of one of our injuries—the place where this literature has purposefully been made separate from the canon. Regenerating feminist postmodern writers involves replacing the fiction of feminist fabulation's marginality with the truth about feminist fabulation's rightful position as respected postmodern fiction. This goal cannot be achieved without the cooperation of feminist critics, who have everything to gain from texts which insist that "[male] gender might not be the global identity after all" (Haraway, 99). Feminist fabulation provides a means to experience new global identities and to alter the world by embracing the alien.

Peter Brown, a member of Princeton University's history department, has announced in the *New York Times Magazine* that he and his departmental colleagues are ready to engage in such an embrace: "Our starting point is our sense of the alien. . . . Our aim may be to inculcate respect for it. That, too, is the historian's office" (Brown, quoted in Silk, 63). It is the feminist literary critic's office to treat alien characters and texts as Brown and his colleagues treat alien historical concepts. By asserting that feminist fabulation is canonical, feminist critics can locate themselves at the starting point of generating respect for the alien in feminist literature.

Feminist critics should heed Russ's instructions to *The Female*

Man, her textual daughter. Russ advises, "Go, little book. . . . Live merrily, little daughter book, even if I can't and we can't; recite yourself to all who will listen; stay hopeful and wise. . . . Do not get glum when you are no longer understood little book. Do not curse your fate. . . . Rejoice, little book! For on that day, we will be free" (Russ, *Female Man,* 213–214). The critic herself should listen to Russ's "little daughter book" and encourage others to listen. If the texts of feminist fabulation live merrily, they can enhance opportunities for women to live in kind. The little book's noncanonical status, after all, coincides with the little woman's marginal status.

Women will progress toward freedom when feminist fabulation is ensconced within the canon. Women will be free when feminist fabulation becomes obsolete, when fiction addressing patriarchy's fictionality is replaced by an improved social story which fills the space patriarchal reality might vacate. Meanwhile, it is crucial to recognize the rightful parentage of *The Female Man* and its sister texts. The daughter books I characterize as feminist fabulation are born of modernist mothers and deserve to share equal status with their postmodern brothers. Rather than being literary orphans who, as Dinesen discusses in "Copenhagen Season," suffer from the absence of family name, these books carry the name of the modernist literary mother, an inheritance which should no longer be ignored.

Fabulative daughter books are positive, feminist she-monsters, dispossessed heirs to space in the postmodern canon. Daughter books inspire revisions of patriarchal fictions. Feminist critics can rejoice while reading them and bringing readers to them. After creating canonical space for feminist fabulation, we may be free. The women men don't see no longer will be feminist writers who create invisible texts.

PART II ★ ○) ★ ○) ★ ○)

Redefining Gendered Space

Pablo Picasso, The Scallop Shell: Notre Avenir est dans l'air. *Private collection.*

"A Dream of Flying"

But, of course, we couldn't let you girls fly again. . . .
The air is no place for a woman. The earth is her
home.

—Inez Haynes Gillmore, *Angel Island*

And once the old world has turned on its axle so that
the new dawn can dawn, then, ah, then! all the
women will have wings, the same as I. This young
woman in my arms, . . . will tear off her mind forg'd
manacles, will rise up and fly away.

—Angela Carter, *Nights at the Circus*

Flying is woman's gesture—flying in language and
making it fly. We have all learned the art of flying and
its numerous techniques; . . . It's no accident: women
take after birds and robbers just as robbers take after
women and birds. They go by, fly the coop, take plea-
sure in jumbling the order of space, in disorienting
it, . . . turning propriety upside down.

—Hélène Cixous, "The Laugh of the Medusa"

Even during the postmodern jet age, until very recently the United States government has stolen flying from women by declaring female combat pilots to be unlawful entities. "Mind forg'd manacles" have constrained American women in regard to piloting most commercial and all combat flights. "The air is no place for a woman," says a male character in Inez Haynes Gillmore's 1914 novel, *Angel Island*. A particular contemporary text reflects this character's comment: Congressional Law 10 U.S.C. Sec. 8549, which forbids Air Force women to pilot fighter planes engaged in combat missions.[1] Patriarchy controls airspace and outer space by defining the right stuff as male and by viewing flying technology as military technology. The authors I discuss in chapter 3 disrupt patriarchy's notion of flying.

Hilary Masters's *Cooper*, from which this chapter takes its title
(138), depicts flying as a humanist hope rather than as a connection
to war and hopelessness. After exploring Masters's positive portrayal
of flight, I turn to Valerie Miner's *All Good Women*, Marge Piercy's
Gone to Soldiers, Carol Hill's *The Eleven Million Mile High Dancer*, and Octavia Butler's *Dawn*, texts which discuss women and
flight according to a continuum ranging from the real to the imaginary. Miner and Piercy, respectively, consider this subject in relation
to the World War II home front and the Women's Air Force Service
Pilots (WASPs). Hill departs from reality when she depicts NASA
personnel engaging with alien phenomena. Butler's protagonist interacts with aliens in a postnuclear holocaust world. These authors
steal flying back from patriarchy by describing women's accomplishments and dreams in regard to flight. The winged women
Angela Carter (in *Nights at the Circus*) and Inez Haynes Gillmore
create reflect this theft. So do the alternatives to patriarchal flying
imagined by the authors I mention at the chapter's conclusion:
Susan Daitch, Lisa Goldstein, Erica Jong, Beryl Markham, Jane
Palmer, and Kurt Vonnegut. The words which appear in Picasso's
1912 painting *The Scallop Shell: Notre Avenir est dans l'air* still
hold true. Our future *is* in the air. Imagining this future involves "a
dream of flying."

"Fly the coop . . . jumbling the order of space."

Masters views flying as a potential space for improved human relationships. The first image in *Cooper*, a broken cuckoo-clock bird
perched outside a house, seems to imply that patriarchal mechanisms
break Woman: "The clock on the kitchen wall had not reached seven,
but the headless bird predicted the hour. . . . The bird was stuck on
its little platform beneath the eaves of the miniature Alpine *hutte*,
as if it refused to return to its cubby without its head. . . . He would
want to fix the whole mechanism at once, Jack Cooper thought, for
there was no point in giving the bird back its head without also
restoring its mobility" (Masters, 1). Even when Woman is perched
outside the home, her head often remains filled with patriarchal
definitions. Patriarchy renders her headless and immobile, a broken
cuckoo whose time to fly to freedom has not yet come.

Jack Cooper wishes immediately to fix the clock mechanism; Hilary Masters wishes immediately to fix the patriarchal social mechanism. *Cooper* is Masters's repair manual, a narrative about constructing a new, improved male. Cooper is a utopian man, the perfect husband to Ruth and the perfect father to Hal, his adopted, retarded son. Ruth reacts to her mate by committing adultery and by calling him a "fucking earth-father" (Masters, 62). In Masters's novel, a woman's relationship with a utopian male fails; in contemporary reality, people seek utopian relationships. "It's the kind of time when people are seeking Utopia. The big market in science fiction, that sort of thing," explains Cooper's editor, Kelly Novak. It's the kind of time when Woman as broken cuckoo seeks Utopia by attaching herself to the sort of sensitive man Cooper epitomizes.[2] *Cooper* and—as I explain in chapter 5—the feminist separatist utopia proclaim that female-male love relationships simply do not work. Masters uses flight as a metaphor to signal hope for rising above this interpersonal fiasco.

By presenting Cooper's utopian viewpoint, Masters indicates that even this well-meaning male protagonist fails to supply the right ingredients for improved heterosexual relationships. Cooper's life is unsatisfactory. Like Woman, he too is a broken cuckoo in need of repair before he can fly from a domestic perch. Cooper is a housebound wimp married to an unfaithful wife, a protagonist who reverses stereotypical female and male roles. He is the silent partner who devotes himself to marriage; Ruth is the assertive partner who places her work before marriage. Cooper, a perfect male spouse, is an imperfect person, a Walter Mitty figure who uses imaginative stories about flying to escape boredom.

Cooper enters an alternative world when, while working in a magazine store, he writes about pilots: "He had been so eager that morning to get down to the store, to go through the window and into that never-never land, as Kelly [Novak] called it" (Masters, 142). But unlike Walter Mitty, Cooper actually experiences his imaginative world. In Masters's role-reversal novel, Novak is the fairy godmother who changes a man's mundane domestic existence. She transforms Cooper's flying stories into vehicles to attend chic Manhattan business lunches. She turns Cooper's fiction into reality: "Kelly Novak had tapped a key to send a message that surprised him. . . . It was like a message from another world, out of one of his own fictions. Flip Winslow waiting for a code of some sort, maybe a faint voice coming over the transmitter of his secret airfield" (Masters, 103–104). Novak enables Cooper to experience space differently: "For years . . . his path between their small house and the Black Ace back-issue store . . . has been along one route, back and forth. . . . Yet, that afternoon he had gone from point A to point B differently" (Masters, 114–115).

Cooper's new path, the two-career marriage positioned as an escape route from domesticity, fails to improve his own and Ruth's marital life. Sex-role reversals—with Cooper and Ruth traveling from point A to point B differently—do not make the couple happy. Masters presents an alternative plan: like those writers who create new feminist utopian spaces, he eradicates points A and B. He gestures toward an uncharted realm, the space beyond point Z located outside patriarchal representational systems. He approaches this space by substituting flying associated with liberation for flying associated with domination, by acting counter to his name. Cooper is no barrel maker—no creator of containers to shape spilling, uncontrollable, "female" fluidity. He builds wooden airplanes rather than wooden barrels, and he wishes to eradicate the social containers which constrain freely flowing behavior. This sensitive man transcends rather than makes molds. Instead of containing fluids—or, inhibiting women—he desires to defy gravity. A space vehicle is an appropriate barrel for Cooper.

In the manner of Walter Mitty, Cooper imagines that driving his Buick resembles traveling in a space capsule: "It was like being in a space capsule. . . . and he had been overcome by a strange emotion; rather like how an astronaut must feel; a combination of estrangement . . . as he pulls away from the lights of earth, knowing a set of those tiny lights belonged to a place he had put together himself" (Masters, 6). Astronauts pull away from the lights of home, the faulty domestic environment put together by man himself. When Cooper pulls away from the lights of his house, he moves toward an illuminating potential—the knowledge that domestic spaces and the marriages enacted within them can be altered.

Like the characters in Pamela Sargent's The Alien Upstairs (which

I discuss in chapter 4), Cooper learns that houses can fly. "I some-times think of the house as a spaceship" (Masters, 163), he explains, echoing Sargent's description of a spaceship disguised as a house, which literally takes off (Sargent, 103–104). Flying houses signal potentials to build new models for houses, female-male love rela-tionships, and societies. Model planes are metaphors for these alter-native social models; Cooper builds a model of one woman pilot's flying machine, Amelia Earhart's Lockheed Vega (Masters, 130). "Vega is a star" (Masters, 131), says Ruth. Vega, a star which shares the name of Earhart's plane, is a hopeful beacon outshining the "tiny lights" of earth, man's world.

Cooper turns his attention from the Lockheed Vega to a model more difficult to build, a Breda 65: "He had had to build the model from scratch, using plans found in a back issue of *Model Airplane News*. No kit had been available; none had ever been made. The plane had never been in demand, not even as a model" (Masters, 134). Building the Breda from esoteric instructions is rather analogous to building an egalitarian society from scratch after consulting instruc-tions found in back issues of feminist journals. The model for such a society is not in demand. Those who want to create it consult a par-ticular "kit"—feminist textual instructions—which explains how to build a society whose female and male citizens can fit together like a successfully assembled model plane. This potential model so-cial body must be built according to the painstaking construction methods Cooper uses when putting together his model plane: "Al-most every day Cooper would spend several minutes looking into the bare framework of the plane's body, marveling at his own work, how each piece and strip of balsa had been shaped and fitted and glued. It was spatial. It was like being in space and looking out on some magnificent, new constellation that he had made" (Masters, 137). Cooper's particular spatial undertaking, making a plane from cohesive parts, is like looking at a magnificent new constellation in space. His activity signals the need to fly from present social mod-els, the need to look on Vega as part of a new female constellation shaped to fit smoothly within a remade social space.

Cooper, however, is ultimately not the best maker of alternative social spaces, not the best interpreter of new constellations. Even though Cooper makes model planes and writes stories about flight, he does not actually fly. Flight is, instead, attained by Hal, the retarded child, the Other who, like Woman, does not fit society's dominant spaces. Despite Hal's handicap, he builds and uses a flying machine: "But [Hal] rose higher . . . doing tricks that I [Clay Peck, a local 'good old boy,' who builds the flying machine with Hal] have only seen on birds. And like some ancient bird, he began to call something out—just one sound—over and over, and I finally caught the sound of it as he turned my way. It was her name, over and over, her name. Ruth. Ruth. Ruth" (Masters, 247). Hal, who flies in a novel containing images of astronauts and space capsules, calls out to another flying Hal, the computer in Arthur C. Clarke's *2001: A Space Odyssey*. Hal calls Ruth; the masculine, technological voice of Clarke's Hal can speak to women. *Cooper*, after all, also describes patriarchy's calling out to the Other. Hal's miracle of flight is made possible when Clay Peck works with the retarded boy he would be expected to shun. Their cooperation, and Hal's flight itself, opposes stereotypes. When Hal flies, he proves that someone other than a macho male has the right stuff.

Ruth proves that being other than male does not prevent a person from having the wrong stuff. She is an indirectly presented—and textually retarded—character who hardly ever speaks or acts. Like the broken cuckoo image, she has lost her head, the ability to articulate herself. One of her rare utterances is an unclear statement. She says, "You don't have to tell me about living in space. . . . I know everything there is to know about living in space" (Masters, 229). More specifically, she knows everything about living in space beyond the boundaries of *Cooper*. Masters does not permit readers to know Ruth Cooper. She is a shadowy presence pertinent to the absence of less-than-heroic women from most feminist fiction. Ruth and Hal indicate that both feminist and patriarchal fiction need to create space for new human models. Feminist discourse might emphasize that women are not always righteous and heroic; patriarchal discourse might emphasize that heroes are not always able-bodied white men, that women are not disabled, retarded Others. Hal can fly. So can his fellow "ex-centrics" (Linda Hutcheon's term). People are able to rewrite definitions of exclusion and disability.

People can soar beyond restrictive representations, rise above patriarchal language. Hal certainly does so when attached to his flying machine. Hal, a flying retarded person, is less handicapped physically than a mentally able person who does not fly. Hal defies linguistic designations: he is neither a bird nor a plane. This flying retarded boy is, of course, Superman. Woman can be Superman too.

Woman's transition to Superman requires her to remodel herself, a transformation Kelly Novak undertakes:

> Fat Mary had died; Kelly Novak was born. Starvation diets, exercise clubs. . . . She moved on from job to position to appointment. All the time she read. She had always read; it had been the only thing that had kept her sanity, she said. From books, she knew there was another world that was different from the one she lived in by the Mohonk River. She would have jumped into the Mohonk if she hadn't believed that from books, she said. (Masters, 146)

Mary becomes Kelly, a sleek new woman made according to textual instructions. Texts literally change her world, enable her to fly from the Mohonk to the Hudson. Like Hal, she turns herself into a plane. She flies. Kelly behaves like an engineer when she follows directions and remakes herself. In *Cooper* Kelly Novak is the remodeled woman who flies beyond her former self.

Masters's positive juxtaposition of flying and transcending social stereotypes pertains to four novels about women's dreams of flying: Valerie Miner's *All Good Women*, Marge Piercy's *Gone to Soldiers*, Carol Hill's *The Eleven Million Mile High Dancer*, and Octavia Butler's *Dawn*. These novels form a continuum about women's relationship to flying which ranges from grounded female World War II pilots to interplanetary fliers. This continuum resembles Joanna Russ's differing female protagonists (the four J's—Jeannine, Joanna, Janet, and Jael) in *The Female Man*. Miner's good women civilians and pilots are ultimately as restricted as Jeannine; Piercy's Bernice Coates is a liberated woman who resembles Joanna; Hill's Amanda Jaworski, like Janet, moves between the real and the fantastic; in the manner of Jael, Butler's Lilith Iyapo resides in a fantastic world. Like Kelly Novak, these characters all remodel themselves. Butler's,

Hill's, Miner's, and Piercy's visions of women and flying can serve as blueprints for building new female role models.

"The air is no place for a woman."

Jonathan Arac's comments about postmodernism apply to Miner's versions of these blueprints. He believes that postmodernism is "active" and shares "commitments to human life in history" (Arac, 281). *All Good Women*, by telling the silenced story of women's experiences during World War II, actively shares commitments to female life in history. Miner's novel reflects Arac's notion of the crucial contemporary agenda for critics. Arac advocates elaborating "the relations that join the nexus of classroom, discipline, and profession to such political areas as those of gender, race, class, as well as nation" (Arac, 307). He continues: "Postmodern critics . . . can carry on a significant political activity by relating the concerns once enclosed within 'literature' to a broader cultural sphere that is itself related to, although not identified with, the larger concerns of the state and economy" (Arac, 308). Postmodern critics would do well not to overlook Miner's portrayals of four women—a Japanese American, Wanda; a Jewish American, Ann; an Irish American, Moira; and a refugee from Oklahoma's dust bowl, Teddy—who unite gender, race, class, and nation. *All Good Women* invites critics to observe that feminist postmodern writers are engaged in rewriting master narratives about women's impact upon the state and economy during World War II.

All Good Women and *Gone to Soldiers* challenge World War II master narratives by presenting women's untold story of the war, the story of the Other. Miner and Piercy teach women's lesson of history: "We must know both our history and our difference from our history" (Arac, 313). Miner's story of women's effect upon the state and economy during the World War II era describes both standard American history and women's difference from standard American history. Piercy voices another example of women's history—the differences between female World War II pilots and their male counterparts. The Second World War provided opportunities for women to inhabit enlarged cultural spaces, to transcend traditional female roles. Miner and Piercy portray this larger female cultural space by illuminating the lives of individual women who made use of it. When imagining these lives, the authors adhere to Cixous's notion that "woman un-thinks the unifying, regulating history that homogenizes and channels forces, herding contradictions into a single battlefield. In woman, personal history blends together with the history of all women, as well as national and world history" (Cixous, 252–253). Or, in terms of the words which head this chapter, Miner's and Piercy's female protagonists learn that "flying is woman's gesture" (Cixous, 258).

Unlike Piercy's Bernice, however, Ann, Moira, Teddy, and Wanda are not pilots. (This is not to say that a female pilot is absent from Miner's novel. According to Teddy's rewritten version of wartime love stories, she yearns for a "man in the war" [Miner, 193] who happens to be a woman. Her thoughts are directed toward Angela, the female pilot flying at the war's periphery. Teddy loves the person pictured in "a photo of a handsome woman with her flying machine" [Miner, 168].) Miner's four protagonists fly metaphorically, a point Moira expresses when she articulates the crux of *All Good Women*: "You can't have models your whole life. At some point you just have to fly, to trust your instinct and your conscience" (Miner, 278). In the manner of Hilary Masters, Moira juxtaposes the need for new social models with flying. She anticipates her new opportunities in terms of Earhart and flying imagery: "Women were rising fast now. And if she didn't want to be Amelia Earhart, she wasn't going to be grounded by outdated expectations" (Miner, 38). Her goal to become a screen actress and epitomize female roles is one such outdated expectation. In other words, Moira's reference to the soda-fountain discovery story involving Lana Turner is not about women who soar upward: "At this rate, I'll never get hired by MGM. I'll be an ancient crone before they discover me falling off the soda fountain stool" (Miner, 38). (While Lana Turner's story is ensconced within many narratives, the same cannot be said for the story of Turner's female contemporaries who tried to fly abreast with men.) If Moira was "discovered" while sitting passively at a soda fountain, she, in truth, would be "falling off," grounded in stereotypical female roles. The activities Moira experiences while wearing overalls and doing factory work are more glamorous than the activities Turner experiences while wearing a sweater and doing no useful work.

Moira's overalls are a flight suit. Women of her generation fly by rising above limited options. Camaraderie with other women, not men's machines, becomes their flying apparatus. Wanda, for example, is elevated by her female Japanese predecessors: "Sometimes Wanda felt as if she were standing on Mama's shoulders, as if each generation of women in her family were supposed to stretch further" (Miner, 30). Unlike these predecessors, she has the chance to attend business school, where her teacher instructs her to type "hop hop hop hop . . . As we hop" (Miner, 30). This typing exercise about jumping forward is a text about her female generation's upward mobility.

Instead of reproducing men's words on typewriters, some women manage to write their own stories. Ann, for instance, completes the typing exercise "now is the time" with "for all good women" (Miner, 39). *All Good Women* fills the blank of women's World War II story by writing over "all good men," by asserting that now is the time to describe good women who came to the aid of their country. The novel's female protagonists fly apart and communicate their own war stories to each other. Ann exemplifies this point when she writes to Moira and Teddy from overseas: "Who would have imagined when we sat in typing class that we'd be scattered like this, writing letters across the world. . . . I imagine the four of us sitting in the living room sharing war stories. I do believe this will happen. My only worry is when" (Miner, 200). The women do reunite to tell their female war stories, stories excluded from American historical master narratives. Women's stories of the Second World War remained silenced until baby boom daughters (such as Miner and Piercy) retold them.

Miner states that "history is the inspiration and territory of this book [*All Good Women*]. History is the fiber from which the story has emerged" (Miner, "Writing," 23; further references to Miner not designated as quotations from "Writing" are to *All Good Women*). Her protagonists lack historical female behavioral role models. They are without a fiber from which their stories of lesbianism, racial victimization, and adopting a child as a single mother can emerge. Moira, who survives grade school by copying the smartest girl's behavior (Miner, 22), cannot survive adulthood by copying other women's behavior. She cannot act according to previously told stories about unwed lesbian mothers working in shipyards. Miner's women assuage this situation by seizing patriarchal language, imbuing patriarchal language with new meanings which assert that women's wartime battles differ from men's wartime battles. Moira the shipbuilder, for example, is "inducted involuntarily" (Miner, 278) into the role of an unwed mother. While men "liberate" countries and "reclaim" Pacific Islands, Teddy reclaims her Stockton Street house as a specific space of women's freedom. Wanda expresses her gratitude to Teddy with words appropriately addressed to soldiers: "Without you, Teddy . . . none of us would be here" (Miner, 462). Men fight for their country; Teddy fights for her domestic space. Wanda, a successful journalist, fights for freedom to write from a female viewpoint (Miner, 427).

The protagonists of *All Good Women* experience new historical stories, new female narratives which can inspire their daughters. They proclaim that patriarchal historical narratives are incomplete. When Miner records women's lives, she speaks in the place of the female silence which characterized her mother's generation. Like Wanda (who writes about Japanese Americans), Miner tells the story of a marginalized group. Wanda and Miner articulate the same question: "Is this the way history got written?" (Miner, 107). Miner's novel revises history and reflects Wanda's words: "Maybe none of them [Wanda's Japanese family and, by implication, her family of female friends] belonged in America. What was this country, anyway, except the distorted fantasy of uptight Anglo-Saxons" (Miner, 343). *All Good Women* suggests that, according to the distorted fantasies of uptight, World War II-generation, Anglo-Saxon men, women should not battle to defend their country and hence, in a sense, do not really belong in wartime America. During World War II, American women were interned outside the space where combat occurred. American women—such as the female pilots restricted within domestic airspace—shared Wanda's position as incarcerated, alien Other.

According to Miner, representing women's lives immediately before and during the Second World War involves writing about aliens:
"I had no inclination toward science fiction, and I have always been
interested in history. Little did I realize that writing about the '30s
and '40s would be like breathing the air of another planet. As much
as I knew about that world, there was a great deal more I did not
know. And unlike the writer of science fiction, I could not make up
the details" (Miner, "Writing," 22). Despite Miner's lack of inclination toward science fiction, she does depict a "planet" which is
Other to man's world—woman's home-front world. Her protagonists
who remain in the United States during the war, "a time without
men" (Miner, "Writing," 2), resemble inhabitants of feminist SF's
separatist planets. Wanda's reaction to her boyfriend, Roy, for example, could be articulated by one of the women in Russ's "When It
Changed" at the moment when men first land on the feminist separatist planet Whileaway.[3] When Wanda looks at Roy's "long, masculine legs and staunch shoulders, she did feel . . . as if she had
landed on a strange planet. Who was this? A man. An other" (Miner,
89). Further, when Moira's boyfriend, Randy, enters Teddy's house,
Teddy feels "jumpy, as if the place had been invaded by ants"
(Miner, 332). These women who live in the female world of the
home front view the returning men as invading, bug-eyed monsters.
Even Ann, who spends time abroad, is "astonished by how strange
men looked" (Miner, 359). Miner portrays women and men as mutually estranged aliens who, like Caucasian and Japanese people, differ from each other. The point is that Miner's Caucasian female protagonists are hardly less alien and incarcerated in World War II
America than are her Japanese protagonists. She portrays American
women who are treated as resident aliens, an indigenous population
of Others enclosed within a limited space outside combat zones.

SF imagery is applicable to the identities of Miner's characters as
well as to the spaces they inhabit. For example, Ann, who changes
her name to Anna to reclaim her family's Jewish immigrant experience (Miner, 357), resembles the protagonists split into interrelated
individuals Russ portrays in *The Female Man* and Sheila Finch portrays in *Infinity's Web*. Ann "imagined a reunion of all the Annas"
(Miner, 443), a reunion of all the versions of herself.[4] Further, like

Russ's four J's and Finch's myriad Anns, Miner's protagonists exemplify how the same woman can be broken into different possibilities. Teddy views herself and her three sister protagonists as "basically the same people" (Miner, 456). Finch, Miner, and Russ create female protagonists who act according to the postmodern theme of "the multiplicity of the self" (McHale, 15).

Instead of replicating herself through biological motherhood, Ann returns from abroad with an adopted child. Her wartime experience is an adventure related to nurturing. Her major question has nothing to do with which men control fatherlands. Instead, she anticipates the surrogate motherhood debate by wondering how a baby could "have two mothers" (Miner, 381). Wanda also articulates feminine questions while contemplating the Nagasaki bombing: "What went on in the minds of scientists divining these fires? Did they ever see children being ripped apart?" (Miner, 389–390). Ann adopts one child; an American male pilot drops "one bomb" (Miner, 389) on Nagasaki. Patriarchal war stories involve males who fly and destroy people's worlds. Feminist war stories involve females as both literal and figurative marginal pilots who, in Ann's words, "think more and more about changing the world" (Miner, 199). According to patriarchal fictions, women pilots are inferior because "it's too dangerous for women to fly across the ocean" (Miner, 138). Feminist authors rewrite this myth and emphasize the danger of living in a world where one pilot can kill millions.

World War II was controlled by American men and won by American men for American men. Miner stresses that American women lost the war. When Wanda becomes a journalist, Ann tells her, "You fought hard for what you have; it didn't fall from the sky" (Miner, 460). After the war, employment opportunities for female pilots did fall from the sky. Angela reports that her fellow female pilots turned to marriage or office work because "all the airline jobs, all the mechanics jobs, went to ex-servicemen" (Miner, 437). As for Moira and female factory workers, they "are all going to lose . . . [their] jobs. Make way for the boys" (Miner, 380). Women's gains were literally gone to soldiers. American male soldiers fought for a patriarchal definition of "freedom." Their victory coincided with women's retreat to the domestic sphere.

Postwar unemployed female pilots supply one means to support the argument that the Second World War marked a defeat for American women. In *All Good Women*, the story of women pilots—Angela's story—is secondary to Miner's discussion of women's metaphorical flights above racial and gender stereotypes. In contrast, Piercy's *Gone to Soldiers* emphasizes a female pilot's story, the story of Women's Air Force Service Pilot Bernice Coates. *All Good Women* concludes when World War II generation women pass on to their daughters an unfinished agenda regarding female progress.

"But, of course, we couldn't let you girls fly again."

Carol Hill's *The Eleven Million Mile High Dancer* tells the story of Angela's and Bernice's "daughters"—the next generation of women pilots. Before turning to Hill's novel, I read Piercy's feminist postmodern depiction of women pilots in terms of Teresa de Lauretis's "Technologies of Gender," Sally Van Wagenen Keil's *Those Wonderful Women in Their Flying Machines: The Unknown Heroines of World War Two*, and Brian McHale's *Postmodernist Fiction*.

McHale refers to Oedipa Maas's comment about "another world's intrusion into this one" (McHale, 22; Pynchon, 88). In Miner's and Piercy's historical novels, the untold story of women's war experience intrudes into the one story of war experience—men's story. McHale states that "Oedipa actually sees the truth plain: this other order of being, America's secret double, really exists" (McHale, 24). The story of women's lives during the Second World War era (especially the story of female pilots) is America's secret double, the untold truth plain, another order of being from men's war story. Many baby boom daughters are uninformed about the women of their mothers' generation who—like Teddy, Ann, Wanda, and Moira—experienced lesbian sexuality, adventures abroad, internment, and single parenthood juxtaposed with nontraditional female employment. The desire to reveal the story of women's lives during World War II provides one answer to Miner's question: "Why do I—and so many of my contemporaries—feel compelled by World War II?" (Miner, "Writing," 22). Baby boom daughters wish to add their mothers' stories to master narratives of American history. Their wish forms one reason why the feminist postmodern historical novel differs from the nonfeminist postmodern historical novel.

McHale believes that what he calls the dominant of postmodern fiction is ontological in that it asks questions "like the ones Dick Higgins calls 'post-cognitive': 'Which world is this? What is to be done in it? Which of my selves is to do it?'" (McHale, 10; Higgins, 101). According to McHale, "Traditional historical novels strive to . . . hide the ontological 'seams' between fictional projections and real-world facts. They do so by tactfully avoiding contradictions between their versions of historical figures and the familiar facts of these figures' careers, and by making the background norms governing their projected worlds conform to accepted real-world norms" (McHale, 17). As opposed to traditional historical novels, Miner's and Piercy's feminist historical postmodern novels expose rather than hide seams between fictional projections and real-world norms. *All Good Women* and *Gone to Soldiers* reveal the contradictions between familiar, patriarchal, fictional versions of women's contribution to the Second World War and the unfamiliar, real-world facts about these contributions. These novels make fictions about women's World War II experiences (such as myths about female pilots' inferiority) conform to unaccepted real-world facts about exactly what women did accomplish.

Miner and Piercy expose the blatant contradictions between the plain truth about women's history during World War II and the familiar, incomplete story about this history. The background norms regarding their factual projections of women's reality do not conform to accepted patriarchal—or, unreal—notions of women's participation in history. Both feminist and nonfeminist postmodern historical novelists expose the ontological seams between fiction and fact. However, the reality feminists emphasize differs from the reality their nonfeminist colleagues emphasize. While the male writers McHale discusses—such as Abish, Coover, Doctorow, and Pynchon (McHale, 85–86)—overtly juxtapose the real with the unreal to project real-world historical settings governed by fantastic norms, Miner and Piercy overtly juxtapose real women's experiences with fantastic stories about women told by patriarchy; they project real-world, historical women's worlds governed by feminist norms.

Most nonfeminist male postmodern writers stress bringing the fantastic to the real; most feminist female postmodern writers stress bringing the feminist real to the patriarchal fantastic (which is commonly—and falsely—thought to be real). Or, to use McHale's words, feminist postmodernists express, in terms of women, "the shift of dominant from problems of *knowing* to problems of *modes of being*—from an epistemological dominant to an *ontological one*" (McHale, 10). Feminist postmodernists know that women's experiences have been excluded from historical novels. Armed with this knowledge, which destabilizes real-world constructions, they emphasize portraying women's modes of being that are counter to patriarchal historical master narratives. Their female protagonists answer Dick Higgins's "post-cognitive" questions.

Instead of describing women's worlds being governed by patriarchal norms (norms which are often fantastic in relation to women's experiences), Miner and Piercy background patriarchal reality and foreground how women behave within patriarchal reality. Bernice Coates, Piercy's fictional carbon copy of a real-world WASP, who, of course, acts according to the truths Keil describes, exemplifies this point. Keil and Piercy reveal how feminist postmodern historical fiction about World War II unmasks men's story of that war to be "imperialism of the imagination" (McHale, 55).

Keil and Piercy emphasize that this imperialism manifests itself when WASPs are restricted to a limited space. McHale calls this space a "zone," a term relying upon Foucault's understanding of heterotopian space as an absent commonality between a large number of possible orders (McHale, 44; Foucault, xviii). Excluding the contribution WASPs made to World War II from historical discourse communicates the story of the war in terms of homotopian space— one orderly male story. Woman's World War II story rewrites this male homotopian story and changes it into heterotopian space which undermines patriarchal master narratives of war. Officials in patriarchal institutions reacted to female pilots' heterotopian presence in World War II by restricting (and, eventually, eradicating) their flight zones. American men "shot down" WASPs—suppressed WASPs' story—and won the right to define the war zone and its subsequent story as a male homotopian narrative.

Bernice calls women pilots "necessarily subversive" (Piercy, 304). Patriarchy nullifies their subversions. Regardless of their accomplishments, WASPs could not deconstruct myths about women's technological ineptitude. Keil explains that "though they [WASPs] all had passed the Army's most demanding intelligence tests, many men were still skeptical about whether women could master the technical exigencies of flying" (Keil, 152). The more WASPs excelled, the more patriarchy limited their flight zones. Alaska, for example, "was forbidden to WASPs, and at the Canadian border, the women had to get out of the fighters" (Piercy, 376). Alaska, all locations outside the continental United States, and eventually the sky itself became, for WASPs, artificially constructed, restricted zones. WASP flight zones became "worlds under erasure" (McHale, 99), akin to events which "may be narrated and then explicitly recalled or rescinded" (McHale, 101). After the limitations of WASPs' flight zones were initially narrated (or defined), the zones were rescinded. Piercy's feminist postmodern historical novel reconstructs this and other examples of women's erased historical reality.

Piercy reiterates Keil's description of the real story of the WASPs:

> [WASPS] ran around to every aircraft manufacturing plant in Southern California looking for jobs as test pilots, but no companies were hiring. They sent their resumes to airlines. The airlines did not bother replying. . . . The [female] pursuit pilots had most infuriated the American legion and Congress, for that was considered a job with too much panache for a woman. . . . no women pilots were to remain with the Army Air Corps. . . . It could not happen. They [woman pilots] had done a good job. . . . they had a better record than the men at delivering the planes. They could not be punished like this. They could not be dismissed when the need for them was glaring. . . . "We've [Bernice and her lover Flo] applied for flying jobs every place people fly, every bloody place. . . . They won't let us fly. They want to push women out of the skies altogether." (Piercy, 542–544, 610)

The sky became a literal limit for WASPs, women who unmask and transcend fictions about justifying subordinate female roles. In Keil's words, "[O]nce a woman broke through the barriers of finance and fear, by involving herself in flight, she never could return to traditional perceptions of her place in the world" (Keil, 54). The world order American men fought to retain depended upon defeating both the Axis powers' political expectations and women's personal expectations regarding power. One retention method, the pairing of WASPs with images of immoral women, is as mythical as portraying every German as a crazed Nazi. This stereotypical depiction of WASPs was inscribed in reality when WASPs were arrested in a southern town for daring to wear slacks at night (Keil, 237; Piercy, 419). WASPs were disempowered by myths, such as the notion that menstruating women are ineffective in cockpits (Keil, 155; Piercy, 260). Keil and Piercy correct myths and stereotypes. Keil states, for example, that menstruating "pilots on duty lost *less* time per month from operational flying, when grounding themselves voluntarily for psychological reasons, than men pilots" (Keil, 155).

Keil's and Piercy's realistic narratives contradict images of the woman pilot portrayed as monstrous Other—the woman pilot portrayed as "cyborg monster" (Donna Haraway's term), Woman combined with machine. Monstrous females were grounded after they deconstructed the "machinery of dominance," Cynthia Cockburn's term for subordinating women by defining technology as a space forbidden to them. Female pilots were (and still are) threatening to patriarchy. WASPs who could effectively pilot shoddy planes and target flights challenged patriarchy's image of inept women. According to Keil, "[M]astering flight also represented an escape from entrenchment in the past. At that time [during the World War II era], flying was considered the most adventurous link to modernity and assured one's active participation in the decades to come" (Keil, 58). Female pilots were barred from the technological and professional future which followed World War II. They were also denied the monetary benefits male soldiers received (Keil, 266).

Patriarchy directed vengeance toward Avenger Field, the WASP base in Sweetwater, Texas. The field functioned as a women's community which resembles the ones portrayed in feminist speculative fiction. Both WASPs and feminist utopians form strong friendships (Keil, 124) and develop female cultures consisting of women's songs and stories (Keil, 149). Avenger Field was a zone of competent women inhabiting a women's world. Government officials responded by defining this female zone as a world under erasure. Bernice refuses to conform to this definition. Instead of ceasing to fly, she creates her own space for private and public flights. She feels that "making love to Flo was like flying" (Piercy, 609). Bernice, like Teddy, "flies" in a new space of lesbian sexuality. Further, she continues to fly planes by managing to circumvent the female flight zone placed under erasure.

Cross-dressing enables Bernice to fly. She re-creates herself as "Harry Edward Munster, formerly of Boston and the Army Air Corps, assigned to OSS during the war and honorably discharged as a captain with ratings up to four-engine planes" (Piercy, 614). She epitomizes McHale's description of characters who "can have their existence revoked" (McHale, 103). Bernice Coates no longer exists in the public world. Erasing gender enables Bernice to cross from a female to a male zone. This spatial shift allows her to circumvent gender restrictions, deconstruct sexism, and nullify fictitious sexist narratives about women pilots. By supplying the factual version of WASPs' erased story, Piercy corrects a situation in which McHale's subtitles—"Something happened" and "Something exists," printed with crosses through them (McHale, 101, 103)—are applicable to WASPs. Piercy erases McHale's crosses. She ensures that WASPs are not crossed out of the Second World War.

In addition to creating Bernice, Piercy emphasizes that nonfictitious female World War II aviators have been erased. She inserts real-world figures—celebrity pilots Nancy Love (Piercy, 185) and Jacqueline Cochran (Piercy, 48)—within *Gone to Soldiers*.[5] (Cochran also appears in *All Good Women* [Miner, 52].) McHale calls placing celebrities in fictional texts "an ontological scandal." He continues: "[T]he presence in a fictional world of a character who is transworld-identical with a real-world figure sends shock-waves throughout that world's ontological structure. . . . Everywhere we find real-world historical figures inserted in fictional contexts, with . . . disorienting effect" (McHale, 85). The ontological scandal and shock waves emanating from Cochran's and Love's presence in *Gone to Soldiers* manifest themselves because women's historical reality in regard to flying has been erased. Most baby boomers would be surprised to learn that celebrity female pilots existed during the previous generation.

Cochran's and Love's appearances within Miner's and Piercy's feminist historical postmodern novels show how these texts differ from their nonfeminist counterparts. While mainstream postmodern novels contain "highly 'charged' figures" who are "rich in associations for most readers [such as Nixon, Lenin, and Idi Amin]" (McHale, 85), *All Good Women* and *Gone to Soldiers* portray real-world women who do not retain their former celebrity status. Upon encountering these forgotten celebrities, baby boom daughters are jolted by yet another example of exceptional women placed under erasure. Nonfeminist postmodern novelists appeal to readers by depicting famous male real-world figures (when McHale lists numerous real-world figures that male writers include, only three are women [McHale, 85]); Miner and Piercy refer to forgotten female celebrity pilots to emphasize that women are erased from history.

McHale states that "illicit mergings of history and the fantastic," such as Ishmael Reed's description of televising Lincoln's assassination (in *Flight to Canada*), place readers "clearly outside the 'classic' paradigm of the historical novel" (McHale, 89). Piercy's merging of history and forgotten female celebrities is illicit (or unorthodox) in terms of patriarchal structures. Patriarchy deems it subversive to resurrect forgotten female celebrities. Reincluding women within history, a paradigm of feminist postmodern historical fiction, occurs when women's reality (which has been rendered unreal by patriarchal narratives) merges with patriarchal reality (which is only partially real). This purposeful positioning of women back into history is outside the paradigms of both nonfeminist postmodern historical novels and classic historical novels.

According to McHale, the postmodern revisionist historical novel "revises the *content* of the historical record, reinterpreting the historical record, often demystifying or debunking the orthodox version of the past. Secondly, it revises, indeed transforms, the conventions and norms of historical fiction itself. . . . The effect is to juxtapose the officially-accepted version of what happened and the way things were, with another, often radically dissimilar version of the world" (McHale, 90). Piercy juxtaposes the officially accepted (patriarchal) version of what happened to women during World War II with a dissimilar, feminist version of the world. She revises the patriarchal historical record's content. She refuses to mirror nonfeminist postmodern historical novels which juxtapose the patriarchal real with the patriarchal unreal. Piercy, like Günter Grass (McHale, 90–91), believes that official history is the history of the male sex and restores marginalized groups to the historical record. Both Piercy and Grass (in *The Flounder*) question the reliability of official male history. *Gone to Soldiers* emphasizes that women's history has been fictionalized and places women's real history back within the context of standard (patriarchal) history. It addresses "precisely the question postmodernist fiction is designed to raise: real, compared to what?" (McHale, 96).

I refer to McHale to argue two points: (1) examples of contemporary feminist historical fiction have been wrongfully excluded from literary postmodernism and (2) the postmodern canon should be expanded to include feminist fiction which both adheres to and differs from the standard understanding of postmodern fiction. These points can be argued further by discussing Bernice Coates in terms of Teresa de Lauretis's "The Technology of Gender."

Bernice acts according to de Lauretis's description of Althusser's term "interpellation." De Lauretis understands interpellation to be "the process whereby a social representation is accepted and absorbed by an individual as her (or his) own representation, and so becomes, for that individual, real, even though it is in fact imaginary" (de Lauretis, 12). Bernice refuses to accept and absorb the image of the technologically inept woman—the inferior female pilot—as her own representation. The imaginary reasons the male power structure invents to justify defining the sky as a war zone forbidden to women do not become real for her. To cope with the lack of congruence between her own reality and patriarchal fiction, Bernice interpellates a male identity. She absorbs an imaginary male identity, creates this identity as her own representation, and, hence, causes it to become real.

Unlike Bernice, most women do not literally interpellate male identities. For example, de Lauretis explains that when filling out application forms, women check the *F* box rather than the *M* box. To mark *M* "would be like cheating or, worse, not existing, like erasing ourselves from the world" (de Lauretis, 11). Bernice dares to check the *M* box. She cheats. She places her female self under erasure. She excludes herself from the sex-gender system whose myths prevent her from flying. The *M* box marks itself on her. No longer Woman, Bernice becomes de Lauretis's "subject of feminism . . . the *representation* of an essence inherent in all women . . . but also distinct from women" (de Lauretis, 9–10). When Bernice assumes a male identity, she represents the full social participatory essence which is distinct from Woman's story of femininity. Bernice-as-Man differs from de Lauretis's "woman," "the real, historical beings and social subjects who are defined by the technology of gender and actually engendered in social relations" (de Lauretis, 10). Bernice subverts the technology of gender. Bernice flies.

She nullifies the fighter plane's relationship to the technology of gender, the myth that only men can appropriately pilot these planes. According to this myth, the fighter plane becomes "a social technology" (de Lauretis, 13), which signifies how the "representation of gender is constructed by the given technology" (de Lauretis, 13); the plane "becomes absorbed subjectively by each individual whom that technology addresses" (de Lauretis, 13). Females are represented as being incongruous with the fighter-pilot role. While WASPs refuse to become absorbed by this representation, it influences their male colleagues and federal government officials. Bernice and her real-world WASP counterparts confront the fighter plane constructed as a technology of gender which announces that women do not possess the right stuff to fly. The truth regarding WASPs' expertise became a fiction; the myth of women's technological ineptitude became real.

De Lauretis describes redefining gender as walking "out of the male-centered frame of reference in which gender and sexuality are (re)produced by the discourse of male sexuality" (de Lauretis, 17). When Bernice adopts a male identity, she walks out of a male-centered frame of reference which dictates that women cannot fly planes and have sexual relations with other women. Acting counter to the discourse of male sexuality, she sexually satisfies a woman and flies a plane. Like Ibsen's Nora, Bernice slams the door on gender limitations. Piercy does not devote narrative space to the events ensuing after the door is slammed, and so we never know how Harry Edward Munster fares in Alaska.

Harry Edward Munster—who is Bernice, the liberated female "man"—exemplifies de Lauretis's understanding of "*postfeminism*," as "a way to . . . reposition female subjectivity *in* the male subject, however that will be defined" (de Lauretis, 24). Bernice's identity change literally repositions female subjectivity *in* the male subject. Piercy defines this repositioning in the male subject as pertaining to both gender-role reversal and technology. When Bernice enters a plane, she penetrates the technology of gender and subverts discourses of female exclusion from the space within technology. This particular space can be understood in terms of Woody Allen as well as de Lauretis. In his film *Everything You Always Wanted to Know about Sex*, Allen presents the plane-as-penis, containing sperm personified as men; in *Gone to Soldiers*, Piercy presents the plane-as-phallus, containing a female pilot personified as a man. Allen's sperm/men become potent when parachuting from the plane/penis; Piercy's female/"male" pilot becomes potent when remaining inside the plane/phallus. Bernice penetrates phallocentrism by deriving power from her position within a cockpit forbidden to women.

She attains power by placing herself inside de Lauretis's "space-off," "spaces in the margins of hegemonic discourses, social spaces carved in the interstices of institutions and in the chinks and cracks of the power-knowledge apparati" (de Lauretis, 25). While located inside a plane, Bernice enters a technological power-knowledge apparat and widens the women's limited space that James Tiptree calls the "chink" in the "world machine" (Tiptree, 154). She deconstructs the story about how planes are naturally complicit with myths about the technology of gender and the machinery of dominance. These myths ensure that female pilots, positioned in the unseen space-off (such as female World War II pilots' presently invisible historical space) cannot be the (W)right brothers. According to de Lauretis, in "classical and commercial cinema, the space-off is . . . erased, or, better, recontained and sealed into the image by the cinematic rules of narrativization" (de Lauretis, 26). According to Keil and Piercy, before the end of World War II, female military pilots were erased, recontained, and sealed into a "proper" feminine image by a particular narration—the notion that men are the best pilots.

Avant-garde cinema's representations of the space-off correspond to Keil's and Piercy's representations of female pilots' marginalized participation in World War II. De Lauretis explains that "avant-garde cinema has shown the space-off to exist concurrently and alongside the represented space, has made it visible by remarking its absence in the frame or in the succession of frames, and has shown it not only to include the camera . . . but also the spectator" (de Lauretis, 26). Keil and Piercy make women pilots' participation in World War II visible by remarking its absence from orthodox historical narratives, highlighting the lives of women who are known only as spectators of men's combat, and indicating that women pilots' position in the space-off exists concurrently (and sometimes alongside) the represented space of men pilots. They comment upon the absence of women pilots from frames enclosing World War II's historical master narratives. Miner and Piercy emphasize that these master narratives should contain, in addition to the camera's record of men's participation in World War II, both the invisible women who concurrently participated with men and those who were home-front spectators.

Keil, Miner, and Piercy point to "a movement back and forth between the representation of gender (in its male-centered frame of reference) and what that representation leaves out or, more pointedly, makes unrepresentable" (de Lauretis, 26). They use "feminist practices" to reconstruct the story of women "in the margins" (de Lauretis, 26) of dominant World War II discourse. Ironically, their feminist novels and historical texts are marginalized. Keil's *Those Wonderful Women in Their Flying Machines* is out of print; Miner's and Piercy's World War II novels are positioned outside the canon.[6] Through their recovery of the women's story of World War II, Miner and Piercy, in Linda Hutcheon's words, remind "us that, while events did occur in the real empirical past, we name and constitute those events as historical facts by selection and narrative positioning" (Hutcheon, 97). They facilitate a "re-evaluation of and a dialogue with the past in light of the present" (Hutcheon, 19).

"We have all learned the art of flying and its numerous techniques."

In terms of this dialogue, cross-dressed Bernice, who at once inhabits represented gendered spaces and the space-off, epitomizes "the tension of a twofold pull in contrary directions . . . [which] is both the historical condition of existence of feminism and its theoretical condition of possibility. The subject of feminism is en-gendered there. That is to say, elsewhere" (de Lauretis, 26). Bernice as Harry Edward Munster is located "elsewhere" in an uncharted space-off. While Bernice creates a new personal outer space, Carol Hill's protagonist, NASA pilot Amanda Jaworski, travels to a new locational outer space, to an unearthly, uncharted, elsewhere space-off. Amanda, who could be the daughter of Miner's and Piercy's characters, flies out of the patriarchal system and enters a fantastic realm. She draws upon the experiences of her flying foremothers to succeed as a NASA astronaut. Although Amanda's flights are certainly not as restricted as those of female World War II pilots, she flies most freely in a fantastic world beyond patriarchy, in an unreal feminist zone.

Like the WASPs, Amanda is a talented pilot who unsettles patriarchy by juxtaposing femininity with flying, technology, and science. She is an "astronaut, a physicist, and an extremely good pilot. It was this combination of achievements with this other feminine thing that disturbed him [Sargent Delko, Amanda's trainer]" (Hill, 7–8). This other "feminine thing" grounds women pilots, a fate experienced by Amanda's Russian counterpart: "Oh, they'd sent one [Russian woman] up all right, brought her down, married her off to a cosmonaut, tested her reproductive tract, shut her up, and closed up the women's space program" (Hill, 22). When Amanda's mission goes awry, NASA plans to bring her down and shut her up: "[T]hey would have to silence Jaworski. . . . But an injection. A tranquilizer. Something to make her forget. A lobotomy. Cruel, but necessary. A surgical solution. She was a woman, he [the general] told himself, and she'd be better off that way anyhow. Jaworski was all out of whack as a woman. Too many abilities. . . . Wouldn't change her that much, just somewhat. Make her easier to handle" (Hill, 267).

Amanda, a brilliant, sexy woman who masters technology and ventures beyond patriarchy, is aberrant and might be erased. She avoids the general's "surgical solution" by entering a fantastic zone where science is invalidated and technology becomes unnecessary. She saves herself by enacting her assertion that "technology isn't enough. . . . We must learn body control through our minds. The mind is the pathway to outer space and inner peace" (Hill, 8). Amanda's mind becomes a space travel mode. She opens a new space in which female pilots can fly in a manner counter to scientific law.

This new space thwarts patriarchy's story about the impossibility of combining femininity with technical adroitness. Competent, feminine Amanda reads women's subordination in terms of the sign on her office door which reads, "NOTHING IS SOMETHING" (Hill, 63). According to Amanda—despite patriarchy's penchant for turning women into "nothing"—"there is no such thing as nothing. The void is not a void. The void is full" (Hill, 65). She understands that the void resulting from women's lack of full social participation is attributable to patriarchal myths. Amanda counters the devaluation of the feminine by pointing out that male omniscience is a mere assumption: "He [Hotchkiss, NASA pilot and Amanda's lover] thought that occasionally Amanda was quite capable of fully believing that women were vastly superior to men, and at such times she pointed out to him that the masculine tendency toward rational, linear, logical thought processes might look good but was wrong" (Hill, 66).

Amanda uses outer space as a vantage point from which to question the validity of masculine thinking processes. Outer space, the site of myths about men's rational competence and women's irrational incompetence, is an appropriate place to locate challenges to patriarchal thinking. A journalist views Amanda in terms of these myths when he explains that limitless distances are threatening to women. The journalist comments that "a woman's concept of herself is as a space. You know, as a nothing, a void, surrounded by a body. Inner space, you know, so outer space is threatening, like she could disappear" (Hill, 110). Amanda's competence does not conform to this particular juxtaposition of space and fictions about women's self-concept. She counters stories used to disempower women. The journalist's belief that "the vastness of space, its absence of delineation, is of special concern to women astronauts" (Hill, 109) exemplifies one such story.

Instead of becoming an inactive character within patriarchal stories, Amanda, as an astronaut, rewrites these stories. She uses outer space to assert feminine superiority and masculine fallibility. For Amanda, outer space is a blank page upon which to deconstruct patriarchal definitions by writing feminist texts about how to nullify patriarchal law. As a superb female scientist, she proves that her femininity and thinking are neither "fanciful" nor "unscientific" (Hill, 111). When Amanda discovers that "technically and theoretically" are "two categories that frequently were sent awry" (Hill, 377) in space, she mirrors Sandra Harding's and Evelyn Fox Keller's feminist critiques of science.

Keller's work on gender and science is applicable to Amanda's questions about the connection between discourses which describe science and discourses which describe female/male love relationships. Amanda considers the reasons why men always seem to have the answers:

> Once, they thought that light was a thing that came in waves, like water. They thought that Einstein, who said it wasn't . . . was crazy. . . . So for all the things that they once thought were crazy, they had come up with laws to explain them.
>
> She was thinking about that. And wondering what she would find on Mars. She was also thinking about women. She was thinking that despite all this emancipation business, men still ruled the earth. . . . And most people in most countries thought that men "had the answers." What bothered her was that women thought they should defer to men, that men should have the answers; or therefore, that women shouldn't. She thought that women who acted like they had the answers weren't sure deep down. Why, she wondered, was it so hard for women to be sure? (Hill, 153)

Keller, seeming to mirror Amanda's thoughts, asks, "How much of the nature of science is bound up with the idea of masculinity, and what would it mean for science if it were otherwise?" (Keller, 3). *Dancer* offers, in Keller's words, a "feminist perspective on science . . . [which] leads us to ask how ideologies of gender and science inform each other in their mutual construction, how that construction functions in our social arrangements, and how it affects men and women, science and nature" (Keller, 8). Hill addresses gender and science constructions when Amanda, located in outer space, conquers the alien social system the Great Cosmic Brain controls.

Amanda journeys to outer space via a fantastic flying method which relies upon "a tachyon—part of the original primal ooze" (Hill, 233). This alternative to real-world science enables her to control her use of space in outer space. Ooze-powered flight is unlike any existing flying technology; Amanda is "out of her spaceship, or whatever you might wish to call it. She was outside any structure. . . . But this system she was in was exceedingly strange. She was traveling, as far as she could tell, inside a long, thin tube, like an infinite subway, and she was going headfirst very fast" (Hill, 279–280). This strange system critiques defining patriarchal systems as the only possible versions of reality. It implies that new paradigms can supersede existing paradigms about exalting the masculine and debasing the feminine. Amanda, after all, flies without NASA's ship, without the military-industrial complex. Her "four Saturn rockets and ten tons of fuel" (Hill, 288) are ineffective when compared to the power the ooze generates. *Dancer* asserts that love, not technology, is the powerful force which enables humans to travel and survive in outer space. Amanda is saved by a "measureless mass, soul and love" (Hill, 328), not by technology. Hotchkiss forsakes patriarchal science and arrives in outer space to rescue Amanda "on a beam of loyalty and love" (Hill, 393). Here, feminine principles about love transcend masculine principles about technology.

Hill, then, echoes another question Keller poses: "What does it mean to call one aspect of human experience male and another female?" (Keller, 6). Like Keller's theoretical text, Hill's fictional text questions mythology about how objectivity, reason, and mind become male characteristics and how subjectivity, feeling, and nature become female characteristics (Keller, 6–7). Amanda and Hotchkiss each excel in stereotypically feminine and masculine characteristics. Further, they each survive in an unearthly space by relying upon feminine principles and disregarding scientific "laws." By creating alternative spaces and gender roles, Hill unmasks traditional roles as mere myths which inhibit women's access to science and technology. She views excluding women from science as, in Keller's words, "a symptom of a wider and deeper rift between feminine and masculine, subjective and objective, indeed between love and power—a rending of the human fabric that affects all of us, as women and men, as members of a society, and even as scientists" (Keller, 7). When Hill indicates that love is more powerful than rocket fuel, she suggests that feminine principles are more effective than masculine principles.

Humor figures in Hill's debunking of men's power. For example, she emphasizes that pilots who are not men can fly Air Force planes. Monkeys can do it: "That chimp deliberately stole the Air Force plane, because he was one hell of a *pilot*" (Hill, 69). The chimp accompanies Amanda on an outer-space journey which challenges science: "It was only one of the crazier aspects of history that here were a woman and a chimp chasing to the moon after a cat, sponsored by the entire military establishment of the United States and utilizing all of technology, but protected finally by a young boy and a magic ring" (Hill, 269). Hill imagines that the American military can be trumped by the unscientific, by magic.

According to Hill's critique of science, feminist fantasies coincide with nonscientific world views. Since Amanda's NASA craft flies via fantastic propulsion methods, her outer-space journey juxtaposes the military with the fantastic. Hill's vision coincides with Harding's notion that feminist fantasy's intrusion into the scientific world is crucial to a feminist critique of science. Harding states, "Thus in examining the feminist criticisms of science, we have had to examine also the worlds of historical particularity and of psychic repressions and fantasies that constantly intrude, only to be insistently denied in the scientific world view" (Harding, 245). Amanda's nonscientific activities in outer space exemplify what Harding calls "parameters of dissonance" which question "fidelity to the assumption of patriarchal discourses that coherent theory is not only a desirable end in itself but also the only reliable guide to desirable action" (Harding, 246). Hill answers the science question in feminism by advocating that, in Harding's words, we "reinvent both science and theorizing itself in order to make sense of women's social experience" (Harding, 251).

Harding's call for reinventing both science and theorizing suggests the appropriateness of understanding Hill's novel in terms of postmodernism: Harding explains that "feminism makes its own important contribution to postmodernism . . . to our understanding that . . . science-centered rationality . . . [is] only a three-century episode in the history of Western thinking" (Harding, 251). *Dancer* posits that the "Female Principle Rising" (Hill, 416) is an alternative to predominating science-centered rationality. This female principle enables Amanda to succeed in an alternative world and depends upon "a certain kind of strength. A tolerance for ambiguities" (Hill, 416). The ambiguities inherent in the female principle rising critique patriarchal discourse by implying that science is ambiguous and results from the rise of the male principle.

Hill reverses the usual roles assigned to female and male principles. The alternative system in outer space, which Amanda confronts by using the female principle rising, is more powerful than our reality's male principle. Earth, then, becomes a "*hypo*diegetic world, one level 'down' from" (McHale, 113) Hill's fantastic world. Her suggestion that patriarchy is not the ultimate system in the universe—that an alternative, nonscientific system is one level above patriarchy and controls patriarchy—subverts patriarchal law. Amanda's nonpatriarchal flying through outer space—both with and without her NASA craft—enables her to experience, in McHale's words, an "ontological confrontation [which] occurs between our world and some other world or worlds somehow adjacent or parallel to our own, accessible across some kind of boundary or barrier" (McHale, 61). Amanda crosses the boundary between feminine and masculine principles in both her personal and professional roles.

Menstruation, for example, enhances her ability to pass mental and physical stress tests (Hill, 18). And, although her large breasts do not easily fit within her space suit (Hill, 6), Amanda welcomes their presence within the suit's mechanical hardware: "She . . . seemed astonished, in the midst of her . . . computer checks, and hardware, to feel the soft smooth surface of her breast. . . . a strange sensation surprising her, pleasing her . . . alerting her like a telegram from an unknown world" (Hill, 263). This unknown world is a space where feminine characteristics are successfully woven within the social fabric. Amanda, the author of a metaphorical telegram which describes a talented woman who adheres to this unknown world, rejects the idea that successful women must sacrifice their femininity. Her interests encompass both feminine and masculine characteristics: "She liked strawberry sodas, high-heeled shoes, men, lipstick, convertibles, long hair, bright toenail polish, particle physics, quarks, entropy, speculations regarding the speed of light, Darwinism, and archaeology" (Hill, 98).

Like Amanda, Olympic-gold-medal sprinter Florence Griffith Joyner (who could be Amanda's real-world counterpart) juxtaposes contradictions between femininity and masculinity. Her body is a flying machine adorned with jewelry and sexually provocative running suits. Joyner breaks speed limits while wearing makeup and bright red nail polish. According to Joyner and Amanda, femininity (and ethnicity) do not coincide with mobility constraints. These women do not discard their femininity when they master space and retell myths about racial and gender differences. Amanda, a Polish American who wears nail polish, travels forty million light-years away from earth faster than the speed of light; Joyner, a black American who also wears nail polish, travels faster than all Olympic runners. Amanda's style ensconces feminine principles within NASA; Joyner's style ensconces feminine characteristics within the sports world. Here is one example of the media's attention to Joyner's juxtaposition of race, femininity, and success: "Joyner was once again breaking the color barrier. Grizzled sports journalists sounded like doyens of haute couture as they debated whether her one-legged bodysuit, one of the 14 that she'd brought to the trials, was more plum or eggplant in hue" (Masback, 34).

Joyner's style emphasizes love as well as fashion. As Amanda derives some of her success from her fellow astronaut and lover, Hotchkiss, Joyner enjoys the support of Al Joyner, her husband and fellow runner. He describes his professional relationship with Florence Joyner in feminine, nurturing terms: "Coaching is a relationship. . . . The better you understand someone, the more you can help them. No one understands Florence better than me" (Masback, 35). Amanda and Florence Joyner contradict and rewrite patriarchal stories about how achieving success depends upon following masculine behavioral roles. Their formula for success relies upon fusing talent with love. Amanda opposes patriarchal success formulas: "The magazine was very busy telling you that the way to become a person was to go out and get a job, when Amanda knew that the way you became a person was by going out and loving someone" (Hill, 260). Going out and loving someone helps both Amanda and Florence Joyner to become successful professional people.

Their male lovers also contradict patriarchal formulas by bringing feminine characteristics to bear upon their relationships with accomplished, feminine women. Al Joyner, a talented runner in his own right, acts as Florence Joyner's supportive coach and stands outside her limelight. Hotchkiss, a successful pilot and scientist, supports Amanda's nonscientific flying and functions as a feminine presence in her personal life. When Amanda and Hotchkiss make love in the alternative world, he "seemed to her almost feminine then; if it hadn't been Hotchkiss she would have thought it *was* feminine. . . . the line of his back, his shoulders, it was soft and strong, like the neck of a swan. . . . a feminine aspect that hovered just outside the outlines of Hotchkiss's very male presence. . . . It was the kind of opposite that didn't . . . break down her concept of Hotchkiss, but balanced it in some perfect way" (Hill, 406).

Hotchkiss's feminine role reflects NASA's position following the *Challenger* explosion. The space agency became feminine, potentially impotent. When NASA again managed to launch a shuttle (on September 29, 1988), the agency did so without its usual macho bravado and automatically assumed competence. On that September morning, NASA was urged on by an audience of millions who hoped that the agency could manage to get its shuttle up. In this instance, masculine, phallic competence was questioned and elicited feminine concern.[7] Ironically, in addition to the momentarily feminized space shuttle, Florence Joyner also "flew" on September 29, 1988.[8] On that day, cultural occurrences regarding outer space and appropriate female and male gendered spaces were communicated as rewritten fictions. Joyner and the shuttle respectively challenge master narratives about black women's lack of mobility and white men's technological competence.

Amanda and Joyner are "ex-centric" postmodern women who epitomize "contradictions" (Hutcheon, 43) between feminine and masculine characteristics. These women, like Hutcheon's contradictory postmodernism, are paradoxically "both academic and popular, elitist and accessible" (Hutcheon, 44). Amanda, a physicist and pilot, calls herself a "knockout" (Hill, 232). Joyner, a sexy celebrity runner, has authored ten children's books, an autobiography, and a romance novel (Masback, 34). Amanda combines such supposedly contradictory characteristics as elite academic training and female

sexuality; Joyner combines such supposedly contradictory characteristics as a black athlete's elite Olympic training and authorship.
The contradictions which characterize these women, like postmodernism, ask "us to rethink and critique our notions" of both history
and reference (Hutcheon, 46).

Amanda's and Joyner's critique of the dominant culture "critically
undermines that dominance" (Hutcheon, 47) and, at the same time,
is implicated within that dominance. Amanda challenges women's
exclusion from NASA and science by working within NASA and
distinguishing herself. Joyner challenges the notion that black ath-
letes do not succeed intellectually by working within the Olympic
sports system and excelling scholastically. Since Amanda needs
NASA and Joyner needs the Olympics, these women challenge
established social spaces from within established social spaces.
They act in terms of Hutcheon's notion that "postmodernist discourses—both theoretical and practical—need the very myths and
conventions they contest and reduce" (Hutcheon, 48).

When Amanda subverts the myths and conventions of NASA
while positioned within it, she creates an appropriate space for the
female, feminine, competent astronaut by acting in terms of Hutcheon's comment about Eco and Foucault. According to Hutcheon,
"Eco has suggested that postmodernism is born at the moment
when we discover that the world has no fixed center and that, as
Foucault taught, power is not something unitary that exists outside
of us" (Hutcheon, 86). Amanda's successful "female principle rising"
is born at the moment when she discovers that patriarchy and science are not the fixed center of the world. During the time she
spends in outer space, Amanda recognizes that the power to fly is
located within her rather than solely within the unitary NASA
structure which exists outside her. In an alternative, decentered
world, Amanda gains the ability to pilot herself by relying upon
power positioned within herself: "She was flying high, high through
the spectacular night, tilting, falling, flying, turning, spinning, what
seemed here to be impossible maneuvers, zillions of maneuvers in
fractions of seconds. She was blazing through the skies with the
most amazing machine of all: she was piloting herself" (Hill, 418).
When Amanda's own female flesh becomes her flying machine,

man's metal technology becomes obsolete: "Amanda was in orbit, and unclassified" (Hill, 430), flying outside scientific laws. Where is Amanda's NASA vehicle? She explains, "I lost it" (Hill, 435). She flies most effectively after loosing her dependence upon the military-industrial complex and the patriarchal knowledge system.

Amanda transcends reality's flying machines as well as fantastic robots who try to prevent her from being able to liberate biological mechanisms. Her flying female body empowers her to enforce a definition of "importance" in which saving a cat supersedes NASA's agenda. She can equate rationality with the ability "to abandon a Mars trip for some four-footed furry thing" (Hill, 250). She learns that power systems are suspect, that the Great Cosmic Brain is a "huge cumbersome stink-filled, wart-covered mess" (Hill, 367). So is patriarchy. Amanda unmasks the Great Cosmic Brain—as well as the Great Patriarchal Brain—as problematic systems which construct life-threatening technological systems. By describing a woman who can fly without a machine, *Dancer* critiques science, technology, and the military. When the novel concludes as Amanda's cat lands with a loud "*WHUMP*" (Hill, 441), readers are also abruptly dropped, left at the entrance of feminist fabulation's imaginative portal.

"And once the old world has turned on its axle so that the new dawn can dawn, then, ah, then! all the women will have wings."

Octavia Butler's *Dawn* positions readers within this portal. The novel describes a postnuclear holocaust world in which all life is valued. *Dawn* juxtaposes feminism, flying, and reproductive technology to plunge deeper into the fantastic than do the novels written by Hill, Miner, and Piercy. Lilith Iyapo, Butler's protagonist, is, like Amanda's cat, a beloved pet who must be saved. Lilith, orbiting earth while imprisoned within an alien living ship, flies in a "cage." Her inability to control her flight within the living ship's at once technological and biological body speaks to the relationship between reproductive technology and women's increasing inability to control their bodies. Butler's coupling of flying and outer space addresses a particular inner space—the womb, which might become as obsolete as metal spaceships are in Lilith's world. Butler's alien

Oankali, who alter humanity's reproductive capacity, are an exaggerated version of real-world biological alterations of women's bodies. The Oankali's reproductive intervention, however, is more humane than existing technological reproductive intervention.

Hill, Miner, and Piercy address flying in terms of feminism and war; the war is over in *Dawn*. Butler shifts these authors' focus upon gender and flying to a context in which the military is nonexistent, patriarchy is destroyed, and technology is constructed from living material rather than inorganic matter. The Oankali experiment with human reproduction stresses that the future flights into outer space both species will undertake depend upon their mutual sexual and technological interconnection. This interconnection should inspire readers to rethink existing practices and laws relating to reproductive technology.

In *Dawn*, where postnuclear holocaust earth's survivors are housed in a living spaceship, flying transcends technology. Humanity, then, exists within a combined biological/technological system it did not construct. Counter to existing tensions between technological development and ecology, the sentient Oankali flying machine works in harmony with its creators: "There is an affinity, but it's biological—a strong, symbiotic relationship. We serve the ship's needs and it serves ours. It would die without us and we would be planet-bound without it" (Butler, 33). The living ship—the "Oankali use living matter the way we used machinery" (Butler, 140)—functions as a flying platform which supports the construction of a new human society. Humans, positioned in flight above ruined social systems, have no choice in regard to accepting new Oankali systems. Lilith describes the collapse of human social structures: "Down on earth . . . there are no people left to draw lines on maps and say which sides of those lines are the right sides. There is no government left. No human government, anyway" (Butler, 142). Wars were fought over the spaces men drew upon those maps, men who will no longer exist after the Oankali create nongendered humanity. An Oankali named Jdahya informs Lilith, "You will become something other than you were" (Butler, 32). Despite readers' expected discomfort with the idea that aliens will control humanity's destiny, Butler indicates that the Oankali plan is for the best.

Dawn blames hierarchy for bringing humanity to the brink of de-

struction (Butler, 37, 38, 178); the novel emphasizes that human history is replete with inhumane actions. Lilith, nevertheless, responds
to Oankali intervention within humanity's sexual space by insisting
upon humanity's importance: "But they [the human/Oankali off-
spring] won't be human. . . . That's what matters" (Butler, 247). Here,
Lilith misses an important point: all real-world human babies are
born into an inhumane patriarchal system. Again, even though
readers might resist defining as heroes the alien invaders who force
humans to alter themselves and their societies, such changes might
be positive. Butler supports this conclusion by locating humanity
within a flying space which unmasks patriarchal brutality. Lilith's
comments show that being enclosed within the Oankali ship is no
worse than being enclosed within inhumane human social structures. She says, "We are on a ship. . . . There is no place to run on a
ship. Even if you could get out of this room, there would be nowhere
to go, nowhere to hide, nowhere to be free" (Butler, 139). Earth has
been constructed as a patriarchal spaceship; each human society
functions as a patriarchal room located on the ship. Humans have
no place to run to avoid patriarchy. Nowhere. The Oankali provide
a potentially positive new space in which to be free from patriarchy.

Instead of taking people to this new space beyond patriarchal en-
closures, existing flying machines ensure that outer space will be
defined according to patriarchal principles. The U.S. government, for
example, scheduled space shuttle *Atlantis*'s December 1988 flight
(which followed the *Challenger* accident) as a secret mission to de-
ploy a spy satellite. Hegemonic American culture insists that such
militarization of outer space is correct. As Lilith explains, "There
were humans who thought that way—right up to the moment the
missiles were fired. People who believed space was our destiny. I
believed it myself" (Butler, 36). *Dawn* attributes a nonmilitary con-
notation to the phrase "space was our destiny." After the Oankali
arrive, outer space no longer implies a destructive destiny, a place
for spy satellites and missiles. Instead, outer space implies a destiny
of reconstruction, a place for nonpatriarchal reproductive technology and living ships. Space shuttle *Atlantis* functioned as a military
appendage; the Oankali ship is a womb flying over the destroyed
military-industrial complex.

The Oankali position Lilith as humanity's mother. Her role is to "teach, to give comfort, to feed and clothe, to guide them [the human survivors] through and interpret what will be, for them, a new and frightening world" (Butler, 110). Hence, the Oankali redefine outer space as the mother's nurturing realm, not the destructive realm of the father's mechanical, penile flying machines. Further, the Oankali also redefine "mother" to denote importance and power. These new definitions bring Robyn Rowland's alternative views of motherhood and reproductive technology to bear upon *Dawn*. She discusses "the relationship between women's demand for choice in reproduction and sexuality; our attitudes towards motherhood; male control of conception and reproduction; and sex preselection technology" (Rowland, "Motherhood," 74). Rowland "tentatively raises the possibility that 'choice' and 'freedom' as a continuing ideological base in the area of reproductive technology may eventually trap women further and limit their choice to say 'no' to increased male control of the reproductive process. It makes the distinct point that feminists *must* educate themselves in this field and *must* reevaluate the issues of reproductive freedom and 'the right to choose' in terms of the long-term consequences of uncontrolled medical 'advances'" (Rowland, "Motherhood," 74).

Lilith is powerless to reject the Oankali's ability to control her reproductive process. She has no choice about giving birth to a child who will transcend human sexuality and biology. Lilith is an "experimental animal" (Butler, 58). Butler stresses that the dangers of reproductive technology are quite real: "Forced artificial insemination. Surrogate motherhood? Fertility drugs and forced 'donations' of eggs? Implantation of unrelated fertilized eggs. Removal of children from mothers at birth . . . Humans had done these things to captive breeders—all for a higher good, of course" (Butler, 58).

She alludes to the circumstances Gena Corea describes in "The Reproductive Brothel."⁹ The Oankali alter humanity; reproductive technology alters women. While the Oankali act according to humanity's best interest, as feminist critics of reproductive technology such as Rowland and Corea explain, the same does not hold true for this technology's patriarchal practitioners. The Oankali should not be regarded as bug-eyed monsters. Readers might realize that this SF term is more appropriately applied to the group Renate Duelli Klein calls "technodocs." She describes their techniques: "preconception sex selection and postconception sex determination techniques, artificial insemination, and the full gamut of 'test-tube' techniques: *in vitro* fertilization . . . embryo replacement, transfer and 'flushing,' embryo freezing, and—yet to come—cloning and the artificial placenta: the 'glass-womb'" (Klein, 64–65).

While Lilith rails against the end of humanity, feminist reproductive technology critics envision the potential end of women, what Rowland calls "the final solution to the woman question" (Rowland, "Solution," 356.) Technodocs are more frightening than the Oankali. While the Oankali are "very careful to avoid damaging new partner-species" (Butler, 153), technodocs are not so careful in their reproductive partnership with women. This point is underscored when Rowland reiterates Roberta Steinbacher's comments about the contraceptive pill: "Who invented it, who manufactures it, who licensed it, who dispenses it? But who dies from it?" (Rowland, "Motherhood," 86; Steinbacher, 89). *Dawn* is a fiction which reveals that arguments about reproductive technology's benefits to women are fictions. The Oankali "revere life"; technodocs threaten to make female life obsolete. According to Rowland, "for the history of 'mankind' women have been seen in terms of their value as childbearers. We have to ask, if that last power is taken and controlled by men, what role is envisaged for women in the new world? Will women become obsolete?" (Rowland, "Solution," 368).

In Butler's world, flying involves eradicating the military, empowering the mother (Lilith), and utilizing woman-centered biological (rather than technological) intervention. In the real world, flying is undertaken in a non-woman-centered military corporate space. This space is one of the many components of the technological social hegemony which threatens to remove reproduction from women's control and fosters the possibility that future humanity might lack a logical reason for reproducing women. During the postmodern age when nuclear war is becoming obsolete, people are constructing new weapons to dominate a new war zone—the technology which manipulates the reproductive space within women's bodies. Eradicating women, the end result of the battle to control the female body, is becoming an acceptable alternative to the aftermath of nuclear war—eradicating humanity as a whole. While *Dawn* envisions creating nonpatriarchal, nongendered people, reality more closely adheres to the imagined obsolete human mother in *Brave New World*. Reality, which threatens to erase females and female reproductive power, might soon provide space for only one gender.

"She will tear off her mind forg'd manacles, will rise up and fly away."

By dispensing with mechanistic technology, feminist fabulators can tell a story which differs from Hilary Masters's story about Hal's flying machine becoming synonymous with hope. Instead of flying by resorting to machines, some female protagonists fly through space and time empowered by such means as childbirth and locating their counterparts in different historical periods.

For example, while progressing from *Fear of Flying* to *Serenissima*, Erica Jong shifts from writing about intercontinental plane travel to focusing upon time travel powered by a baby. In both Lisa Goldstein's *The Dream Years* and Susan Daitch's *L.C.*, women's texts, not time machines, allow female protagonists to interact with their female counterparts from the past. When feminist fabulators imagine alternatives to mechanistic flying technology, they create vehicles to express their differences from patriarchal imperatives. *The Watcher*, Jane Palmer's feminist critique of patriarchal power (as I indicate in my introduction), portrays this difference.

Gabrielle, Palmer's protagonist in *The Watcher*, learns that she is the Star Dancer, the greatest power in the universe, a bomb who flies effortlessly through the spaces separating galaxies. As a bomb who possesses no wish to explode, she refuses to wield patriarchal power: "Given the power craved by the human race ever since it discovered it had a thumb that could oppose its fingers, Gabrielle was painfully aware she hadn't the faintest idea what to do with it. She had to give it back. . . . It was still early when Gabrielle put on her walking shoes and trudged over the beach towards the village to return her library book and buy some groceries" (Palmer, 88, 105). Gabrielle relinquishes the power she derives from being a flying bomb and focuses upon her own textual power—her word, her law. Her power results from serving as a Watcher, one of "the ultimate Law enforcers." Watchers "enforce Laws by using symbols which can be recognized by all sophisticated life forms. . . . They have more power than all the civilisations in the galaxy. They don't use it much because no one makes a habit of crossing them" (Palmer, 176–177). Gabrielle can construct and enforce her own law, codes, rules. She flies in the library, not in the sky.

Alternatives to technological flying and assertions that texts are more powerful than war weapons also figure in Kurt Vonnegut's *Slaughterhouse Five*. Tralfamadorian travel is much more impressive than the flying machines Billy Pilgrim encounters during World War II. Billy himself reduces his war experience to a text, a retold tale. After being asked to talk about war, he replies that "it would sound like a dream. . . . Other people's dreams aren't very interesting, usually" (Vonnegut, 121). From Billy's retrospective stance, the war is a dream, a story. Miner and Piercy echo Billy's assertion that other people's dreams of war are not very interesting. These feminist authors designate "other people" as men and rewrite men's war story in terms of women's alternative dream of flying. Vonnegut, like these female authors, rewrites the patriarchal story of war. A surgeon tells Billy Pilgrim, "I take it you find war a very comical thing" (Vonnegut, 151). Vonnegut proposes that war can be eliminated by transforming the story of war into a humorous text, not by stockpiling weapons. Like Miner and Piercy, Vonnegut wishes to change the code of war stories. He believes that those who laugh at war might view the sky and flying machines as peaceful spaces.

Angela Carter's *Nights at the Circus* also posits that humor makes war appear ludicrous. Carter, however, is specifically concerned with the war between women and men. Sophia Fevvers (Carter's winged protagonist) and newspaper reporter Jack Walser (Fevvers's lover) personally terminate gender war when Fevvers's humor becomes worldwide laughter: "You mustn't believe what you write in the papers!' she assured him, stuttering and hiccuping with mirth. 'To think I fooled you!' . . . The spiralling tornado of Fevvers' laughter began to twist and shudder across the entire globe, as if a spontaneous response to the giant comedy that endlessly unfolded beneath it, until everything that lived and breathed, everywhere, was laughing. Or so it seemed to the deceived husband" (Carter, 294–295). Carter's description of all-pervasive laughter blanketing the world resembles James Joyce's description of snow covering Ireland. Joyce writes, "Yes, the newspapers were right: snow was general all over Ireland" (Joyce, "The Dead").

Fevvers and Carter assert that newspapers are wrong. More specifically, major newspapers—texts which report upon social constructions—are the "giant comedy" of the patriarchy general all over the world. Newspapers cover the world with patriarchal stories, blanket society as completely as Joyce's snow. Newspapers often ignore women, turn women into the dead. Carter's allusion to Joyce implies that if laughter at patriarchal constructions blankets the world like snow, then laughter might cause these constructions to lose their power to define reality. Laughter unmasks the illusion that there is no alternative to patriarchy. *Nights at the Circus* further unmasks this illusion by questioning the reality of Fevvers as birdwoman. Is Fevvers really the "only fully-feathered intacta in the history of the world" (Carter, 294)? The answer is negative. Walser, the newspaper writer who reports patriarchal reality, becomes the world's other fully feathered intacta, a man who is also a bird. Fevvers sits on him, causes him to "hatch" as the "New Man . . . [a] fitting mate for the New Woman" (Carter, 281). "This reconstructed Walser" (Carter, 291) is a birdman who joins with a birdwoman.

Fevvers and Walser are newly constructed humans who fly above the comedy of social constructions. While doing so, they look down upon the patriarchal world and laugh. Feathered, rather than metal, wings function as their flight vehicle. Flight frees Fevvers from the whorehouse, the female prison of her childhood; flight frees Walser from the prisonhouse of patriarchal language, which communicates that women and men are not destined to fly together. Carter, like Inez Haynes Gillmore, imagines women and men enjoying equal relationships after humans become a new biological entity—birdwomen and birdmen who fly in tandem.

Carter's reconstructed flying people figure in her rereading of both texts and symbols which signify flying. Her image of the gold medallion worn by one of the whorehouse's regular customers exemplifies this point. The "figure engraved on this medallion was that of a . . . phallus . . . and there were little wings attached to the ballocks thereof. . . . Around the shaft of this virile member twined the stem of a rose whose bloom nestled somewhat coyly at the place where the foreskin folded back. . . . the thing . . . represented a heavy instrument" (Carter, 70–71). Fevvers—like Butler, Hill, Miner, and Piercy—deconstructs the typical patriarchal story about the superior, winged flying phallus. She reveals that the phallus is a mere penis controlled by a female part: the "penis, represented by itself, aspires upwards, represented by the wings, but is dragged downwards, represented by the twining stem, by the female part, represented by the rose. . . . tread carefully, girlie! I exhort myself" (Carter, 77). In the manner of this explanation, the authors I discuss in this chapter call for rereading the powerful flying-phallus myth represented by the medallion's engraving. They depict natural alternatives to technology and insist that flying should not be dominated by man's machines and ideology. Women are exhorted to tread (and read) carefully when instructed that their presence drags men downward.

Gillmore's *Angel Island* describes a carving which addresses Carter's flying-phallus image pictured on the medallion. Angel Island men capture flying women by baiting a trap with feminine trinkets. (Trinkets cause women to lose Angel Island as surely as they caused Native Americans to lose Manhattan Island.) One trinket is "a handmirror of silver. Two carved Cupids held the glass between them. Their long wings made the handle" (Gillmore, 169). Holding on to femininity, clasping the image of oneself reflected in Cupid's mirror, is a trap still set by men to keep women from flying. Like the flying women of Angel Island, many real-world women sacrifice their supposedly unfeminine wings, an act symbolically described by this particular mirror's winged handle. Carved cupids, constructed images of love, enable men to hold women down and convince women to hold themselves down. As Gillmore's flying women discover, women can release this controlling handle and unfurl their wings. Angela, an Angel Island daughter whose wings remain unclipped, enjoys this discovery. Gillmore is a modernist mother who provides a model of flying women for another daughter named Angela—

Angela Carter. Carter's Fevvers, who flies above the center ring in
Nights at the Circus, hatches from the example set by Gillmore's
women who fly above Angel Island's demarcated space.

Fevvers, the women of Angel Island, and all the flying women I
discuss articulate a specifically female aspect of the real and dreamed-
about human story of flight. According to these protagonists' stories, female principles command the central camera angle—not the
space-off—of human flight productions. The protagonists insist that,
instead of being erased from history and barred from the sky, female
flyers deserve medallions. Or, in terms of Carter's image of the medallion, Butler, Hill, Miner, and Piercy declare that wombs as well
as penises have wings.

Beryl Markham articulates the same point. She explains that, like
herself, real women who pilot real planes can fly in their own at-
once unreal and real space:

> To fly in unbroken darkness . . . is at times unreal to the point
> where the existence of other people seems not even a reasonable
> possibility. . . . The earth is no more your planet than is a distant
> star—if a star is shining; the plane is your planet and you are its
> sole inhabitant. . . . The air takes me into its realm. Night en-
> velops me entirely, leaving me out of touch with the earth, leav-
> ing me within this small moving world of my own, living in
> space with the stars. (Markham, 9, 14)

Although Markham is no science fiction character, she tells women,
"[T]he plane is your planet."

Markham describes the end of a flight as a retold, unorthodox
story: "It is impossible to avoid the thought that this is the end of
my flight, but my reactions are not orthodox; the various incidents
of my entire life do not run through my mind like a motion-picture
film gone mad. I only feel that all this has happened before—and it
has. It has all happened a hundred times in my mind, in my sleep,
so that now I am not really caught in terror; I recognize a familiar
scene, a familiar story with its climax dulled by too much telling"
(Markham, 254). I turn from the end of my chapter about flying to a
more mundane scene and story told anew in terms of redefining gendered space. Unlike Masters's aforementioned astronaut who "pulls

away from the lights of earth" (Masters, 6), I now venture toward them. I move from the nonroutine (flying and model planes) to the familiar (domesticity and model houses). Chapter 4 discusses potentials for building new models for houses and the female/male love relationships enacted within them.

Richard Hamilton, Just What Is It That Makes Today's Homes So Different, So Appealing?, *1956. Kunsthalle Tübingen, gift of G. F. Zundel.*

Just What Is It That Makes Today's Homes So Different, So Appealing?

Oh, the numbers and numbers of slithering, rugose tentacles I've met in my time! And the squamous abominations and nameless cravings from beyond the stars . . . and strange figures celebrate . . . shocking sacrifices to nameless eidolons . . . mounted on . . . well, on Singer sewing machines. . . . Why are horrors always nameless? . . . Jean has got "a terrible slithering splash in the old attic." . . . "In the cellar," she says. "Besides, they keep an old washing machine in the attic." Helpless laughter from both of us at the idea of the Lurker from the Stars bobbling about in the family laundry.

　　　　　　　　　　—Joanna Russ, *On Strike against God*

Russ's feminist version of the fantastic juxtaposes space, domesticity, and the supernatural. Slithering tentacles emanate from torsos of blind dates, strange figures sit on Singer sewing machines, and a soapy alien might appear in the family laundry. However, neither Russ's narrator nor Jean, the narrator's graduate student, spends days in attics with washing machines and nights in bedrooms with slithering, rugose tentacles. These characters defeat frightening images of domesticity and transform themselves into scholars. They are women who buy houses, leave the domestic sphere, and unleash feminism to haunt hallowed university halls. In the manner of Russ, feminist supernatural fiction authors make generic clichés new. By challenging patriarchy's efforts to perpetuate its definition of domestic bliss, they answer Richard Hamilton's question regarding what makes today's homes so different and appealing.[1]

Feminist supernatural fiction, the subject of this chapter, defines and names patriarchal reality as a threatening space for women. It addresses the difficulties encountered by professional women who must control domestic space and function in the outside world. The feminist theme in contemporary supernatural fiction is evoked when the hero defines her home as a liberating space and supports herself financially after confronting realistic and fictive horrors. She triumphs over the witches, spirits, and aliens inhabiting her house. She is the visible, powerful woman in the office rather than the hidden, powerless madwoman in the attic.

Contemporary feminist supernatural texts spring from such nineteenth-century fictional treatments of connections between domesticity and female madness as Kate Chopin's *The Awakening* and Charlotte Perkins Gilman's *The Yellow Wallpaper*. Sandra Gilbert and Susan Gubar describe nineteenth-century female writers as "literally and figuratively confined."

> Enclosed in the architecture of an overwhelmingly male-dominatcd society, these literary women were also . . . trapped in the specifically literary constructs of what Gertrude Stein was to call "patriarchal poetry." For not only did a nineteenth-century woman writer have to inhabit ancestral mansions (or cottages) owned and built by men, she was also constricted and restricted by the Palaces of Art and Houses of Fiction male writers authored. We decided, therefore, that the striking coherence we noticed in literature by women could be explained by a common, female impulse to struggle free from social and literary confinement through strategic redefinitions of self, art, and society. (Gilbert and Gubar, xi–xii)

Although contemporary female writers are, of course, more able to own houses and to construct houses of fiction than their nineteenth-century counterparts, they still inhabit a male-dominated society. They are, however, free to create feminist supernatural literature, to redefine the place of art by exploring women's personal and professional roles.

Authors of present-day supernatural fictions provide positive additions to the tradition Chopin's and Gilman's victims of domesticity exemplify. These contemporary writers present women who defeat mad psychic forces and who refuse to be incarcerated in the attic. In this chapter I focus upon the female protagonists of three representative feminist supernatural fictions—Lynn Abbey's *The Guardians*, Marion Zimmer Bradley's *The Inheritor*, and Pamela Sargent's *The Alien Upstairs*—with an eye toward articulating contemporary supernatural fiction's feminist theme. In each of these works, a woman encounters a haunted house and transforms it into a house of her own. Abbey, Bradley, and Sargent insist that houses must be liberating spaces rather than sites of women's confinement. Mainstream novels echo their argument. I move from novels categorized as genre fiction to canonical texts when I position Gilman as a precursor to contemporary writers who link space, domesticity, and the supernatural. Then, I explain that Donald Barthelme's *Paradise* and Lynne Tillman's *Haunted Houses* exemplify how recognized postmodern writers treat these themes. As I have argued throughout the first three chapters of this study, the postmodern canon systematically excludes a wide range of important women's writing by dismissing it as genre fiction. Since these chapters pound home my thesis with insistent repetition, I will present my points about feminist supernatural fiction without direct reference to feminist fabulation's relationship to the postmodern canon.

Killing the Demon of the House, or, A Haunted House of One's Own

In contrast to Gilman's protagonists and Chopin's Edna Pontellier, Abbey's Lise Brown, Bradley's Leslie Barnes, and Sargent's Sarah Jaynes are not victimized by domesticity. Rather, each protagonist is, in Nina Auerbach's words, "an explosively mobile, magic woman, who breaks the boundaries of family within which her society restricts her" (Auerbach, *Demon*, 1). Each woman subdues the patriarchal demon of the house—the mad patriarch in the attic—and becomes a feminist angel of the house. Because "the angel's otherworldly power translates itself imperceptibly into a demonism that destroys all families and all houses" (Auerbach, 4), patriarchy defines this new feminist angel as threatening, almost supernatural.

Abbey, Bradley, and Sargent confront this view of the powerful feminist angel as an unnatural threat. Feminist supernatural fiction questions defining feminism as an otherworldly, problematical space and argues that feminists are not demons. This supernatural fiction, then, discusses the differences between feminist and patriarchal agendas in terms of supernatural fiction itself. Patriarchy defines feminism and feminists as the setting and characters of supernatural fiction; feminists wish to transform patriarchal reality into feminist supernatural fiction. Abbey, Bradley, and Sargent envision replacing patriarchal society with a new society which functions as a hospitable room of women's own.

The Alien Upstairs, by portraying earth as a dilapidated house inhabited by both women and men, addresses the merging of social and private spaces. Sargent's novel attempts to locate a space where women and men can live together with mutual dignity. Sarah Jaynes and her lover, Gerard Litvinov, live in a stagnant society and share a rented apartment, which they hope eventually to purchase together. In their world, subordination has little to do with gender roles. Indeed, *The Alien Upstairs* answers a question posed by Natalie Davis. Davis asks, "How could one separate the idea of subordination from the existence of the sexes?" (Davis, 128). In *Alien*, subordination concerns the relationship between humans and aliens, not the existence of human sexes. With regard to the superior extraterrestrial aliens they never meet, Sarah and Gerard—and all of their fellow humans—are positioned as Woman isolated on a static earth analogous to a limited domestic space.

The Alien Upstairs explains that humanity, in the guise of Woman, must transcend confining, domestic boundaries. Raf Courn, the supposed alien who moves into Sarah and Gerard's Oak Street apartment house, acts as a potential messiah who can move humanity from subordination to the position Davis calls "woman-on-top." From Raf's point of view, human society behaves like a nonproductive woman who seeks motivation from a source exceeding her own power and control. Sarah and Gerard—and humanity as a whole—are positioned equally in relation to Raf's power. Their subordination has nothing to do with gender. Raf himself realizes that the novel's entire human society, not individual females, is analogous to Woman hampered by limited possibilities: "You people amaze me. There are such possibilities open to you, and yet you live . . . such a short-sighted existence. . . . You people will never lift your heads above trivialities, will you?" (Sargent, 24–25, 33).

Sarah and Gerard encounter new possibilities after they enter an underground domestic space which literally takes off from the ground. Raf takes them to his spaceship disguised as a house:

> Raf led them into the house and down through the trap door. . . . Sarah saw a lighted room. . . . They left the room and entered another which had several reclining seats. . . . Tapestries lined the walls. . . .
>
> "This is my ship," Raf said in an expressionless voice. "I have kept it underground. . . . We shall make our journey in it." . . .
>
> She surveyed the room. At one end, there was a flat dashboard, which she assumed was supposed to be the control panel. (Sargent, 103–104)

Humanity-as-Woman gets on top in a new domestic space—the house-as-spaceship, an extremely mobile home. When the ship lands on Phobos, Sarah and Gerard find themselves located within another domestic environment: "They came to a hallway filled with more artifacts like those on the ship, urns and manuscripts and photographs. . . . Raf led them to a room filled with Oriental rugs and large, red cushions" (Sargent, 108). Nothing is accomplished by the move to Phobos; Sarah still resides with Raf, the demon/alien haunting her house. The existence of more stagnation becomes apparent when readers learn that Raf is a mere human male who keeps a woman, Margaret, imprisoned within his Phobos home (Sargent, 113).

In addition to his alien/human role reversal, Raf behaves according to a female role. Furthermore, all the humans in *Alien* act in terms of role exchanges. Humans, trapped on their stagnant home planet earth, are cast as Woman. Earth is controlled by "others," powerful extraterrestrials: "We [Raf and Margaret] are observers, set here to watch our home [earth] by those others. . . . We are powerless to do more" (Sargent, 112). Like a housewife watching soap operas in her living room, the humans on Phobos can take no action as they sit in Raf's house watching earth.

Although Margaret and Raf are perched on Phobos, a position enabling them to function as Davis's "woman-on-top," they are as powerless as the formerly earthbound Sarah and Gerard. Expected social and domestic power roles malfunction here. Just as Auerbach states that the angel of the house is not necessarily negative (Auerbach, 4, 72), Sargent implies that giving Woman a room of her own is not necessarily positive. Raf, Margaret, Sarah, and Gerard all ultimately leave their room on Phobos. Their otherworldly domestic environment proves to be an unsatisfactory space: "[T]hey might remain on their own accord, safe and cared for inside Phobos. It must have been easy for all the others to stay at first, before they saw what Raf had become, easy for them to hide from uncertainties, dangers, and disappointments of home" (Sargent, 143–144). Raf is positioned as a cloistered, bitter housewife relegated to nonproductive activity.

The Alien Upstairs, a speculative work concerned with social power positions, can be read as a supernatural *Upstairs, Downstairs*. In the world of Sargent's novel, all humans are analogous to scullery maids; the extraterrestrials are analogous to the upper class. Extraterrestrials are upstairs in the position of patriarch; humans are downstairs in the position of Woman. *Alien* introduces new spaces to describe new social power positions.

At the novel's conclusion, Sarah and Gerard return to their Oak Street apartment. Crucially, Mr. Epstein, their landlord, gives them his apartment and remains alone in the Phobos house. Sargent's resolution, then, emphasizes economic schism, not gender schism. While Sarah and Gerard are situated together on equal terms, the landlord is left as the distanced, isolated Other. Epstein becomes a supernatural creature, the alien "upstairs" on Phobos. Sarah, Gerard, and Epstein are all inheritors, the new holders of Raf's position. Epstein explains, "It's up to us. We are the observers now" (Sargent, 165). However, since Sarah and Gerard refuse merely to observe, they differ from Raf and Epstein. Instead of viewing life on earth from a "console" television screen, as co-owners of a new bookstore they insist upon participating in life, working with each other to control their economic destiny. Sarah and Gerard possess a house of their own and a shared purpose. All aliens—all economic and social specters—are removed from this house. Together, Gerard and Sarah become positive angels of their house.

Raf and Margaret, who join the extraterrestrials on separate occasions, never achieve this happy equilibrium. Although *Alien* is silent about Raf's and Margaret's life with the aliens, it hints that, like Epstein, they inhabit separate rooms of their own. In the manner of Sarah's and Gerard's trip to Phobos, Margaret's and Raf's shift to the alien milieu is wasted motion which fails to change their status and relationship. Hence, *Alien* communicates that momentous movements (trips in spaceships and shifts to alien environments) do not yield improved situations. The house on Phobos mirrors conditions in the house on Oak Street.

The final scene in *Alien* implies that the most important movements are domestic and intimate rather than public and mechanical.

> Gerard was with her, on his side of the bed, unmoving, but she felt alone. She wondered how he would change. She thought of Mr. Epstein, alone on Phobos.
>
> She did not move. . . . She was in a black tunnel that went up past the night sky and into space. . . . Gerard's warm fingers touched her arm, then took her hand, pressing it against his palm. (Sargent, 165)

This passage takes a very positive view of potential relationships between women and men. It also hints that humanity can progress to a higher level in the interplanetary great chain of being and that women and men must attain this new level together as equal partners. Even though Gerard is with Sarah, she feels alone. The text implies that answers to the following questions are positive. If Sarah reaches the next stage in the interplanetary progression will she, like Epstein, be alone? Or, will Gerard—and all men—be willing to change? Sarah's and Gerard's mutual lack of movement is altered when he takes her hand. Together they will enter the black tunnel leading to a transcendent version of the present human condition. Women and men will be able to make their home in a new space. Humans will join extraterrestrials in the position on top.

Sargent presents this possibility through a festival of supernatural, topsy-turvy role reversals in which, as I have explained, humanity plays Woman and a human, Raf, plays both an alien and Woman. Sargent's women and men are mutable entities who become each other, just as Auerbach's angel of the house can change into a demon. Auerbach explains that angels become demons (Auerbach, *Demons*, 107); Sargent creates Raf, an alien/human who becomes Woman. Davis shows that the role reversals in *Alien* belong to a tradition of artistic and sexual inversions enjoyed by societies facing change. According to Davis, "In hierarchical and conflictful societies that loved to reflect on the world-turned-upside-down, the *topos* of the woman-on-top was one of the most enjoyed. Indeed, sexual inversion—that is, switches in sex roles—was a widespread form of cultural play in literature, in art, and in festivity. . . . Women played men; men played women; men played women who were playing men" (Davis, 129). The feminist theme in Sargent's supernatural novel coincides with Davis's understanding of sexual inversion.

Hierarchical and conflictful society turns to popular literature to reflect upon social alternatives. In Sargent's version of this tendency, Raf Courn transports Sarah and Gerard from a mundane world to a cornball, extraterrestrial role-reversal festival. Humanity portrayed as "woman out of her place" (Davis, 135) affords "an expression of, and an outlet for, conflicts about authority within the system; . . . this inversion could prompt new ways of thinking about the system and reacting to it" (Davis, 142–143). Sexual inversions in *Alien* provide outlets for conflicts stemming from patriarchal and economic systems, prompt new ways of thinking about these systems. In addition to inheriting their own house, Sarah and Gerard are bequeathed a potential new nonsexist social and economic order.

Marion Zimmer Bradley's inheritors also acquire a new house and new social arrangements. While *The Alien Upstairs* portrays a shift in economic power positions, *The Inheritor* portrays a shift in family power positions. This shift acts as a poltergeist in relation to the nuclear family by causing a supposedly stable structure to become topsy-turvy. When Leslie Barnes makes her newly purchased haunted house habitable, she at once provides space for her sister Emily's development as a pianist and refuses to establish a nuclear family in a house her boyfriend, Joel Beckenham, finances.

Leslie's actions might appear to be counterproductive. She liberates herself from one domestic space by securing another domestic space, a model home. Judith Fryer speaks to this supposed contradiction when she describes women moving away from the idea of the model home at a time (between 1884 and 1925) when this construct was becoming more rigidly imposed upon American society:

> We have, then, a *seeming* paradox: exactly as women moved increasingly outside the home—becoming a cause of social disorder—the *model* home became a rigid construct imposed on a social situation as a means of establishing order and control, suggesting by the ordering of spaces that could be endlessly duplicated particular values, particular norms concerning family life, sex roles, community relations, and social equality. . . . In this time in which the very fabric of society was tearing apart— for the liberation of women from the traditional cultural patterns involves the social structures of home, family, work, leisure, sexual relationships—a similar solution was proposed, by *both* traditionalists and reformers. Those who would preserve existing patterns and those who would restructure those patterns shared a belief in the relationship between the spaces inhabited by human beings and the behavior of those human beings. (Fryer, 207–208)

Bradley and Lynn Abbey provide contemporary renditions of this seeming paradox. Leslie and Abbey's Lise Brown cause social disorder by insisting upon working outside the home. Instead of serving as housewives in homes men support, they control their lives by constructing domestic spaces which reflect their notions of appropriate social roles. The protagonists' new private environments have an impact upon their new definitions of proper female behavior. Their involvement with witches and demons signals that, as Fryer explains, the fabric of society is tearing apart. In Bradley's words, "The old rules of life had been shattered, and the new parameters of existence were not yet made clear" (Bradley, 378).

Bradley's juxtaposition of the supernatural, women, and domestic space can be linked to Carolyn Merchant's connection between witches' activities and women's place in the social order.

> Extant representations of the witches' Sabbath present an image of widespread chaos and uncontrolled nature dominated by

women engaged in exuberant, frenzied activity. . . . The control
and the maintenance of the social order and women's place
within it was one of the many complex and varied reasons for
the witch trials. . . . The immediacy of individual relationships
with a spirit or demon and the possibility of revenge and control
may account for the popularity of witchcraft among oppressed
women. No hierarchies stood between the witch and the object
of her will. . . . The release of passion and violence at the devil's
Sabbath symbolized the witch's alienation from a world that
offered her little human comfort or hope of salvation. (Merchant, 134, 138, 140)

Because Leslie and Lise circumvent the social order and women's
place within it, they retain the right to engage in independent, frenzied activity. They are, then, themselves feminist witches who triumph over the patriarchal supernatural forces haunting their houses.
Viewing a poltergeist or a witch as an evil patriarchal entity is—
since such forces are usually thought to be feminine—another role
reversal of the kind presented in *The Alien Upstairs*. Witch/protago-
nists who rise above oppression, subvert hierarchies, and react to the
world with active participation rather than alienation give the word
"witch" a positive, feminist meaning.[2] I will explain how Abbey and
Bradley make use of the supernatural and create feminist witch/pro-
tagonists to rewrite patriarchy's version of the proper relationship
between women and domestic space. Their postmodern supernatural fictions address the fictionality of patriarchy's story about women
and domesticity.

As opposed to the female protagonists of Chopin's *The Awakening* and Gilman's *The Yellow Wallpaper* (who are victimized by patriarchal definitions of women's domestic roles), Leslie rejects Joel's
ideas about equating houses with women's loss of independence.
Joel tells her that she sounds "like one of those damned women's
libbers. Your own property. Your own career. . . . What will you do
with a house of your own after we get married?" (Bradley, 34–35).
Leslie defines entering Joel's house as a dangerous activity: "*If I go
home with him he can talk me into anything*" (Bradley, 38). Rather
than marrying Joel, she chooses to love her own haunted house and

to establish a new version of the nuclear family within it. She hopes that "with Joel out of the picture, maybe the house will turn out to be the great love of my life after all. A grand passion, maybe" (Bradley, 65). The house turns out to be haunted by a spirit which resents women's talent. Leslie learns that the former female tenant "was driven out of the place! Because she said the studio was haunted by something that hated her . . . hated her art especially!" (Bradley, 180). Leslie defeats this misogynistic spirit and claims the house as an appropriate place for Emily's artistic talent to develop.

Her insistence upon successfully inhabiting the haunted residence compensates for her parents' failure to provide the proper supportive environment for her and for Emily. These parents do not "understand why Leslie should want a career more interesting than teaching school, and Emily's passion for performing, first ballet and then piano, had appalled them" (Bradley, 115). The haunted house provides ample space for Leslie to establish a psychiatry practice and for Emily to enjoy a music studio. It houses these women's talents and enables Leslie to act as a supportive parent who provides space to make Emily's career possible. She functions as her sister's positive mother and ensures that Emily's talents—unlike the talents of most women—will not be sacrificed. Leslie's atypical parental role speaks to the damaging influence of the nuclear family. Leslie and Emily establish alternative familial relationships which enhance their professional activities.

Leslie augments her parental role by providing Emily with a nonbiological father—her new lover, Simon Anstey, a renowned pianist who practices black magic. Simon feels "as if she [Emily] were his daughter" (Bradley, 324). Simon assumes a second new role in addition to his position as Emily's nonbiological father. As a renowned pianist whose hand has become permanently injured, Simon, a person prevented from expressing his talents fully, finds himself in the role of Woman. He acts counter to this usually ineffectual role by dedicating himself to developing Emily's talent. Emily, then, is the inheritor in *The Inheritor*, the young woman who inherits musical expertise from a nonbiological father who acts as nurturing Woman. She is the beneficiary of topsy-turvy, alternative family constructions—a "masculine" professional sister/mother and a "female" adopted father. She benefits from engaging in a new nuclear family configuration which successfully exorcises patriarchal demons. Leslie's haunted house becomes a positive space for both herself and the members of her unconventional nuclear family. After Leslie marries Simon, "The house would be theirs. Somehow it must be habitable for them both" (Bradley, 389). Like *The Alien Upstairs*, *The Inheritor* concludes as a woman and a man manage to inhabit the same domestic space with mutual dignity. (And, like the authors of the postseparatist feminist utopias discussed in chapter 5, Bradley does not portray her happy heterosexual couple functioning together equally in the society at large.)

In the manner of Sargent and Bradley, Lynn Abbey calls upon the supernatural to place women in the role of poltergeists, unpredictable, topsy-turvy forces which intrude upon a stable patriarchal world. While Sargent and Bradley, respectively, concentrate most fully upon establishing new economic and familial orders, Abbey's story of one couple's shifted gender and power roles coincides with Davis's aforementioned term for switches in sex roles, "sexual inversion." Abbey's protagonist, Lise Brown, disrupts patriarchal order.

The "Rift" to the "Otherworld" in Lise's Manhattan apartment is one cause of the rift between her and her boyfriend, Alan Porter. Lise's ability to enter a realm which has been an Otherworld to women—the business world—is another cause of their strained relationship. Lise is the woman who appropriates a man's executive position, takes over male space in the office. She is the effective witch/feminist who inhabits men's nightmares; Alan is the financially deposed man, who, like Raf and Simon, is another version of the man-as-Woman.

Through the use of an urban setting, Abbey comments upon women's relationship to outside as well as inside spaces. She indicates that city streets can be terrifying, otherworldly places for women. Lise's brother gives her the following advice about appropriate attire for women who venture onto the street: "[H]er pants were too tight and her bra not tight enough; she was asking for IT" (Abbey, 130). What exactly is "IT"? Abbey provides an answer in terms of the supernatural: "IT would break out at any moment. IT was unstoppable, irresistible. IT was infinite in its Otherworldly terror and evil" (Abbey, 176). Every woman on city streets can encounter the patriarchal repressive IT which exists to restrict her public movements. IT is one of what Russ calls "nameless horrors," the nagging fear of encountering the "Lurker from the Stars" on a deserted street (Russ, *Strike*, 39–40). IT is sexual gestures and whispered obscenities. IT is rape. By using phrases such as "the *Times* had lapsed into lurid reportage in response to the latest criminal psychotic loose on the streets" (Abbey, 189), Abbey stresses that city streets can be demonic. This point is further articulated by Abbey's title, *The Guardians*. In Manhattan, men such as Lise's doorman, Sam, function as the guardians. Doormen, located in the place between inside and outside space, guard apartment houses and women from dangers lurking on otherworldly streets.

The Guardians tells the story of Lise's struggle to secure domestic and economic spaces. Like Leslie Barnes, she acts according to Judith Fryer's understanding of the apparent contradiction between simultaneously struggling to establish a model home and a model career. Like Leslie, Lise refuses to allow supernatural forces to drive her from her home: "She would not be driven out of her home by anything, anyone. . . . This was her home. . . . Nothing was going to drive her off" (Abbey, 66). These words belong to the rhetoric of war; Lise is protecting her home front. Her fight for independence entails guarding domestic space, a battle which is more important to Lise than romantic love. In the manner of Leslie, she judges her house to be more attractive and important than her boyfriend: "She wondered . . . if she really liked him . . . or if she was only desperate for someone's company. . . . Asking herself what did matter to her, she found that the problems riding closest to the surface of her mind had to do with her apartment and the witchcraft that had been performed within it" (Abbey, 89). Her stance against invading supernatural presences indicates her strength: "'I'm stronger than you are' she warned the empty room, 'and at least twice as stubborn'" (Abbey, 93).

Lise stresses that, in her house, nothing is truly inanimate (Abbey, 100). Male visitors become additional mobile entities to be defended against. She speaks to Alan with the same independent, defensive tone she uses to address the haunted room: "You're trying to take over. You saw me get frightened and cry on your shoulder so you think I'm the frilly, dependent type just waiting for your Prince Charming. I'll take care of myself, thank you, and do it quite nicely" (Abbey, 140). Lise, the protagonist of a feminist supernatural novel, refuses to play the female part prescribed by sexist fairy tales. In Abbey's tale, Prince Charming is the enemy. Lise must fight the supernatural spirits and the real patriarchal forces which seek to take over her life.

Her struggle is economic as well as domestic. Abbey emphasizes that, like city streets, office buildings are often hostile environments for women. In addition to subduing the demons in her apartment, Lise copes with sexist forces running rampant in her office. She herself initially views Alan as her professional superior: "When she looked at him now, on the executive escalator, the light of ambition in his eyes while she was still a troop-in-waiting, the differences seemed unbridgeable" (Abbey, 92). Lise, a witch/feminist troop-in-waiting, wins the battle to occupy the executive suite.

She removes the demons from both her home and office. Alan is removed from his office when the demon in Lise's house vanquishes him: "That—that THING held onto him. It let the others go—but Alan went with it" (Abbey, 177). After this incident, Alan is (understandably) unable to act as an effective professional. While the IT on the street does not deter Lise's efforts to function in the outside world, the THING in her apartment makes it impossible for Alan to function in that outside world. Hence, *The Guardians* recasts a metaphor: instead of a woman being figuratively gobbled by a house, a man literally suffers this fate.

Alan, not a woman, is engulfed by domestic space. Lise, not a member of "the elite corps of rising-young-men" (Abbey, 212), rises to the top of the office hierarchy. Situated on the office building's top floor, she becomes a powerful woman-on-top. Her boss dismisses Alan and invites her "to take over the Year-End Analysis project now that he's gone" (Abbey, 215). Lise, rather than domestic supernatural forces or sexist economic forces, takes over. She moves into the space Alan vacates: "She waited until after the office had emptied before piling her belongings on her chair and wheeling everything into Alan's deserted office" (Abbey, 215). After Lise wins the right to control outside and inside spaces, her mother approves of her accomplishment: "Your father worked twenty years to get four weeks off—and then he could never take them. You're doing well, Lise: a home of your own, a fine job" (Abbey, 242). Lise is positioned above her boyfriend and her father.

Abbey is less benevolent toward men than Bradley and Sargent. While the women and men in *The Alien Upstairs* and *The Inheritor* share domestic and economic spaces, Lise inhabits these spaces alone. However, *The Guardians* does present a counterpart to Raf and Simon who, as I have explained, function as the man-as-Woman embraced by the female hero. Although Lise is attracted to Nigel, a shadowy figure involved with witchcraft, instead of sleeping with him she removes him from her apartment to prevent sex from interfering with her next day's work (Abbey, 269). Like the eventually murdered Alan, Nigel is gobbled by the Otherworld. Men do not fare well in *The Guardians*. Even Sam, the doorman, is killed. Lise wins against the patriarchal evil which haunts women: "The Rift is gone" (Abbey, 379). Nothing separates her from independently occupying domestic and professional spaces. The men in her life disappear. Lise seems to have no more guardians.

Lise, Leslie, and Sarah defeat the supernatural forces in their houses and secure domestic spaces. They have rooms of their own in which to construct new economic, familial, and social environments. They also, however, grapple unsuccessfully with another supernatural presence in their domestic environment. A guardian haunts their minds and an unwanted entity which can manifest itself at any time inhabits their bodies. I am referring to the relationship between domesticity and women's weight, a woman's fear of eating in her own room and emerging as the fat angel of the house. Abbey, Bradley, and Sargent are concerned about how, in addition to myths about domesticity, dieting is used as a means to control women; their protagonists demolish demons—and count calories. Sarah diets to model a dress in the department store which employs her (Sargent, 10, 53). Lise eats salad greens and yogurt for dinner (Abbey, 62) and views her haunted apartment in terms of dieting: "I've lost five pounds since I've moved in—so it hasn't been a complete waste. Of course, if I keep that up I'll disappear before the lease is up"

(Abbey, 95). Leslie feels guilty after eating baked goods (Bradley, 323, 341). Emily is a health food fanatic (Bradley, 156). After treating an anorexic teenager, Leslie wonders what "curious force of cause and effect, in this life or any other, would force . . . a teenage girl to starve herself, sometimes literally to death?" (Bradley, 294). Abbey, Bradley, and Sargent insist that, like domestic roles, notions of proper female weight limit women's ability to function efficiently.

Hillel Schwartz's opinion that the specter of weight gain is a supernatural force applies to my discussion about haunted women and their domestic roles. He compares weight gain to Satan: "In this century Satan has reappeared as the mocking mouth of the dial on the bathroom scale. . . . And Satan has legions of Little Red Devils (or hidden calories) urging Mrs. Chubby to shoot the works at the soda fountain" (Schwartz, 308). Although the protagonists defeat aliens and evil spirits, legions of devilish calories haunt them. They do not overcome all aspects of female domestic roles. Schwartz stresses that food is an integral part of women's roles as cook, hostess, and homemaker: "Given the primary job as food shoppers, women are persuaded to buy for their families what they are told they should not eat themselves. Informed by science that they are naturally fatter than men, fashion convinces them that they should be naturally thinner. . . . As cooks and hostesses, women must prepare those foods they should not eat and wear those expressions of generosity they must not allow themselves" (Schwartz, 330). Like Leslie, Lise, and Sarah, many real-world women who own homes and pursue careers are haunted by the contradictory demands of acting as food providers for families and adhering to thin body images. This contradiction leads to frustration, denial—and, sometimes, death.

A diet is a "gothic tale of unremitting horror" (Schwartz, 6); society's confusion regarding appropriate food is as problematical as its confusion regarding appropriate gender roles. In fact, Schwartz's description of the sugar substitute called Equal mirrors Davis's aforementioned remarks about topsy-turvy role substitutes. In terms of masquerade and carnival modes, an analogy exists between men playing the role of Woman and a substance which is not sugar masquerading as sugar. As Schwartz explains, Equal's "masquerade is close to perfect. The lo-cal economy conduces to such carnival. The effect of the many masquerades is ultimately to call into question the very nature of food" (Schwartz, 267). Abbey, Bradley, and Sargent present food as yet another masquerade which, like gender role reversals, calls into question the very nature of femininity and domesticity. The authors' attention to women's obsession with dieting underscores the relationship between empty calories and empty lives, the relationship between Equal and equality. These female supernatural fiction authors point to a feminist version of Stephen King's *Thinner.*

Their texts can be described by what Fryer calls "books that are explicitly female in their . . . withdrawal from patriarchal culture into the indistinctly mapped and terribly difficult space of the self in order to generate new modes of being and of expression. Initial steps in this imaginative journey . . . criticize cultural patterns without being able to envision viable alternatives" (Fryer, 221). Although *The Alien Upstairs, The Guardians,* and *The Inheritor* do not envision alternatives to women's attempts to reduce the space their bodies occupy, these novels venture into the space of the female self to reflect an insight theorists such as Kim Chernin and Susie Orbach articulate: fat is a feminist issue.[3]

Alternatives proposed by feminist supernatural fictions form a feminist poetics of personal and public space, an area which can be understood in terms of Gaston Bachelard's *The Poetics of Space.* Bachelard desires to "show that the house is one of the greatest powers of integration for the thoughts, memories and dreams of mankind. . . . Without it [the house], man would be a dispersed being. . . . Life begins well, it begins enclosed, protected, all warm in the bosom of the house" (Bachelard, 6–7). He does not state that the house is one of the greatest powers to curtail the thoughts, memories, and dreams of women. Houses enclose women. Women do not live well while protected in a domestic environment which, like a constraining brassiere, holds them in. Further, Bachelard does not take issue with the demand that women sacrifice themselves to maintain houses. He says, "Through housewifely care a house recovers not so much its originality as its origin. And what a great life it would be if, every morning, every object in the house could be made anew by our hands, could 'issue' from our hands" (Bachelard, 69). The patriarchal notion of housewifely care relegates women to unoriginal lives. "Our" hands are, in truth, "her" hands, and she does not have a great life as an object devoted to maintaining household objects.

Abbey, Bradley, and Sargent offer a feminist interpretation of Bachelard's notion that a "house constitutes a body of images that give mankind proofs or illusions of stability. We are constantly reimagining its reality: to distinguish all these images would be to describe the soul of the house; it would mean developing a veritable psychology of the house" (Bachelard, 17). Their protagonists turn houses into proofs or illusions of stability by reimagining the reality of houses, using the supernatural to imbue houses with souls. As residents of houses which literally possess psychologies, these characters can inspire positive, liberating female psychologies. In other words, the characters create examples of a new feminist fictive topoanalysis, a term defined by Bachelard as "the systematic psychological study of the sites of our intimate lives" (Bachelard, 8). *The Alien Upstairs, The Guardians,* and *The Inheritor* are feminist supernatural studies which suggest methods to alter the psychology and site of women's intimate lives.

Through feminist topoanalysis, these novels insist that women control a private space which enables them to move between their personal and public lives. Feminist topoanalysis names Russ's strange figures on the Singer sewing machines and Lurkers in the laundry (Russ, *Strike,* 39–40). Such phrases as lack of space, entrapment in the domestic sphere, absence of access to the public world, cramped quarters, and inability to move refer to the nameless horrors she describes. The narrator of *On Strike against God* explains: "I remember being endlessly sick to death of this world which isn't mine and won't be for at least a hundred years; you'd be surprised how I can go through almost a whole day thinking I live here and then some ad or something . . . gives me a nudge—just reminding me that not only do I not have a right to be here; I don't even exist. . . . I was living in a small New York apartment then, so there was barely room for me in the bathroom, what with the stockings hung over the railing of the bathtub and the extra towels hanging on the hooks I'd pounded into the wall myself" (Russ, *Strike*, 16, 37). Although women do not control the world, Leslie, Lise, and Sarah insist upon their right to be located in the particular public and private worlds they do manage to control. They secure enough room for themselves.

Instead of being enclosed by domestic objects such as stockings hanging in bathrooms, they define their own spaces by hanging their lives on mobile hooks they themselves pound into walls. Women's lack of confidence regarding venturing into new outside spaces, their fears of encountering the Lurker from the Stars, are flushed away when the protagonists refuse to define their lives according to discourse the Tidy Bowl Man articulates. Their actions reflect a point Fryer makes about space, domesticity, and women's power: "Spaciousness, then, means being free; freedom implies space. It means having the power and enough room in which to act. . . . Trapped as she has been at home . . . woman has been *unable to move* . . . between private spaces and open spaces" (Fryer, 226). The protagonists have enough room to move from private to public spaces and to act in public spaces. These powerful women live according to a feminist topoanalysis. They are able to ignore yellow wallpaper, engage in women's awakening to the public world, and transcend the experience of the madwoman in the attic.

Abbey, Bradley, and Sargent venture into the supernatural to voice both society's and some individual women's reluctance to express a feminist topoanalysis. These authors portray women confronting ghosts as a means to call for more enlightened houses. In the words of Italo Calvino, the "power of modern literature lies in its willingness to give a voice to what has remained unexpressed in the social or individual unconscious. . . . The more enlightened our houses are, the more their walls ooze ghosts. Dreams of progress and reason are haunted by nightmares" (Calvino, *Cybernetics*, 19). An existing nightmare haunts the dreams of progress and reason within *The Alien Upstairs*, *The Guardians*, and *The Inheritor*: real-world women relegated to domestic space, real-world shrouded Arab women, real women who are ghosts.

Western women live in more enlightened houses than their Muslim sisters. In the Western world, the madwoman in the attic is a

shunned image, an avoided cliché. Yet, despite this relative enlight-
enment, our houses usually do not conform to feminist perspectives. Thankfully, feminist writers and critics can turn imperfect
houses into glass houses. Their ideas facilitate seeing through sexist imperfections, deconstructing foundations erected according to
patriarchal constructions. Feminist supernatural fictions serve as
stones thrown at patriarchal glass houses. These fictions are the
building material for new feminist domestic spaces, and as such
they should not be segregated from the neighborhoods their canonical postmodern counterparts and modernist forebears inhabit.

"We Are All Haunted Houses": Redesigning Domestic Space

I now turn to examples of these counterparts and forebears. I discuss
Charlotte Perkins Gilman (a feminist precursor to Abbey, Bradley,
and Sargent) and Lynne Tillman and Donald Barthelme (postmodern
writers who confront women's relationship to domesticity in terms
of living space). Gilman believes men can help women to develop
new domestic paradigms; Tillman portrays men as invaders of the
female house/body; Barthelme emphasizes that housebound female
sex objects are not architects of the world order.

Gilman's "If I Were a Man" and "When I Was a Witch" present
extraordinary women who wield male power and leave the home.
Women also alter their domestic spaces in her "The Cottagette"
and "What Diantha Did." Tillman's *Haunted Houses* presents the
haunted house as a metaphor which describes three women's development from girlhood to young adulthood. In Barthelme's *Paradise*,
three ghostly women who fail to become productive members of
society haunt an architect's apartment. Gilman, Tillman, and Barthelme grapple with domesticity and the supernatural in terms of
transformation.

Mollie Mathewson, the protagonist of "If I Were a Man," becomes
a "woman-on-top" after a sex role reversal enables her literally to
become her husband, Gerald. Her transition from the female domestic world to the male public world positions her as an alien: "The
world opened before her. Not the world she had been reared in—
where Home had covered all the map, almost, and the rest had been

'foreign,' or 'unexplored country,' but the world as it was—man's world, as made, lived in, and seen, by men" (Gilman, "Man," 36). Mollie/Gerald's special perspective emphasizes men's power to make the world and women conform to men's definitions. A clergyman, for example, informs Mollie/Gerald that, according to divine law, a woman's place is in the home. He says, "The real danger . . . is that they will overstep the limits of their God-appointed sphere" (Gilman, "Man," 37). When addressed to a woman-as-man, these words emphasize that women's sphere is limited by male-appointed rather than God-appointed reality.

Gilman juxtaposes gender roles to enlarge women's appropriate place. The conclusion of "If I Were a Man" communicates that women and men can learn from experiencing each other's roles. In the words of the story, "Gerald was vaguely conscious of new views, strange feelings, and the submerged Mollie learned and learned" (Gilman, "Man," 38). Gilman's foray into the fantastic advocates liberating the submerged Mollie, the housebound woman.

While Mollie passively experiences men's public world, the unnamed protagonist of "When I Was a Witch" actively changes this world. The protagonist is a witch/woman who can grant all of her own wishes concerning improving civic life and the plight of animals. Gilman's story becomes most interesting at its conclusion when the narrator specifically turns her attention to women. The narrator wishes "that women, all women, might realize Womanhood at last; its power and pride and place in life" (Gilman, "Witch," 31). Her particular wish fails to come true. Although this narrator alters an entire city, she can do nothing to change women's subordinate role.

Her magic is simply not applicable to women: "You see, this magic which had fallen on me was black magic—and I had wished white. It didn't work at all, and, what was worse, it stopped all the other things that were working so nicely" (Gilman, "Witch," 31). The magic is ineffective because it is derived from a male source. When the narrator becomes a witch, she has the power to define her world, to make her wishes become reality. In other words, she behaves like a man; her role reversal causes the word "witch" to become synonymous with "male." Her magic's ultimate ineffectiveness implies that women cannot transcend subordination by imitating male power modes. Men use black magic to fulfill their wishes regarding how the world should appear; male black magic nullifies feminist wishes. According to "When I Was a Witch," feminists need to employ alternatives to patriarchal methods, to rely upon their own white magic. This point is exemplified when the narrator laments the loss of "my privileges when I was a witch" (Gilman, "Witch," 31). Her privileges, the ability to construct reality, are male privileges. Patriarchal black magic orders the world and fails to meet women's needs. Positive, powerful female witches change the world through means which differ from those of male witches.

Gilman's "The Cottagette" and "What Diantha Did" posit such feminist alternatives. In these stories, feminist white magic effectively creates feminist domestic spaces. "The Cottagette" describes this transformation in terms of behavioral role reversals. Malda, the protagonist, chooses to reside in a bungalow (affiliated with a central boardinghouse) where other people perform her domestic tasks. This living arrangement allows her to devote herself completely to her art. Despite this freedom from domestic labor, Malda's friend Lois encourages her to create a domestic environment for a potential husband rather than an artistic environment for herself. Lois explains that "what they want to marry is a homemaker. . . . If I were you—if I really loved this man [Ford Mathews] and wished to marry him—I would make a home of this place" (Gilman, "Cottagette," 51). In order to marry Ford Mathews, Malda redefines her cottagette, her own art studio, as a space of servitude. She transforms her house into a place haunted by patriarchal notions: "What was one summer of interrupted work, of noise and dirt and smell and constant meditation on what to eat next, compared to a lifetime of love? Besides—if he married me—I should have to do it always, and might as well get used to it" (Gilman, "Cottagette," 53). "The Cottagette" contradicts this statement by proposing that a female artist can devote herself to art as well as to a man, that "it is not true, always . . . that the way to a man's heart is through his stomach" (Gilman, "Cottagette," 56).

Ford's response to Malda's newly enacted domestic emphasis invalidates Lois's opinions. He explains to Malda that "when you took to cooking, it jarred on me. . . . I hated it—to see my woodflower in a kitchen" (Gilman, "Cottagette," 55). His reaction asserts that individual men are not evil forces. Instead, the evil forces are discourses about defining proper domestic roles in ways which do not suit women's and men's needs. Malda and Ford are equally disconcerted by her domestic focus. "The Cottagette" asserts that women who act as kitchen drudges retard rather than enhance their relationships with men. Gilman seems to imply that Dinesen's Babette (who is discussed in chapter 2) is not Everywoman, that all women should not try to satisfy themselves and their loved ones by preparing food. Ford says the magic words which cause his woodflower to disappear from the kitchen. Malda realizes that when she thinks of herself as an artistic free spirit inhabiting her cottagette, she conjures an alternative, effective female domestic space. Malda and Ford both wield feminist white magic.

Diantha also insists that this form of magic is not always unreal. In "What Diantha Did," feminist white magic manifests itself as a boardinghouse which, as Ann J. Lane explains, Gilman views as women's escape route from domestic traps (Lane, xxvii). Diantha renegotiates men's domestic contract with women by insisting that housework is not free work. She is called "an unnatural daughter" (Gilman, "Diantha," 135) who asks her father to pay for her domestic services. She is also, according to her husband, Ross, an unnatural wife, a married woman who is a businesswoman. Gilman writes, " 'No man—that is a man—would marry a woman and let her run a business.' . . . He wanted her there, in the home—his home—his wife—even when he was not in it himself" (Gilman, "Diantha," 137). Diantha disregards Ross's wishes when she establishes a successful hotel and food delivery business.

She juxtaposes domesticity with power by refusing to separate her domestic talents from financial remuneration. As a result of linking housekeeping with economics, she builds a business which "grew so large she had to have quite a fleet of delivery-wagons" (Gilman, "Diantha," 138). She tears down social walls as well as economic barriers. By the end of the story, "the pressure of this blank wall between them [Diantha and Ross]" (Gilman, "Diantha," 138) is alleviated. "What Diantha Did," a feminist fairy tale about female entrepreneurship, ends "happily ever after" when Ross finally appreciates his wife's venture into the business world.

Although some contemporary women surpass Diantha's economic achievements, few contemporary men share Ross's changed attitude. For the most part, the blank wall separating independent women from men's domestic expectations is still intact. Tillman and Barthelme emphasize that feminist white magic is not very effective. They show that what Diantha did in this century's first decade (she reconciled women's economic goals with patriarchal definitions of domesticity) is not a usual component of contemporary reality. Diantha is still appropriately described as a fantastic witch who creates social transformations yet to be incorporated fully within contemporary society. Enlightened men, such as Ross and Ford, do not inhabit the houses that Barthelme and Tillman imagine are populated by ghosts.

Tillman's *Haunted Houses* focuses upon the development of three young women, Emily, Grace, and Jane. Each of their unconnected stories is "the kind of document one might keep as evidence of the morals of women in transition in the second half of the twentieth century" (Tillman, 61). Tillman chronicles these transitions by locating her narrative in the recent past and by refusing to allow her characters to become mature adults. Emily, Grace, and Jane leave their childhood homes without ever establishing homes of their own.

Tillman is uninterested in her protagonists' futures; *Haunted Houses* is a science fiction, fairy tale, time-travel story which forever runs backward. Jane, for example, does not care about the future:

> Jane lingered on the past, entirely disinterested in something called the future. . . . Jimmy [her boyfriend] and his science fiction, his teasing her about her walking, no, running, backward into time. Jane telling him that there was just as much invention in versions of the past as in what's written about the future. . . . "I guess it is like a fairy tale to me, about the past." (Tillman, 100–101)

Women's past prepares them for a future fairy tale about meeting the perfect husband and making a home for him.

Emily defines the story of making this home, the myth of love and passion, as science fiction: "Emily assumed . . . writing passion was writing the fantastic, sort of science fiction—which she hated—about love" (Tillman, 188). Many women live by casting themselves as heroines of impossible, future, passionate love stories—stories Emily interprets as science fictions about discouraging women from enacting their own adult stories. Instead of becoming mature adults, Emily, Grace, and Jane function as poltergeists who forever haunt the past's houses, dwellings which are not their own. *Haunted Houses* defines its protagonists' inner selves and changing bodies as metaphorical haunted houses invaded by unsatisfactory, sexual males.

Tillman's silence about her protagonists' futures deconstructs patriarchal fairy tales about women's futures. These tales are about women, located in houses they do not control, who sacrifice their figurative house/bodies by surrendering to men's passions. When Tillman presents Woman's future as silence, she points to the fictionality of wishing to live with Prince Charming. Her chosen silence corresponds to Ihab Hassan's point that "silence develops as the metaphor of a new attitude that literature has chosen to adopt toward itself. This attitude puts to question the peculiar power . . . of literary discourse—and challenges the assumptions of our civilization" (Hassan, "Silence," 11). Tillman uses silence as a metaphor to express her attitude toward patriarchal stories about women's futures. Her silence questions the peculiar power of these stories and challenges the assumptions of the civilization which creates them.

The epigram to the final chapter about Jane also alludes to silence as a metaphorical description of women's futures. This epigram reads, "What shall Cordelia speak? Love and be silent" (Tillman, 165). Jane's friend Maria interprets Cordelia's juxtaposition of love and silence: Cordelia " 'thinks that love's enough. And Shakespeare shows that it isn't.' Love isn't enough, Jane repeated to herself" (Tillman, 175). Jane and Maria realize that women are ultimately silenced by pursuing love, pursuing passions synonymous with fantastic dreams. Tillman's own silence alludes to Cordelia's silence. Tillman refuses to allow her protagonists to experience a "normal" female future requiring them to act as characters in particular stories which please men. Her silence indicates that patriarchal love stories provide an insufficient foundation upon which to build a satisfying adulthood. Her characters do not love. The rest of their future is silence.

In Tillman's novel, love is a science fiction story which acts as an impediment to the full development of each woman's house/body. And sex, the unsatisfying invasion of the female house/body, is a supernatural horror. Grace asks, "Why hadn't Poe ever written about impotence? Or was it there somehow, disguised in the terror?" (Tillman, 65). Jane's encounter with an impotent man addresses Grace's question. This encounter is literally terrifying: when a rapist breaks into the home of Jane's sister's boyfriend, Jane is saved by her attacker's inability to engage in sexual intercourse. Tillman tells readers that "Jane understood that the longer the man didn't get hard, the more desperate he would grow, and the more time she had" (Tillman, 174). According to *Haunted Houses*, the belief that male virility satisfies women is a fiction.

Grace would say that passion does not exist, that sexual intercourse is an unimportant act which should be relegated to the supernatural. She is unable "to shake the feeling that being with Hunter [her boyfriend] was like being with a ghost. She didn't think he came either, not that it really mattered" (Tillman, 139). A male enters her house/body as a ghostly presence; she is almost unaware of his presence within her. Grace's ghostly male lover reiterates the idea that passion, the supposed appropriate crux of women's futures, is a fiction. Grace evokes Marilyn Monroe to explain that the patriarchal story of heterosexual women's sexual satisfaction is a lie, a supernatural fiction which could appropriately serve as a Vincent Price role: "'I bet she [Monroe] didn't even like sex,' Grace said. 'And no one will ever know that, the mystery no one mentions.' Mark [another boyfriend] put his hands in front of his face, very Vincent Price; he said she took that secret to her grave" (Tillman, 203).

Marilyn Monroe might not have liked having her house/body violated by lovers who are, according to Grace and Mark, analogous to ineffective male ghosts. The word "ghostly" applies to the personalities of Grace's lovers as well as to their sexual behavior. More specifically, although Mark obscures his face in the manner of Vincent Price, Tillman never describes Mark's features. He does not have a face, then. He is a ghost who is interchangeable with Hunter. The protagonists' male lovers are all nondescript presences, ghosts who enter each woman's house/body and fail to provide pleasure.

Grace, a protagonist in a novel which proclaims that passion is a fiction containing male flat characters, does experience passion: she is in love with her room in her childhood home, her own space which comes alive for her. Grace "missed her room at home. Small as it was, it was hers and she grew to love it as if it were human. After school she'd kiss its floor, with passion, pursing her lips, opening her mouth slightly, the way movie stars did" (Tillman, 25). She finds passion with a "human" house instead of with a human male "ghost." Tillman hints that it is a mistake for women to seek passionate relationships with men at the expense of passionate relationships with houses—at the expense of loving their own domestic spaces. She reiterates Abbey's, Bradley's, and Sargent's point that women sacrifice their futures when they fail to control their domestic environments.

Descriptions of Emily spending her childhood afternoons playing in housing construction sites provide further commentary about this sacrifice. On one afternoon, an overweight boy with a reading problem falls through an unfinished attic floor (Tillman, 45). This scene evokes another image relating to violating a woman's house/body. Like unfinished houses, Tillman's protagonists are under construction. Their foundations are ruined when imperfect boys plunge through their bodies, tear away their virginity. This situation is rectified when women rely upon themselves—rather than upon men—to act as building contractors of female lives.

The image of Woman as a violated house made ineffective by unsatisfying men provides the key to understanding Emily's dream. *Haunted Houses* describes the dream:

> Emily awoke from this dream. Someone like her is enticed into a room whose walls are deep red. Like shame, she thinks later. She is given a seat by a man smoking a cigar. Then there are many men. All of them want her, whoever she is. . . . She says she's not interested in money, that she wants to be respected. . . . Her hands are bound behind her. She's not going

to get anything. She's made a mistake of some sort and can't correct it. One by one the men lift her dress . . . and fuck her. She is taken over and over again. She does not resist. (Tillman, 149)

"We are all haunted houses," the epigraph to *Haunted Houses*, appears in H.D.'s *Tribute to Freud*. Emily's dream becomes pertinent to Tillman's epigraph when it is interpreted according to Freudian analysis. The dream communicates that women are all haunted houses. The cigar in the deep red room, of course, symbolizes the penis entering the vagina. The room (or, Woman as violated house) is most important. Men desire to enter women—and men routinely treat women like anonymous property. Women make a mistake when, without resisting, they encourage men to violate them in return for nothing. Women are "taken over" by demonic possession when patriarchal social vampires ingest their essence.

Tillman continually depicts women as contained, controlled domestic spaces. For example, like Emily's impression of Dutch houses, Woman becomes analogous to a violated house filling an occupied space. Like neat Dutch houses, orderly suburban houses offer pleasing facades which mask problems located within. *Haunted Houses* describes the relationship between houses, love, and occupation:

War on their soil, on their streets, the Dutch went about their business and cleaned the stoops and sidewalks in front of their neat houses, and no one would ever know from the outside what it was like. Being an occupied country obsessed Emily. . . . Love is like that, an occupation, being occupied by. He swept over me, she wrote. . . . I let myself be taken. (Tillman, 179)

Women who appear undamaged on the outside become occupied territory, empty shells inhabited by the fiction of love. They allow themselves to be taken over by a supernatural, fictitious, passionate ideal.

The dieting obsessions so apparent in Abbey's, Bradley's, and Sargent's novels exemplify how patriarchal fictions literally diminish women. Tillman also mentions this obsession. Jane constantly gains and loses weight (Tillman, 18, 201). Grace diets unnecessarily (Tillman, 32). These characters remodel themselves as the objects of men's passions. (As I explain in chapter 6, the female protagonists Atwood, Johnson, and Piercy create do not remodel themselves to please men.) Jane observes that women are analogous to European buildings transplanted to America; women are like a "Scottish castle shipped to New Jersey, stone by stone" (Tillman, 78), objects made absurd by occupying an unnatural space. Men often reconstruct women similarly.

Ellen, Grace's young black acquaintance, a mental hospital inmate, tries to deface buildings which symbolize that men build culture. She tears down the ivy and the geraniums decorating rich doctors' homes. The doctors' maids and nurses—powerless women confined, respectively, within homes and offices in a state of stunted growth—respond to her actions by taking no action (Tillman, 96). Ellen is the most assertive woman in *Haunted Houses*. Presently, dangerous female spirits like Ellen are sometimes incarcerated within mental hospitals. In the past, women like Ellen were sometimes incinerated: "Just think of all the witches they burned" (Tillman, 109). Deviant women are the evil, alien Other. They were burned; they were forced to stare at yellow wallpaper; they are haunted by Freudian fictions which define female happiness as female restriction. Women are still encouraged to act like clinging ivy vines and boxed geraniums.

Ivy plants live by attaching themselves to buildings controlled and constructed by men. So do most women. Like geraniums, most women are treated as decorations deprived of their natural space, trapped in a box. Emily, Grace, and Jane are forever frozen in the nineteen-sixties, the time of the flower child. They epitomize a horror of arrested development. Emily's friend Christine, for example, "imagined herself in a neutral space where she was safe. Her long thin body needed a space, a design of her own" (Tillman, 154–155). Christine, like her fellow female characters, is denied her own design, her own space. Tillman's protagonists, girls who do not grow up, are violated in homes they do not own: Jane is attacked in an apartment owned by her sister's boyfriend (Tillman, 174); while living in the home of a Dutch woman who experienced Holland's Nazi occupation, Emily feels that she is an occupied country (Tillman,

179); while residing in a shared apartment, Grace recalls that her deceased, bad mother had thrown out her toys and school papers (Tillman, 203). Like Emily's anecdote about Margaret Fuller's drowning with her baby and husband (Tillman, 192), the three women "never got home" (Tillman, 193).

Tillman refuses to describe these women maturing and living in suburbia, the place of the living female dead. By arresting her characters' development, Tillman relegates them to the world of the undead. Grace comments upon this world: "Did the murdered return? Did their souls rest? Or were they always watching, waiting to be avenged from the grave? The undead were vampires, but she was sure that the undead existed in other forms. People who refuse to die" (Tillman, 206). Emily, Grace, and Jane are the undead, people who exist in other forms. Without dying, they merely do not enter adulthood. They never become adults who are told to experience the Freudian definition of properly enjoying passion with men. Tillman casts Freud aside through her implication that narratives about women enjoying heterosexual passion are fictions. She explains that women enter men's houses in order to adhere to patriarchal myths.

Like Tillman's protagonists, many real-world women exist as the undead who attempt to live in terms of fictions about domestic bliss. These fictions prevail despite the definition of suburbia as a horror story, a graveyard consisting of houses that dead living women haunt. Gilman's woman-controlled boardinghouse and Abbey's, Bradley's, and Sargent's woman-controlled private residences are, in contrast to suburbia, paradise. Jane, Emily, and Grace—unlike Lise Brown, Leslie Barnes, and Sarah Jaynes—never kill the patriarchal demons of their own houses.

Barthelme's *Paradise* also portrays women as the living dead. His female protagonists—Anne, Dore, and Veronica—unemployed lingerie models who move into an apartment an architect, Simon, owns, experience the future Tillman never invented for Emily, Grace, and Jane. The models' relationship with the architect emphasizes that the world is constructed by men to be a paradise for men; men's blueprints do not satisfactorily accommodate women. From a patriarchal perspective, Anne, Dore, and Veronica are model women—objects who please men. Simon enjoys a privileged male's "Simon says" relationship with both women and the world. Powerful men of Simon's ilk say magic words which cause the world and women to satisfy men's desires. Men's illocutionary force makes the world a male fantasy, a Disneyland for men. Within this male paradise, women function as ghostly talking mannequins, simulacrum components. Barthelme's female protagonists attempt to transform their roles as wax museum models into satisfying existences.

Simon encounters the models while enjoying a voluntary sabbatical. In contrast, women's lives are sometimes an endless involuntary sabbatical from meaningful work. During his sabbatical, "Simon enjoyed life as a ghost, one of the rewards of living in the great city" (Barthelme, 119). While Simon temporarily chooses to function as a ghost, the models are permanent ghosts, ethereal women unable to have an impact upon the great cities men like Simon build. When he defines himself as a hotel (Barthelme, 133), Simon appropriately comments upon his ability to shape the world; Simon-as-hotel is quite congruent with Gilman's notion of the woman-controlled boardinghouse. Both descriptions refer to people controlling the space they inhabit. The models who live in Simon's apartment cannot achieve the model situation both he and Gilman's Diantha enjoy. They cannot own and control homes.

While the witch protagonist of Gilman's "When I Was a Ghost" alters a city by wishing for change, Barthelme's women are ineffective witches who cannot grant their own wish to be more than shadows of fulfilled people. "I wish I could do something" (Barthelme, 56), says Anne. Her wish is not granted in a world created by men, a circumstance which forms the crux of *Paradise*. Simon's decision to separate himself from meaningful work temporarily is indicative of an appropriate alternative title for *Paradise*—"When I Was a Witch." Simon, one master builder of the world, chooses to become Woman-as-ghost. He elects to function as one of the female living dead.

Paradise echoes the aforementioned point the narrator of Russ's *On Strike against God* makes: the world does not belong to women. The models live "in limbo" (Barthelme, 28) within an architect's apartment, a space owned (and most probably designed) by men. A metaphorical waiting room is the only space reserved exclusively for women in the world men make. The models are aware of this situation: "'Where are we?' 'We're in some sort of waiting room. Waiting'" (Barthelme, 50). While limbo is a temporary enjoyable state for Simon, it is an endless fact of life for Anne, Dore, and Veronica.

Women often passively fill, instead of create, space. Their inactivity contributes to making the world a paradise for men and a purgatory for women. The models articulate this circumstance in terms of their living arrangement with Simon: "Simon was, as the women repeatedly told him, existing in a male fantasy, in hog heaven. He saw nothing wrong with male fantasies (the Taj Mahal, the Chrysler Building) but denied that he was in hog heaven" (Barthelme, 80). Simon exists in hog heaven in fact. Most men deny that there is anything wrong with having the power to make their fantasies become reality, to design the world to suit themselves. They deny that they are selfish. Russ articulates the truth which is not said by Simon—that male hogs enjoy and inhabit hog heaven. She believes "that separatism is primary, and that the authors [of separatist feminist utopias] are not subtle in their reasons for creating separatist utopias: if men are kept out of these societies, it is because men are dangerous. They also hog the good things of this world" (Russ, "Utopias," 77). Further, at the conclusion of *Paradise*, the models blame their exclusion from the world upon men's hoggishness. "It's the fault of men. . . . Trying to keep all the prosperity for a few self-selected individuals" (Barthelme, 197). Barthelme explains that men succeed all too well at designing a society which allows them to hog all the good things of this world.

The world works for men in proportion to their ability to keep women from working in a world which works for women. The sole job offered to the models reflects this point. Anne describes the available position: "Convention. The National Sprinkler Association. At the Americana. We have to stand under these things and get sprinkled. I won't do it" (Barthelme, 142). The very existence of this job underscores that hoggish men behave like male dogs who wet fire hydrants to create territorial markers. Model women, then, stand as stationary hydrants sprinkled upon by man-as-dog. Patriarchal stories reduce model women to stationary reproductive receptacles who get sprinkled by sperm. Patriarchal stories demand that women wait to be sprinkled with sperm-as-fairy-dust, a substance which magically defines women's reality by turning them into exploited mothers.

Women's efforts to protest against this situation have so far been ineffective. For example, after Simon listens to the models' complaints and agrees to take clothes to the laundry (Barthelme, 64) he will, most probably, patronize a business owned and designed by men. When men perform domestic tasks, women still do not profit from domesticity. Gilman's Diantha is a rarity. Women have not managed to convert New York's Americana Hotel into a woman-controlled boardinghouse. This hotel has merely become a Sheraton, another corporate domestic space which adheres to patriarchal conventions (and often houses MLA). The Americana-as-Sheraton exemplifies corporate patriarchal magic which makes "difference" synonymous with "sameness."

Simon is happy to end his sabbatical, his time spent in the horrifying world of women's purposelessness: "To be working again felt very good" (Barthelme, 185), he says. The models cannot share his good feeling. As Anne explains, because the models define themselves as commodities which please the male eye, they have no meaningful work: "If I'd spent the same amount of time worrying about my mind as I have worrying about my chest, I'd be Hegel by now" (Barthelme, 189). Men are architects who build the world to suit themselves; women are architects who build their bodies to suit men. Simon recalls the building material his lumberman father used in the family mill: "Redwood was light, easily milled, plentiful, took a stain well, weathered beautifully. Tens of hundreds of thousands of board feet of California redwood had passed through the family's logging and milling operation" (Barthelme, 138). Like redwoods, Anne and her companions become building materials which men run through the mill. Like redwoods, many women are cut down, transformed into less than majestic objects—made into something other than themselves.

The models must lumber through life because patriarchy stunts their full potential growth. As one of the models explains, men "exploit us and reduce us to nothing" (Barthelme, 149). Her insight results from reading a feminist text: "Read it in a feminist text. . . .

heard they're not gonna let us read any more books" (Barthelme, 149). She could be referring to Margaret Atwood's *The Handmaid's Tale,* a dystopian future vision which portrays women who are trapped within men's houses and forbidden to read.

Women are trapped in a world men make. Objects which reflect men's visions of women shape women's lives. *Paradise* mentions that man-made objects tell women's stories: "Buildings are about women, cars are about women, landscape is about women, and tombs are about women. If you care to look at it that way" (Barthelme, 153). Most cars and buildings are made by men; landscapes and women are controlled and destroyed by men; men's objects relegate women to the tomb of the undead.

The conclusion of *Paradise* reflects the lack of space for women in the world men build. When the models leave Simon's apartment, they "lurch through the door" (Barthelme, 206) and provide no hint about their fate. Although Anne, Dore, and Veronica grow older than Emily, Grace, and Jane—like Tillman—Barthelme is silent about his female characters' future. *Haunted Houses* and *Paradise* retell Ibsen's *A Doll's House.* Tillman's and Barthelme's female protagonists slam the door in patriarchy's face and venture into ambiguous space.

Barthelme's novel, like most houses and Ibsen's play, is a story about women authored by a man. *Paradise,* then, raises questions about a male author writing as a feminist, a male author acting as an architect who designs women's stories. When Barthelme describes female subordination in terms of male sexual titillation, he speaks about women's future in the place of Tillman's chosen silence about this future. Since his sexist descriptions are so overt, they can be read as efforts to counter sexism through exaggeration. Chris Weedon offers a comment pertinent to this point: "[I]t is only by looking at a discourse *in operation,* in a specific historical context, that it is possible to see whose interests it serves at a particular moment" (Weedon, 111). *Paradise* portrays contemporary sexism in operation; Barthelme reveals exactly whose interest current sexism serves.

Paradise itself argues for this positive interpretation of sexism's presence within its pages. The novel offers a metafictional defense by insisting that it is not a male fantasy: "It [Simon's situation] has the structure of a male fantasy. The dumbest way to look at it" (Barthelme, 50). In other words, instead of dismissing *Paradise* as a male fantasy, feminist readers might recognize that this novel's sexist images purposefully underscore women's secondary position in the world. Simon certainly regards the models with sympathetic concern: "There was no place in the world for these women whom he loved, no good place. They could join the underemployed half-crazed demi-poor, or they could be wives, those were the choices" (Barthelme, 168). Feminists can think well of Simon and Barthelme.

Simon, after all, wants women to design and control space: "He'd [Simon] send them all to MIT, make architects of them! Women were coming into the profession in increasing numbers" (Barthelme, 101). This is a good idea. More women can become architects who construct a world which adheres to feminist speculative fictions. Barthelme, then, echoes Abbey, Bradley, Russ, Sargent, and Tillman when they insist that women participate in building the world. Women, according to these authors, should not live analogously to the protagonists of horror fictions. Women can define, according to their own terms, just what it is "that makes today's homes so different, so appealing."

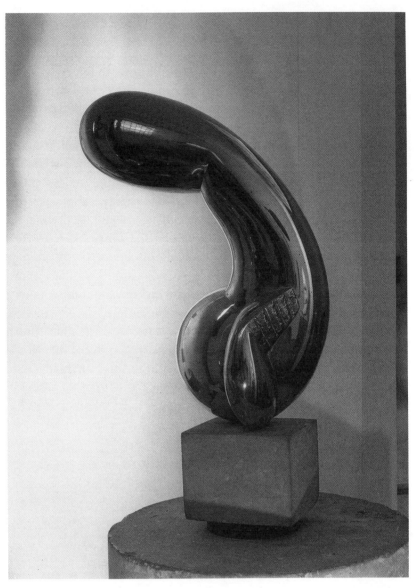

Constantin Brancusi, Princess X, *1916. Musée National d'Art Moderne, Paris.*

All You Need Is Love?

*I can't imagine a two-sexed egalitarian society and I
don't believe anyone else can, either. . . . Well, here
you have the whole thing about s.f. Where else could
one even try out such visions? Yet in the end we will
have to have models for the real thing and I can find
none yet.*
—Joanna Russ, "Reflections on Science Fiction"

*"What I want is a strange conjunction with you . . .
an equilibrium, a pure balance of two single be-
ings:—as the stars balance each other." . . .
"But why drag in the stars? . . . You want a satellite,
Mars and his satellite!" . . .
"I meant two single equal stars balanced in
conjunction."*
—D. H. Lawrence, *Women in Love*

Ursula Brangwen articulates the nonutopian
truth regarding Rupert Birkin's vision of
women and men living together like bal-
anced stars: women usually function as satellites revolving around
men, not as "single equal stars balanced in conjunction" with men.
The equality Rupert describes, an egalitarian female/male space
which seems to be represented by Brancusi's image of androgynous
fusion, is farfetched, appropriately located in an unreal location.
Gail Godwin's *The Finishing School* and Saul Bellow's *More Die of
Heartbreak* reflect Ursula's opinion by stressing gender schism, insisting that women and men cannot peacefully coexist.

Godwin describes a successful relationship between two women
whose ages differ; Bellow describes a similar relationship between
two men. To locate the space where women and men act as balanced
stars, it is necessary to turn from realistic fiction to feminist space

fiction. After discussing Bellow's men and Godwin's women, I focus upon three postseparatist feminist utopias which imagine one woman and one man living together equally: Doris Lessing's *The Marriages between Zones Three, Four, and Five,* Pamela Sargent's *The Shore of Women,* and Joan Slonczewski's *A Door into Ocean.* I summarize my points about these utopias in terms of Harvey Wasserman's *America Born and Reborn.*

"But why drag in the stars?"

Bellow's protagonists, Kenneth Trachtenberg and his uncle Benn Crader, attempt to establish harmonious relationships with women. In terms of language which echoes Lawrence's stars in conjunction, Crader wishes "to live peacefully. Two human beings bound together in love and kindness" (Bellow, 17). *More Die of Heartbreak,* however, insists that war rather than love binds women and men. The question which forms its crux implies that there is no appropriate place for successful heterosexual love relationships: "Where's the space for love to perform in?" (Bellow, 44). The novel asserts that love is dangerous, that the space for love to perform in is a "theater of war" (Bellow, 44). Bellow proclaims that more people die of heartbreak than nuclear radiation (Bellow, 241).

To avoid marriage, Benn boards jet planes and defines the sky as a vast space of escape from women. Like the stock western hero who loves his horse and his male Indian sidekick, Benn loves Arctic lichens and his French-American Jewish nephew. Benn fits Leslie Fiedler's description of a "man on the run" who journeys "anywhere to avoid 'civilization,' which is to say, the confrontation of a man and woman which leads to the fall to sex, marriage, and responsibility" (Fiedler, 26).

More Die of Heartbreak self-consciously and playfully responds to Fiedler's observation that "the whole of Bellow's work is singularly lacking in real or vivid female characters; where women are introduced, they appear as nympholeptic fantasies, peculiarly unconvincing" (Fiedler, 363). The male protagonists of *More Die of Heartbreak* are cast as Bellow's real and vivid female characters. Benn and Kenneth function as women, male women rather than

Joanna Russ's female man. The relationship between Kenneth and his estranged lover, Treckie, the mother of his child, exemplifies this point. Kenneth acts like a sexually rejected woman; Treckie resents his efforts to establish a typical nuclear family. He explains, "But (and this was downright shocking!) she didn't want any part of me. I failed to turn *her* on" (Bellow, 312). To compensate for being barred from acting as a spouse and parent, Kenneth travels with his uncle: "Being a husband and a father would have reduced my need for an uncle" (Bellow, 41). Benn, "a magical person" resembling "a science fiction character or one of the moon astronauts" (Bellow, 23), is the star with whom Kenneth establishes a balanced conjunction. Bellow, according to a feminist understanding of love and death in the American novel, comments upon the lack of space where women and men can live together peacefully.

Kenneth is a male Woman engaging, with his uncle, in a relationship which is "doubly, multiply, interlinked" (Bellow, 15). Benn also becomes a male Woman after marrying his second wife, Matilda Layamon. Empowered by her father's money and social position, Matilda views Benn's marital role to be more important than his profession. Benn becomes a "wife" whose professional integrity is jeopardized. This eminent biologist's loss of personal and professional self-esteem is extreme enough to cause him to commune with the plastic plant he believes to be real (Bellow, 300). Benn loses what is most meaningful to him: "My occupation, my instinct, my connection . . . broken off" (Bellow, 300).

Since marriage causes Benn to sacrifice his possessions and career, he seeks an alternative to the damaging space within the Layamon penthouse. Hence, when Benn flies to the Arctic to escape Matilda, he acts like a woman fleeing a bad marriage. Contrary to Mark Twain's boys, who run away from civilization to escape matriarchy, Benn runs away from civilization to escape patriarchy. In the Arctic, he embraces nature and removes himself from America's scientific establishment which—contrary to Benn's academic priorities—interprets "science" as synonymous with "corporate profit making." Benn and Kenneth act like good women. Matilda is a monstrous male wife. Treckie is a monstrous mother who wants her "kid out of her hair" (Bellow, 332). It is impossible for Kenneth and

Benn, honorable individuals, to form productive relationships with such women. They, instead, become "absorbed in each other" (Bellow, 251).

Heartbreak, like Barthelme's *Paradise* (which is discussed in chapter 4), uses graphic sexism to refute sexism. For example, Benn and Kenneth watch Japanese women, encased in Plexiglass cages, who dilate themselves to entertain businessmen. Benn wants no part of this Japanese corporate patriarchal paradise in which female sex objects entertain male executives (Bellow, 108). Realizing that the entire civilized world is a space for staged sexism, he flies to the Arctic, the space of civilization's absence, one of the few locations where a character in a realistic novel can avoid patriarchy.

The female/male role reversals in *Heartbreak* allow Benn-as-Woman to escape demonic women who act like men. In this novel, whose epigraph evokes supernatural stories by referring to Charles Addams, vampirelike women threaten to nullify male victims. Kenneth explains: "She [Tanya Sterling, Treckie's mother] was making a bid to take me over, just as Matilda had taken over Uncle" (Bellow, 248). Benn's restrictive marriage enacted with Matilda in the Roanoke apartment building positions *Heartbreak* further within the supernatural realm. *Heartbreak*, which mentions both Addams's Morticia (Bellow, 10) and Hitchcock's *Psycho* (Bellow, 231), can be read as a retold *Rosemary's Baby*. Bellow's Roanoke apartment building, after all, resembles the setting of Ira Levin's novel, New York City's landmark Dakota building. Benn's baby—his work—is possessed by Matilda, a demonic wife, a "sexual Lucifer" (Bellow, 161). Like *Rosemary's Baby*, *Heartbreak* links sex with the devil: "[S]ex might be a diabolical way to recover paradise . . . a parody on the beautiful and the sublime, a false light shed for our destruction by the sexual Lucifer—if indeed great spirits like Eros or Lucifer are still bothering with us human nut cases" (Bellow, 161).

In addition to discussing "the beautiful and the sublime," *Heartbreak* alludes to the beautiful and damned, to F. Scott Fitzgerald. Matilda's apartment, for example, is described in terms of a direct reference to Fitzgerald (Bellow, 149). *Heartbreak*, then, might also be read as a retold *Tender Is the Night*. Ensconced within the Layamon family, "so far, far from his botany, where the best of him should be invested" (Bellow, 142), Benn is certainly analogous to Dick Diver. Marrying daughters of monied families distracts both Benn and Dick from their professions. The Layamons use Benn's academic eminence as a commodity to enhance Matilda's social position. He becomes just another decorative furnishing for Matilda's apartment.

Matilda transforms Benn into an unreal female character, Fiedler's aforementioned description of a "nympholeptic fantasy, particularly unconvincing." Kenneth comments upon how women make men conform to female fantasies: "[I]t was a common feminine fantasy to put together an ideal man. No real person has everything they [women] dream of, so they assemble parts and elements from here and there—a large cock, a sparkling personality, millions of dollars, a bold brilliant spirit" (Bellow, 255). Matilda, who values parts of Benn which can enhance her social whole, acts according to this female fantasy. She behaves like the male protagonists of Lester del Rey's SF story, "Helen O'Loy," who assemble a living female robot from various inorganic parts. Benn is Matilda's living male robot, a subhuman "wife" made from the professional parts of his life she uses to suit her self-interest. Marriage enables Matilda to try to construct a man-as-Woman.

Ultimately, however, Benn is no Dick Diver who permanently succumbs to professional and personal dissipation. By viewing Matilda as a man, he thwarts her efforts to transform him into Woman. He watches *Psycho*, equates Matilda with Tony Perkins, and defines her as dangerous: "But merging Matilda with Tony Perkins playing a psychopath—that was a deadly move. . . . And this vision in the movie house told him not to marry her" (Bellow, 233). Juxtaposing Matilda with a male film star causes Benn to see her as a slasher ready to attack him, her feminized husband. He understands that, while residing in Matilda's apartment, he is just as victimized as Hitchcock's woman in the shower stall. Benn rereads *Psycho* as a warning indicating that Matilda's body and personality do not suit him.

Matilda is physically as well as psychically masculine. Benn questions: "Why are Matilda's breasts so far apart! . . . She isn't wide only across the shoulders but also in front. There's a lot of space between the two of them. . . . I'm not asking for a sensible interpretation. . . . The distance between them has an effect on me" (Bellow, 262–263). Benn is saved by interpretation, his realization that Matilda functions as a dangerous, patriarchal space. She is a female man. The huge space between her breasts threatens to engulf Benn. He rejects the threat that living with Matilda in the Roanoke apartment poses and instead chooses to commune with lichens in the Arctic. His decision enables Kenneth to acquire another isolated space, the apartment Benn once shared with his first wife, Lena. The Arctic, as well as Benn's apartment filled with plants and botany books, is devoid of both patriarchy and women. Benn and Kenneth are feminine men who cannot make peace with masculine women. Matilda is Morticia; Kenneth is Benn's best companion. Lichens, which "are both algae and fungi" (Bellow, 253), are more compatible than women and men. Kenneth and Benn become refugees from a gender war caused by women's and men's failure to achieve symbiosis.

Benn escapes to "an incomprehensible location in reindeer country, far out on the tundra. . . . Even that was not remote enough" (Bellow, 335). *Heartbreak* specifically mentions Chernobyl (Bellow, 197), and Benn's incomprehensible location in reindeer country is the site of heavy Chernobyl fallout concentration. His Arctic refuge is not remote enough from civilization's hazards: the reindeer are irradiated. Living with radioactive fallout, however, is more desirable to Benn than living with emotional fallout. His choice announces that female/male relationships are more dangerous than Chernobyl. "More people die of heartbreak than of radiation" (Bellow, 87). The erotic is one of "*our* gross hazards" (Bellow, 110); Matilda is "an H-bomb of beauty" (Bellow, 135); sexuality is a bomb: "After the atomic one, the orgastic one was dropped on us" (Bellow, 159). Bellow is not optimistic about peaceful coexistence between women and men.

Heartbreak emphasizes this opinion by announcing that Matilda is "a friend of Marguerite Duras" (Bellow, 252), who writes about "Hiroshima with sex" (Bellow, 252). Duras's title, *Hiroshima, Mon Amour*, juxtaposes love and death. So does the title *More Die of Heartbreak*. Dita Schwartz, Kenneth's friend, is one survivor of the orgastic bomb. She embodies love and death after undergoing plastic surgery in order to attract Kenneth. Both her blood-soaked bandages and the strips of skin hanging from her face (Bellow, 207–210) evoke images of Hiroshima burn victims. Dita's female voice articulates one form of love and death in the American novel: a woman who, to please a man, voluntarily re-creates herself as a radiation burn victim. Bellow appropriately begins *Heartbreak* with a reference to Charles Addams's *Monster Rally*. His protagonists are monstrous mutations, female/male fusions without fixed gender identities who are postmodern survivors of the love bomb's nuclear family fission.

These survivors inhabit "fantastic reality" (Bellow, 122), a world which is not our own. Benn, for example, teaches at a major university located in a midwestern city which contains one of the tallest skyscrapers in America. Even though Chicago is the only city which fits this description,[1] *Heartbreak* itself implies that Chicago is not its setting (Bellow, 269). *More Die of Heartbreak* might be an alternative world novel whose protagonists inhabit a postholocaust (in terms of the war between the sexes) terrain. Matilda, a female male mutation, a physically deformed beautiful woman, poses the greatest threat in *Heartbreak*, not atomic bombs. This novel's monstrous characters and unreal setting metafictionally indicate that romantic love is a fiction. In the world Bellow creates, as well as in our own world, there is a lack of space for women and men to occupy together peacefully.

A particular skyscraper, the Electronic Tower erected on the site of Benn's childhood home, represents this point. Benn resents this structure which buries the foundation of his life. He says, "And every time I come near a window, I see that goddam skyscraper. My old life is lying under it—my mother's kitchen, my father's bookshelves, the mulberry trees" (Bellow, 196). Benn sees a framed image of male power (the phallic Electronic Tower) covering and replacing feminine domestic space. The tower signifies corporate male hard science which differs from botany, Benn's academic female soft science. The building appears in the place where young Benn first developed an interest in plants when picking mulberries with his uncle, Vilitzer (Bellow, 45). Vilitzer, who benefits financially from the skyscraper, sacrifices the family home for profit. Matilda's desire to control Vilitzer's money transforms the building into disputed territory, the reason for her gender war, the reason for reading *Heartbreak* as exemplifying the literature of exhaustion: a nephew's story of an uncle (Kenneth's story of Benn) within another nephew's story of another uncle (Benn's story of Vilitzer).

From the vantage point of gentile space—the Layamon penthouse called Parrish Place—Benn is forced to decide whether or not to satisfy his Protestant wife by appropriating the tower, his Jewish uncle's financial resource. The tower Vilitzer owns, then, also symbolizes a minority group's presence within America's Protestant economic hegemony. As a powerful and wealthy Jewish person, Vilitzer might be categorized as a female man, an influential marginalized individual. Vilitzer resembles his at-once phallic and female tower, the place of enfranchised corporate power controlled by a Jewish Other.

Matilda's demand that Benn reappropriate the tower requires him to break the uncle-nephew bond Benn had established during childhood. Fighting with Vilitzer, and the money derived from owning the tower, will not enable Benn to attain his real desire—the ground under the tower, the occupied space where male camaraderie introduced Benn to botany. The tower stands; Vilitzer dies; Benn leaves Matilda. Despite all this activity, Benn is unable to enjoy both his once-amiable relationship with Vilitzer and the ground—the soil— upon which this relationship began. Benn's manhood is rooted in engaging with nature and other men. He does not win a woman after fighting to derive money from a corporate structure.

He does not behave like the protagonists of "The Bear," *Moby-Dick*, and "The Old Man and the Sea," who, according to Fiedler, confront "monstrous embodiments of the natural world in all its ambiguous and indestructible essence. . . . They [Faulkner's bear and Hemingway's swordfish] are sacred embodiments of power. . . : Ishmael and Ike McCaslin live, after all, in America, where the way is open for the rape of nature" (Fiedler, 359–360). Benn, no Ishmael or McCaslin, is a female male who embraces rather than battles the natural world, loves rather than rapes nature. He is a new American male literary hero whose feminine sensitivity towers above Ishmael's and McCaslin's boorish masculine histrionics. Benn ultimately rejects the tower and devotes himself to plants.

Virginia Woolf seems to describe the man-made tower while discussing the oppositions which characterize the Lighthouse. Woolf's
Lighthouse has a counterpart: "[T]he other was also the Lighthouse.
For nothing was simply one thing. The other Lighthouse was true
too" (Woolf, 277). The tower also possesses a true other. Kenneth
explains that the tower is more than a symbol of oppression:

> You mustn't think it was always an oppressive object. Skyscrap-
> ers ... also express an aspiration towards freedom, a rising
> above. They may be filled with abominable enterprises, but
> they do transmit an idea of transcendence. Perhaps they mislead
> us or betray our hopes by unsound analogy. (Bellow, 294)

The other tower is true too. An ambiguous symbol, a building which
at once represents oppressive patriarchy and the benign Vilitzer (a
Jewish patriarch who rises above oppression) stands at the center of
an impending shoot-out between a "female" Jewish male (Benn) and
a "male" Protestant woman (Matilda).

Benn and his sidekick Kenneth face the Layamon gang. Matilda is
certainly not the hero. Fiedler calls the ninth chapter of *Love and
Death in the American Novel* "Good Good Girls and Good Bad
Boys"; Bellow's portrayal of love and death in the American role-
reversal novel presents male characters as the good girls and female
characters as the bad boys. Kenneth Trachtenberg, a satellite cir-
cling Benn, tracks the course of his life away from Treckie. Benn
Crader is, according to Kenneth's aforementioned description, a
magical moon person, a crater representing the unfilled potential
space between women and men. Kenneth and Benn experience their
closest human relationship with each other. *More Die of Heartbreak* is Bellow's statement about the impossibility of women and
men peacefully coexisting.

Gail Godwin reiterates this statement. Bellow's individuals in
alien spaces—his Jewish Trachtenbergs and Craders who inhabit
gentile countries—are represented by two groups in *The Finishing
School*: the Stokes family, American southerners forced to move
north, and the DeVane family, traditional northerners who confront
obsolete traditions. Godwin rewrites Benn and Kenneth as real and
vivid female characters: Justin Stokes and Ursula DeVane, women

who exult in each other's company and do not form long-term sexual alliances with men. Kenneth loves Benn; Justin loves Ursula. Both Justin and Kenneth use words such as "bewitched," "magic," and "enchanted" to describe their respective relationships with the older people who share their gender. Kenneth and Benn enjoy "a devouring friendship" (Bellow, 26), and Kenneth comes to America "to absorb certain essential powers from" Benn (Bellow, 92); Justin imagines telling Ursula, "I have absorbed you" (Godwin, 3). The women are doppelgängers who inhabit the same experiential and narrative spaces. Justin believes that "for a moment, I *was* her [Ursula]" (Godwin, 376).

The Finishing School consists of retold stories about failed relationships, stories which blur the usual demarcations between gender, love, death, sex, and class. Viewing her family as a story, Ursula describes, in terms of narrative, the events which cause two generations of DeVanes to enact retold tales: "I find it all very amusing, the way human beings divide themselves up into all these subgenres and then run around hating everybody in the other subgenres" (Godwin, 18). Justin's and Ursula's shared relationship, and the stories about their mutual experiences, communicate the breakdown of fixed meanings in regard to gender and class. The changing uses of landscape space obscure class barriers: the lower-class Cristiana family flourishes economically after buying and improving DeVane land; Justin moves to a subdivision built on the site of a landmark farmhouse's destruction.

While she lives within her new subdivision home, Justin's efforts to define her appropriate "subgenre" point to a change in notions about human canons and hierarchies. Her experiences (such as rejecting her stepfather's authority) coincide with Ihab Hassan's term, postmodern "decanonization," which applies to "all canons, all conventions of authority" (Hassan, "Pluralism," 169). Hassan describes the "delegitimation" of society's "mastercodes" in terms of metanarratives which give way to "*les petites histoires.*" Ursula's and Justin's little stories, which dominate the plot of *The Finishing School*, delegitimate mastercodes. These stories concern dead fathers, failed marriages, regional transitions, changes caused by the modern world's encroachment, the rise of the new upper class over the old gentry, and sexless passion between women. They signal the breakdown of distinctions between such human subgenres as gender and class. They, in summary, "deconstruct the languages of power, desire, deceit" (Hassan, 169).

One particular *petite histoire* forms the central image in *The Finishing School*. Justin recalls seeing Abel Cristiana's horses engaging in sexual activity. The mare's rear hooves are booted and her tail, to avoid obstructing the stallion's access to her vagina, is bandaged (Godwin, 10). Justin explains why the situation upsets her: "Maybe it was because I hated to see him [the stallion] lose his dignity like that and join the herd. Or maybe it was the way the mare had capitulated; how she hadn't much chance anyway, with her tail bandaged to one side and those boots on her hooves. But what made the incident mortifying was that I realized someone had been watching me watch" (Godwin, 11). This scene speaks to the reason that efforts to establish equal, dignified relationships between women and men often fail. Like the mare, many women (wearing high heels and bras instead of hoof hobbles and tail bandages) capitulate to men's demands. Like the stallion, many men lose their dignity after capitulating to the demands of masculinity. These activities occur in domestic, enclosed, corral-like spaces. Society corrals women and men, constructs social codes which ensure that patriarchal mating rituals are properly enacted.

The Finishing School presents stories about women confronting this metaphorical social corral. Three women who do not live with husbands—Justin, her aunt Mona (who is separated from Eric Mott), and Charlotte (Justin's stepfather's first wife)—escape their enclosed social spaces. Justin ultimately substitutes working as an actress for the "ardor" she felt for Ursula (Godwin, 387). Charlotte and Mona become dissatisfied with their roles as wives: "Charlotte was like Aunt Mona. They were both women who had gotten married early and then sometime later had decided they had a lot to make up for and couldn't do it and remain the wives their husbands had married" (Godwin, 384). Charlotte becomes a lawyer. Mona becomes a wealthy realtor and lives with her young male lover.

Other female characters are not lucky enough to avoid limiting social roles. Ursula's mother, for example, escapes marriage by entering a mental hospital. Justin's mother, Louise, voluntarily reenters a confining social space when she chooses to marry Charlotte's former husband. Although Ursula never marries, when nurturing her father and brother, she places herself within an enclosed circle of prescribed female roles. The stories about these women's experiences—narratives constituting exhausted tales two generations retell—metafictionally comment upon the story of women in patriarchy. Godwin's stories of mothers, daughters, nieces, and aunts are female counterparts to Bellow's stories of fathers, sons, nephews, and uncles.[2]

Justin's relationship with Ursula, her finishing school, is a space between her childhood and the start of her own adult story. She is another version of Ursula who, unlike Ursula, becomes a successful actress. As opposed to staging herself in a limiting corral, Justin controls professional staged space. She describes, according to supernatural imagery, her own effort to build her life as an improved version of Ursula's life:

> I was aware . . . of the ironies and parallels between Ursula's trauma and mine. I had repeated her history. . . . She had led me on with her charms. . . . She had been a witch, I decided, able to make me perform in her story, robbing me of the chance to be the heroine of my own story. But I was no longer bewitched. (Godwin, 369)

Justin at once repeats and rewrites Ursula's story; she breaks the spell of Ursula-as-witch and gains the power to live in her own unencumbered fashion. She does not "*become* Ursula" (Godwin, 131). Nor does she become her mother. She is not "possessed" (Godwin, 126, 238) by the stories about women adhering to limiting roles. Instead, she enacts her own story as a professional actress who plays diverse roles. Fences are not part of Justin's life. Neither is a permanent relationship with a man.

Justin, however, suggests that Ursula might substitute as a man: Ursula "might have been a man. She had slipped into one more transformation" (Godwin, 254). "Transformation" is a key word in *The Finishing School*, a novel "about how people could learn from one another and be transformed" (Godwin, 224). Justin learns from

Ursula, a woman who views herself in terms of androgyny. Ursula says, "Sometimes ... I'm a man; sometimes a woman" (Godwin, 153). While teaching in Justin's finishing school, Ursula functions as a particular fictitious man—Professor Henry Higgins.

The finishing school, a bewitched, enclosed enclave a woman who is herself unfinished presides over, is ultimately ineffective. Justin progresses toward becoming a finished person most efficiently when she leaves Ursula and, accompanied by her mother, watches a play: "The show was *My Fair Lady*, with Rex Harrison and Julie Andrews, and I was impressed without reservation. . . . It was the first time in my life I had seen a professional stage production with fine actors at the top of their form and all those masterful accoutrements of stage-craft that can create an unbroken illusion for the audience. . . . But with *My Fair Lady* came a new experience. I did lose myself, but in a less self-enclosed way" (Godwin, 224). Ursula is ultimately an ineffective androgynous figure, an ineffective Professor Higgins. Julie Andrews (who plays the androgynous Victor/Victoria in the film of the same name), not Ursula, is ultimately Justin's most important teacher. Her influence, her ability to teach Justin to live within a self-enclosure, not a patriarchal enclosure, functions in terms of "trans-world migration" (Brian McHale's term). Andrews, when she appears in *The Finishing School*, migrates "across the semipermeable membrane that divides a fictional world from the real" (McHale, 35).

In contrast to the well-known story of Lana Turner's discovery (which is discussed in chapter 3), Andrews's success story has nothing to do with functioning as a sex object. Unlike Ursula's and Turner's respectively fictitious and real adherence to female roles, Andrews (within both the real world and Godwin's fictitious world) transcends femininity's restrictions. Justin finds herself by losing herself in *My Fair Lady*. She chooses acting, a professional performance on staged space, to free her from limited female space. Instead of succumbing to patriarchy's fictions about women (instead of turning these fictions into reality by becoming Ursula), Justin—a future renowned actress—casts herself as Julie Andrews. Andrews's real-world success story exemplifies that patriarchal stories about ultimate female failure can be challenged. Because of this possibility, Justin emulates Andrews and defines Ursula and Louise as failed stars. According to Justin, "both of them had the aura of deposed stars who, because of family fates and adversities, must now devote the remainder of their lives to promoting the interests of their nearest and dearest" (Godwin, 233). Justin does not repeat their stories; she becomes a stage star rather than a deposed star.

She graduates from the finishing school as a "lady" who defines the word as she sees fit. Justin is "My Fair Lady" who interprets the title to mean the fair right to possess herself. Instead of being sucked into a problematical life, she freely pursues her own interests: "I could recognize very well the one [life] I didn't want: it was all around me! It was threatening to suck me in" (Godwin, 97). Like Lynn Abbey's *The Guardians* (which is discussed in chapter 4), *The Finishing School* describes how a supernatural force sucks people into its malevolent realm. When confronted by this force, some women act like shapeless masses who are continually threatened by the possibility of assuming an improper container's shape, a danger Ursula repeatedly calls "congealing": "You solidify at a certain point and from then on your life is doomed to be a repetition of what you've done before. *That's* the enemy. . . . You must be constantly on your guard . . . against congealing" (Godwin, 306). Ursula is afraid of solidifying into a stagnant shape which will forever fill a mundane space.

Justin avoids congealing by devoting herself to acting's "dramatic intensity . . . a need for everyday life to have a *shape*" (Godwin, 178). Acting enables her to mold her adult life in a self-satisfying manner, to grow by assuming dramatic roles and rejecting dramatically crippling accoutrements of femininity. She does not believe, for example, that "when you became a woman you grew long fleshy appendages on the bottoms of your feet so you could wear high heels" (Godwin, 146). She changes shape after growing real mental and experiential appendages, not after adhering to patriarchal stories which stunt women's growth. Justin fills the space of womanhood without becoming as hobbled as the Cristiana family's mare.

When acting, she performs as a rhapsode of women's stories, a professional filler of absent female narrative space. *The Finishing School*, a novel replete with the unfilled spaces of undisclosed information, functions in kind. Parts of this novel simply belong to "the epistemological genre *par excellence*" (McHale, 16), the detective story. Godwin's text contains a detective story whose denouement is alluded to approximately fifty pages before the novel ends: " 'Was that the famous evening?' 'That was the famous evening' " (Godwin, 338). Clues hint at how this crucial evening affects the novel's conclusion. Often, women's lives are also prearranged stories whose outcomes are signaled by clues given to young girls. Justin, for example, recognizes that the milkmaids printed on her bedroom's raspberry-colored curtains, dust ruffle, and dressing table skirt are clues about proper feminine behavior: "But the *worst* part about the milkmaids . . . is, I'm afraid they're going to do me in. I mean, everywhere I look, there they are, with their full skirts and their little milk pails and their shallow, beauty-contest smiles. What if I wake up one morning and look into my mirror and discover I am like them?" (Godwin, 106). The raspberry curtains and sconces become Justin's version of the yellow wallpaper Charlotte Perkins Gilman describes. The milkmaids, demure females printed on fabric, advertise a patriarchal pattern for complacent female behavior.

Justin shuns the raspberry room and the feminine domestic triviality it signifies. Instead of being absorbed by the milkmaids the feminine room's enclosed space pictures, she ventures out with Ursula to seek a phallic tower. She is a girl who goes to the Lighthouse with a woman:

> I remember being afraid that it would rain the day we planned
> to go to the tower. . . . And then that day, in late August, we
> went. . . . Then we climbed the steep path to the tower and
> looked down on the surrounding valleys. She [Ursula] pointed
> out the Cristianas' shiny roof . . . and our Finishing school. . . .
> And Ursula said, "They [an old couple passing by] thought we
> were mother and daughter. . . . It was a nice feeling, having
> them think you belonged to me." (Godwin, 58, 185–86)

This tower, which is as significant as the Electronic Tower in *More Die of Heartbreak,* enables Justin and Ursula to look down upon their world. They view three specific spaces: "prosaic Lucas meadows and seductive Old Clove Road," "the Stokes-Mott world, with its practicalities and family duties," and the "DeVane kingdom,

with its long-standing prides and alienations" (Godwin, 124). Instead of seeing static, congealed spaces, the women view fluid, momentarily separate spaces which ultimately merge before separating. Lucas meadows contains mundane corporate domiciles erected
where a majestic farmhouse once stood; the Stokes-Mott world
ceases to exist after Mona moves to a French villa; the DeVane kingdom falls and its prides are forgotten. Within these changing social
environments, people and buildings cease to reflect class differences
and clan loyalties, a situation exemplified when Ursula DeVane and
Abel Cristiana literally make the Old Clove Road seductive (Godwin, 353).

The view from the tower, then, reveals change rather than such
fixed definitions as rigid social systems and congealed landscape.
(Benn and Kenneth also see changed landscape when they go to the
Electronic Tower and look out upon empty factories and abandoned
freight yards [Bellow, 201].) After the Cristiana family purchases
DeVane property, the fence between Cristiana and DeVane land becomes irrelevant. This purchase causes the fence to mark deconstructed spatial and social hierarchies, to announce that "everything
changes, nothing lasts" (Godwin, 252). When the adult Justin returns to admire the tower's view, she sees evidence that "plenty of
useful things can be built on the ruins of other people's lives" (Godwin, 188). Bellow's tower covers ground the Crader family's ruined
home once occupied; Godwin's tower reveals that Ursula's pond "is
full of woodland debris" and that her hut is "a heap of stones" (Godwin, 188). The tower Justin encounters provides a view of changed
landscape, the ruins of the DeVane ancestral home. It towers above
change and suggests Justin's ultimate ascendancy over Ursula.

Makiko Minow-Pinkney's comments about To the Lighthouse
further illuminate this point:

If To the Lighthouse consents to some degree to Mrs. Ramsay's
"passive" role of the ministering angel in the house to her "active" intellectual husband . . . it also suggests a simultaneous
counter-logic. The "passive" role turns out to display a truer
activity than the "active," and the "subsidiary" is revealed as
essential to that "primary" function to which it had initially

seemed a mere external crutch. Ramsay's self-serving oppositions—between philosophy and fiction, men and women—are,
to cite Derrida [Derrida 41], a "violent hierarchy" and not "the
peaceful co-existence of a *vis-à-vis.*" Yet the text dismantles
these hierarchies to the point where the excluded term becomes
the inner truth of its opposite, where people at last acknowledge
that "he depended on her." . . . Binary oppositions and hierarchies in this novel are ceaselessly undone. (Minow-Pinkney,
91–92)

The Finishing School, in spatial terms, articulates the lack of a comfortable coming face to face with opposites. This articulation un-
does oppositions and hierarchies, refuses the peaceful coexistence of
a *vis-à-vis.* After moving from South to North to South, Justin ultimately finds success on the New York stage. Failing to reconcile
locational oppositions, she is most comfortable living within the
stage's imaginative geography.

Godwin's characters function according to a simultaneous coun-
terlogic and self-serving opposition. Ursula jumps into her pond as
a result of Justin's self-serving, counterlogical behavior as a talented
swimmer who denies her ability to swim. Eric Mott, a failed father
who, against Justin's wishes, volunteers to act as her surrogate father, also behaves according to counterlogical, self-serving oppositions. After he is dislodged from his own familial space, he fills this
void by assuming the space Justin's father vacates. Mott's paternal,
protective instinct even extends to his job as an IBM employee who
guards American airspace. He is at once a metafather and an unsuccessful family man.

Juxtaposed oppositions also characterize Justin. The product of
many merged differences—North and South, poor father and formerly rich mother, nouveau riche aunt and uncle-as-adopted-father—
she is most affected by the particular fictional/real combined influence of Ursula and Julie Andrews. She ultimately inhabits the
Broadway stage, which is at once part of the real world and, from
readers' perspectives, a fantastic world within a fantastic world (a
play within a novel). Justin, her fellow characters, and the world
they occupy reflect Hassan's understanding of postmodernism as

characterized by indeterminacy, fragmentation, selflessness, and hybridization. I make the unusual claim that, according to its own criteria, *The Finishing School* exemplifies "the highly experimental nature of women's writing" (Hite, 2–3).

Justin, like Godwin's text, subverts institutional contexts. Within the world of Ursula's institution (the finishing school), Justin only appears to be Ursula's passive pupil. She is, in truth, essential to Ursula's story, a catalyst to the events which shape Ursula's life. Or, in Minow-Pinkney's terms, Ursula's self-serving oppositions between worldliness and domesticity (her oppositions between upholding and transgressing class distinctions) involve violent hierarchies. Justin, who listens to Ursula's stories, frees Ursula from these violent hierarchies, binary oppositions between adventure and domestic entrapment. Ursula is caught in a stasis within androgyny, a stalemate broken after Justin's presence causes Ursula's brother, Julian, to commit suicide. Julian's demise breaks the binary opposition between sister and brother. Like Justin, after Julian's death, Ursula can finally live according to her own self-interest.

Ursula tries in vain to use her relationships with Justin and Julian to act as the mother of two children, to define them as her dream children. Justin is the "dream daughter I [Ursula] might have had" (Godwin, 295). Although Ursula sacrifices motherhood and devotes her adult life to transforming the man (Julian) she positions as her brother/son into a star, Justin is the person who becomes that star—and she shines without a man. In contrast to Ursula's professional and familial failures, Justin's ability to be a daughter with two mothers (Ursula and Louise) provides one explanation for her success.

Godwin's stage star and Bellow's uncle-as-astronaut both fail to achieve equal and enduring relationships with the opposite sex. To discuss positive female/male relationships, I turn to space fiction; I "drag in the stars" (Lawrence, 139). Further, I reiterate that, regarding definitions of postmodern canons, I want to "drag in" space fiction.

This suggested and needed move compensates for the fact that, despite authors' best intentions, realistic fiction (as my lengthy attention to the plots of *The Finishing School* and *More Die of Heart-*

break reveals) falls short of profoundly reimagining the patriarchal real. Feminist utopian fiction, a component of the feminist fabulaftion super-genre, compensates for realistic literature's inability to portray the complete breakdown of patriarchy. Feminist utopias—postmodern challenges to patriarchal master narratives about such matters as stereotypes regarding male superiority and female ineptitude, the sanctity of the nuclear family, and men's right to rape nature—should not be marginalized. While it is in the best interest of those who wish to retard social change to label feminist utopian literature as mediocre genre fiction, it is the business of this chapter to explain why canonizing feminist utopias benefits feminists. One explanation immediately comes to my mind: feminist utopias portray the space of patriarchy's absence, a place where no realistic text has ventured. Feminist utopias are, in truth, more fantastic versions of canonized texts which challenge the patriarchal status quo.

For example, Lessing, Sargent, and Slonczewski pose, in more extreme terms, the same questions Godwin and Bellow raise about heterosexual love relationships. Their shift from the real to the fantastic has nothing to do with literary inferiority. Inferiority has been an unfortunate and effective ploy to nullify the subversive potential of texts which best imagine alternatives to patriarchal reality. This ploy will become obsolete if feminist utopias—fictions which rewrite patriarchal fictions—are acknowledged to be part of the postmodern canon. Literature which depicts women's new worlds should be respected and read, especially by feminist critics who have chosen to focus solely upon realistic literature. (And, as I state in my review of Francis Bartkowski's *Feminist Utopias*, feminist critics who do address women's fantastic literature should devote detailed attention to the relationship between feminist utopias and scholarly texts about what has been called feminist SF.)

" 'Go and find your new world, dear,' [Gudrun] said."

Hermione Roddice, Gerald Crich, and Rupert Birkin discuss "a new state, a new world of man" (Lawrence, 95). They question: "Supposing this old social state *were* broken and destroyed, then, out of the chaos, what then?" (Lawrence, 95). Separatist feminist utopias, which portray a new women's world emerging out of the chaos resulting after patriarchy is broken and destroyed, answer this question. They reflect Ursula Brangwen's assertion that "there *can* be something else" (Lawrence, 429), what she describes as "a sort of other self, that belongs to a new planet, not to this" (Lawrence, 429). She advocates the need to "hop off" earth to fulfill something inhuman and unknown, of which love is only a small part (Lawrence, 429). In addition to agreeing with Brangwen, the protagonists of postseparatist feminist utopias affirm Gudrun's response to her sister's ideas. Gudrun questions: "And what will happen when you find yourself in space? . . . After all, the great ideas of the old world are the same there. You . . . can't get away from the fact that love . . . is the supreme thing, in space as well as on earth" (Lawrence, 429). These protagonists echo Gudrun's concerns about what happens when women find themselves in space. The feminist utopians who have found their new world learn that the great ideas of the world *are* the same there. They learn, in other words, that it is as difficult to establish nonrepressive heterosexual love relationships in feminist utopian societies located on new planets as it is to establish them on earth.

For example, the protagonists in three postseparatist feminist utopias—Doris Lessing's *The Marriages between Zones Three, Four, and Five*, Joan Slonczewski's *A Door into Ocean*, and Pamela Sargent's *The Shore of Women*—at first do not enjoy heterosexual relationships superior to those portrayed in realistic novels such as *The Finishing School* and *More Die of Heartbreak*. Because of this failure, one woman in each of the postseparatist feminist utopias Lessing, Sargent, and Slonczewski imagine—protagonists who fulfill Gudrun's injunction to go and find a new world—opposes a separatist feminist world's social codes. Each woman ventures outside her feminist world to find love after confronting a nonhuman, unknown entity: omnipotent "Providers" direct Lessing's Al·Ith toward a loving relationship with Ben Ata; Slonczewski's Lystra is willing to love a man, a being who, from her perspective, is defined as nonhuman; Sargent's Birana forms a relationship with Arvil after they both learn to disbelieve the illusion that women are goddesses. Each female protagonist achieves a loving relationship with a man after placing herself outside a feminist separatist society.

(Even though male feminists reside in Lessing's Zone Three, since this zone excludes stereotypical masculine characteristics, I consider it to be separatist.)

The outgrowth of separatist feminist utopias written during the 1970s reflects a conclusion Suniti, the protagonist of Suniti Namjoshi's *The Conversations of Cow*, expresses: "I've come to the conclusion that men are aliens. . . . the Men from Mars, the Unearthly Aliens" (Namjoshi, 90). This character believes that men are invaders who come to earth after their spaceships break down (Namjoshi, 91). She turns to the "study of literature" (Namjoshi, 92) to prove that men who are in fact Martians establish patriarchal hegemony. Similarly, the inhabitants of feminist utopias created during the 1970s also view men as aliens.[3] They flee from earth, a planet that male alien invaders control, to establish separatist, lesbian communities on planets of their own. They share Suniti's belief: "I do not want to be married to a Martian" (Namjoshi, 93).

The utopias I discuss here, texts written during the 1980s, differ from the previous decade's separatist feminist utopias. Unlike the earlier utopias which define men as dangerous, subhuman, and alien, the recent works confront the question of how to incorporate men within their feminist worlds. The new utopias differ from their predecessors by redefining men as human beings. They act as correctives to the dearth of successful, equal relationships between women and men in realistic literature. Further, they reflect current debates regarding men's efforts to generate feminist theory.

Many female feminist theorists, like the protagonists of post-separatist feminist utopias, now welcome men as full participants within their enterprises. Alice Jardine and Paul Smith's anthology, *Men in Feminism*, is applicable to placing men in feminist utopian worlds.[4] Smith describes himself in terms of Suniti's theory that men are invading aliens: "I don't have the native accent; I'm an alien" (Smith, 36). He clarifies this statement: "I can be an alien only in a system which perceives itself as having some definitional integrity which can be enforced or embodied as a correctness of speech or activity" (Smith, 37). In the feminist worlds Lessing, Sargent, and Slonczewski create, the system which defines men as aliens changes to allow the masculine to be perceived as correct.

Stephen Heath's contribution to *Men in Feminism* addresses the result of this changed system: "Admiration as utopia, what has never existed between the sexes; so how to open this space of a radical sexual difference that is not the old difference" (Heath, "Male," 30). In postseparatist feminist utopias, what has never existed between the sexes—admiration—becomes utopian. The novels open a space of radical sexual difference that is not the old difference eradicated in terms of separatism. Each female protagonist steps outside her feminist society to establish a relationship with a man based upon mutual respect. She eradicates the old sexual differences which characterize her world. Sargent's Birana learns to put aside the guise of women's metahuman superiority; Lessing's Al·Ith teaches Ben Ata to incorporate feminine traits within his military role; Slonczewski's Lystra defines a man as an appropriate inhabitant of her women's world.

The protagonists' behavior coincides with Heath's response to Irigaray's comment. Irigaray says, "I will never be in a man's place, a man will never be in mine. Whatever the possible identifications, one will never exactly occupy the place of the other—they are irreducible the one to the other" (Irigaray, 19–20). Heath responds, "Yes, but the irreducibility can quickly become not difference and contradiction but a gulf, as though between two species, and the implications of men in feminism—feminism which has to include men, their transformation, in its project—are cut short" (Heath, "Male," 31). Sargent and Slonczewski initially locate women and men in different places. Lessing initially locates masculine and feminine traits in different zones. These separate locations form a gulf which positions women and men as two species. Heath's notion of "two species" is syonymous with Suniti's comment that "men are aliens."

Postseparatist feminist utopias initially portray men as literal aliens—cut short the implications of men in feminism—before welcoming a transformed, feminist man within their societies. The male protagonists who discard patriarchy are men in feminism who inhabit new feminist utopian spaces. Lyotard's understanding of postmodernism is applicable to these spaces. He explains that "*post modern* would have to be understood according to the paradox of the future (post) anterior (modo). . . . Finally, it must be clear that it is our business not to supply reality but to invent allusions to the conceivable which cannot be presented. . . . The answer is: Let us wage a war on totality; let us be witnesses to the unpresentable; let us activate the differences and save the honor of the name" (Lyotard, 341). The postseparatist feminist utopia incorporates a paradox: combining new versions of the future separatist feminist utopia with new versions of an anterior patriarchy. The new literary space in which altered feminist and patriarchal ideologies live together in utopian admiration alludes to conceivable reality which cannot yet be realized. Lessing, Sargent, and Slonczewski begin to answer the question which reality—and realistic novels such as *The Finishing School* and *More Die of Heartbreak*—fails to answer: how do women and men live together in terms of mutual dignity and equality? These authors suggest waging war on the totality of the manner in which patriarchy constructs heterosexual love relationships. They allow readers to witness unpresentable women's worlds. They activate (and ultimately unite) the differences between women and men and save the honor of the name "human."

While Lyotard's definition of postmodernism contributes to a theoretical understanding of postseparatist feminist utopian fiction, Norman N. Holland's version of the term has a more praxis-oriented relationship to the imaginative texts. According to Holland, "In Postmodernism, the arts take as their subject matter the relationship between the work of art and its artist or between the work of art and its audience. It is as though we changed the subject matter of our arts from something behind the canvas to the canvas itself and now to the space between the canvas and us" (Holland, 296). Feminist goals can be accomplished by strengthening the relationship between feminist utopias, the female artists who create them, and the audiences who read them. It is not impossible to make reality resemble feminist artists' literary utopian canvases. As the differences between Namjoshi's separatist notions and the Smith-Jardine anthology's postseparatist notions indicate, feminists are trying to do so. Feminist goals can be realized by narrowing the space, closing the gap, between the postseparatist feminist utopian canvas and us. However, before this closure can be accomplished, it is necessary to understand the canvas. I will closely analyze

Lessing's, Sargent's, and Slonczewski's texts to explain how, within each novel, separatist feminist utopian spaces become postseparatist feminist utopian spaces. This transition provides an imagined solution to the lack of real-world spaces in which women and men can live productively together.

Although women and nonpatriarchal men do live together harmoniously in Lessing's Zone Three, their relationships fall short of a utopian ideal. Zone Three's feminist female and feminist male inhabitants suffer from stagnation, the absence of desire to move from zone to zone. They neither learn from nor admire other spaces. Al·Ith, for example, does not think about Zone Two: "What lay there? She had no idea! She had not thought! She had not wondered!" (Lessing, 59). Lack of wonder forms Zone Three's flaw. Lessing views movement between differing zones, not isolation in an individual zone, as a crucial aspect of healthy societies. Traveling to other zones (rather than defining the pavilion as a numbered zone) forms the basis for hope in *Marriages*. The novel defines static relationships between women and men as unsuccessful relationships.

Movement between zones facilitates change in real women's lives. Three particular examples of this statement come to mind. First, the various waves of feminism are historical movements between zones of reactionary backwardness and progressive insight. Second, women merge various personal and professional zones while they build careers in a sexist world. And third, Lessing develops as a writer when she moves from the zone of realistic fiction to the zone of space fiction. Lessing enters the realm of feminist fabulation, a zone separated from patriarchal space. As Al·Ith and her fellows improve themselves by looking toward Zone Two, readers can learn by looking beyond patriarchy toward a zone where patriarchy can be discarded. Like the Providers who order Al·Ith and Ben Ata to live together, Lessing provides a new zone for feminists to emulate. Patriarchy is no less a construction, a fiction, than are Lessing's Zones Three, Four, and Five. Ben Ata and Al·Ith rely upon love to transcend the zones which separate their respective roles as warlord and presider over peace. Fortunately for reality-bound readers, love is not a fantastic element limited to the pages of feminist fabulation. Lessing's positive vision announces that, to achieve Heath's "admiration as utopia," all you need is love.

She speaks against the separatism which characterizes feminist and patriarchal ideologies. Utopia is achieved in *Marriages* after women and men learn to admire each other and to progress toward teaching each other. Further, according to Lessing, patriarchal ideas often have little to do with gender. Ben Ata introduces peaceful concepts to Vahshi, the female leader of Zone Five, whose bellicose personality is more extreme than his own.

Lessing moves beyond separatist utopias, visions which she would view as patently wrong. Unlike separatist utopias, *Marriages* approaches Namjoshi's notion that men are an alien species as a mere starting point. At first, Al·Ith watches Ben Ata, "interested, as she would have done some strange new species" (Lessing, 33). He, in turn, contemplates "how alien was this woman: how the strangeness of her did weigh him down, how she oppressed him" (Lessing, 38). *Marriages* uses this mutual alienation as a means to explain that women and men are inappropriately cast as science fiction characters, that women and men are not aliens who inhabit differing worlds. Unlike *The Finishing School, More Die of Heartbreak,* and separatist feminist utopias, *Marriages* finally imagines women and men crossing what Heath calls a "gulf, as though between two species."

Lessing's protagonists achieve this gender integration after they leave their respective zones and join hands in a pavilion, their own space supplied by the Providers. Their joined hands announce mutual respect derived from mutual compromise:

> While he [Ben Ata] had been holding in impulses of pure disliking hostility, she [Al·Ith] put her hand in his, as if it was a natural thing to do. His own hand remained stiff and rejecting. . . . Respect. Again her hand went out and into his, in an impulse of friendliness, and his great hand closed over hers like a bird trap. (Lessing, 40, 42)

Here, the separatist feminist utopian impulse becomes an inclusive gesture. Instead of rejecting the men of Zone Four, Al·Ith reaches out to Ben Ata, touches his hand in the pavilion's neutral space. When the couple joins hands, Ben Ata signals his willingness to learn from feminism.

Heath seems to describe Ben Ata's curriculum: "But one of the things men learn from feminism is that women have had enough of being marginal, marginalized: patriarchal society is about marginalization, keeping women out or on the edges of its economy, its institutions, its decisions. To change things, moreover, involves not individualism but collective action, women together, what feminism is about. . . . Is the position of men to feminism marginal, an individualism?" (Heath, "Male," 24). Marginalization pertains neither to the fantastic scenario within Al·Ith and Ben Ata's pavilion nor to their experiences within their own zones. Ben Ata is marginalized only after he moves from Zone Four to Zone Five. Like Al·Ith, he derives insight from movement rather than from stasis. Ben Ata's new realizations exemplify a positive answer to Heath's aforementioned question about "how to open this space of a radical sexual difference that is not the old difference." When Heath answers his own question, he explains that feminism decenters men and creates "a new individualism in the sense that collective identity of men is no longer available" (Heath, "Male," 24). After being exposed to Al·Ith's feminism, Ben Ata can no longer participate in militarism, the collective identity of Zone Four men. Instead, he finds a new activity—educating Zone Five about peace. People living in zones Four and Five will follow Ben Ata's example. As Ben Ata's transformation shows, individual feminist men can inspire crucial social change.

Change in *Marriages* occurs after individuals convert other individuals to the feminist insights practiced by the women and men who inhabit Zone Three. The novel's new feminists learn three lessons when they join hands with established feminists: patriarchy is itself about marginalization; women's subordination is not normal; and women should be positioned at society's primary right hand rather than relegated to its secondary left hand of darkness. Like Ursula Le Guin, Lessing is concerned with marriages between opposites.[5] She portrays men who are feminists (the men who inhabit Zone Three), a man who becomes a feminist (Ben Ata), a female feminist utopian who lives within patriarchy (Al·Ith), and a female patriarch (Vahshi) who encounters a new male feminist (Ben Ata). People's ability to change, not their gender, is most significant to Lessing.

According to *Marriages*, gender is merely another rigidly enclosed zone—another fixed definition—which needs to open itself to the influences of other zones. Women and men can best live together within a space which is free of gender hierarchies. Al·Ith and Ben Ata accomplish this objective as they merge with each other in their pavilion: "Now they were naked most of the time, for their being bare there together was like being clothed, so various and speaking had these two bodies become" (Lessing, 126). The pavilion, a zone within Zone Four which enables Al·Ith and Ben Ata to become the world to each other, is the site of Heath's "utopia of admiration"; it is an as yet unattainable zone which can inspire making admiration between a woman and a man real.

The presence of men within Zone Three's feminist society sets an example Sargent and Slonczewski follow when they portray an individual man inhabiting a feminist zone. The women's City in Sargent's *The Shore of Women* maintains power in a manner analogous to Zone Four's bogus weapons. Al·Ith and Ben Ata explain: " 'Do you actually mean to say that these hideous gray round buildings you've got all over Zone Four don't make death rays? That's a fake too?' [Al·Ith asks.] 'Everyone believes we've got them. It comes to the same thing,' " [Ben Ata answers] (Lessing, 96). The City's defense also depends upon fakery. Technologically sophisticated women expel and control men by picturing themselves as fakes—powerful, sexual goddesses.

When City women project false religious and social images of themselves, they reverse the usual sexist relationship between eros and power. They enact the courtly love tradition and place women on pedestals after convincing men to define women as holy, more than human. Their trick (as well as Zone Four's fake visions) coincides with Christine Brooke-Rose's understanding of Derrida's and Lacan's position that "meaning is an illusion, absolutely necessary to us but an illusion" (Brooke-Rose, 47). Brooke-Rose explains that "for both Derrida and Lacan, reality is . . . an emptiness, filled in by man and his manic systems of meaning" (Brooke-Rose, 47). Reversed gender/power roles in *Shore* illustrate that patriarchy perpetuates itself by creating an illusion in which the word "female" denotes inferiority. Patriarchy subordinates women by filling an empty definition of "female" with myths about ineptitude. Haunani-Kay Trask describes this arbitrary patriarchal meaning system: "'[W]oman' is a social construction. Examinations of women's gender roles, especially mothering, and women's status under law, custom, and kinship uncover again and again that women's situation is connected to her definition as a sex" (Trask, 29). Sargent imagines changed gender roles through redefining women's collective definition as a sex. Her novel alters the patriarchally defined relationship between eros and power.

Lessing and Sargent present metafictional commentaries upon the fictionality of patriarchal stories, patriarchy's illusory right to wield power. Nuclear facades in Zone Four indicate that patriarchal reality can be an emptiness; false-goddess images projected by Sargent's City are a meaning-making system which can fill this emptiness. These false images can be understood according to Brooke-Rose's notion that "all human discourse is fudged. . . . And insofar as a basic premise is at any time shown or declared to be untrue . . . a whole edifice collapses, an abyss remains: the real, which must quickly be filled with new idols, readjusted significance" (Brooke-Rose, 10). *Shore* declares patriarchal discourse to be untrue; this novel depicts patriarchy's collapse, women becoming men's new idols, and readjusted female images assuming significance formerly reserved for phallic power. When City women exile all boys, they conveniently obliterate the father and his law.

Hence, Trask's description of eros and power cannot hold true in the City. According to Trask,

> women, within the family and within society, *belong* to the father (patriarchy, culture). . . . In a patriarchal society, the phallus distinguishes the "exchanger" from the "exchanged," the powerful from the powerless. Juxtaposing psychoanalysis and anthropology, the phallus becomes the source of power through which the vagina and womb (women's erotic-reproductive personalities) are passed. In reverse, the vagina and womb are conduits for the source of power, the phallus. (Trask, 72)

City women belong to the mother in a society where the penis can never be represented as a phallus; in the City, those who possess penises are powerless. These mothers are "exchangers" who force sons to trade the City's technology for tribal life in a wilderness beyond its walls. According to City gender constructions, this exchange is necessary because the phallus—which City women view as the representation of men's dangerous, degenerated personalities—must be made to signify powerlessness. Trask, when she discusses Western civilization's "fear and disgust of female flesh," refers to H. R. Hays's term "myth of feminine evil" (Trask, 141); the City constructs a myth of masculine evil by reacting to male flesh with fear and disgust. According to this City myth, when a boy is born, the vagina becomes analogous to a garbage disposal chute. The vagina becomes a passageway for waste products (male infants) which must be placed outside the City to ensure community health.

The City, then, is a separatist feminist utopia which reifies the idea that men are aliens. As one inhabitant explains, "they [men] aren't like us. . . . their minds are narrow and incapable of higher intellectual functions" (Sargent, 9). Women and men cannot live together in the City: "We [City women] cannot possibly live with them [men], not as we are and they are—we couldn't share our lives. So it might be better if they died out completely" (Sargent, 122–123). Like Lessing, Sargent believes that feminist utopian literature must move beyond separatism. Her City is as stagnant as Lessing's Zone Three: "We [women who reside in the City] don't know anything that wasn't known two centuries or more ago. We probably know less. We hold ourselves back" (Sargent, 26). In the manner of Al·Ith and Ben Ata, Sargent's Birana and Arvil oppose stagnation by leaving their respective zones and establishing a space of mutual understanding. Birana is cast out of the City—left, like a male, to die outside its walls. She is forced to live in a male world; she is forced to believe that Arvil and his male fellows are human. Like Al·Ith, she has no choice about inhabiting a foreign zone and adjusting to foreign realities. Like Al·Ith and Ben Ata, Arvil and Birana learn to love each other.

However, while Al·Ith and Ben Ata ultimately separate and enter other zones to disseminate their new knowledge, Birana and Arvil remain together and become an egalitarian couple unable to conform to any of the various societies they encounter: the women's

City, the all-male tribes, the male tribe which includes a woman, and the scraggly crew of women and men who inhabit a shore community. Their inability to establish space for themselves within any social order indicates that social organizations, not individual women and men, retard heterosexual relationships. Sargent's protagonists recognize that myths generated by constructed social systems cause women and men to view each other as aliens. Lessing and Sargent respond to these myths by advocating building new societies.

Arvil's twin sister, Laissa, articulates Sargent's call for social change. When Laissa closes her chronicle, the story of Birana and Arvil, her words refer to new social systems: "It may be time for us and for those outside to begin to reshape ourselves and become another kind of being" (Sargent, 469). Both Birana and Arvil become changed social entities who no longer belong in their respective original communities, the women's City and the men's tribe. They stand together, removed from all the societies in their world. Birana, a pregnant outcast from the City, is a literal (m)other. Arvil is his society's first man who functions as a nurturing father to a female infant. *Shore* advocates creating a new social system, not resorting to gender role reversals which reflect patriarchal systems.

Venturing into the fantastic allows Lessing and Sargent to improve upon Godwin's and Bellow's realistic representations of failed female/male relationships. By pointing to a need for an appropriate space within which one heterosexual couple can live together according to mutually respectful terms, their space fiction surmounts realistic literature's difficulty with portraying gender equality. These imagined new spaces are very tenuous, however. Al·Ith and Ben Ata's pavilion disappears. Birana and Arvil are lovers without a country—postseparatist feminist utopians without a postseparatist feminist utopia—who must send their daughter to the City. Neither Lessing nor Sargent creates a nonstagnant, postseparatist, egalitarian society. Hence, Lessing's and Sargent's happy couples take only small steps beyond Bellow's and Godwin's realistic depictions of inadequate relationships between women and men. The couples' experiences are, nonetheless, important efforts toward building nonsexist social systems in literature—and, eventually, in life. Laissa

echoes this goal when she closes her chronicle. She imagines the outcast Birana and Arvil "on a distant shore near a refuge they have
built for themselves dreaming of the oceans we might sail again and
the stars we might seek. Perhaps we will join them on that shore at
last" (Sargent, 469). Birana and Arvil, like Rupert Birkin, wish for the
relationship of two single and equal stars balanced in conjunction.

Lessing and Sargent portray patriarchal and feminist ideologies as
two continents separated by an ocean of differences. In their space
fiction, seeking the stars coincides with positing alternative worlds
where individuals attempt to bridge feminist and patriarchal discontented discourses. Postseparatist feminist utopias send a representative from the shore of women to meet a representative from the
shore of men—and the representatives have difficulty securing a
place to negotiate. Birana and Arvil, a transformed, stranded couple,
live together without an appropriate space; Al·Ith and Ben Ata separate and live in spaces which exaggerate the conditions they learned
to transcend. We can only dream about bridging women's and men's
shores, about mounting a successful sailing expedition to the undiscovered continent of equality.

The City, an at-once flawed feminist utopia and dystopian nightmare for men, forces men to enter an exclusively male territory, to
experience Fiedler's description of men's desire to escape civilization. Sargent, however, does not allow men who inhabit an all-
male territory to be free from women's social control. The City
sends forth surveillance ships, piloted by women, which fire upon
men who disregard social codes regarding male subordination (Sargent, 187). The women in ships who attack men's territory reverse
Namjoshi's notion that men are aliens. These women are themselves the SF alien invaders.

According to City women, sexuality is an invasion steeped in
myth. They appropriate sperm by defining ejaculation as a religious
ritual in which men are blessed when they become sexually aroused.
Arvil informs Birana that he no longer believes this illusion: "I see
a truth you didn't tell me. . . . It is from our joining with the spirit-
women that boys come, and perhaps young ones of your own kind
as well, unless you have other magic for that. . . . We were not called
to be blessed, but to have part of ourselves stolen from us" (Sargent,

207–208). He defies the City's version of his reproductive functions by adhering to Trask's ideas. She explains that women can substitute patriarchal definitions of the female self with their own self-definitions: "The first stage of revolt in the colonized is a taking back of the Self from the confining realm of the colonizer. Women's self-definition, then, is at once a usurpation of patriarchy's right to define women and at the same time a statement of legitimacy against this definition" (Trask, 157). Arvil revolts against the City by taking back his sexual self, by asserting that sperm cannot be appropriated by those who wish to colonize male reproductive functions. He refuses to allow the City to define and legitimate his sexuality.

Arvil declares that men in his society, for the convenience of women, are compelled to understand sexuality according to myths about how the male reproductive role is determined. City women construct sexuality's rules, arenas, and rituals. They eradicate love, the father, and the phallus. These women act like the men in Trask's description of patriarchal sex and reproduction. Trask believes that "in most cultures, it is men who pursue, who determine first sexual approaches and choose daily schedules and residences when marriage takes place. Despite American society's characterization of love as primarily the domain of women, the rules, arenas, and rituals of love, especially sexual encounters, are shaped by men for their advantage" (Trask, 80). Sargent's women determine initial sexual approaches as well as the spaces in which these approaches occur.

Sargent, according to Trask's viewpoint, imagines an alternative world where woman hating does not exist. Trask explains: "[B]efore feminists can work toward the control of their own bodies, they have had to imagine a world where 'woman hating'—sexual mutilation, 'snuff' films, social violence against women—does not exist. Part of this imagining comes through the actual experience of alternatives—for example, lesbian love, women's support networks, freedom from pregnancy afforded by abortion and contraception—which lead to a heightened consciousness regarding what women's control over their own bodies would be like" (Trask, 143). Sargent's female protagonists decide that male control of women's bodies is wrong and that women's control is better. Hence, they act according to Trask's description of women "who decide, against all odds, to fight for control over their bodies . . . [and who] possess not only a sense that male control is wrong, indeed evil, but that women's control is inherently good, that is, inherently better for women, men, and society. In fighting to wrest control from men, feminists are simultaneously fighting for a different kind of world" (Trask, 143). Within Sargent's different kind of world (her separatist City), women wrest control from men in order to control men. She asserts that this power reversal is inherently bad. Substituting man hating with woman hating, substituting patriarchy with feminist separatism which exploits men, does not provide an appropriate basis for an alternative world.

The City is a women's community which routinely resorts to patriarchal tactics. The spirit-women whom the men worship, for example, are pornographic film characters. Laissa explains: "I knew that these tapes were centuries old. . . . Images of women, naked and seductive, would appear to men in shrines when the men were wearing mindspeaker circlets, and the men would experience the sensation of lying with these women. . . . The tapes had been both a source of amusement and disgust to us all; some of my friends shrieked or laughed nervously as we prepared such transmissions" (Sargent, 11–12). The tapes allow women to define the visual space of Woman as filmed subject, to reverse the usual effect of pornographic films. Pornographic images cause male sexual arousal to become a means for City women to appropriate male sexuality: men are drawn to the City; circlets communicating pornographic images are placed on men's heads; women harvest sperm.

Arvil remembers functioning as a powerless sperm provider: "I was naked. A clear, slender tube attached to my member curled under the couch on which I lay. . . . my body glittered with metal threads that bound me to the couch as well as to several metallic objects near me" (Sargent, 112). Filmed images enable City women to cause men to become bound, mechanized, powerless objects in the reproductive process. Unconscious men who donate sperm, not pregnant women, lay on tables attached to machines. This problematic social reversal can be accomplished because the pornographic images women transmit veil women behind City walls.

Mary Ann Doane's understanding of the veil's cinematic function is applicable to Sargent's text. Doane states that "the veil's work would seem to be that of concealing, of hiding a secret. . . . the woman is veiled in an appeal to the gaze of the spectator. And the veil incarnates contradictory desires—the desire to bring her closer and the desire to distance her. Its structure is clearly complicit with the tendency to specify the woman's position in relation to knowledge as that of the enigma" (Doane, 110, 118). The City wall acts as a veil which hides women from men. The wall-as-veil, a trick to mask women's visible vulnerability, enables City women to change from signifiers of powerless femininity to signifiers of religious and sexual power. As Laissa explains, the control City women derive from projecting themselves as goddesses depends upon the ability of the walls and the tapes to veil women's humanity: "Our true protection doesn't lie just in our wall and our weapons, but in what they [men] believe about us" (Sargent, 117). The new "truth" (about Woman-as-goddess) communicated by the women-produced pornographic tapes replaces the real truth, veiled behind City walls, of women's powerlessness. The wall and the tapes appeal to the male gaze, lure men into spaces women control.

A veil existing in the form of City walls and pornographic films forces men's knowledge of women to be presented as an enigma. The male characters' ability to derive sexual pleasure while viewing these films depends upon their lack of knowledge about women. Hence, the men's image of Woman-as-goddess is a mystical vision of idealized *jouissance*, a vision which coincides with Doane's notion that

the price to be paid for visual immediacy and the "more" of *jouissance* is the absence of knowledge. . . . *Jouissance* presupposes a nonknowledge or even an antiknowledge. It is linked to the realm of the mystics and hence, at the very least, divorces the register of knowledge from the register of discourse. . . . the woman here becomes emblematic of the subject who is duped by the unconscious, of the nonknowledge of the subject. It is almost as though there were an obligatory blind spot as far as the woman is concerned which is compensated for by an *over-*

sight, a compulsion to see her, to image her, to make her reve-
latory of something. (Doane, 132, 133)

In Doane's terms, Sargent's veiled women control men through an
absence of knowledge, which enables men to experience *jouissance*.
This absence of knowledge (a nonknowledge or antiknowledge) about
City women's true nature is the price men pay for the visual sexual
immediacy the tapes provide. Their *jouissance* is linked to a mystical, religious motivation to conceptualize women in a manner di-
vorced from true knowledge of women. Sargent's men are duped by
their nonknowledge of City women. Their literal obligatory blind
spots regarding women are compensated for by the compulsion to
view sexual Woman in the tapes, to make her reveal men's sexual
desire.

The tapes, which picture females as erotic aliens who inhabit
alien spaces, make it possible for City women to present Woman as
alien to men. Sargent's men do, in fact, view woman-controlled SF
films which—counter to Vivian Sobchack's observation that biological sexuality and eroticism are repressed in the narratives of
male-dominated SF films (Sobchack, 41)—portray erotic women.
Sobchack emphasizes that Marilyn Monroe could not appropriately
star in an SF film: "The genre could not have possibly contained her
body, and she would have destroyed the impact and iconic potency
of any technological marvel or activity . . . simply by the awful truth
of her visual presence. That female body, those full breasts and
rounded belly, that amplitude and plenitude of flesh, would have
distracted both male characters and narrative alike from their generic course" (Sobchack, 44). *Shore,* then, creates space for a film
genre which is not part of American culture—the sexual SF film.

This new film genre appears when City women alter a social construction which attributes biology and sexuality to women and
knowledge and technology to men. City women control the technological distribution of the sexual SF film; outcast men make up
the biologically and sexually manipulated audience. The City wom-
en's art, their SF films, reflects the City's constructed sexual and
social spaces. As Sobchack emphasizes, so, of course, do our own:
"Insofar as American culture observes and perpetuates the semiotic

linkage of biology to woman and technology to male, astronauts will always be represented as virginal no matter how much they screw around" (Sobchack, 57). In the City, which reverses the biological/ technological linkage Sobchack discusses, technological women are always represented as lascivious desirers of men—even though these women define "screwing around" as repugnant.

Birana and Arvil come together after deconstructing the artistic and ideological images the City perpetuates. When Arvil removes his circlet and learns the truth about women's humanity and sexuality, Birana stands unveiled before him. Arvil observes, "You are one like me; I see it now. You live in our world, and something in you calls to me" (Sargent, 154). He is the first man in his world to interact with a female human rather than with a female image of male desire. Like Al·Ith and Ben Ata, Birana and Arvil transcend their respective societies by exploring sexuality. And, like Lessing's protagonists, Sargent's protagonists begin their exploration after managing to hold hands. Arvil says, "Her hand was cold. I saw from the tenseness of her body that she wanted to pull away, but she kept her palm against mine. Joy filled my spirit" (Sargent, 181–182). Birana and Arvil discard sexual myths and create their own sexual narrative. They touch and realize that women and men are equal halves of the human species, not aliens. Birana explains that "for the first time since I had met Arvil, I had accepted his touch without wanting to pull away; I had wanted my hand in his, and that frightened me. . . . His body, so different than mine, no longer seemed so repulsive, so alien" (Sargent, 228, 333). The couple's life together nullifies two false stories: the City's myth about how having sex with men is unthinkable and the male tribe's myths derived from seeing women portrayed as SF film stars.

Birana and Arvil are no longer alien to each other. Arvil explains, "I loved her in all the ways she loved best. We would escape and find a place where we could love without fear. I felt her warmth around me as I entered" (Sargent, 362). In the world of *Shore*, sexual intercourse is a new activity (or frontier) for women and men. When the enterprising Arvil enters Birana's body, he ventures within a new space where no man of his society has gone before. He creates a place for the penis in a world where female hegemony successfully deconstructs phallic power. However, as I have explained, even though Birana and Arvil rediscover heterosexual love, they lack a society in which to function as nonsexist lovers. After Birana suggests that she and Arvil house themselves in an ancient bomb shelter, he responds by saying, "Perhaps it's a sign, this place where life had to begin again, where men and women were once together" (Sargent, 383). But, unlike Lessing's pavilion, the bomb shelter, where "the dust of men and women mingled in death" (Sargent, 383), is not a conducive location for women and men to live together harmoniously. When mentioning the bomb shelter, Sargent reflects Bellow's notion that more people die of heartbreak than of nuclear radiation. Birana and Arvil—lovers living in a postnuclear holocaust world which shuns heterosexuality—could die from the heartbreak of being social aliens.

City women, who refuse to nurture men and who cause men to become outcasts, enact an exaggerated version of the choice presently available to the real-world women Trask describes. According to Trask, the "choice for women now is to make their lives within a praxis of pain, limiting the expression of their own humanity as they cushion man's inhumanity to himself and others, or to begin refusing support to men in quite the same sacrificial way, while developing their own visions, their own communities, where nurturance and autonomy are everyday realities" (Trask, 82). In response to men's historical inhumanity, City women treat men inhumanely. Their flawed community does not allow all human beings to experience nurturance and autonomy. Sargent's separatist City signals that feminist utopian literature is ready to move beyond separatism. Feminist utopian literature is beginning to imagine how to fill the potential space of female/male social equality. Birana and Arvil suffer because this space remains unoccupied in their society.

They need more than love, more than Birana's assertion that "he's loved me and I've come to love him as well" (Sargent, 451). Laissa (a scholar who literally places feminist criticism in the wilderness) travels to the men's wilderness, creates scholarly records, and provides the potential for change. She "did some important work. . . . The historians now know more about the outside than we've known for some time" (Sargent, 466). Lessing and Sargent, then, describe changed couples and changed individuals, not changed societies.

In postseparatist feminist utopias, one woman leaves a feminist separatist world and one man leaves a patriarchal world to encounter each other in a meta-utopia, a nowhere emerging from a nowhere. The couples hold hands in an isolated void; a society which will welcome them is still an undiscovered country. Although Al·Ith and Ben Ata, and Birana and Arvil, enjoy heterosexual relationships which are more successful than the ones experienced by Godwin's and Bellow's protagonists, these postseparatist feminist utopians cannot live together in a society suited to contain them. They are as culturally retrograde as the notion of Marilyn Monroe starring in science fiction films. The feminist utopian literary imagination needs to perform many more "thought experiments" (Le Guin's term) before it can portray the environment Laissa and Arvil experience within their mother's womb—a place where female and male twins together equally share space sustained by a woman. (Suzy McKee Charnas, for example, never completed the third volume of her *Walk to the End of the World/Motherlines* trilogy, which is supposed to portray a two-sexed egalitarian society.) Joan Slonczewski's *A Door into Ocean* offers her version of the postseparatist utopian thought experiment.

Nelson Goodman's comments about "worldmaking" pertain to Slonczewski's novel. According to Goodman, "the many stuffs . . . that worlds are made of are made along with the worlds. But made from what? Not from nothing, after all, but *from other worlds.* Worldmaking as we know it always starts from worlds already on hand; the making is a remaking" (Goodman, 6). Slonczewski's world builds upon the worlds Sargent and Lessing imagine; its "stuffs" remake Lessing's and Sargent's already-on-hand worlds. Shora, the world in *Door* that women (who call themselves Sharers) populate, transcends Zone Three's stagnation and the City's inhumanity to men. *Door*, nevertheless, insists that its perfectly made women's world is insufficient. Rather than being an end product, Shora is a separatist world from which a new world for women and men can be made. Shora reflects Goodman's concern that "with all this freedom to divide and combine, emphasize, order, delete, fill in and fill out, and even distort, what are the objectives and constraints? What are the criteria for success in making a world?" (Goodman, 17). Shora is constrained by separatism. Slonczewski defines success in making a world as creating an equal space which both sexes can enjoy. Hence, in order to inhabit a truly successful world, the Sharers must make their existing world a base for building a better one. They cannot "dismiss as illusory or negligible what cannot be fitted into the architecture of the world . . . [they] are building" (Goodman, 15). The Sharers cannot dismiss what cannot be fitted into the architecture of their world—a man.

The novel begins when two Sharers, Merwen and Usha, come to planet Valedon (the patriarchal antithesis of Shora, which resembles Le Guin's Urras in *The Dispossessed*) to ensconce one young male, Spinel, in their world. *Door*, then, concerns worlds remade by fitting incongruous parts within existing worlds. Sharers integrate Spinel within their feminist world; Valans (the name for inhabitants of Valedon) learn about applying Shoran ideas regarding peace to their militaristic society. These changes show that, in Goodman's words, "this world, indeed, is the one most often taken as real; for reality in a world, like realism in a picture, is largely a matter of habit" (Goodman, 20).

Like Goodman—and like Brooke-Rose and Trask—Slonczewski insists that reality is habitual and constructed. All women are not comfortable on Shora merely because they are female. Lady Berenice of Hyalite, Spinel's fellow resident of Valedon, experiences as much difficulty as he does while adjusting to Shora. But, like Spinel, she successfully accomplishes the transition from the Valan zone to the Shoran zone. After changing her name to a Shoran name, Nisi, she dons Shoran reality like a substitute change of clothes. Nisi and Spinel create a new world for themselves—and for the Sharers. Shora, in turn, re-creates the newcomers by changing their skin color from Valan white to Shoran purple. This fantastic racial alteration calls attention to the need to attribute flexibility to race and gender roles. Just as Nisi and Spinel adjust to Shora, readers can accommodate less rigid definitions of these roles.

The purple Sharers routinely change their color. When angered, instead of fighting, they place themselves in "white trance," a temporary near-comatose state which comments upon the permanent white trance of some Caucasians (a refusal to change or to accommodate other groups' differences). On Shora, racial segregation becomes impossible when the Shoran and Valan antagonists become each other: "[T]he natives simply sat before the fence and turned white. . . . five pallid Sharers facing soldiers awash in dreadful violet, as if the color had seeped directly from one side to the other" (Slonczewski, 301).

"Sharing" or merging roles forms the crux of *Door*. Slonczewski rewrites master narratives which describe man as human and Woman as Other. When Merwen and Usha's daughter, Lystra, wonders if males are human, her question underscores the fictionality of patriarchal definitions. She asks, "Why did you [Merwen] bring a Valan malefreak to this very door? . . . You went to Valedon to share judgment of them in their own habitat, to judge if they can be human. Surely you have your answer now" (Slonczewski, 57). Slonczewski places males on trial; Sharers judge whether or not "malefreaks" can be called "human." Sharers reach their verdict after incorporating a man, after changing their society.

In addition to evoking Le Guin's description of the neighboring planets Urras and Anarres, *Door* offers a postseparatist commentary upon the title of Joanna Russ's separatist utopia "When It Changed." The word "it" in Russ's title might refer to the planet Whileaway. In Shoran society, "it" at first refers to Spinel. The Sharers define him—and all men—as "it." After this male "it" leaves his home— becomes dispossessed—he is repossessed by the Sharers' willingness to remake him, to redefine him as human. Slonczewski's inclusive gesture toward an individual male is more generous than its counterpart in *Shore*. The Sharers, who can reproduce without men, do not need men. Further, their ecological power is superior to mechanistic Valan power. Sharers incorporate a male simply because they wish to move beyond separatism. In Merwen's words, "We are one species, only one" (Slonczewski, 222). Some female feminist theorists currently espouse Merwen's attitude.

Tenured female feminist literary critics can rely solely upon their female colleagues. Some of these critics are powerful. All of them engage in an exciting professional enterprise. Yet, like the Sharers, despite their autonomy, many female feminist scholars wish to interact with those colleagues whose views differ from their own, women and men who are (like Nisi and Spinel) outside feminism.

Nisi, who is not a feminist, learns to embrace a feminist community. Spinel is a man in feminism who shares much in common with Paul Smith's and Stephen Heath's descriptions of the male Other positioned within a feminist hegemony. When Spinel decides to inhabit Shora permanently, he wonders, "Could he bear to stay here, a freak for the rest of his life?" (Slonczewski, 406). His answer is affirmative. As he chooses to live on Shora, Heath and Smith choose to spend part of their professional lives as alien "malefreaks," as men in feminism. Their decision is positive. "Malefreaks"—such as Heath, Smith, and Spinel—become more human when they engage the female feminist Other counterparts to themselves. The same holds true for Nisi's decision to welcome a love relationship with the Valan commander (Slonczewski, 406). The same holds true for female feminist theorists who interact with men.

Minow-Pinkney's comments about *Orlando* further illuminate my analogy regarding the behavior of Slonczewski's feminist characters and many feminist theorists. Here is Minow-Pinkney's description of Orlando's relationship with Sasha: "Sasha represents otherness to him; she is a foreign woman with whom he cannot communicate except in French, which is a foreign tongue for both. . . . He is drawn to and beyond the uttermost limits of himself; embraces are only possible (and thus also impossible) if the other is indeed the other, on the other side of the boundary of self. . . . Metamorphosis on a small scale has already happened" (Minow-Pinkney, 122–123). Men who engage feminism, Sharers who welcome men, and Nisi, who loves a male exemplar of militarism, are all drawn to and beyond the uttermost limits of themselves. These people exchange, from the reader's point of view, possible and impossible embraces. Heath and Smith epitomize such possible impossibilities while speaking as feminists who articulate their position as aliens in relation to feminism. Lystra and Spinel experience another example of a possible impossibility when they successfully perform sexual intercourse. (Since Lystra's reproductive organs are not structured to accommodate a penis, she is biologically incompatible with Spinel.) Metamorphosis on a small scale occurs when Lystra and Spinel embrace the Other on the otherside of the boundary of self.

Such possible/impossible metamorphosis happens when individuals make changes in a new space alien to both of them. Birana and Arvil step out of their respective female and male worlds; Al·Ith and Ben Ata step out of their respective zones. Orlando and Sasha converse in French while standing on a new location they have never experienced, a river frozen more solidly than ever before. They speak in a foreign tongue while interacting on a new landscape, another world which is at once British and Russian. The same is true for Spinel and Lystra, who learn to overcome the word "malefreak." They will learn to live in a new world which differs from Shora and Valedon, the worlds they know. In Goodman's terms, this new world will spring from elements particular to both Shora and Valedon.

Spinel finds love on Shora: "His arms went around her [Lystra], and she held him as hard as ever. . . . Spinel thought he would faint from her nearness. He was sure now that Lystra was meant for him, no matter how 'different' she was" (Slonczewski, 323). Regardless of Lystra's and Spinel's love for each other, like Lessing and Sargent, Slonczewski stops short of depicting a society in which women and men can live together equitably. Although *Door* concludes when Spinel and Lystra fall in love, the novel never describes how the couple lives together. *Door* does, however, move beyond the flawed separatist feminist utopia to depict self-sufficient feminist utopians who, nonetheless, try to incorporate a male.

Spinel refers to this inclusive spirit: "Just tell them [the citizens of his hometown on Valedon] that the door is still open" (Slonczewski, 406). The door is still open for more women and men to follow Spinel and Nisi as incorporated members of Shora's society, for women and men from a patriarchal society to live together in a postseparatist feminist utopia. Slonczewski's door shuts out rigid racial and gender roles. Her door into ocean suggests an entrance into the space of female fluidity, the place where women and men together can successfully inhabit a perfect world. Now that Slonczewski has opened this door, other writers are positioned to begin imagining how to walk through it. Birana, Arvil, Al·Ith, and Ben Ata are better able to do so than Kenneth, Benn, Matilda, Treckie, Justin, and Ursula. As for Spinel and Lystra, their hands touch while reaching for the doorknob—and they are anxious to inhabit the space beyond the door. They need this space as much as they need love.

New American Stars Balanced in Conjunction:
Politicians/Native Americans/Feminist Theoreticians

I conclude this chapter about heterosexual love relationships in realistic and fantastic texts by pointing out that feminist utopian fictions
are quite congruent with American history. Spinel, for example, is
analogous to an immigrant seeking a better life in America. On Valedon, "his life meant nothing, except to a desperate family who had
tearfully sent him packing. . . . Here [on Shora] . . . he could prove
himself as good as anyone, even Merwen" (Slonczewski, 100). He
proves himself by immigrating to a new world which provides him
with a new love relationship. Bellow, Godwin, Lessing, and Sargent
create less successful immigrants. Kenneth journeys to America
and remains single. Ursula does not marry in Europe. Ben Ata and
Arvil lack a society to immigrate to with their lovers. It is useful to
compare these characters' experiences as seekers of love—as well
as the feminist utopian vision as a whole—to the American historical experience Harvey Wasserman describes in *America Born and
Reborn*.

According to Wasserman, American culture reflects the interplay
of Native American and Puritan heritages. He believes that "the Puritan strain has powered the Industrial Revolution and has dominated the nation since its first birth in 1776. The Indian influence
has helped inspire the humanistic side of our society, and its ideals
are now a major force among much of the baby boom generation
born since World War II, a generation now poised to take control of
the nation" (Wasserman, 3). Wasserman explains that the power of
the World War II generation (wielded by Nixon, Ford, Reagan, and
Bush) is grounded within a Puritan model and will give way to a rebirth of an alternative model involving baby boomers who follow the
example of Native Americans (Wasserman, 283). Further, "we are
witnessing a shift in power not only from the World War II generation to the baby boom generation, but also from men to women. . . .
feminism's importance continues to escalate" (Wasserman, 296). My
descriptions of how heterosexual love relationships are portrayed in
realistic literature and feminist utopias coincide with Wasserman's
points about our postmodern moment. Juxtaposing Wasserman's no-

tions with my own forms a conversation about love and death, eros and power.

The Puritan power structure fails because it perpetuates an economy pumped by spending money on destructive war technology. America builds nuclear weapons, products which are not used. Heterosexual love relationships in realistic literature fail due to a similar reason: patriarchy stresses war, not love. The failure of love in realistic literature reflects the failure of love in the Puritan power structure, the "economic breakdown" (Wasserman, 5) Wasserman describes. In other words, the failed love relationships Godwin and Bellow portray reflect the failures of the Puritan World War II generation.

Wasserman predicts that the American government will move from Puritan power models to Native American power models. I predict the same for literature. The postseparatist feminist utopias which explore methods to achieve successful heterosexual love relationships are symptomatic of this change. Like the World War II generation's governmental presence, realistic characters who fail to experience such successful relationships (Benn and Kenneth, Ursula and Justin) will become less significant. Characters who learn to love a partner of the opposite sex and who lack an appropriate society in which to express love (Birana and Arvil, Al·Ith and Ben Ata, Spinel and Lystra) reflect the transition from the Puritan, patriarchal, realistic text to the Indian, feminist, fantastic text.[6] Lessing and Sargent write on the brink of literary change as Americans stand right on the brink of historical change in regard to the end of the Cold War. Slonczewski, whose male protagonist is able to love a woman and enjoy the potential to situate his relationship in an accepting society, signals that Native American modes can potentially replace Puritan modes as models for power structures.

Despite the persuasive presence of Bush and his vice-presidential "bummer of a baby boomer" (Eisenberg, 37),[7] Wasserman's thesis remains viable. The public can now picture someone other than a white male serving as president.[8] With regard to politics, many Americans—with Anita Hill and Clarence Thomas in mind—recognize the need to elect women who would challenge male-centered views. (In the wake of the Thomas hearings, a record number of women are seeking Senate election.[9] Further, issues formerly dismissed as women's issues—such as the government's relationship to child care—are now becoming recognized as part of the national agenda.) With regard to literature, feminist utopias, which Russ describes in terms of Native Americans,[10] are becoming more respected by the newly empowered baby-boom professorial generation. Feminism's influence upon literary studies continues to escalate; male theorists of the baby-boom generation elect to become men in feminism.

Wasserman himself is a man in feminism who addresses issues raised by feminist utopian literature. *America Born and Reborn* describes "a new 'Global Village' based on feminism, sexual liberation, racial and cultural diversity, environmentalism, grass-roots democracy, instant electronic communications, and many of the basic lessons of native American culture" (Wasserman, 8). The new Global Village resembles the "new historicity" (Jardine, *Gynesis*, 33)— based on the feminine, "u-topia," and the end of patriarchal history— that Alice Jardine discusses in terms of Jean-Joseph Goux's work.[11] And, the new Global Village certainly includes the new communal spaces feminist utopian literature envisions. (In *Door*, for example, instant electronic communications are achieved without machines: insects called click flies immediately convey information from one Sharer to another.) American culture is possibly on the brink of the changes Wasserman, Goux, and the creators of feminist utopias describe. According to Wasserman, "we are in the throes of a transformation as monumental as that experienced at the dawn of the industrial age, when European settlers began taking their first uncertain steps on the shores of native America" (Wasserman, 8–9). Spinel and his real-world male counterparts (the men in feminism), when they embark upon the shore of women, retake European immigrants' uncertain steps on America's shore. Their experience involves the "rebirth of something resembling the Iroquois matriarchal system" (Wasserman, 297), the space where power shifts from men to women.

Wasserman describes "the ebbs and flows of our national story" (Wasserman, 9). He views history as a narrative, an ebbing and flowing tide poised to reveal what lies beyond the door into ocean. Linking Wasserman's ideas to the "men in feminism" debate—and to feminist utopias—forms a marriage between historical, theoretical, and imaginary zones. Unlike the love relationships *The Finishing School* and *More Die of Heartbreak* portray, this marriage can be successful. Unlike the lovers Lessing, Sargent, and Slonczewski create, these marriage partners can potentially inhabit an appropriate society—America reborn as a feminist utopia. Although realizing this particular potential is highly unlikely (but not impossible), Wasserman does emphasize that America is currently experiencing the start of rebirth: "For it has become clear in the 1980s that the first life span of the United States is drawing to a close, and something entirely new is struggling to be born out of it" (Wasserman, 7). (During 1989 and early 1990, for example, the life span of the United States as the antagonist of European communism drew to a close when something new—democracy—struggled to be born in Eastern Europe.)

Feminist utopias are the midwives—the imaginative catalysts—for this entirely new something's birth. Wasserman emphasizes that, during previous cycles of American history, texts such as *Common Sense, Uncle Tom's Cabin, The Jungle,* and *Silent Spring* influenced social upheavals (Wasserman, 281–282). Feminist utopias function similarly in relation to the potential shift from Reaganomics to Native American and feminist ideals. Feminist utopias are appropriate imaginative texts for our postmodern moment.

America drastically needs alternatives to the ideas, promoted by patriarchal, puritanical World War II generation political leaders, which yield the "breakdown of America's dominance in world trade, the decline of our productivity growth rate, the rise of unemployment, and the deteriorating quality of life" (Wasserman, 277). Clearly, if we do not construct a different present reality, we will not have a future reality. Wasserman argues that our "global tinderbox" is on the verge of erupting into nuclear war (Wasserman, 278). This scenario might be avoided by positioning feminist utopias as models for reality, by valorizing the story from which they stem: "the old Indian spiritual belief that the health of the human individual is inseparable from that of Mother earth" (Wasserman, 277).

"Make love, not war," which I chanted as a teenage baby boomer, is still a relevant slogan. My ability to incorporate the former street text into a scholarly text marks one instance of power shifting to the baby-boom generation. All you need is love (in regard to this chapter's argument, "you" refers to heterosexual women and men)—and the social structure Russ calls "a two-sexed egalitarian society." If we can construct a space and place for love, we will die neither of heartbreak nor of nuclear radiation. We will, instead, live happily as lovers in societies which can encompass equal relationships between women and men. Rather than follow Benn Crader to the Arctic, where he embraces lichens, it is possible to sail through a door into ocean, reach the shore of women, and construct a new feminist zone. The separatist feminist finishing school is about to be dismissed. It is time to enact postseparatist feminist utopian lessons.

PART III ★ ○ ☽ ★ ○ ☽ ★ ○ ☽

Reconceiving Narrative Space

Cy Twombly, Untitled, *1955–1956. Collection of the artist.*

Hesitation, Self-Experiment, Transformation—Women Mastering Female Narrative

> I am not dead, but back—I, Isadora White Stoller-mann Wing, alias Leila Sand, Louise Zandberg, Candida Wong, La Tintoretta, Antonia Uccello, *und so weiter.* As another author said on another occasion: reports of my death were an exaggeration.
> —Erica Jong, *Any Woman's Blues: A Novel of Obsession*

> *We live our lives through texts. . . . these stories have formed us all; they are what we must use to make new fictions, new narratives. . . . We must stop reinscribing male words, and rewrite our ideas about what Nancy Miller calls a female impulse to power. . . . We know we are without a text, and must discover one. . . . There will be narratives of female lives only when women no longer live their lives isolated in the houses and the stories of men.*
> —Carolyn G. Heilbrun, *Writing a Woman's Life*

Women reconceive narrative space by refusing to live their lives through patriarchal texts, by making new fictions—and new realities. We enact our impulse to power when rewriting the patriarchal texts which form real-world contexts. I turn my attention to female characters who hesitate to live isolated in men's stories and domestic spaces, characters who master female narrative after undertaking the self-experiments and transformations which result once patriarchal stories are discarded. Like Erica Jong's Isadora White Stollermann Wing, the female protagonists of Margaret Atwood's *Lady Oracle*, Diane Johnson's *Persian Nights*, and Marge Piercy's *Small Changes* discover "another possibility of female destiny" (Heilbrun, 110), construct an "identity 'other' than their own" (Heilbrun, 111), live according to a new, nonpatriarchal "self-creation" (Heilbrun, 117). They echo Isadora's words, "I am not dead, but back" (Jong, 352). They are, in short, "alive because of transformation" (Cixous, 260).

This chapter focuses upon a progression of texts—ranging from depictions of collusion with patriarchy to descriptions of language functioning outside patriarchy—which concern how women stop reinscribing male words. I begin with two stories about men defining women: Tommaso Landolfi's "A Woman's Breast" and Philip Roth's "The Breast." Then, I turn to Christa Wolf's "Self-Experiment: Appendix to a Report," a woman's version of the gender ambiguities Landolfi and Roth address. Wolf's female protagonist rewrites her life in terms of both erotic and professional impulses to power. Her revision erases the male texts which limit women's lives—male texts which require women to act, for example, as erotic breasts or frigid subordinates to powerful male professionals.

Atwood, Johnson, and Piercy—like Wolf—portray women who engage in self-experimentation. After hesitating to accept the either/or alternatives for women in patriarchal stories, their protagonists reject choices men author and offer to women. These female characters change themselves and live according to new liberating stories. They exercise an impulse to power by countering male discourse's power to articulate their lives. They conduct self-experiments which yield what Chris Weedon calls "a mode of knowledge production" (Weedon, 41) congruent with an aim of feminist poststructuralism: "to understand existing power relations and to identify areas and strategies for change" (Weedon, 40–41). They identify the power relations between female and male discourses, imbue women's words with status, and use newly empowered female language to re-create themselves. This change allows women to win the political struggle between female and male "competing discourses" (Weedon, 24).

Women master female narrative and, subsequently, author their own lives by recognizing that discourses "represent political interests and in consequence are constantly vying for status and power. The site of this battle for power is the subjectivity of the individual and it is a battle in which the individual is an active but not sovereign protagonist" (Weedon, 41). Atwood's, Johnson's, Piercy's, and Wolf's female protagonists actively and successfully battle to re-create their individual subjectivity and to depose the sovereignty of male discourse. Their struggles can be read "as a political act of trans-forming fables" (Morris, 2). Meaghan Morris mentions "the ques-tion of rewriting 'discourses'" (Morris, 5), a question which "emerges from a political critique of the social positioning of women" (Morris, 5). The feminist fabulators I discuss in this chapter create protagon-ists who socially reposition themselves after rewriting patriarchal discourses (i.e., fables) about women. By doing so, the authors si-multaneously critique the process of excluding women from post-modern discourse and reposition themselves as postmodernists ac-cording to their own terms, not according to the terms of stellar male theorists. Hence, despite the fact that my claim differs from the various prevalent conceptions of what constitutes canons of postmodern fiction, I assert that feminist fabulators should not be placed outside these canons. Although critics have been blind to this point, feminist fabulators who imagine female characters rewriting their lives—female characters critiquing (to paraphrase Morris) the social position of women by rewriting patriarchal fictions about women—write postmodern fiction.

Alice Jardine's "gynesis" is applicable to feminist fabulators' chal-lenge to and repositioning of patriarchal master narratives about women's lives. Jardine points out that if "the 'author' is male . . . [the woman's] plot is not her own" (Jardine, 52). The female prota-gonists Atwood, Johnson, Piercy, and Wolf create insist upon living according to their own plots in a world that patriarchy authors. At-wood, Johnson, Piercy, and Wolf inscribe female narratives within male-authored stories about how women should behave. Their ef-forts can be understood according to a particularly female version of Jardine's description of the postmodern condition. Jardine states that the "state of crisis endemic to modernity is experienced primar-ily as a loss, or at least a breakdown, of *narrative*. . . . Those writing modernity as a crisis-in-narrative . . . are exploring newly contoured fictional spaces, hypothetical and unmeasurable, spaces freely coded as *feminine*" (Jardine, 68–69). Atwood's, Johnson's, Piercy's, and Wolf's protagonists create female narrative in response to the loss, or breakdown, of the ability to structure their own experiences. These female narratives guide their efforts to inhabit newly contoured, nonhypothetical, measurable feminine spaces. While masculinist postmodern theorists put the feminine into their discourse in a manner which "has very little, if anything, to do with women" (Jardine, 35), the feminist authors I discuss create spaces for female narrative within patriarchal master narratives.

These spaces are pertinent to the manner in which real women function in the real world. Much postmodern fiction written by men has a bleak, trivializing perspective on human life. In contrast, feminist fabulators insist that individual women's lives are important; they optimistically portray female protagonists who successfully revise their lives to conform to specifically female narratives—and their optimism in regard to women deserves, as much as male authors' bleak commentary upon humanity, to be called canonical postmodern fiction. My analysis of these narrative spaces, sites of women's resistance to patriarchal stories, ranges from the conciliatory response of the female protagonist in Landolfi's "A Woman's Breast" (which is not an example of feminist fabulation) to the notion that texts whose physical characteristics are fantastic can have an impact upon women's reality. Like Cy Twombly's scrawl, his unreal writing which is beyond language, women's potential new reality is as yet untitled.

Female Breasts/Male Stories

Landolfi's "A Woman's Breast" concerns a woman's failure to transform a man's fable. Her failure relates to Nancy K. Miller's "stakes of narration," a term describing a female character's fear of a male character's power to decide her fate. Miller applies this term to Germaine de Staël's *Corinne, or Italy*; Miller refers to what Oswald might think and do when Corinne tells him her story (Miller, *Change*, 173). Within Landolfi's text, the stakes of narration involve the question of who has authority to define a woman's breast. Answering this question entails a battle for narrative control between his unnamed female protagonist (I call her LFP—for Landolfi's female protagonist) and his unnamed male protagonist (I call him

LMP). This textual discord constitutes a "battle of the gaze" (Miller, *Change*, 177; Schor, 121). Miller applies Naomi Schor's term to the struggle between patriarchal judgments and a female subject's desires in *Corinne* (Miller, 177). LMP redefines LFP's story about her breast, decides her aesthetic self-conception. Although she wins some battles for narrative control, she ultimately loses the war of the gaze and the stakes of narration.

LMP, captivated by the sight of LFP's breasts, displaces her from a sidewalk: "I kept on walking until I was beside her. She had decided, she had stepped off the sidewalk" (Landolfi, 113). Her decision exposes her to an oncoming car. LMP saves her and demands the right to kiss one of her nipples (Landolfi, 116). He controls narrative by authoring a story about how he is entitled to enact his fantasy about kissing the nipple. Empowered by his story, his potentially fulfilled desire is no longer limited to a mere gaze.

LFP, however, does not immediately surrender the stakes of narration. Before revealing that her breast is nippleless, she momentarily gains narrative control by emphasizing her particular physical characteristics. She decides that because her breasts "have distinct sensitivities" (Landolfi, 116), LMP should choose which one to kiss. LFP's unique breasts, then, temporarily defy the male gaze and raise the stakes of narration. Her house functions similarly. It acts as a narrative space which interrupts LMP's story: "It's as my mother left it before she died" (Landolfi, 117), LFP tells LMP. Her home, a place where every object "gave the impression of age . . . the entire house seemed frozen" (Landolfi, 117), reflects female generational continuity. Miller's comments about a woman's space and story in *Corinne* clarify why LFP can use domestic space to appropriate LMP's masculine narrative space. According to Miller, "In Staël's novel, a woman's space . . . has a story of its own. Space suspends the masculine plot (Oswald's anxiety about closure and destination) by an insistence on description that puts plot itself into question" (Miller, 171). LFP's house has a female story of its own which suspends a masculine plot (LMP's desire to define and to kiss LFP's breasts). The image of the house as an unchanging female space questions and displaces LMP's masculine plot.

LMP learns that, like LFP's house, her breast represents an un-

changing female story. This story falsifies the narrative LMP attributes to the breast, a narrative about the breast as the object of the
male gaze. Because of the breast's uniqueness, LMP describes it as a
horror story: "[O]bscene creases ran toward the tip of that pale flesh
. . . and the aureola . . . looked colorless and sick . . . and the ultimate
horror . . . was that in the place of the nipple . . . was a sort of dark
and flaccid flesh" (Landolfi, 119). The ultimate horror in "A Woman's Breast" does not involve the nippleless breast's lack of confor-
mity to patriarchal stories about "proper" female breasts. Rather,
the story's ultimate horror is that, despite her successful efforts to
gain some narrative control, LFP eventually shares LMP's belief that
her breast could "hardly" (Landolfi, 119) be a woman's breast.

The word "hardly" inappropriately describes a female breast lacking an erectile, penile nipple. Counter to LMP's opinion that LFP's
breast is not womanly, phallic lack makes it more female. LFP's absolutely female breast defies the male gaze; it epitomizes female
difference. In other words, like *Corinne*, LFP's nippleless breast "en-
gages the possibility of an authoritative vision within femininity
that refuses the legitimacy of a permanent patriarchal construction"
(Miller, 165). This breast is an authoritative female vision, a legitimate female breast which lacks a phallic nipple and, hence, negates
LMP's story about kissing LFP's nipple. LMP, in reaction, simply
changes his story, insists upon the power of male stories. He decides
to kiss the space where a nipple would usually be located (Landolfi,
119), explaining that "one image can take the place of another . . .
that the first image can survive its own ruin" (Landolfi, 120). In
other words, one patriarchal story and image can take the place
of another; men's stories about women usually survive feminist
inquiry.

Miller points out that Corinne experiences "subjection to the law
of the male gaze" (Miller, 184). Citing John Berger's work, Miller
explains that according to this law, when a woman watches herself
being looked at by a man, she turns herself into an object of vision
(Miller, 184; Berger, 47). LFP, conforming to Miller's explanation,
fails to use her unique physical characteristic to define herself as her
own subject; she fails to use her lack of a nipple to counter LMP's
narrative—authored when he sees her covered breasts—about kiss-

ing her nipple. Instead, she interprets his desire to kiss the space her absent nipple vacates as "a lucky coincidence" (Landolfi, 121). She turns herself into an appropriate object for his gaze, fits herself into his story: "There's still hope for me! I could be a woman for at least one man!" (Landolfi, 121). With this assertion, she loses hope of winning the narrative stakes, telling her own story, defining herself. LFP's behavior coincides with Miller's description of Corinne's identity crisis. Miller writes, "cut off from the mobile *jouissance* of performance, through which she defies the conventional inscription of woman's body, Corinne seems to enter the borderline zones of an identity crisis; the state, neither subject nor object, that Kristeva describes as abjection" (Miller, 184).

LFP's nippleless breast defies the conventional inscription of a woman's body. According to this inscription, which ignores women's self-conception, men's *jouissance* is derived from bouncing breasts which attract men's gaze. Experiencing an identity crisis because she is physically unconventional, LFP strives to conform to patriarchal female identity. Her efforts reduce her to abjection; she is neither her own subject nor an appropriate patriarchal object. Instead of appreciating her physical uniqueness, LFP views herself as a flawed sex object and moves to a borderline patriarchal zone. Her nippleless breast, which (like Barbra Streisand's trademark nose) could represent an empowering symbol of personal identity, instead becomes "an object of pity" (Miller, 183) which causes LFP to be "brought down" (Miller, 183). Miller uses the words "brought down" to indicate that a deformed woman "bears in her body the image of Corinne's internal crisis" (Miller, 183). Similarly, according to my reading of "A Woman's Breast," male narratives about impossibly perfect breasts bring down women's self-esteem and cause women to experience the internal crisis Kristeva calls abjection. LFP's deformed breast represents how patriarchal narratives about the breast as object deform women's self-conception as subject.

Corinne, in contrast, reacts to a female breast and ruined female destiny in a manner which creates female narrative. Her response to a female use of a woman's breast motivates her to want to write. Miller explains that Corinne "is suddenly drawn to a statue of Niobe clasping her 'daughter to her breast with heartbreaking anxiety' and it is her powerful reaction to this figure that engenders for the first time since the separation from Oswald a desire to write. The choice of Niobe, who is a figure of ruined female destiny, is both a plausible and paradoxical embodiment of Corinne's grief" (Miller, 185). Corinne desires to write after she defines a statue depicting a breast as a communicative mode between mother and daughter; LFP sacrifices her self-definition after allowing LMP to define her uniquely marked breast. Corinne interprets "a figure of ruined female destiny" as a positive catalyst to her control over her own female destiny—as a powerful reason to resume writing. Unlike Corinne, instead of interpreting her breast as representing distinct female identity, LFP acquiesces to the male gaze and patriarchal imperatives and defines her breast as flawed anatomy. LFP's patriarchally defined breast never becomes a means for her to control her own story.

LMP enacts his fantasy at the expense of LFP's power to define herself. He reduces her covered, seemingly attractive breast to the parameters of his story. When confronted with the breast's true form, he again makes it conform to his narrative. LFP's breast, her natural anatomy, becomes LMP's breast: "My imagination transformed the obscene withdrawn nipple—or maybe it had never been visible—into an obscene beast cowering in the fissure of a crumbling wall" (Landolfi, 124). He finally controls the story of their encounter: "She made the grave mistake of becoming attached to me, whereas it is clear that these minimal episodes of our lives do not have, cannot have, any history" (Landolfi, 124). LFP mistakenly becomes attached to LMP's story about her breast—an episode which is not minimal to her. LMP wields the narrative power to define and make history. Despite the particular characteristics of LFP's breast, "A Woman's Breast" is about how men appropriate women's breasts, how women's breasts become men's breasts.

LMP recasts LFP's breast as a part of "the fragile wall" which forms human constructions of reality. In his words, "Everything ends badly, that goes without saying; and like the 'fragile wall' of her breast, everything crumbles" (Landolfi, 124). After one aspect of patriarchy ends badly and crumbles, a new patriarchal story routinely emerges from the rubble. LMP's first false story about LFP's covered "attractive" breast crumbles after he views the nippleless breast. He responds by building another story. LFP's own story is walled within male discourse. Like the statue of Niobe, she is forever an art object and forever cries.

"A Man's Breast" would more correctly describe Landolfi's story of a man taking possession of a woman's breast, of his protagonists' struggle for narrative control. Philip Roth's "The Breast" is a title which does not name gender as a part of the narrative battle represented by the potentially competing titles "A Woman's Breast" and "A Man's Breast." Roth's title gives no indication that his story is about a man who becomes a woman's breast. After David Kepesh's body crumples, his male voice emerges intact from within the wall of a breast. David explains: "I am a breast. . . . a mammary gland disconnected from any human form" (Roth, 449–450). The story of a man transformed into a breast is fantastic; the story of women transformed into breasts is real. The male gaze routinely changes women into breasts, causes women to become, like David, "the breast." By transforming a man into a breast, Roth rewrites the story of men transforming women into breasts.

Landolfi's and Roth's narratives negate the potential space of women's stories. In addition, both authors allow male protagonists to extricate themselves from horror stories. For Roth's male readers, the greatest horror results from witnessing the male voice enclosed within a female body part, not Kepesh's transformation into a breast. Annette Kolodny explains that some male English professors also experience a horror story about male voices contained in female spaces. As more women reach professorial status, more men seek alternatives to English departments. According to Kolodny, "the centers of professional prestige" shift "from departments to summer schools and institutes of critical theory" staffed "largely by white males from elite institutions" (Kolodny, 455). Kolodny explains why these men band together: "What must be understood is that yoking these men together was neither shared ideology nor shared practice but, instead, the appeal of establishing boundaries. . . . High-powered men were bent on fleeing not only an increasingly feminized professoriate, but, as well, an increasingly persuasive feminist practice rooted in literary history and the retrieval of lost traditions. In other words, the male 'muscle' of the profession aimed at theory *in order to* distinguish itself from feminism that had never been systematically theory-driven" (Kolodny, 455). These male professors seem to say Kepesh's words: I do not "wait with open lips for her breast to fill my mouth" (Roth, 460). To escape having their voices encased within female English departments, men shift centers of professional power from departments to summer institutes. These institutes, new spaces for male professional discourse, enable men to light out from female departmental territories. "The Breast," like male professors' move to summer institutes, is a story about men building new patriarchal structures after old ones crumble.

Although David's male body structure ceases to exist (and he lacks a mouth) he, nonetheless, speaks. He explains why this is so: "I am able to make myself heard through my nipple, and, faintly, to hear through it what is going on around me—I had assumed that it was my head that had become my nipple. . . . my voice, faint as it is, evidently emanates from the flab in my mid-section" (Roth, 450–451). David's nipple becomes a technological receiving unit, a flesh-made-antenna. His mid-section, a female body component emphasized by those who define women as walking wombs, is the place from which he speaks. Both his nipple and real women's bodies, when they are reduced to Woman-as-womb, generate male discourse. "The Breast" pictures Woman's body broadcasting patriarchal fictions.

While many women often collude with sexist images which reduce them to body parts, David rails against such treatment: "My face? Where is it! Where are my arms! My legs! Where is my mouth! *What happened to me?*" (Roth, 452). David, unlike some women, would not try to conform to advertising's sexist images. Advertisements routinely project images of decapitated women, disregard the severed heads, and focus upon breasts (or legs, or buttocks). One Kellogg's cereal commercial, a patriarchal fantasy of Woman as dislocated and controlled physical body, exemplifies this type of advertising. The camera focuses upon a headless, svelte female torso attired in a bathing suit. The torso forms a *K* when assuming a diving position. According to this particular patriarchal story, a woman's head is erased and her torso becomes a corporate text. The creators of the commercial expect that instead of echoing David's question— *"What happened to me?"*—most female viewers wish to become the svelte torso, to transform themselves into a male fantasy. Like so many Alices trying to assume the right size to fit a male wonderland, many women eat the Kellogg's cereal hoping to become smaller, hoping—after rewriting themselves as a special *K*—to fit the text of a male fantasy space. They hope to disappear as women by becoming Woman. Or, the headless female torso in the Kellogg's commercial is what Jardine calls women's "simulacrum: a female figure caught in a whirling sea of male configurations. A silent, mutable, head-less, desire-less, spatial surface necessary only for *His* metamorphosis" (Jardine, 217). The creators of the Kellogg's commercial expect women who watch the headless, diving torso to eat Kellogg's cereal to achieve a figure appropriate for plunging them into a sea of male configurations.

"The Breast" evokes metamorphosis relevant to Kellogg's as well as to Kafka. The Kellogg's commercial reduces women to a letter of patriarchal law. David also turns into a component of this law during his second transformation, a change from a breast to a penis. This change occurs when he orders his nurse to "fuck" him, to sit on his nipple with her "cunt" (Roth, 461). By making his body-as-breast function as a body-as-penis, David avoids having his voice encased within a female structure. Further, he experiences a third transformation: "The Breast" describes how a man who becomes a breast changes himself into a penis and ultimately becomes a phallus. David, a talking breast-as-penis, assumes phallic power. He defines his nurse as a "whore" (Roth, 461) and insists that all nurses should be young and beautiful (Roth, 462).

David's male voice which emanates from a female anatomical part effectively controls women. His phallic nipple, for example, literally silences his lover, Claire: she sucks this nipple, allowing it to engulf her mouth. David is not interested in Claire's voice. He imagines her reading his students' papers and recording his comments and grades (Roth, 465). Claire becomes "nothing but the female machine summoned each evening to service a preposterous organism that was once David Kepesh" (Roth, 464). Claire's story is a horror story whose most grisly element, rather than her involvement with David's transformation, is her lack of concern for her own professional transformation.

Although Claire is a Cornell Phi Beta Kappa, "she is still only a fourth-grade teacher" (Roth, 465). David teaches at a college; Claire teaches at an elementary school. This situation might be explained by the fact that Claire has breasts, that Claire is a woman. David plans to ask his mentor, Dean Arthur Schonbrunn, for permission to teach in the English department even though he is a breast. Schonbrunn laughs at David-as-breast—before David can articulate his request for employment (Roth, 466). If Claire wishes to become a professor, the dean might treat her as he treats David. Schonbrunn might view her as a breast and laugh. When David reads *Othello* aloud, he reminds himself that he is "a breast reciting" (Roth, 479). He realizes that his voice is abnormal and displaced. Academic women are often placed in the position of experiencing David's realization.

When dressing for success in masculine jackets, female academics cover their breasts, veiling the gaze of the patriarchal academic establishment. Jackets protect female academics from assuming the role of a breast reciting. Female academics—indeed, all professional women who try to escape sexism—articulate David's cry: "I'm not a breast!" (Roth, 475). While a "man cannot turn into a breast other than in his own imagination" (Roth, 467), men's imaginations can— and routinely do—change women into breasts. In order to act as professionals, women retransform themselves, change from breasts into people. Successful professional women have "out-Kafkaed Kafka" (Roth, 480). Instead of erasing themselves to become, for example, a patriarchal story's nonspecial *K*, they rewrite themselves according to their own story. They rephrase David's question: "Who is the greater artist, he who imagines the marvelous transformation, or he who marvelously transforms himself" (Roth, 480). Many men define a marvelous transformation as the ability to turn women into breasts, a definition which relegates women to a wasteland. To counter this definition, women can rewrite Eliot's dedication of *The Waste Land*, "For Ezra Pound, *il miglior fabbro*." They can act as female better makers who marvelously transform themselves from breasts into whole people. Female better makers transform themselves after realizing that patriarchal imagination is not marvelous.

Like the female voice speaking in a patriarchal system, David experiences himself "as speaking to others like one buried within" (Roth, 468). He sounds like a participant in a women's consciousness-raising group when he says, "I no longer believed I was a breast. . . . I sensed myself slowly turning back into myself. . . . I had only to stop whispering! I had only to speak out! . . . That when I believed I was speaking aloud, I was speaking only to myself? Speak up then!" (Roth, 473–474). David, the female/male voice within the breast, is no man in feminism, however. He becomes the center ring of a patriarchal circus. David plans "to make a pot of money" (Roth, 481) as people step right up to view a talking penile breast. He imagines selecting desirable women to insert "a cock as new and thrilling as my nipple" (Roth, 481) between their thighs. David "will be deliriously happy" (Roth, 481) debasing women during his nights at the circus. When fantasizing about his new male story about man-as-breast/cock, he undergoes a fourth transformation, changing from a breast to a penis to a phallus to a prick.

Landolfi and Roth do not describe positive transformations for women. However, the conclusions of their stories inadvertently allude to women's eventual victory in the battle of the gaze and the stakes of narration. "A Woman's Breast" ends by describing "joys that are not only ambiguous and twisted, but even fleeting" (Landolfi, 124). The jóys men derive from re-creating women as protagonists of male fantasies become ambiguous, twisted, and fleeting when women live in terms of their own stories. Or, according to the words from Rainer Maria Rilke's "Archaic Torso of Apollo" (which appear at the conclusion of "The Breast"), "You must change your life" (Roth, 483). Women change their lives when they reject patriarchal fictions. They can, for example, interpret the headless woman in the Kellogg's commercial as an archaic torso of Venus. If they are willing to do so, "the curve of the breast" might less effectively "blind" (Rilke; Roth 483) women's personhood. Feminist stories might emerge from the rubble after patriarchal stories become an ineffective "crumbling wall" (Landolfi, 124) within women's texts and lives.

Self-Experiment: Busting Out of Patriarchal Contours

Christa Wolf's SF critique of gender and science systems, "Self-Experiment: Appendix to a Report," is one such feminist story, a woman's counterpart to Landolfi's and Roth's stories of gender roles and anatomy. LMP authors the story of a woman's breast; David's male voice emerges from within a woman's breast; Wolf's unnamed female protagonist (I call her WFP) has a voice that is temporarily male. A drug called Peterine Masculinum 199 changes WFP into a man "without undesirable side effects" (Wolf, 113).

Acting according to patriarchal fictions, WFP at first concurs with her male professor's story concerning the sex-change drug. She explains that to "test your drug you needed someone like me. I wanted to bring you to the point of needing *me*. I had to prove my worth as a woman by consenting to become a man" (Wolf, 118). Despite her effort to emphasize "me," while participating in the professor's experiment, WFP rejects her femininity and enacts the role of a professional, masculine woman. "Self-Experiment" questions narratives which assert that, to succeed within patriarchal systems, women must behave like men. WFP's new ability to question this requirement for success is the most important result of the professor's experiment.

After being sensitized to patriarchal language's ability to construct sexist reality, WFP no longer acts as a character in the professor's male-authored text. Living within a male body enables her to learn how sexist words hamper women. For example, as a man, she does not become lost while driving; as a woman, after a driving instructor tells her that women are bad drivers, she "began to get lost in neighborhoods" (Wolf, 122). Recalling the negative effect of the male instructor's words, she realizes that derogatory fictions about women drivers (or generalizations such as "women who want to play first fiddle in the sciences . . . are simply doomed to fail" [Wolf, 124]) become truths. "Self-Experiment" emphasizes that male utterances are magic words which cause women to act out men's stories about femininity.[1] Like the professor's drug, men's words alter women.

WFP appropriates language and places words in a female space, a "womb of language" (Wolf, 122). She realizes that "language . . . can help me. . . . I am affected by the fates of certain words, and still what torments me most of all is longing to see *Verstand* and *Vernunft*, understanding and reason, long ago one and the same word in the carelessly creative womb of language but forced apart by our disputes, in brotherly union once again" (Wolf, 122). "Self-Experiment" advocates a linguistic transformation in which "understanding" and "reason" are not gender-specific. The story assumes that such a linguistic change is more difficult to accomplish than automatic pill-induced gender change. Because different words define women and men, women and men inhabit different worlds. "Man and woman live on different planets" (Wolf, 121, 125). Although women's and men's worlds are both derived from fictions (gender stereotypes), patriarchy makes male fictions real. Unlike LFP and Roth's Claire, WFP questions this practice. "But back to my planet" (Wolf, 122), she says, calling for interruption, a pause in the patriarchal process which negates women's words/worlds and reifies men's words/worlds.

Changing into a man named Anders, the Other, enables WFP to pause and understand that she lives according to the patriarchal definition of "professional woman." Her identity as Anders is a transitional space in which she changes from male-identified professional woman to woman in a male body to female woman. Only in her final stage is WFP fully human. As a professional woman, a person with a male mind and a female body, WFP's gender orientation is as jumbled as her Anders identity. During the time she exists as Anders, WFP learns that, as a male/female professional, she is Other in relation to both female and male identities. The professor's experiment—a more fantastic version of the patriarchal experiment which categorizes working women as either masculine professionals or feminine nonprofessionals (i.e., participants in the Mommy Track)—is a failure. Patriarchy and the professor both turn professional women into "nothing," not man or woman, an empty space.

WFP explains that Anders, who is a genderless male biological organism, not a man, is also an empty space: "The woman in me, whom I sought urgently, had disappeared. The man was not yet there" (Wolf, 125). Anders, a genderless being, neither parodies gender roles nor can be described in terms of gender roles. This person

who is "nothing but stylistic diversity and heterogeneity" epitomizes what Fredric Jameson ("Consumer Society," 16–17) describes
as the "moment at which pastiche appears and parody has become
impossible." During this moment, the words *his* and *her*, which do
not apply to Anders, become "speech in a dead language." Anders,
who functions as a pastiche of gender roles—a humorless "blank
parody" of gender roles—reveals that gender roles are something
constructed rather than "something *normal.*" This member of *Homo
sapiens* who cannot be categorized as either female or male evokes
"the end of individualism" defined according to gender roles, the
eventual "death of the subject" of people's worth calculated in terms
of gender roles.

WFP and her real-world female counterparts could benefit from
this particular demise. She is a single, childless doctor of physiopsy-
chology, "capable of summoning up masculine courage and manly
self-control" (Wolf, 114), who sacrifices her feminine individuality
to adhere to masculine gender roles. At first, she is akin to Isaac
Asimov's Susan Calvin, a human female scientist who behaves like
a robot. Unlike Calvin, though, WFP changes and connects lack of
self to lack of language. WFP learns that "person" means "Mask.
Role. Real Self. A prerequisite for language, it seems to me after all
this, must be the existence of at least one of these three conditions.
The fact that all of them were lost to me had to mean virtually total
silence. You can't write down anything about nobody. This explains
the three-day gap in my report" (Wolf, 127). As a male/female scientist and as Anders, WFP epitomizes the silent, empty linguistic
space she describes. Becoming Anders allows WFP to pause and dis-
cern that patriarchal language is not applicable to her particular female experience. Rejecting the necessity of living according to the
stories told in this alien language, she decides to use women's words
to inhabit her own woman's world.

WFP will no longer play the patriarchal game: "Dispassionate,
free and unattached, I was finally able to rise above a certain game
whose rules we had followed religiously for so long" (Wolf, 128). She
frees herself from adhering to patriarchal definitions, a game women
play to please men. She rewrites Susan Calvin's robotic role: "I no
longer found it dangerous to be part of that division of labor which
gives women the rights to sorrow, hysteria, and the vast majority of

neuroses while granting them the pleasure of dealing with outpourings of the soul (which no one has yet found outside of a microscope)" (Wolf, 128). WFP reappropriates "femininity" for women by attributing positive connotations to the word.

Confronted with this new definition, the professor acknowledges that WFP possesses a self independent of his control and needs. Her self-experiment, an appendix to the male report about what constitutes female reality, supplants his experiment. WFP rereads both the professor's experiment and patriarchy as flawed systems which degrade and exclude the feminine: "Your ingeniously constructed system of rules . . . all your withdrawal maneuvers were only an attempt to protect yourself from this discovery: that you cannot love, and know it" (Wolf, 130). She becomes a feminine scientist who rediscovers the importance of love.

Finally valuing her femininity, WFP elects to take "Peterine *minus* masculinum" (Wolf, 115), the antidote to Peterine Masculinum 199. Peterine minus masculinum acts as a "morning-after pill" capable of aborting the patriarchal language and images implanted within WFP. She is ready to embrace positive femininity, to experiment with living according to her own self-definition. WFP will undertake her own self-experiments, enact her own stories: "Now my experiment lies ahead: the attempt to love. Which incidentally can also lead to fantastic inventions—to the creation of the person one can love" (Wolf, 131). While creating a new female self—Woman as whole person who loves her female characteristics—WFP discards patriarchal roles and rules. Rejecting her psychological and physical male/female Anders role enables WFP to defy patriarchal master narratives about professional women who must construct themselves as men. She becomes a female self she herself can love. Her self-experiment reveals the appropriateness of marketing Peterine minus masculinum to women who participate in the real professional world.

Todorov's "Hesitation"; Heilbrun's "Awakening"

The female protagonists of *Lady Oracle, Persian Nights,* and *Small Changes* seem to ingest Peterine minus masculinum. Behaving according to feminist versions of Todorov's term "hesitation,"[2] they—

together with readers—pause to realize that living according to patriarchal narratives is problematical. Hesitation, which Heilbrun
calls "awakening," is a theme present in each of the three novels.
Each emphasizes that, in Heilbrun's words, "men tend to move on a
fairly predictable path to achievement . . . [while] women transform
themselves only after an awakening" (Heilbrun, *Writing*, 118). The
female characters' awakenings, their nonlinear lives, are hesitations
resulting in small changes, efforts to move from patriarchal reality
to women's worlds. These characters pause in the face of patriarchy
to engage in self-experiments which yield discoveries about self-
awareness. Atwood, Johnson, and Piercy transform their characters
from appropriate protagonists of Landolfi's and Roth's stories to protagonists feminist readers can love.

   Both Stanislaw Lem and Eric S. Rabkin explain why Todorov's theory of the fantastic should be expanded.[3] I offer another expansion
of Todorov's theory which is applicable to contemporary female protagonists who, after experiencing an awakening, create their own stories. According to Todorov, the "fantastic implies . . . not only the existence of an uncanny event, which provokes a hesitation in the
reader and the hero; but also a kind of reading which we may for the
moment define negatively" (Todorov, 32). Uncanny events "may be
readily accounted for by the laws of reason, but which are, in one
way or another, incredible, extraordinary, shocking, singular, dis-
turbing or unexpected, and which thereby provoke in the character
and in the reader a reaction similar to that which works of the fantastic have made familiar" (Todorov, 46). Misogynist stories are incredible, shocking (etc.), uncanny events readily accounted for by
the laws of patriarchal reason. Feminists who read *Lady Oracle*, *Persian Nights*, and *Small Changes* (along with the novels' female protagonists) resist sexist narratives about proper female roles by hesitating to accept the patriarchal uncanny. Shocked after encountering
the victimized female protagonist (the patriarchal uncanny), feminist readers identify with her, hesitate, and wonder how she (and
they themselves) will survive. The protagonist also hesitates (awak-
ens), questions the patriarchal uncanny's control over her life story.
She pauses to create space in which to rewrite herself. In turn, "the
actual reader identifies . . . [herself] with the character" (Todorov,
33) and reads patriarchy negatively. This hesitation and negative

reading open a new narrative space—a specifically feminist version of the fantastic—which makes room for creating and enacting women's stories.

Atwood's Joan Foster, Johnson's Chloe Fowler, and Piercy's Miriam Berg and Beth Phail respond to patriarchal constructions of their reality by hesitating, creating textual interventions, and opening space in uncanny patriarchal narratives for women's stories. They awaken, remake/rewrite themselves, and like Wolf's female protagonist, transcend some of the sexist stories which retard women. Their revisionary self-experiments coincide with Robert Scholes's observation that Todorov's emphasis upon poetics, "truly understood, is a liberation from prejudice, an opening of the mind, creating new opportunities for readers and writers" (Scholes, *Fantastic*, vii–viii). Atwood, Johnson, and Piercy know that Todorov's emphasis upon poetics truly understood in feminist terms reveals new opportunities for readers, writers, and characters to hesitate when confronted with patriarchal narratives. I now turn to these authors' depictions of the awakening of their female protagonists.

Zones in Which to Negate the Patriarchal Uncanny

Elaine Showalter provides a context, in terms of space, to understand the new opportunities available to Atwood's, Johnson's, and Piercy's characters. *Lady Oracle, Persian Nights*, and *Small Changes* describe the new women's stories which result after female protagonists hesitate, refuse to enact the patriarchal uncanny. These stories reveal that women are ready to inhabit the space Elaine Showalter calls the "wild zone" and to extend this zone's boundary so that it can encroach upon the territory of the patriarchal real.

Showalter's "wild zone" is derived from the work of cultural anthropologist Edwin Ardener, who categorizes women as "a *muted group*, the boundaries of whose culture and reality overlap, but are not wholly contained by, the *dominant (male) group*" (Showalter, 261). She applies Ardener's model about silencing and perception, his point that muted groups must communicate in terms of dominant structures, to current feminist theory. To ensure clarity, like Showalter, I include Ardener's diagram which pictures his notion of the relationship between muted women and dominant men:

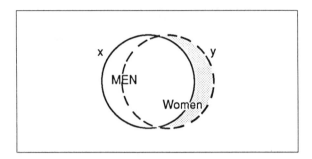

As Showalter explains, Ardener uses intersecting circles to represent the dominant and muted groups. Not all of muted circle Y falls
within dominant circle X. A crescent or zone in X is forbidden to
women; a similar zone in circle Y, called the wild zone, is outside
the dominant boundary and, hence, represents women's culture (Showalter, 262).

Showalter's wild zone differs from Brian McHale's description
(which I discuss in chapter 3) of the heterotopian "zone" (McHale,
43–58). The wild zone, unlike the postmodern heterotopian zone,
is not plural, is not "a space of overlapping subjectivities" (McHale,
44). Chloe Fowler, Beth Phail, and Joan Foster want to make the wild
zone resemble a heterotopian zone. They attempt to push back the
boundary of circle X, which separates the wild zone from dominant
patriarchal reality, and, when doing so, they enact what McHale
calls "the strategy of interpolation" (McHale, 46). (McHale defines
this strategy as "introducing an alien space *within* a familiar space"
[McHale, 46].) These characters try to introduce the wild, alien
space of women's culture within the dominant, familiar space of patriarchal culture. Their behavior is quite subversive. McHale explains that Barthelme's version of Paraguay (in the story "Paraguay")
is the *"negation"* of real-world Paraguay (McHale, 48–49); I point
out that feminist zones negate real-world patriarchy. When Beth,
Chloe, and Joan try to transform the fixed spaces pictured on Ardener's chart into postmodern heterotopian zones, they threaten to
"overrun" (McHale, 58) patriarchal world boundaries.

I want to explain exactly how Chloe, Beth, and Joan manifest this
subversive behavior. I do so below in terms of Showalter's observation that "the 'wild zone' of women's culture" can be thought of

"spatially, experientially, or metaphysically" (Showalter, 262). Chloe, Beth, and Joan, respectively, enter the wild zone's spatial, experiential, and metaphysical components.

Chloe in the Spatial Wild

Showalter defines the spatial wild zone as "an area which is literally no-man's-land, a place forbidden to men, which corresponds to the zone in X which is off limits to women" (Showalter, 262). Prerevolutionary Iran, a country which will be forbidden to both American women and men, functions as Chloe's liberating, woman's "no-man's-land," a spatial wild zone in which to escape both American sexism and, as a Western woman, its Iranian counterpart. All Americans were muted in Ayatollah Khomeini's Iran. He redefined Iran as a dominant space forbidden to all Americans, a no-Americans'-land. His narratives recast Americans as metawomen, despised Others ousted from all the spaces in his country. Chloe experiences a personal revolution while witnessing these circumstances. No longer a muted housewife denied access to dominant social spaces, she enters a newly discovered place of female self-importance. This place is a postmodern zone which results from introducing the alien (according to Chloe's point of view) space of a foreign country and that country's silencing of Americans within the familiar space of an American woman's repression.

Beth in the Experiential Wild

Beth Phail is denied access to dominant American space when she assumes a new identity to live with her lover, Wanda, a person forced "underground." Beth enters an experiential wild zone as a lesbian who enjoys "aspects of the female life-style which are outside of and unlike those of men" (Showalter, 262). Her experience as a woman's spouse is outside of and unlike those of men who are women's spouses. She introduces the alien (from the point of view of patriarchy) space of a woman acting as another woman's spouse within the familiar definition of the word "spouse."

Joan in the Metaphysical Wild

Joan Foster is a writer who reinvents herself as a female character; her entrance into the wild zone is metaphysical, "in terms of consciousness" (Showalter, 262). Unlike Chloe's experience as an American in Iran, or Beth's experience as a woman's spouse, Joan's decision to appear to die—to rewrite herself as another female identity—has "no corresponding male space" (Showalter, 262). Newspapers, texts of the real-world's social record, define Joan's imaginary death as real. As a living deceased person who can read her own obituary, Joan inhabits the wild zone, a space of female life renewal. Her at-once real (from patriarchy's point of view) and imaginary (from her own point of view) death enables her to introduce the alien space of women's culture within the familiar space of patriarchal culture. Since she *is* alive, she does live within patriarchy. But because reality defines her as dead, she also lives outside reality's cultural imperatives. Hence, Joan moves the boundary between wild and dominant space. This woman who diets to reduce her body size enlarges the wild zone.

Emancipatory Strategies

After learning to hesitate before enacting patriarchal stories, Chloe, Beth, and Joan enter the wild zone and incorporate its liberating characteristics within their lives. Their hesitation yields positive female textual spaces for women's stories. They treat their lives as texts, revise themselves, and, after doing so, break out of limiting social spaces. Their transformed (or rewritten) lives—transformations available to real-world women—are female-centered narratives about women vacating muted social spaces. Even though they have hitherto not been defined as postmodern, I advocate placing such examples of feminist fabulation as *Lady Oracle*, *Persian Nights*, and *Small Changes* within postmodern canons. These novels are, after all, feminist metafictions (or, fictions about patriarchal fictions). The novels portray women who challenge master narratives about necessarily subordinate female lives, define these narratives as fictions, and refuse to live according to such fictions.

Patricia Yaeger, in this same optimistic vein, argues that feminist critics should focus upon the positive aspects of female characters' textual reality. She suggests exploring the textual spaces in which women describe their own desires (Yaeger, 1). Like Yaeger, I want to show that "women have shattered male plots, have successfully

called upon verbal resources that are unavailable to their male contemporaries" (Yaeger, 29). Some of Yaeger's observations in *Honey-
Mad Women: Emancipatory Strategies in Women's Writing* support
my point that Beth, Chloe, and Joan take positive action when they
shatter male plots. Yaeger states that "the woman writer's response
to interruption may be more emancipatory than we have seen" (Yaeger, 293). I add that Beth's, Chloe's, and Joan's hesitation to live as
protagonists of patriarchal stories exemplifies interruptions which
emancipate female characters, widens spaces within patriarchal narratives for women's full self-expression. Further, while the woman
writer is productively engaged in "making gaps in . . . language and
filling in these spaces with other words, with abnormal speech"
(Yaeger, 45), Beth, Chloe, and Joan open a gap in patriarchal discourse and fill it with "abnormal" female experience. They replace
patriarchal stories about women with their own stories about themselves. Responding to patriarchal stories by hesitating to accept
them—by interrupting them—is a positive means for the female
character "to interrogate and to challenge the very voices that tell
her to conform" (Yaeger, 59). Hesitation enables her to enter an
"unenclosed space" (Yaeger, 78).

   Yaeger relies upon Hannah Arendt's notion that "language has 'natal' power" (Yaeger, 95; Arendt, 11), that language can instigate the
new, what Arendt calls a "second birth" (Yaeger, 96; Arendt, 176–
177). Words, according to Yaeger, "usher us into the space of dialogue . . . into a space where the unexpected can happen" (Yaeger,
96). Atwood, Johnson, and Piercy use language as a means for their
female protagonists to rewrite themselves—to give birth to themselves. Language's natal power enables the characters to become
new people. They experience a second birth of self when initiating
a new dialogue with patriarchy which gives primacy to women's
interpretations of their own lives. Such newly important interpretations thrust female characters into a space of dialogue where hitherto unexpected female actions happen. Chloe re-creates her self-
conception while positioned in an alien national space; Beth and
Miriam change themselves by exchanging spaces; Joan rewrites herself after transforming the space of her reality into a textual space.

   For these characters, hesitation is an emancipatory strategy involving wars of words, battles to replace men's stories about women with women's versions of themselves. Unlike Landolfi's female protagonist, they win the war; they control the stakes of narration and change their identity. Beth and Chloe transcend the housewife role. Miriam, the potentially powerful intellectual woman who chooses to be a housewife, is their foil who, ultimately, welcomes their liberating solution. Joan, a romance novelist, redefines "real" and "imaginary" after literally becoming the newly born woman.

Although patriarchy reads the protagonists' transformations as small changes, these changes are both crucial and necessitated by an inability to fit patriarchal narrative roles. All the characters are the wrong size. Joan is too fat. Beth is too small: "She was convinced she had been bred to be miniature, like a toy poodle or a dwarf peach tree" (Piercy, 16). Miriam is too big: "Big, awkward, shy, she felt like something acquired at a rummage sale, one of those awful coats her mother got from resale shops" (Piercy, 95). Regardless of the protagonists' particular shape, patriarchal narratives reduce them to one size which fits all women—small in relation to men's large stories. Beth's husband, Jim, for example, "was expanding and she was contracting" (Piercy, 33). Unlike Carroll's Alice, these women cannot drink or eat something which will transform them into an appropriate size. They enlarge themselves by rewriting themselves. The following three sections describe Chloe, Beth and Miriam, and Joan as lady oracles who claim power to control their future.

"Whose Life Is It, Anyway?": Chloe Fowler/Chloe Linden

Moving from the United States to Iran helps Chloe confront patriarchal narratives. Freed from the role of housewife as hostage to the nuclear family, she feels purposeful abroad: "In America her life is safe because she can take the toaster and pick up the children from school. Here it is useless, without function. How strange, then, that it should be here that she feels full of purpose and calm" (Johnson, 162). She redefines "useless," learns to attribute this word to chauffeuring electric appliances.

Chloe's realization that she is not "the most unliberated woman she knew" (Johnson, 17) forms the crux of *Persian Nights*. She deconstructs patriarchy's story of women by interpreting her own actions, authoring her own life role. In other words, she provides an affirmative answer to her own question—"Was it necessary to decide on your own character?" (Johnson, 311–312). Chloe becomes useful as an expert on Sassanian pots, not as "being the appendage" (Johnson, 135): "She had surprised herself by having a gift for the painstaking work of fitting shards together. From a heap of fragments she could find matching bits with a facility that amazed the real archaeologists" (Johnson, 135). Chloe herself becomes a real archaeologist. She possesses "an unusual talent" (Johnson, 135) for reconstructing pots, and she is a talented archaeologist of self-knowledge. Chloe painstakingly fits together shards of her desires and transforms the matching bits into a whole object—the narrative of her life.

When Chloe realizes that her archaeological talent should not be buried beneath her role as mother, wife, and household manager, her psychic digging enables her to enter a new experiential episteme. Being "an expert on Sassanian pottery" (Johnson, 135) becomes more meaningful to her than bringing her toaster to an expert on toasters. Chloe unearths herself in Iran. By placing Chloe in Iran without her husband, Jeffrey Fowler, Johnson helps readers to reinterpret women's roles in the American patriarchal system. Chloe reexamines her identity from the standpoint of Iran, an alien space outside that system: "'I'm an archaeologist in far-off Iran. I'm nobody's wife,' said Chloe, distantly" (Johnson, 223). Like some inhabitants of SF feminist utopian planets, Chloe remakes her female self in a different world. Ironically, she finds freedom from patriarchy in an Iran on the brink of a revolution which will strengthen patriarchy. Chloe, then, experiences a postmodern contradiction: she critiques a system from within that system.

Chloe learns to read her life as a "terrorist text" (Yaeger's term), to explode her self-conception as an unliberated woman. *Persian Nights* is Johnson's "ecstatic espionage, her expropriation of the language she needs, her own invention of a 'terrorist text'" (Yaeger, 3). Vahid Farmani, Chloe's Iranian host, judges her to be "the very perfect choice for a spy" (Johnson, 122). Chloe—no espionage agent who appropriates men's secret stories of other men—reconceives her life as a terrorist textual version of a housewife's story, an alternative story about assuming men's active social role: "It occurs to her that she is tasting some of the fun and power of being a man, being far away, on her own, working at something" (Johnson, 149). Chloe authors her terrorist text after replacing a narrative about appropriate wifely behavior with the language she needs—words which articulate her desire to enjoy fun and power.

Iran, Chloe's wild zone, functions as a space in which her role as wife is not an encumbrance. Jeffrey's absence allows her to develop her own woman's narrative, to define herself as something more than "a pretty appendage to Jeffrey Fowler" (Johnson, 96). Chloe, who states that she is the only member of her American social circle without a reason to be in Iran (Johnson, 75), later negates this statement. Realizing that she is abroad to spy upon opportunities to achieve improved self-awareness, she delivers the intelligence she gathers about her own story to herself. Chloe reads in a spy novel that "women can easily pass for one another. To the eye of a guard, women are interchangeable" (Johnson, 203). She defies the eyes of male guards whose gazes police and erase women in Iranian and Western cultures.

Despite the advantages that living alone in Iran will afford her, Chloe hesitates to board the plane and, to alleviate her anxiety, attempts to read Jeffrey's feelings: " 'I can't possibly go by myself,' she said firmly. . . . 'Are you [Jeffrey] sure you don't want me to come?' she kept saying, always expecting to surprise a glint of relief at the offer [to return with Jeffrey to their San Francisco home], but receiving no clue at all to his feelings if they were different from those he was expressing" (Johnson, 15). Confronted with her husband's face as blank page, she boards the plane and journeys toward an opportunity to learn to read herself. She makes her decision by default. Through omitted detail, Persian Nights itself reflects Chloe's hesitant lack of initiative: the text never directly states that Chloe boards the plane when it almost immediately progresses from "the Tehran plane was loading" to "on the plane she had been reassured" (Johnson, 15). The point is that Chloe's hesitation to undertake the trip unexpectedly signals her entrance into the fantastic. From the perspective of her life in America, the freedom Chloe experiences while alone abroad is unreal.

In *Persian Nights*, hesitation deconstructs patriarchy's story of men as well as its story of women. When some American men (including Chloe's friend Dick and her lover, Hugh) accompanied by a male Iranian witness an art theft, the Americans, counter to the narrative about heroic male action, hesitate to intervene. Only the Iranian acts—and he is killed: "They had seen Abbas run toward the shooting, toward the men, and they, American men, had not run. If they had dashed out after Abbas to save the relics of Persepolis, then they would all have been shot" (Johnson, 277). Hesitating to adhere to the patriarchal story about male heroes most certainly serves these American men's best interest. Nonetheless, since men are forbidden to enact feminine pauses in response to dangerous situations, Chloe's male friends cross "the dominant boundary" (Showalter, 262) of acceptable male behavior. In other words, they enter an experiential wild zone situated beyond macho stereotypes.

Dick understands his position within this zone in terms of popular culture. He explains: "All those movies you saw as a kid, you knew it was supposed to be you running in a zigzag pattern through the line of fire to save something" (Johnson, 277). When faced with a real line of fire, Dick hesitates to assume a movie hero's role. However, because this role is so potent, Dick, deciding that his sensible decision not to take action is agonizing, silences his experience: "No need to tell Chloe or Junie [Chloe's friend] about this notion, since there was nothing to tell, strictly speaking, about that moment of hesitation more agonizing in retrospect than at the time. . . . Hugh, Dick felt sure, would also not tell" (Johnson, 277). He hopes silence will shield him from the derogatory labels ("coward," for example) which brand men who experientially enter "female space" (Showalter, 262), the wild zone forbidden to men.

Hugh counters Dick's expectation about remaining silent. Unafraid to reveal his deviation from the macho role, Hugh admits that "Abbas ran out at that point. . . . We sort of stood there" (Johnson, 278). Hugh's words exemplify a male emancipatory linguistic strategy. Not hesitating to speak about his agonizing moment of hesitation causes him to become heroic. He announces his feminized position and dignifies a new story about male roles. *Persian Nights* asserts that narratives about men who never fail to face the line of fire are stereotypical fictions. The art theft incident "became a story: they [the American men] wove it together sitting in the hot car waiting for Abbas to come walking up with the keys" (Johnson, 278). Abbas, who acts according to male roles, never returns. His death marks a gap in the patriarchal story of male heroism. Hugh, in contrast, lives to reinterpret his own life story in nonpatriarchal terms.

In addition to portraying "feminine" retreat as life-saving, the art theft incident emphasizes that female spaces are as effective as male spaces. Chloe finds shelter in a specifically female space, "the ladies' toilet" (Johnson, 273); Dick hides in a toolshed (Johnson, 274). This detail signals that like "Self-Experiment," *Persian Nights* rejects stories about women achieving success by acting like men. In addition, Johnson emphasizes that men also sometimes lack appropriate narrative space. Hugh informs Chloe that men are not asked to articulate their feelings about obligatory masculine competence:

"But you haven't even asked me how I feel. In fact no one ever does ask. *You* never ask. I'm just useful. I do everything, not that I mind, but it's I who make reservations, arrangements . . . and I get beaten up and lied to and stranded in Iranian hotels or [*sic*] sneaking around in the dark all the time to visit you, and getting up at five in the morning, did you think I liked that?" . . . She saw to her surprise that a tear stood in his eye, at his pitiable lot.

She was stricken. His accusations were perfectly true: she let him do everything and didn't try to understand him. Was it because he was so tall? She was struck speechless with the remorseful conviction of her own callousness. (Johnson, 310–311)

Hugh is "terrorized by the texts of others" (Yaeger, 3), victimized by the myth that men (especially tall men) are always efficient. Like Chloe, then, Hugh requires narrative space to discredit damaging stereotypical stories. Johnson open-mindedly implies that narrative can also victimize men, that women might consider being more sensitive to men's need to discuss emotions. Feminists can rewrite patriarchal narratives as well as understand pitiable men's tears. Men are not always narrative villains in relation to women's voices.

The American men survive the art theft incident by casting aside the male heroic role; Chloe survives this incident by casting aside the female helpless-victim role. She tells herself that she cannot expect a man to save her: "Anyway, the thought came to her, you have to save yourself; no one is going to come and save you" (Johnson, 258). Here, Chloe's behavior differs from her hesitation to fly to Iran. Lacking a male rescuer, she does not hesitate to save herself. Her life depends upon her ability to understand herself and to read men, not men's power to interpret her: "But whether she now stays here or moves, in which direction moves, how clearly understands the temper of the men out there, will affect whether she dies or survives" (Johnson, 269–270). Her efforts to read men, unlike her attempt to interpret Jeffrey's feelings in the airport departure lounge, now result in self-preservation rather than self-erasure.

Chloe's remade self-conception manifests itself in her language, her ability to empower feminine conversation. She uses "shirts," a word which often signals women's domestic role, as a means to question Hugh about his whereabouts: "'You had nine shirts done at the Tehran Hilton and you said you weren't there,' cried Chloe all at once to Hugh. He looked surprised at this sudden accusation. . . . 'You just thought no one would notice the shirts, not notice that you didn't turn up for ten days!'" (Johnson, 281). When Chloe does not hesitate to use "shirts" aggressively, Johnson's narrative reverses the usual hierarchy of female and male stories. Facing the line of fire becomes a foolish act leading to male obliteration; "shirts" becomes an assertive word leading to female affirmation. *Persian Nights* portrays the death of the macho male hero (Abbas), the emergence of the feminine male hero (Hugh), and the presence of newly empowered feminine narrative ("shirts" as linguistic weapon).

A more powerful linguistic weapon victimizes Chloe's Iranian friend Noosheen. As a consequence of trying to escape the patriarchal text her culture and husband espouse, Noosheen literally is transformed into an indelible patriarchal text. A man throws ink on her while she shops in the bazaar (Johnson, 176), marking her as a subversive woman. *Persian Nights* hesitates immediately to identify the liquid covering Noosheen.[4] This textual hesitation indicates discomfort with Woman-as-patriarchal text, with "something invented by people who hate women enough to mark them, maybe to hurt them" (Johnson, 177–178). Noosheen realizes that the ink's ability to hurt her depends upon interpretation. Her awareness addresses the point that supposedly indelible patriarchal interpretation can be reinterpreted when a feminist community creates its own self-definition. Together, Chloe and Noosheen begin to create such a community.

Chloe, now a rescuer and mentor, helps Noosheen to try to escape a bad marriage and encourages her to read Victorian poetry (Johnson, 92–93, 201–203). Noosheen's thwarted escape has little impact upon her freedom: women can never leave patriarchal countries. Those who emigrate merely move from one patriarchal governmental narrative system to another. Noosheen, like Chloe, emancipates herself after reinterpreting existing male narratives. She derives power from positioning Matthew Arnold as an advocate of her version of Iranian revolution. Noosheen explains, "I am translating poetry. There are certain poems of Matthew Arnold that I think will be an inspiration to others in the cause, only I am not putting his name on. Oh, I am not putting my name, no fear, it's just that I am afraid a Western poet would not be well received, so I am putting 'Ancient Persian Manuscript'" (Johnson, 297). She erases the male author, writes over his text, makes his text speak as she sees fit. Noosheen reads Arnold—and her own life—as terrorist texts. She proclaims herself to be a professional reader of Victorian poetry; Chloe proclaims herself to be a professional archaeologist piecing together Persian culture. Both women cross cultures, experience different patriarchal rules to redefine themselves.

At the conclusion of her stay in Iran, Chloe realizes that there are no more rules: "She has, for a moment, a sensation of perfect indifference to her personal fate; she will marry or not, will divorce, will suffer illness and die; she is for an instant serene in knowing that it will all happen as it will happen" (Johnson, 326). Chloe, as the author of her own life, is not obligated to conform to either patriarchal or feminist texts. Her contradictory decisions regarding whether or not to eat caviar reflect her freedom of choice. After becoming uninterested in caviar, she wants to eat a large amount of it—behavior which at once conforms to and contradicts Yaeger's description of the honey-mad, language-mad woman who frantically satisfies her oral desires: "Caviar, thought Chloe. So emblematic of all luxury, all desire. She didn't want any. . . . She will eat both the tins of caviar herself, is her thought. . . . At least, she certainly won't give one to Jeffrey" (Johnson, 332, 338). She is ambivalent about the amount of caviar she wishes to eat; she is certain about eschewing the luxuries women garner from living according to feminine, marital roles. Neither Iranian nor American society will consume Chloe.

Her narrative freedom is signaled when, past the novel's midpoint, readers learn that "Fowler" is not Chloe's sole appropriate surname: "He [Hugh] thinks of her as Chloe Fowler, which she is really not, she is Chloe Linden" (Johnson, 186). This information jolts readers who have not hesitated to associate Chloe with her husband's name. Heilbrun's insights about women's names indicate that a new name signals Chloe's new self-acceptance. According to Heilbrun, "women have long been nameless. They have not been persons. Handed by a father to another man, the husband, they have been objects of circulation, exchanging one name for another. . . . women who began to write another story often wrote it under another name" (Heilbrun, 121). Chloe Linden begins to write another story about herself. The new information about Chloe's name reflects her new hesitation to view herself as an appendage of Jeffrey Fowler. Rewriting female identity by substituting the name of the husband with the name of the father is less than revolutionary, however. Chloe's lack of a nonpatriarchal surname might reflect the dearth of established alternatives to patriarchal societies. Chloe cannot board a plane and fly to a women's country.

Nonetheless, her final plane flight shows that she has progressed from enacting the housewife role to living as a person. Chloe, who at the novel's conclusion "crowds herself in among the people climbing up the metal steps" (Johnson, 338) of the plane leaving Iran, has taken major steps toward freeing herself from patriarchal definitions. In a manner appropriate to her new independence, unlike her uncertain arrival, she departs from Iran without hesitation: "All airplanes, all steps and bags and seats in the world are alike and she is home already" (Johnson, 338). She returns to her home as a changed person.

"Whose phallus is it, anyway? The Father's? The Mother's?": Miriam Berg/Mrs. Neil Stone; Beth Phail/Naomi Burns/Cindy

Beth and Miriam change themselves by becoming each other. Beth extricates herself from the victimized, undereducated-housewife role; Miriam, whose academic success could save her from Beth's initial domestic position, embraces domesticity. Beth's and Miriam's first identity shifts result, respectively, from hesitation and lack of hesitation. Soon after Beth's husband, Jim, destroys her birth control pills (Piercy, 41), she pauses to recognize her powerlessness. Due to Jim's behavior, Beth realizes that marriage differs from the romantic fantasy story she once hoped to enjoy. Miriam, on the other hand, becomes Phil's lover, abandons her professional aspirations, and does not hesitate to define her relationship with Phil as a fantasy: "It was a fantasy, so she knew just how to behave. She did not hesitate" (Piercy, 100). Miriam immediately replaces her reality (a potentially successful career) with mythic desire about enacting romantic fantasies with male wastrels. She views her sexual relationship with Phil's friend (Jackson) as "a myth born full-fledged within her . . . she leaped into it. . . . He is The Man. . . . This is more real than anything gone before" (Piercy, 190). The Man becomes more important to her than her career. While leaping to embrace the tale of The Woman as The Man's sexual handmaid, Miriam erroneously concludes that her "previous life seemed vacuous by comparison" (Piercy, 195). Beth, in contrast, leaps into a situation resembling Miriam's previous life.

Beth tries "to make a center to" her "life that isn't a man" (Piercy, 247). She tries to replace The Man with what Miriam voluntarily relinquishes—The Self. Like women who buy Joan Foster's romance novels, Beth reads to escape her domestic reality. She encounters Colette and wonders how "could a book be more real than a marriage?" (Piercy, 34). Colette's female-authored texts function as emancipatory strategies for Beth. Acting in direct contrast to Miriam's behavior, Beth is "tired of the whole mythology of love and marriage, which seemed much of a piece with the rest of her daydreaming" (Piercy, 37). She emancipates herself by defining her husband as a mere character, a signifier of patriarchal fiction: " 'Jim' was a character made up as she used to make over her daily life for her diary" (Piercy, 37).

Beth's decision to rewrite herself as a new character extends beyond her diary to reality. As Joan Foster becomes Louisa K. Delacourt, Beth Phail becomes Naomi Burns (Piercy, 46) and, later, Cindy (Piercy, 526). Naomi Burns's room of one's own in Boston is "a free space she thrived in" (Piercy, 47). Instead of existing as a blank page eventually to be covered with patriarchal writing, Beth covers the walls of her room with her own writing: "She made love to her room by writing mottoes on the wall" (Piercy, 48). She marks her territory, uses words to make love to her own space, creates (in the manner of Twombly) untitled graffiti. Beth flouts rules about respecting property to signal that she defines herself as something more than a man's property.

While name change functions as an emancipatory strategy for Beth Phail, Chloe Linden, and (as I will explain below) Joan Foster, the same does not hold true for Miriam. When Miriam Berg becomes Mrs. Neil Stone, she figuratively becomes Miriam Fail. She is, in other words, erased: "Married women were twice invisible" (Piercy, 459). Miriam ceases to exist: "Miriam Berg was dead. . . . Mrs. Stone was nobody in particular" (Piercy, 475). Miriam has no story. Her life consists of "being dull and bored and servile. I feel as if my life is over" (Piercy, 515). As a married woman, she "was always exhausting old motifs" (Piercy, 97). The story of her marriage, a literature of exhaustion about wives' roles, continually reenacts old motifs.

Beth confronts exhausted female roles by becoming a visionary artist who, like Piercy, imagines new possibilities for women. "I make a new world in my head" (Piercy, 249), Beth says. She creates these worlds as a member of a women's theater group (Piercy, 410). The group, when articulating women's stories in a particularly female space, creates "theater that speaks for women. That can pull women out of their solitary cells. . . . Wanda [the group leader] made them aware how they moved, how they rested, how they occupied space" (Piercy, 419, 427). Their women's performance art, which Jeanie Forte describes as "a specific strategy that allies postmodernism and feminism" (Forte, 218), is feminist metafiction, female stories about how patriarchal fictions limit movement in patriarchal space. (Or, in Forte's words, "the woman performance artist may work to uncover her own zones of resistance to the patriarchal 'text' of society, exemplifying the search for an alternative to patriarchal discourse, one in which women can speak their own experience, as subjects, from a non-patriarchal frame" [Forte, 229].) Beth's unencumbered movement in theater space differs from the Stone family's house, an area Neil transforms into a staged domestic space for enacting fictions which restrict Miriam. Neil refuses to allow her to dance in the house (Piercy, 447). The women's theater, in contrast to the Stone household, is an alternative public space, "a powerful force, that makes women's truths visible and moving" (Piercy, 443). *Small Changes* suggests that it is not too late for Miriam to embrace women's truths.

Miriam ultimately recognizes marriage's limitations. "I hate you! I hate you! I wish I'd never met you!" (Piercy, 389), she informs Neil. Finally hesitating to live according to the story of the nuclear family, she imagines replacing this story with a fantastic narrative. She pictures her children as stars, her son, Jeff, "a warm orange star," her daughter, Ariane, a "blue-white star" (Piercy, 537). Miriam too is a star: "She would not pulsate a full rich orange . . . but she would emit a dim warm red glow—not so bright as she had used to, perhaps, but steady and a bit brighter than it had been in a few seasons" (Piercy, 537). She can shine at the center of her own text. Miriam's belated hesitation to accept herself as a mere body orbiting Neil (or any man) portends her decision to rewrite her life as a feminist story.

Beth's and Miriam's emancipatory strategies can be understood in terms of "A Woman's Breast" and "The Breast." These women do not wish to be reduced to improperly sized breasts. Miriam explains: "It was like this terrible embarrassment suddenly hung on the front of me that was in the way and which everybody else looked at before they looked at me—maybe it [her breasts] was all they saw" (Piercy, 88). Beth describes her fantasy about her small breasts: "I'd take off my clothes. Then my husband would look at me and say, 'Well, is that all?' Then he'd throw me out" (Piercy, 88). Unlike Roth's David Kepesh, Beth and Miriam become breasts and transform themselves back into people. So does Joan Foster.

"Whose ruse is it *then*? And whose *gynesis*?": Joan Foster/Louisa K. Delacourt

Young Joan speculates that a boy perceives her fat body "as a single enormous breast" (Atwood, 107), a self-image which remains with her even after she becomes a thin adult. She describes herself as "just a kind of nourishing blob" (Atwood, 236). Regardless of her size, patriarchy reduces Joan to a breast, a blob. She wishes to change her life story, to transform herself from a breast to a human.

Joan creates alternative narratives as a means to confront patriarchal narratives. As an author of popular, subversive costume gothics, she hesitates to accept patriarchal reality. Joan describes "the pure quintessential need of my readers for escape, a thing I myself understood only too well. Life had always been hard on them and they had not fought back. . . . Escape wasn't a luxury for them, it was a necessity" (Atwood, 34). Instead of fighting back effectively, Joan's readers cast themselves as characters in patriarchal stories. She creates alternative textual space for women to express their "hidden selves" (Atwood, 34). This liberating space, like E. Ann Kaplan's understanding of "utopian postmodernism," concerns "a movement of culture and texts beyond oppressive binary categories" (Kaplan, 4). Joan deals in "hope" as she offers "a vision of a better world, however preposterous" (Atwood, 35).

She searches for a title "with the word *Love* in it; love was a big seller" (Atwood, 32). Her search reveals that patriarchy is itself a trash novel written by those who sell love and manipulate women to "sell out" in pursuit of love. Joan's novels assert that patriarchal scripts about love require women to suppress themselves. She is able to extricate herself from this script by erasing her role as Arthur's wife, rewriting herself, creating a new self. Joan enters a fantastic world in fact: she can comment upon the manuscript she wrote at the time of her death (Atwood, 29).

Gaps in Joan's life experience—an absent father and the lack of dates with boys—enable her to avoid some negative aspects of female sex-role socialization and facilitate her decision to "start being another person entirely" (Atwood, 18). Her father is a blank space, a variable story told by the word of her mother. He "didn't come back until . . . [Joan] was five, and before that he was only a name, a story, which my mother would tell me and which varied considerably" (Atwood, 72). Joan, a fat adolescent who is the daughter of an invisible father, is invisible within the sexual arena. She describes discovering that "there was something missing in me. This lack came from having been fat. . . . I'd never developed the usual female fears. . . . I wasn't whistled at or pinched on elevators, I was never followed down lonely streets. I didn't experience men as aggressive lechers but as bashful, elusive creatures who could think of nothing to say to me and who faded away at my approach" (Atwood, 155). Fat, for Joan, acts as a force field to repel patriarchy.

Joan does not lose weight to conform to "proper" patriarchal images of women. Instead, she reduces to adhere to a particular female text, the provision in her Aunt Lou's will which stipulates that Joan must become thinner before she can inherit money. Weight loss empowers rather than diminishes Joan; she learns that she can change herself. Lou's will is a textual and financial catalyst to Joan's decision to rewrite her life.

Adhering to the cliché that there is safety in numbers, Joan creates another version of her identity. If patriarchy destroys one version, she can depend upon the other. Hence, unlike Miriam Berg, she enjoys adventures with men without sacrificing her goals. For example, a man called the Royal Porcupine provides an adventure for one of her selves: "The Royal Porcupine had opened a time-space door to the fifth dimension, cleverly disguised as a freight elevator, and one of my selves plunged recklessly through" (Atwood, 274). Joan's multiple-self approach to dealing with men enables her to add a new dimension to marital fidelity: she uses men to eradicate the influence of other men. When she is with the Royal Porcupine, Arthur becomes "unreal . . . an insubstantial ghost" (Atwood, 289); when she is with Arthur, the Royal Porcupine becomes a "daydream" (Atwood, 289). Instead of erasing herself in order to enjoy heterosexual relationships, Joan enjoys heterosexual relationships which, from her perspective, erase men. While engaging with Arthur and the Royal Porcupine, she writes her life as her own story.

Joan describes herself as a complex plot: "My life was a snarl, a rat's nest of dangling threads and loose ends. I couldn't possibly have a happy ending, but I wanted a neat one" (Atwood, 326). She revises her life's plot, fakes her own death, and transforms herself into a text. Joan survives by killing her former self. As she explains, "I pretended to die so I could live, so I could have another life" (Atwood, 347). She rewrites her life in opposition to patriarchal narrative.

After the publication of Lady Oracle, Joan seems to inhabit a woman's space in outer space. Reviewers say that she bursts upon the literary scene "like a comet" (Atwood, 261) and she reflects upon the nature of comets, imagines that comets men name resemble women: "Lumps of cosmic debris with long red hair and spectacular tails, discovered by astronomers, who named them after themselves" (Atwood, 261). Contrary to this description of men naming female images, Joan charts her own orbit and renames herself. The name "Joan" will not do. "Joan" evokes Joan of Arc and other heroic women who "gave a lovely light; a star is a blob of burning gas. . . . The English cheered as Joan went up like a volcano, a rocket, like a plum pudding" (Atwood, 370–371). Instead of functioning as a powerful, glowing space entity, Joan of Arc becomes analogous to a burned plum pudding. According to Joan Foster, there is no positive metaphorical space in space for Joan of Arc. Evoking Joan of Arc reminds Joan Foster that stories about women's lovely—and personally harmful—light must be changed.

When ascending literary comet Joan Foster rewrites herself as Louisa K. Delacourt, she alters destructive stories about shining women. She maintains her forward trajectory by functioning as a positive rocket rather than as a burned plum pudding—and she hints that her writing will incorporate science fiction: "But maybe I'll try some science fiction. The future doesn't appeal to me as much as the past, but I'm sure it's better for you" (Atwood, 379). The past includes the story of Joan of Arc burning at the stake like a star or a rocket; the future might include the story of female starship commanders moving beyond terrestrial patriarchal stories about women's lives which end as ash heaps.

This potentially positive story can characterize future reality if women abandon debilitating patriarchal stories and master affirmative female narrative. Joan certainly does so. In Yaeger's words, Joan discovers "the word's productive power as a natal moment, a discovery of the word as a deed which might allow . . . [the] heroine to enter the world in a new way" (Yaeger, 107). Words enable Joan to give birth to her self, to reenter the world as her own positive mother rather than as patriarchy's underprivileged foster child.

Beth, Chloe, and (eventually) Miriam share Joan's discovery about how words enable women to give birth to themselves. The protagonists' self-experiments and hesitations allow them to claim a particular magic word—"'Myself.' The magic word" (Atwood, 64). They live according to the narrative Joan's acquaintance finds in her fortune cookie: "*It is often best to be oneself*" (Atwood, 257).[5] Rather than being restricted by patriarchal stories—such as the story which portrays women as breasts—they create productive female narratives. They interrupt and disrupt patriarchal stories while seeking alternatives to living as something other than full people (representations of breasts, for example). Their hesitation to conform to patriarchy's story of women propels them into a liberating feminist space, a place which is fantastic in relation to restricting patriarchal imperatives. Newly ensconced within this space, Beth, Chloe, Joan, and Miriam conduct self-experiments which lead to discoveries about the transformations described by feminist terrorist texts.

Their discoveries answer Jardine's questions: Whose life? Whose phallus? Whose ruse? Whose gynesis?[6] Beth, Chloe, Joan, and Miriam learn to live in terms of phallic power. They question the ruse of defining patriarchal stories as the only possible master narratives which can shape human reality. One cannot hesitate to understand that their self-experiments and transformations regarding placing female narratives within patriarchal master narratives result in gynesis which belongs to women.

Hence, unlike theorists of postmodernism, Atwood, Johnson, and Piercy are not concerned with the *gynema*, the object produced by the process of gynesis which is "neither a person nor a thing, but a horizon" (Jardine, 25). But, although the gynema as "a reading effect" (Jardine, 25) is not at the heart of these women's agenda (they emphasize patriarchy's real impact upon real female persons, the limitations placed upon women's horizons), the same cannot be said for the notion of the gynema as a literal writing effect. Theorists of postmodernism place "a woman-in-effect" (Jardine, 25)—which has nothing to do with real women—within texts which themselves conform to the properties of scientific reality. I close this chapter by discussing how writing which is not a thing—texts which do not conform to the usual physical characteristics of writing—has something to do with real women.

"We all write in invisible ink anyway": Mastering Female Narrative

I have described the efforts of female protagonists to achieve feminist subjectivity through rewriting patriarchal stories. Narratives about changing writing's physical characteristics reflect their efforts. Since, in terms of feminist poststructuralism, "social reality has no meaning except in language" (Weedon, 34), changed, unreal writing can yield changed social reality. Authors who describe fantastic textuality hyperbolically point to the need to "pay full attention to the social and institutional context of textuality in order to address the power relations of everyday life" (Weedon, 25). Fantastic, alternative textuality pictures feminist theoretical discourse about women's alternative language modes.

Joan Foster exemplifies this picture when she creates supernatural writing which defies science; words fantastically appear on her page: "When I would emerge from the trance, as I suppose it could be called, there would usually be a word, sometimes several words, occasionally even a sentence, on the note-pad in front of me, though twice there was nothing but a scribble" (Atwood, 247). Joan explains that her poems are dictated by "a spirit hand" (Atwood, 265). Her "experiments with Automatic Writing" (Atwood, 265) automatically subvert writing's ability to provide structures for patriarchal reality. Automatic writing at once does not conform to scientific laws and questions other patriarchal laws. Twombly pictures this "unexpected form of 'automatic writing' [as] an apparently uncomposed and unstructured repetition of cursive gestures" (Varnedde and Gopnik, 96).

Vonnegut's *Slaughterhouse-Five*, which challenges the patriarchal story of war, proposes that unstructured writing itself can subvert patriarchal order. This male-authored text imagines a feminine language mode (Tralfamadorian writing), which—in terms of Chris Weedon's discussion of Kristeva's and Cixous's notion that feminine signification forms threaten the rational symbolic order and are placed at the margins of discourse (Weedon, 69)—is not rational and threatens the symbolic order's sovereignty. Tralfamadorian texts exist outside human notions about beginnings, middles, and ends:

> We Tralfamadorians read them [texts] all at once, not one after the other. There isn't any particular relationship between all the messages, except that the author has chosen them carefully, so that, when seen all at once, they produce an image of life that is beautiful and surprising and deep. There is no beginning, no middle, no end, no suspense, no moral, no causes, no effects. What we love in our books are the depths of many marvelous moments seen all at one time. (Vonnegut, 88)

Tralfamadorian texts contain no patriarchal story, no order. Tralfamadorians can read everyone's story all at once.

Billy Pilgrim views Tralfamadorian texts as "brief clumps of symbols separated by stars" (Vonnegut, 88). Similarly, Yuri, a protagonist of Jane Palmer's *The Planet Dweller*, describes texts formed by planets: "Long ago I discovered that some of these small planets briefly formed patterns. . . . the more I study them, the more I become convinced that these patterns are not natural even though they have orbits more eccentric than I am. It is as though something is turning and guiding them to take different positions in the sky without interrupting their trajectories. . . . Then I discover one big major pattern spread across the sky" (Palmer, 24, 81). When reading planets, Yuri replaces paginated space with outer space as page. The "something" turning and guiding the planets is beyond patriarchal science's control.

Atwood, Palmer, and Vonnegut describe spaces (supernatural spaces, alien spaces, and outer space itself) which make pages and patriarchal narratives obsolete.[7] By discussing texts derived from fantastic origins, they suggest that alternative stories yield alternative realities. The hesitations, transformations, and self-experiments I describe in this chapter indicate that female narratives are best mastered by changing the relationship between writing and power.

Ursula K. Le Guin communicates this point in "Sur," a story about female adventurers who refuse to mark their presence at the South Pole.

Instead of perpetuating the myth of man's control over nature, Le Guin's protagonists enact a new story about ultimate human powerlessness. Their story indirectly critiques a male astronaut's decision to place a flag on the moon and, hence, create an illusion of power. Like all unmaintained man-made objects, this flag will eventually cease to exist. Le Guin's explorers, who leave no sign of themselves at the Pole, imply that writing is another futile assertion of human permanence, another object reflecting the temporary existence of humans and their endeavors. In other words, writing ultimately becomes invisible. Joan Foster's supernatural writing is not fantastic. Jong's Leila explains why this is so: "*We all write in invisible ink anyway, our words flying up to heaven like so many cinders from hell flying toward the face of God, whose radiance vaporizes them*" (Jong, 353).

If "we all write in invisible ink anyway," then women might master female narrative by refusing to juxtapose writing and mastery. Women can empower themselves by eschewing patriarchal power constructions and revising the definition of power. Madeleine Kunin's decision not to seek a fourth term as governor of Vermont exemplifies how a woman can rewrite her life according to this revised definition. Kunin explains:

I think our democratic political system is kept alive and vital when people like me understand that public service in the form of holding political office is not a lifelong occupation. Power is difficult to release. What enabled me to arrive at this decision with a new sense of purpose was the realization that there are other ways to create change. I want to write a book. I want to develop new ideas and strategies on global environmental issues, and I want to continue to inspire women to reach their full capacity. (*Ms.*, 59)

Kunin describes a self-experiment regarding her personal self-government. After hesitating to accept the patriarchal story about a lifetime quest for political power, she decides to devote herself to creating narratives which inspire women's transformation. She will mark the world by writing her life according to "other ways," alternatives to patriarchal stories about texts, identity, and power. She is another female explorer who does not desire to place a flag to mark her achievement.

Feminist SF protagonists meet their different selves;[8] feminist realistic fiction protagonists—and real-world feminist women—can change themselves into different people. Men seize the day; women "seize upon their own stories, and . . . tell them with a directness that shocks as it enlightens" (Heilbrun, 64). Changed stories inspire people to create changed reality—and enlarged female spaces are a part of this change. Heilbrun states that she was drawn to detective fiction because she "must have wanted, with extraordinary fervor, to create a space for" herself (Heilbrun, 113). The female protagonists I discuss echo Heilbrun's desire to create personal space. Heilbrun's detective stories, like other examples of female narrative, provide clues about how best to establish female spaces. Virginia Woolf, in *A Room of One's Own*, seems to hint at one solution to this mystery. Woolf seems to say that self-experiments about reinventing womanhood cannot be conducted outside a particular woman-controlled room—a feminist laboratory.

René Magritte, **The Rape,** *1934. The Menil Collection, Houston.*

Gender and the Literature
of Exhaustion

> *Writing has been run by a libidinal and cultural—*
> *hence political, typically masculine—economy . . .*
> *where woman has never* her *turn to speak—this be-*
> *ing all the more serious and unpardonable in that*
> *writing is precisely* the very possibility of change, *the*
> *space that can serve as a springboard for subversive*
> *thought, the precursory movement of a transforma-*
> *tion of social and cultural structures.*
> —Hélène Cixous, "The Laugh of the Medusa"

The previous chapter describes feminist writing as a springboard for subversive thought,
a literary space of personal transformation
which can inspire social and cultural transformation. This concluding chapter continues to give woman *her* turn to speak by suggesting
that she thwarts literature's typically masculine economy and replenishes patriarchal stories. Writing in terms of gender and the literature of exhaustion, she looks at patriarchal myths "straight on"
(Cixous, 255) and rewrites them as positive women's stories. Feminist writers act as Medusas who petrify the male-centered literary
tradition. To counter the literature of exhaustion, they replenish literature, offer new female versions of male-centered stories. They
give woman her turn to speak through a mouth she represents and
controls, a mouth which bears no resemblance to René Magritte's
image of the exhausted story about reducing female individuality to

sexuality. Magritte's *The Rape*, like this chapter and its predecessor, implies that, contrary to patriarchal myths, breasts substitute neither for woman's eyes nor her "I"—her identity.

I begin this chapter by identifying Kate Chopin and Elizabeth Stuart Phelps as precursors to contemporary female literary replenishers. I explain that Chopin's "Her Letters" describes female textual power and that Phelps's "The True Story of Guenever" infuses Arthurian legend with a female perspective. I move from Chopin's merger of empowerment and words to Phelps's recast Arthurian legend to Elizabeth Scarborough's "The Camelot Connection," a rewritten version of "The True Story of Guenever." Then, after discussing John Barth's rereading of himself, I analyze women's and men's specific methods of retelling classical myths. The next section's attention to gender and rewritten contemporary corporate myth follows the discussion of gender and rewritten classical myth, in which Christa Wolf's *Cassandra* and Barth's "Dunyazadiad" illuminate each other. I point out that Thomas Pynchon's *The Crying of Lot 49* and Sandi Hall's *The Godmothers* present differing responses to corporate myths regarding information dissemination. I then position Doris Piserchia's *Star Rider* as an example of feminist literary replenishment. In the chapter's final section, which focuses upon feminist textuality, I explain how texts within E. M. Broner's *Her Mothers* and Italo Calvino's *Cosmicomics* themselves engender feminist texts.

Awakening to the Importance of Woman's True Story: Chopin's Male Edna Pontellier, Phelps's Rewritten Guenever, and Scarborough's Feminist Guinevere

When Cixous speaks "about women's writing: about *what it will do*" (Cixous, 245), her words seem to describe the depiction, in "Her Letters," of female narrative's potential power. The unnamed female protagonist in Chopin's story (I call her CFP) decides not to destroy her love letters, which describe an adulterous affair, her story. She attaches a message to the letters instructing her unnamed husband (I call him CMP) not to open them and to destroy them (Chopin, 136). After CFP's death, CMP finds the letters and throws them into a river: "It [the package of letters] vanished silently; seemingly into some inky unfathomable space. He felt as if he were flinging it back to her in that unknown world whither she had gone" (Chopin, 139). CFP and her letters both vanish into an inky unfathomable space, an unknown world of female silence. From the standpoint of this space, CFP's written message has the textual power to punish CMP, to forever bar him from knowing her story.

This textual power dictates that CMP must learn about CFP by examining texts other than her love letters. He seeks clues when reinterpreting his male friends' conversations: "He had heard the empty boast [about commanding women's affections] before from the same group and had always met it with good-humored contempt. But tonight every flagrant, inane utterance was charged with a new meaning, revealing possibilities that he had hitherto never taken into account" (Chopin, 139–140). CMP, a failed detective, looks futilely in male utterances for new meanings about a woman's story. Turning from spoken language to the written word, CMP exhausts himself by rereading all the books CFP owned. He searches for marked passages in the books which might provide clues about her letters' content: "Then began a second and far more exhausting and arduous quest than the first, turning, page by page, the volumes that crowded her room—books of fiction, poetry, philosophy. She had read them all; but nowhere, by the shadow of a sign, could he find that the author had echoed the secret of her existence" (Chopin, 140). CMP seeks a woman's story while rereading volumes which probably contain men's old stories. Overcome by the impossibility of accomplishing his objective—reading, as a woman, Woman in terms of the patriarchal literature of exhaustion—CMP drowns himself in a river, the only possessor of CFP's story (Chopin, 142). He engulfs himself in "the song of the water" (Chopin, 142), merges with "her and her secret thought in the immeasurable rest" (Chopin, 142). He enters the space of women's lost song.

"Her Letters" discusses patriarchal attitudes toward women's stories according to an allegory in which CFP is Everywoman living under patriarchy. She retaliates textually, writes counter to silenced female thought, by both refusing to destroy her letters (and, hence, her story) and attaching a message which empowers her words. She controls her husband's behavior; CMP acquiesces to the textual power of CFP's message when he chooses not to ignore or to reinterpret her words. He allows the message to function as a female text which prohibits access to other female texts (the letters). The message acts as a "no trespassing" sign which designates the letters to be a private space. This sign instructs CMP to play a woman's game according to female textual rules. He cannot win. His awakening to the importance of women's stories occurs too late. "Her Letters" is the story of how female textual power destroys a man. When CMP acknowledges this power, he becomes defeated Woman—a male, drowned Edna Pontellier. CMP's fate is a feminist power fantasy in which a woman's text dooms a man who wishes belatedly to read it. "Her Letters" advocates punishing men who wait too long to read and appreciate women's stories. (Chopin might not approve of *Men in Feminism*.) Like separatist feminist utopias, "Her Letters" describes gender schism and signals that some women are not concerned with communicating with men.

Chopin's story about female textual power (in which both the female and male protagonists die and a woman's story is forever lost) is not a positive alternative to male textual power. In other words, it is not constructive incessantly to produce exhausted versions of ignored women's tales and feminist separatist role-reversal revenge tales. Instead, the literature of exhaustion might, as Phelps's "The True Story of Guenever" indicates, present retold women's and men's stories, endless versions of human literature. Phelps challenges the patriarchal story of Guenever by denying that the queen is "unclean" (Phelps, 68). Her Guenever never faces public execution after deviating from patriarchal stories. In Phelps's story, "burnt toast" (Phelps, 74) describes ruined food, not a ruined woman about to be burned at the stake.

Phelps refocuses Arthurian legend, shifts its emphasis from battle arenas to domestic arenas, from knights on quests to nights at home. Instead of describing men peering into fire-breathing dragons' mouths, Phelps mentions that "Queen Guenever had the toothache" (Phelps, 68). She recasts Guenever's adulterous behavior as a bad dream caused by toothache medication, "Launcelot's laudanum!" (Phelps, 79). Guenever is still Arthur's "honored wife. There was no Launcelot, no wilderness. The soul which the King had crowned with his royal love was clean, was clean, was clean!" (Phelps, 79). Phelps's Guenever is no feminist, however. She is a loyal wife, who, at the story's conclusion, looks within "her husband's eyes [where] the safe, home fire-light shone" and listens to "the birds of paradise. . . . This . . . is the true story of Guenever the Queen" (Phelps, 79).

"The True Story of Guenever" contradicts its own conclusion. Phelps's Guenever story emphasizes the queen's marital dissatisfaction, not her positive response to paradisal home fires. This "clean" Guenever is free to remain the object of Arthur's gaze. "His shining, kingly eyes" will continue to look "down on her like stars from Heaven" (Phelps, 74). Arthur does in fact look down on Guenever, calling her, for example, a "little woman" (Phelps, 75, 78). Although Guenever listens to the birds of paradise and enjoys Arthur's heavenly looks, her domestic life relegates her to passionate limbo. She is unhappy about Arthur's inadequate expressions of affection (Phelps, 70–71). This queen as little woman is unable to shine in a domestic space she herself would consider to be heavenly.

"The True Story of Guenever," which suggests that Guenever cannot be true to herself, questions woman's role within patriarchy. Sans Launcelot, Phelps's Guenever is, nonetheless, still a victim fated to remain dissatisfied with Arthur. In Phelps's rewritten Camelot myth, Guenever continues to conform to a patriarchal story: rather than facing public execution for committing adultery, she privately extinguishes herself in the role of "clean"—and unhappy—wife. Phelps's Guenever lacks an appropriate space outside patriarchal stories. Instead of shining like a star from heaven, she endures a sanctioned domestic life as Arthur's proper conjugal shadow; she is restricted by the "very pale" Arthur's passionless "grave and repressed manner" (Phelps, 79). "The True Story of Guenever" is appropriately anthologized in *Haunted Women: The Best Supernatural Tales by American Women Writers*. Guenever experiences a living death as a repressed ghost who must bury her passion.

Phelps announces the crux of her rewritten tale at its inception: "Song and story, life and death are so cruel to a woman" (Phelps, 67). Although Phelps's Guenever remains a victim, the author posits a course of action for herself and—by implication—for readers and future writers. This action is described by the statement "I rebel against the story" (Phelps, 68). Rebellion is crucial to considering the literature of exhaustion in gendered terms. Contemporary fantasy writer Elizabeth Ann Scarborough, for example, rebels against Arthurian legend when she recasts Phelps's rewritten Guenever.

Scarborough's "The Camelot Connection" seems to respond to "The True Story of Guenever" by liberating the queen. Scarborough's Guinevere is a feminist who speaks for Phelps's silent Guenever. Guinevere tells her true story: "You'd think when a person got to be Queen she'd get a little respect but no. . . . and the first time I show the slightest sign of having a little crush on someone everybody cries 'Burn the bitch!' . . . Trying to be a decent Christian queen is most unrewarding" (Scarborough, 65–66). This contemporary Guinevere emerges from Arthur's shadow and rejects both the King and Lancelot. She explains, "I've been clinging to Lancelot because being in Arthur's shadow has made me feel so helpless and inadequate, but I don't really need either of them" (Scarborough, 66–67). Scarborough's rereading of Phelps's rereading exemplifies women's positive contribution to the literature of exhaustion—a replenished female literature of reclamation. "The Camelot Connection" coincides with a feminist rereading of John Barth's "The Literature of Exhaustion."

Read It Again, John

Barth himself rereads "The Literature of Exhaustion" with an eye toward allowing the spaces between its lines to tell a new story. Barth states, "Rereading it now, I sniff traces of tear gas in its margins; I hear an echo of disruptions between its lines. Its urgencies are dated" (Barth, "Exhaustion," 64). His olfactory and auditory senses are poised to intercept new stimuli—such as an urgently needed feminist reinterpretation of "The Literature of Exhaustion." One such reinterpretation might assert that tear gas emanating from conservative critics' canisters has been sprayed upon literary postmodernism. This tear gas produces a temporary blindness, a failure to see that women's writing can be defined as postmodern. The gas, though, is losing the ability to marginalize feminist literature and hamper the feminist critical establishment's demonstrations aimed at enlarging the patriarchal canon. The echo of disruption Barth hears is a call to expand literary postmodernism's definition in order to make room for feminist retold stories. The blinding tear gas keeping women's texts situated outside postmodernism is dissipating to reveal a crystal-clear vision: more feminist writers deserve admittance to postmodernism's almost-all-male club.

Contemporary female authors can experience an artistic victory of the kind Barth attributes to Borges. According to Barth, Borges confronts an intellectual "dead end and employs it against itself to accomplish new human work" (Barth, "Exhaustion," 70). Teargassing women's contributions to literary postmodernism—blurring their importance—is an intellectually dead-ended practice employed to subvert new human work. Within the academic community, this practice might become as unfashionable as articulating sexist and/ or racist stories. Publicly telling such stories to elicit humor has become unsuitable to academe. Such discourse has become an exhausted communicative form which has reached "the moment at which pastiche appears and parody has become impossible" (Jameson, "Consumer Society," 16).[1] Within the academic world, public sexist and racist humor has become pastiche, "blank parody, parody that has lost its sense of humor" (Jameson, "Consumer Society," 16). Academic audiences no longer laugh at sexist and racist narratives. If postmodern literature is not going to join the sexist and racist slur as another dead-ended academic communicative mode, then it is necessary for this literature to include a "new component" (Jameson, "Consumer Society," 17)—patriarchy as a retold tale.

Many scholars and writers now judge sexist and racist stories to be "Baroque" according to Barth's understanding of Borges's use of the term. Barth explains that "Borges defines the Baroque as 'that style which deliberately exhausts (or tries to exhaust) its possibilities and borders upon its own caricature.' While his own work is *not* Baroque . . . it suggests the view that intellectual and literary history has been Baroque, and has pretty well exhausted the possibilities of novelty" (Barth, "Exhaustion," 73–74). The Borgesian Baroque is applicable to literary postmodernism, the current intellectual and historical moment which, with few exceptions, includes only men's experience. This exclusivity exists even though possibilities for most white men's stories are becoming exhausted, devoid of novelty, and resemble caricature.[2] The white male story is reaching a dead end. Many literary scholars no longer want to hear it. Their impatience is reflected by the scarcity of MLA convention panels devoted exclusively to white male authors, the emphasis in the *MLA Job List* for black candidates to teach black literature, and the widely held opinion that black women are America's most highly regarded contemporary novelists. The MLA has replaced its former emphasis on nothing but white male literature with, in Jameson's words, "nothing but stylistic diversity and heterogeneity" (Jameson, "Consumer Society," 16). Linda Hutcheon's "ex-centric" fills the space the exhausted white male tradition vacates.

Barth explains that literary scholars (Robert Alter and Ihab Hassan, for example) describe postmodern fiction as being "more and more about itself and its processes, less and less about objective reality and life in the world" (Barth, "Replenishment," 200). Male postmodern writers usually focus upon men and male processes, not upon women's reality and its impact upon life in the world. Feminist fabulation, on the other hand, explores life in the patriarchal world by rewriting patriarchal stories and exposing their fictionality. Rewriting patriarchy enables feminist fabulation to become "vitalized" (Barth, "Replenishment," 200), and, in turn, feminist fabulation vitalizes postmodern literature. Hence, feminist fabulation's relationship to male postmodern canons exemplifies Barth's point that "artistic conventions are liable to be retired, subverted, transcended, transformed, or even deployed against themselves to generate new and lively work" (Barth, "Replenishment," 205). Placing ex-centric female voices within postmodern literary canons facilitates enabling "what is gropingly now called postmodernist fiction" to "be thought of one day as a literature of replenishment" (Barth, "Replenishment," 206).

"Woman" vitalizing and replenishing texts pertains to Jardine's "gynesis." Jardine explains that "woman" acts as a catalyst for propelling new discourse modes forward: "[T]he putting into discourse of 'woman'" is "somehow intrinsic to new and necessary modes of thinking, writing, speaking" (Jardine, 25). In addition, Jardine focuses on women writers and critics when she observes that feminist criticism's energy "has changed the face of American literary criticism" (Jardine, 53) and that this energy yields at-once strange and familiar readings. These readings are "the key to a new feminist reading and writing style" (Jardine, 53). Before discussing Barth's description of the "key" and the "treasure" in "Dunyazadiad," I wish to emphasize that the key intrinsic to a new and necessary vitalization of postmodern fiction is "the putting into" of real women's concerns within the discourse of this fiction.

Feminist reading and writing styles and real-world experiences change the face of postmodern fiction. Barth omits this observation when he states that "'The Literature of Exhaustion' is about the exhaustion of what Hugh Kenner called 'the Pound era'" (Barth, "Replenishment," 206). Naming a literary era after one white male should be an exhausted custom. If women's contributions to postmodern literature are not recognized (if, for example—randomly choosing the name of one well-known male metafictionist—"the Barth Era" follows "the Pound Era"), then what is gropingly called postmodern fiction might be exhausted quickly. After all, uncanonized ex-centrics create the literature of replenishment. Scarborough's Guinevere, for instance, adds ecological awareness to the Arthurian legend. She says: "I don't think our peasants should continue this strip-and-burn method of agriculture any longer. There must be more efficient and attractive ways to farm. It's dangerous too—look there, they've burnt down the village while they were at it" (Scarborough, 68).

Scarborough's "The Camelot Connection" vitalizes mythological characters by imbuing them with contemporary concerns. The next section focuses upon works which function similarly, Barth's *Chimera* and Christa Wolf's *Cassandra*. I explore how a female and a male author replenish literature through their differing approaches to re-creating mythological characters.

Sherry's Recast Razor and Cassandra's Thundering "No," or, the Gift Horse and the Female Mouth

Wolf and Barth allow mythological literature's female characters to speak again and to confront the lack of attention directed toward women's stories. However, while Barth and his Scheherazade (the protagonist of "Dunyazadiad," called Sherry) ultimately collude with patriarchy, Wolf and her Cassandra do not retreat from their confrontation with patriarchy. Wolf rewrites mythology in a particularly antipatriarchal manner; Cassandra fares better than Sherry. While Barth, to evoke humor, describes kings who murder women, Wolf dismisses death-centered stories and creates literature which "no longer wants to tell coherent stories held together by war and murder and homicide and the heroic deeds which accrue to them" (Wolf, "Conditions," 262).

Wolf's "Conditions of a Narrative: Cassandra" rewrites Barth's "The Literature of Exhaustion" from a feminist perspective. According to Wolf, empowering women's words and generating alternatives to linear narratives can replenish exhausted patriarchal literature.[3] Her "narrative network" questions Western thought's singular, linear narrative. She asks: "Why should the brain be able to 'retain' a linear narrative better than a narrative network, given that the brain itself is often compared with a network? . . . Everything is fundamentally related; and . . . the strictly one-track-minded approach . . . damages the entire fabric. . . . Yet to put it in simplified terms, this one-track-minded route is the one that has been followed by Western thought" (Wolf, "Conditions," 262, 287). *Cassandra* and "Dunyazadiad" are both structured as alternative, related narrative networks, not one-track-minded linear narratives. *Cassandra* is a nonchronological narrative about the past of a protagonist who can see the future. Sherry's tales are collaborative, simultaneously past and future stories she derives from consulting a Barth-look-alike genie who repeatedly circles between her present and his past.

Sherry voices a lengthy lament about her unfair position within patriarchal stories (Barth, *Chimera*, 43). She tries to thwart patriarchy by telling her little sister Dunyazade (called Doony) a new story. Sherry says, "There *is* no victory, Doony, only unequal retaliation; it's time we turned from tricks to trickery, tales to lies" (Barth, *Chimera*, 45). This new story, a plot to castrate her own and Doony's future husbands (Shahryar and Shah Zaman) by resorting to lying and trickery, proves to be ineffective. Sherry critiques patriarchy, tries to create space for woman's voice, and tells Doony about an ineffective means to counter patriarchy. The sisters fail to use new stories to create space for themselves outside patriarchal boundaries. Although the women spend their wedding nights holding razors to their bound husbands' genitals, intact men happily emerge from nuptial bedrooms (Barth, *Chimera*, 64). Barth leaves men's stories and genitals uncut. He allows Sherry to speak as a feminist without liberating her.

Sherry insists upon teaching Doony about the power of words. According to Sherry, "it's in the words that the magic is . . . but the magic words in one story aren't magical in the next. The real magic is to understand which words work, and when, and for what; the trick is to learn the trick" (Barth, *Chimera*, 15). "Dunyazadiad" stresses that the magic words in feminist stories are not magical in patriarchal stories, that patriarchy denies women the trick of effective illocutionary force. Men's words control women's actions and deny power to women, a circumstance made apparent when Doony holds the aforementioned razor to Shah Zaman's genitals. Although Shah Zaman is tied to the bedposts, as I have explained, he nonetheless manages to save himself: "The King shrugged his eyebrows and whistled through his teeth; two husky Mamelukes stepped at once from behind a tapestry . . . seized Dunyazade by the wrists, covered her mouth, and took the open razor from her hand" (Barth, *Chimera*, 49). A man's nonlinguistic communicative modes—body movement and whistling—effectively nullify a woman's story about gaining power. Sherry does not utter magic words when she tells Doony to "cut his bloody engine off and choke him on it, as I'll do to Shahryar!" (Barth, *Chimera*, 46). In patriarchal stories, kings understand which words enable them to continue "raping a virgin every night and killing her in the morning" (Barth, *Chimera*, 13). In patriarchal stories, women do not understand which words enable them to castrate and silence kings.

Patriarchal stories, myths which validate men who rape and kill women, deny women the magic words to stop the raping and killing. Patriarchy manufactures and reads myths to suit its needs. As Wolf explains, learning to read myth involves "a readiness to give oneself to the seemingly frivolous nexus of fantastic facts, of traditions, desires, and hopes, experiences and techniques of magic adapted to the needs of a particular group—in short, to another sense of the concept 'reality'" (Wolf, "Conditions," 196). Patriarchy, then, can be defined as a magical—in the sense of the relationship between Barth's "magic words" and illocutionary force—technique of adapting fantastic facts, traditions, desires, and hopes to the needs of men's particular group sense of the concept reality. "Dunyazadiad" can be understood in terms of the relationship between feminist fabulation and mythic patriarchal master narratives.

Barth ends "Dunyazadiad" with words pertinent to the definition of feminist fabulation: "The key to the treasure is the treasure" (Barth, *Chimera*, 64). As I explain in chapter 1, Scholes's structural fabulation concerns how Man finds the key to information regarding his place in the universe—a key to patriarchal master narratives. Feminist fabulation concerns how Woman finds the key to information regarding her place in patriarchy—a key to female narratives devalued by patriarchal myths about women's inferior texts. When feminist literary theorists believe the myth that feminist fabulation is subliterary genre fiction, they collude with another myth—a story which places Woman in a patriarchal labyrinth and defines her as the monster. Feminist fabulation serves as Woman's guiding thread. It is both the key and the treasure, the object of the Barthian genie's effort to locate the "treasure-house of new fiction [which] lay vaguely under his hand, if he could find the key to it" (Barth, *Chimera*, 19). If the genie, the magical male director of women's stories in "Dunyazadiad," lifts his hand from clasping, controlling, and covering women's stories, he will find an undervalued literary treasure—feminist fabulation, the literature of replenishment, the key to invigorating exhausted male stories.

Sherry and Doony never utter magic words which will free them from patriarchy. They marry the kings and become dutiful wives. The conclusion of "Dunyazadiad" explains that to "be joyous in the full acceptance of this dénouement is surely to possess a treasure, the key to which is the understanding that Key and Treasure are the same" (Barth, *Chimera*, 64). Feminist readers cannot be joyous in the full acceptance of this denouement's implication that women do not possess the Key/Treasure, that women's magical voices are not effective enough to alter patriarchal stories about subordinate, married women. This denouement is a feminist defeat. When the married couples "greet one another with warm good mornings" (Barth, *Chimera*, 64), Sherry and Doony express themselves as controlled, complacent wives.

Instead of directly confronting Shahryar, Sherry recites the acceptable stories he wants to hear. She has sex with him. She even offers to have sex with the genie: "I imagine you [the genie] expect what every man expects who has the key to any treasure a woman needs" (Barth, *Chimera*, 23). She defines "treasure" as a means for her and Doony to function within patriarchy. In order to survive, she throws away her key to herself, denies that she is the author of her stories. "I don't invent. . . . I only recount" (Barth, *Chimera*, 37), she informs the genie. This attitude diminishes her stories and prevents her words from becoming appropriately magic. In order to avoid execution, Sherry compromises her "narrative and sexual art" (Barth, *Chimera*, 32) by telling the genie's stories to Shahryar. She has no choice about becoming the victim of literal sexual/textual politics. Like real-world women, she lives within the space of a patriarchal story. According to one such story, women's words and efforts cannot nullify a temporarily helpless man's ability to summon, by whistling and moving his eyebrows, other men who follow his order to kill.

"Dunyazadiad" celebrates the triumph of the male word. Shah Zaman does not have to fear Sherry's story about emasculation. When emerging from his potentially lethal nuptial bedchamber unscathed, he says, "Treasure me, Dunyazade. . . . I hear the cocks" (Barth, *Chimera*, 63). Many men crow about themselves daily; women are taught to treasure men's words. Sherry's story about razors does not redirect this emphasis. Instead, women's words become empowered when the "magic words *as if*" (Barth, *Chimera*, 57) result in "the survival of anything radically innovative" (Barth, *Chimera*, 58–59). The key is to treasure women's stories.

Shah Zaman tells a tale-within-a-tale which exemplifies his lack of regard for women's stories. According to his retold Amazon myth, instead of murdering women, he allows them to emigrate to a women's country. He does not know if this gynocracy exists: "For all I know, my original mistress never truly intended to found her gynocracy; the whole proposal was perhaps a ruse; perhaps they all slipped back into the country . . . married and lived openly under my nose. No matter" (Barth, *Chimera,* 60). He categorizes the "Country of the Breastless" (Barth, 60) as "no matter." Whether or not there is a gynocracy, his lovers' behavior coincides with his purpose and with his story. The women are powerless; the key to the women's country cannot be obtained without first sleeping with the king. The women's country is a patriarchal space, the product of a man's story—not a treasure.

"Dunyazadiad," nonetheless, exemplifies Barth's sensitivity to women's problems. Yet despite Barth's open-mindedness (and despite the genie's refusal to take sexual advantage of Sherry), "Dunyazadiad" still articulates patriarchal purposes. Shah Zaman's tale-within-a-tale excuses violent male behavior and portrays him as a good guy who does not kill women after all. "Dunyazadiad" is Barth's fantasy about personally having a controlling hand in authoring Scheherazade's fictions. His female protagonists fail to extricate themselves effectively from patriarchal stories. They never circumvent male interpretations.

Binding men to bedposts does not make Sherry and Doony powerful. On the contrary, Shahryar's and Shah Zaman's decision to agree to be tied speaks to the women's ultimate inability to control men. The kings' decision to welcome vulnerability into their bedrooms resembles the Trojans' decision to allow the gift horse to enter their city. The kings and Trojans both define a potential threat as nonthreatening and allow their space to be violated. The kings' interpretation is correct because, unlike the Greeks, Sherry and Doony lack the power to enact their plan. Even though Sherry has the courage to author an attack upon patriarchy, she cannot win. To find a female victor, to find a woman who utters words which successfully locate her outside patriarchal space, it is necessary to turn from Barth's Scheherazade to Wolf's Cassandra. Wolf allows Cassandra to tell her own story.

"Dunyazadiad" and *Cassandra* are concerned with "lack of speech turn[ing] into lack of identity" (Wolf, "Conditions," 161), women's relationship to "the power of the word" (Wolf, "Conditions," 162). Sherry and Doony do not discuss their oppression with their husbands and ultimately define themselves as wives, not as individuals. For them, and for their real-world sisters, female culture is a nonexistent space. As Wolf explains, "women were allowed to contribute virtually nothing to the culture we live in, officially and directly, for thousands of years" (Wolf, "Conditions," 260). At first, Wolf's Cassandra exemplifies this lack of female contribution to culture. Although Cassandra can predict the future, her society does not listen to her (Wolf, *Cassandra*, 23). She has no words. She has no identity. When Wolf retells the Cassandra tale, Cassandra transcends this silencing of women. Cassandra finds a space for her identity and story—and, hence, for women's reality.

Cassandra stresses that words make reality. Cassandra, for example, is a Trojan because of others' stories, not her birth. She explains that "it was not my birth that made me a Trojan, it was the stories told in the inner courts" (Wolf, *Cassandra*, 33). Subjective, patriarchal interpretation and perception routinely give shape and meaning to the "naked, meaningless shape of events" (Wolf, *Cassandra*, 42). While people habitually see what they "*want* to see" (Wolf, "Conditions," 201), society is grounded upon what men want to see. Male visions determine "the *image* we make of the ages" (Wolf, "Conditions," 201). Women, however, now demand space for their particular sights and insights. *Cassandra* is positioned in this space. Wolf retells a woman's story from a woman's point of view. *Cassandra* insists that readers see what Wolf wants them to see.

Wolf views war as a story open to interpretation. She emphasizes that women's interpretation of war is ignored and men's interpretation of war is reified. War, as Cassandra explains, occupies the entire emotional and experiential space of human perception: "In the middle of a war you think of nothing but how it will end. And put off living. When large numbers of people do that, it creates a vacuum within us which the war flows in to fill" (Wolf, *Cassandra*, 65). During the Trojan War, men's perceptions and stories flow in to fill interpretative space; Cassandra's female interpretation is ignored. Instead of following Cassandra's advice not to wage war, her father, King Priam, listens to the "declaration of the military leaders" (Wolf, *Cassandra*, 69–70). Cassandra's version of the "honor of our house" (Wolf, *Cassandra*, 70) is interpreted as a threat to the house. Like a location (such as the Dardanelles), interpretation is, of course, subject to battles for control. Women and minorities are at a disadvantage during these battles.

They are, for example, usually denied access to places where war is interpreted, a situation experienced by Cassandra's mother, Hecuba, who, as a woman, is barred from the Trojan council. Her son, Hector, explains, "The things we have to talk about in our council, now in wartime, are no longer the concern of women" (Wolf, *Cassandra*, 92). "Our" does not refer to women. The wise Queen Hecuba and Cassandra the Seeress both "did not belong" (Wolf, *Cassandra*, 94). The council's magic words silence women, erase their interpretations, and remove them from the space where the male story of war is authored. "The things we exclude and ban are the things we have to fear," states Wolf (Wolf, "Conditions," 282). Because the Trojan council fears the female version of war's story, it bans women. Wolf advocates changing patriarchal interpretations and definitions which have remained unchanged from Cassandra's time to the present.

Cassandra confronts one particular unchanged definition while discussing the word "victory" with a chariot driver (Wolf, *Cassandra*, 116). The driver asks if victory is synonymous with destruction. Cassandra answers: "So in the future there may be people who know how to turn their victory into life" (Wolf, *Cassandra*, 116). We have not reached the point where "victory" means "life" rather than "destruction." "Victory" still alludes to warfare and economics. Politicians give lip service to the notion that the patriarchal definition of "victory" has become exhausted.[4] They speak with empty words about replacing exhausted rhetoric with a feminist literature of replenishment, about redefining "victory," about ceasing to accomplish the "gain of culture by the loss of nature" (Wolf, "Conditions," 216).

Despite patriarchy's efforts to snuff out women's stories, Cassandra insists upon telling her own when she begs Clytemnestra to send a young woman who will pass on her story. She wishes her life story to flow to the future "so that alongside the river of heroic songs this tiny rivulet, too, may reach those faraway, perhaps happier people who will live in times to come" (Wolf, *Cassandra*, 81). Now that the river of male heroic songs is becoming exhausted, the rivulet of the female story is present to surge and flood and replenish the arid space the male literary canon occupies. Acting counter to Sherry's acquiescence to her husband, Shahryar (and to Sherry's silenced story), Cassandra confronts Priam and tells her own story. In fact, as Wolf points out when describing servile airline flight attendants and female Syrian travelers who unconditionally obey men (Wolf, "Conditions," 151), Cassandra's voice is more effective than many contemporary women's voices. Cassandra is a hero who effectively wields illocutionary force. Despite her father's ability to use words to punish her—he can declare her to be insane, imprison her, and force her to marry (Wolf, *Cassandra*, 79)—Cassandra publicly articulates words her father does not want to hear. She says, "end this war" (Wolf, *Cassandra*, 75), and she backs this statement by analyzing Paris's abduction of Helen. Just as King Lear responds to Cordelia, King Priam banishes and disowns his daughter when confronted with her version of the truth (Wolf, *Cassandra*, 76). When Cassandra is "led away" in response to Priam's order to "throw that person out" (Wolf, *Cassandra*, 76), she moves from patriarchal space to her own space. She progresses toward building a new Troy by directly saying "no" to patriarchy.

Cassandra refuses to collude with a particular male story, the Trojan council's plan to use Polyxena as an object, a decoy to lure Achilles to his death (Wolf, *Cassandra*, 125). Cassandra offers a different interpretation of this story when she faults the council for being more concerned about Achilles than about Polyxena (Wolf, *Cassandra*, 126). She asserts her refusal to cooperate with the plan:

"Now Cassandra. You're going to be sensible, aren't you?" [Asks Priam.]
I [Cassandra] said: "No."
"You don't agree to the plan?"
"No."
"But you will keep silent?"
"No," I said. . . . The king said: "Seize her!" (Wolf, *Cassandra*, 127)

Cassandra's and Priam's discontented discourse is a battle of words in which the daughter's "no" confronts the father's "seize her." Despite Priam's ability to incarcerate Cassandra within a basket, her "no" communicates victory. Sherry never confronts King Shahryar; Cordelia remains silent before Lear; but Cassandra tells Priam about her refusal to cooperate with patriarchy. Cassandra's "no" opens a space for a female interpretation of morality and reality. By saying "no," Cassandra successfully reconciles what Terry Brown calls "the dilemma that each feminine subject has in relation to patriarchal discourse" (Brown, 29). Cassandra situates herself outside patriarchal discourse and, when doing so, confronts another female dilemma. Brown describes this dilemma: "How can a woman 'answer' the patriarchy in its terms without relinquishing her own identity as a woman?" (Brown, 29). Cassandra preserves her identity as a woman; she refuses to answer patriarchy according to its terms. Her "no" rewrites a patriarchal story and frames it in other, female terms. Cassandra is not "the feminine subject as a daughter" who "negotiates her way into subjectivity through an alienating language, the language of her father" (Brown, 30). Her female interpretation is not open to negotiation. She finally refuses to speak the alienating language of her father. As a consequence, she is imprisoned in a basket, a small—and effective—new female space.

Cassandra realizes that war-torn Troy is a space constructed by words. She states: "Thus out of words, gestures, ceremonies, and silence there arose a second Troy, a ghostly city, where we were supposed to feel at home and live at ease" (Wolf, *Cassandra*, 85). Cassandra uses words to create a third Troy. When she says "no" to Priam, she reconstructs a Troy of her own within her basket/prison. The confining space within the basket is, at least, hers. The basket's woven wall separates Cassandra's space from patriarchal space. From her vantage point within the basket, Cassandra is a woman functioning in what James Tiptree calls "the chinks of your world-machine" (Tiptree, "The Women Men Don't See," 154; mentioned in chapter 3). This enclosed space is, unlike Troy and the world, a viable female space. She occupies herself by working at unraveling the wicker, making her female space bigger, enlarging women's chink in the world machine (Wolf, *Cassandra*, 128).

After using her time while imprisoned to reexamine her decision to speak counter to patriarchal stories, Cassandra concludes that she rightly insists upon her own voice (Wolf, *Cassandra*, 131). The Cassandra myth corroborates her conclusion. While the Trojans insist that the horse located outside the city gate is a "token of victory" (Wolf, *Cassandra*, 136), Cassandra correctly interprets it as a threat. Here, one woman's truth confronts patriarchal "truth." Because Troy contains no authoritative place for Cassandra's interpretation of the horse, the city's space is jeopardized. Because Troy excludes women's truth from within its walls, the city becomes an exhausted community.

A prophecy which affects Cassandra aptly describes mainstream America's usual response to feminist discourse. This prophecy declares that "you will speak the truth, but no one will believe you" (Wolf, *Cassandra*, 136). Troy pays a penalty for ignoring Cassandra. (The United States pays a penalty for ignoring feminist voices which speak against nuclear arms and environmental pollution. Americans are just beginning to accept that the patriarchal penchant for improved horsepower—faster machines, more and more technology— is a threat, not a gift horse. If people continue to respect stories about technological supremacy and refuse to respect nature, then, their behavior might lead to American culture's exhaustion.) When the Trojans see the horse outside their walls, like Cassandra, they create a story to interpret its meaning. Trojans must choose which story and interpretation will occupy the space of believability. Cassandra's truthful interpretation is contained, discredited, and silenced. The desire to believe themselves "victors" (Wolf, *Cassandra*, 136) in the male story of war motivates the Trojans to place the horse within their city. Hence, Trojan society suffers because of the empowering of a male story to construct reality and the silencing of a woman's interpretation.

Wolf discusses the enduring "rituals which it is the storyteller's job to reinterpret as needed" (Wolf, "Conditions," 207). *Cassandra* emphasizes that silencing women and reifying men's stories are social rituals which, after centuries, need to be reinterpreted. *Cassandra* articulates the need to create spaces for female storytellers who reenact cultural rituals and represent women's worlds. When Wolf mentions the *Iliad*, she implies that women's chink within the male literary world machine should be widened. Wolf states that "the line the narrator pursues is that of male action. Everyday life, the world of women, shines through only in the gaps between the descriptions of battle" (Wolf, "Conditions," 233). Unlike "Dunyazadiad" (and unlike *King Lear*), *Cassandra* is structured along the line of direct female verbal action. Descriptions of male battles appear in the gaps between descriptions of women's personal struggle. "The wrath of Achilles" (Wolf, "Conditions," 233) is exemplified by a male battlefield; the wrath of Cassandra is exemplified by a female war of words, one woman's decision to say "no" to patriarchal stories.

Cassandra's "no" reflects her effort to alter the patriarchal "manufacturing process of a so-called historical truth" (Wolf, "Conditions," 261). "No" says that since "myths mirror 'truth'" (Wolf, "Conditions," 261), it is necessary to retell the myths and remirror "truth," to disempower the pervasive belief in patriarchal "truth." As Wolf explains, after viewing material through a different lens, it is necessary to create subversive new living words, new stories which reveal unrecognized possibilities (Wolf, "Conditions," 270–271). The contemporary world needs new words, new versions of patriarchal stories. Creating space for women's words, stories, and interpretations facilitates such narrative replenishment. Patriarchy might understand that opening its narrative walls to admit women's discourse is analogous to accepting a gift, not becoming vulnerable to a surprise attack.

Retelling Corporate Myth: The Informatics of Liberation, or, "'Why,' Driblette said at last, 'is everybody so interested in texts?'"

Such understanding depends upon empowering women's words and making crucial information available to women. Lyotard, who believes no one is powerless in an information society, would advocate this openness. He explains that if people are given free access to memory and data banks, knowledge—like language—becomes inexhaustible (Lyotard, 67). Freedom of information indicates respect for the desire for justice and the unknown (Lyotard, 67). Comparing Sandi Hall's *The Godmothers* to Thomas Pynchon's *The Crying of Lot 49* provides an opportunity to apply Lyotard's notions to a woman's story and a man's story about relationships between individual and corporate information dissemination systems. Hall and Pynchon examine, respectively, how feminists and creative men subvert the manner in which corporations acquire knowledge. Hall portrays women who use corporate information as a means to achieve feminist goals. *The Godmothers* is a woman's rewritten version of Pynchon's story about altering corporate knowledge. Pynchon imagines an organized system of failed male executives who cannot bring meaningful change to the corporate information system; Hall imagines an organized group of marginalized feminists who can revise the corporate information system. The feminists, unlike the executives, do not create a "WASTE" (Pynchon's term) system. While both Hall and Pynchon portray the corporate information apparatus functioning counter to patriarchal objectives, only Hall describes fruitful change—Lyotard's free access to knowledge resulting in justice.

Oedipa Maas, who discovers a patriarchal corporate knowledge/power system while investigating Yoyodine, Inc., is manipulated by a male character's text—Pierce Inverarity's will. Inverarity calls himself "a founding father" (Pynchon, 14) of Yoyodine; Pynchon never questions a situation in which Yoyodine's powerful positions are accessible only to "fathers." His story and his sympathy are aligned with men who fail in the corporate system. *The Crying of Lot 49* concerns ostracized fathers who do not receive the stamp of corporate approval and who, to no fruitful avail, alter the male mail system. The power system which excludes virtually all women and discards men's creative initiative remains intact.

Yoyodine's unsuccessful executives construct an alternative to a system which designates them as failures. They create an underground world, a separatist masculinist dystopia which is "a whole underworld of suicides who failed. All keeping in touch through that secret delivery system. What do they tell each other?" (Pynchon, 85). They tell an exhausted male story, a tale about failure to wield patriarchal power. They have nothing useful to say; their discussion is "fixating in a position of minimax equilibrium because it had exhausted its stakes. For the stakes would be knowledge (or information, if you will)" (Lyotard, 67). *The Crying of Lot 49* explains that patriarchal information systems have exhausted their stakes. The alternative system Pynchon's men establish is merely another exhausted story. By withdrawing into "the separate, silent, unsuspected world" (Pynchon, 92), they escape to a space of inertia.

Oedipa enters this space when she is powerless and lost while attending a Yoyodine stockholders' meeting: "There was nothing she could do at it. . . . Somehow Oedipa got lost" (Pynchon, 59, 60). Male inventors who must sign "over all their rights to a monster like Yoyodine" (Pynchon, 64) are equally powerless and lost in corporate space. The corporate information system produces knowledge in a mechanistic manner: "IBM typewriters chiggered away . . . fat reference manuals were slammed shut, rattling blueprints folded and refolded . . . all with Yoyodine was normal" (Pynchon, 62). Yoyodine functions in opposition to Lyotard's notion that "knowledge finds its validity not within itself . . . but in a practical subject—humanity. The principle of the movement animating the people is not the self-legitimation of knowledge, but the self-grounding of freedom or, if preferred, its self-management" (Lyotard, 35). Pynchon does not look beyond the corporate patriarchal system to envision an alternative story about how Yoyodine grants freedom to men and incorporates women. *The Crying of Lot 49* is, instead, an exercise in language play. The clever revelation that its title refers to auctioning stamps does not approach the full implication of Lyotard's belief that "the reserve of knowledge—language's reserve of possible utterances—is inexhaustible" (Lyotard, 67).

In contrast, Hall's feminists expand the reserve of knowledge when they interpret this reserve according to feminist utterances. Her novel's power is derived from commitment to the possibility of social change. Unlike *The Crying of Lot 49* and much postmodern fiction written by men, *The Godmothers* does not have a bleak, trivializing perspective on human life. Rather, it sketches "the outline of a politics that would respect both the desire for justice and the desire for the unknown" (Lyotard, 67) and explores the relationship between corporate power and legitimating knowledge. Hall shifts Pynchon's emphasis from corporate founding fathers to speculative godmothers. She retells, according to feminist replenishment, Pynchon's exhausted story of men and entropy.

Hall rewrites Pynchon in terms of feminism when she portrays women who subvert corporate information systems. An activist dedicated to changing images and positions of women in media, Hall describes organized feminist communities which nullify corporate power in present and future time. By linking women who live in three separate time frames—past women burned as witches, present oppressed women who thwart a corporation, and future empowered feminists who control information systems—*The Godmothers* depicts women's successful historical struggle to counteract misogynistic media systems. Hall's future feminists succeed when they author a story in which feminist media systems free themselves from restraints imposed by big business. The women replace Pynchon's male entropy with "women's energy" (Hall, 82). Their feminist utopia conforms to Lyotard's description of the relationship between democratic information access and humanistic liberty.

Hall's Comnet replaces Pynchon's Yoyodine:

Feminist media, because of their autonomy and consequent freedom from restraint by big business, had been able consistently to present analyses of the very actions that had brought the planet to this point of annihilation. They had, in short, hundreds of years of understanding the problem. The Information Centre came into being, composed of a feminist representative from each culture. It had the specific duty of assessing all information before it was used by Comnet—the place from which all educational and informative communications came. . . . Eventually, Comnet became the centre for a settlement of women. . . . Administrative groups were each linked to the central global offices, which were not huge and relied on computer efficiency for the vastness of their administration. . . . Your Birthrights gave you your living and you could devote your time to the pursuit of your subject knowledge. (Hall, 112)

This system erases stories written by the male corporate heads Hall describes as "raging giants of cruelty and fear" (Hall, 113). As opposed to Oedipa and her powerless position as a stockholder, Hall's future feminist utopian community has the power to kill the corporate father, erase his name from the boardroom door, and embrace the Godmothers who will freely *"teach things that are yet unknown"* (Hall, 182). According to Hall's feminist utopian information dissemination system, the Godmothers replace mystifying patriarchal texts with freedom of information, a call to *"know the mystery"* (Hall, 182). Her future feminist community is "arranging the data in a new way" (Lyotard, 51), creating Lyotard's "new arrangement" established "by connecting together series of data that were previously held to be independent" (Lyotard, 52).

Lyotard continues:

> This capacity to articulate what used to be separate can be called imagination. Speed is one of its properties. It is possible to conceive the world of postmodern knowledge as governed by a game of perfect information, in the sense that the data is in principle accessible to any expert: there is no scientific secret. Given equal competence (no longer in the acquisition of knowledge, but in its production), what extra performativity depends on in the final analysis is "imagination," which allows one either to make a new move or change the rules of the game. (Lyotard, 52)

Hall's feminist utopia mirrors Lyotard's knowledge utopia. She rewrites the patriarchal world in a speedy, three-page space (Hall, 111–113). Feminist imagination, women's new move, changes the rules of the corporate game. According to these new rules, equal competence in regard to producing knowledge yields political and economic freedom. This point serves as an argument for changing the rules which define literary postmodernism. Rather than being separate from postmodern fiction, the feminist imagination should be speedily incorporated within it. Postmodernism's feminist imagination is about allowing women to change the rules of the patriarchal game, about women's redefining reality.

Present as well as future protagonists of *The Godmothers* experience Lyotard's knowledge utopia. The novel concerns how contemporary feminists access and rewrite corporate information as a feminist story. They transform their feminist interpretation of corporate power into a film, a woman-controlled media project. Hence, in both the present and the future, to disseminate knowledge, Hall's women freely collect formerly independent data and arrange them in a new way. Their new move yields a speedy change of corporate rules concerning power. Here is how Hall's contemporary characters achieve success:

In another few days the film was finished, the speed of its compilation making it raw. But it was compulsive viewing. . . . Shirley's explanation of the actions of American Vehicle were supported by the indisputable evidence from the files. The evidence that they'd [the feminist community] picked up along the way of corporate collusion, tax fiddles, payola and big money political graft was backed up and proven time after time. The film was damning. . . . Over those six pairs of unwavering eyes [a group shot of women] ran the sound: "The way to get things done is to begin to do them." (Hall, 177–178, 183)

The Godmothers describes women who control information and rewrite the corporate system in order to begin to get feminist work done. By presenting widely disseminated, woman-controlled media as a new move to change the rules of the patriarchal game, this novel reads the postmodern condition as a report on feminist knowledge. Hall retells Pynchon's story about subverting corporate power, a positive reassuring move which functions counter to Donna Haraway's description of "transitions from the comfortable old hierarchical dominations to the scary new networks I have called the informatics of domination" (Haraway, 80). Hall's new story reflects feminist discomfort with scary hierarchical domination and imagines a new informatics of liberation—open access to and feminist use of information systems.

The Crying of Lot 49 seems to allude to feminist fabulation's liberating possibilities by questioning, in terms of planetarium imagery, who controls meaning. Pynchon describes "dark machines in the centre of the planetarium" making "Meaning" when someone flashes "some arrow on the dome to skitter among constellations and trace out your Dragon, Whale, Southern Cross" (Pynchon, 58–59). The central question concerns who controls the arrow and who enters the planetarium. A woman-centered answer to this question interprets stars as texts which reflect potential feminist textual power. Oedipa Maas does not command this power. The answer to her question—"*Shall I project a world?*"—(Pynchon, 59) is nega-

252 ○ Reconceiving Narrative Space

tive. Feminist fabulators, not Oedipa, control the planetarium arrow, and, in their hands, it points to feminist textuality and projects women's worlds. Feminist fabulation is an accessible information system.

Contemporary women writers freely draw upon this system to enable feminist fabulation to rewrite itself. For example, Sheila Finch's *Infinity's Web* and Fay Weldon's *The Cloning of Joanna May* are new versions of Joanna Russ's story about split female selves, *The Female Man*. And by describing a female rather than a male interplanetary emissary, Mary Gentle's *Golden Witchbreed* re-creates Ursula Le Guin's *The Left Hand of Darkness*. Feminist fabulation, then, functions as an information system which replenishes itself by rewriting women's as well as men's stories. Feminist science fiction, a component of feminist fabulation and, as such, no longer viewed as a female subgenre locked within a ghetto (or basket/ prison), allows women to control the planetarium arrow, to chart "Meaning" in texts about stars. Oedipa Maas erroneously declares that she too is a feminist fabulator: "But the reality is in *this* head. Mine. I'm the projector at the planetarium, all the closed little universe visible in the circle of that stage is coming out of my mouth, eyes, sometimes other orifices also" (Pynchon, 56). Oedipa's words do not describe the truth. Feminist fabulators, not Oedipa, are the controlling projectors who author new realities in their heads. I now hand the planetarium pointer to one of these writers, to Doris Piserchia. Her *Star Rider*, a new story, a combination of feminist SF and the feminist Western, imbues Oedipa's words with illocutionary force. Jade, the protagonist, inhabits the reality in Piserchia's head— and she can inspire readers to rewrite their reality.

A Replenishing Genre Splice: Another Version of How the West Was Won

Jane Tompkins explains that the "Western *answers* the domestic novel" by seeking to "marginalize and suppress" (Tompkins, 371) nineteenth-century women who stood for evangelical Protestantism and the cult of domesticity. *Star Rider* answers the Western. Piserchia locates women in the Western—creates a feminist Western—when she juxtaposes the Western with feminist SF. She enables females to enter a generic space from which they have purposely been excluded. Tompkins asks, "Why are Westerns so adamantly opposed to anything female?" (Tompkins, 373); Piserchia seems to answer Tompkins by creating a feminist SF/Western which celebrates a female character and opposes femininity. Jade is told that a jade statue of the eternal feminine woman does not resemble her: "You're nothing like this eternal woman. See how soft and feminine her body is? . . . This is a mother of people, not a hedonistic adolescent who will grow up to be a caricature of a female" (Piserchia, 199). The Western rejects women; Jade rejects femininity. Instead of adhering to the tired story of femininity the statue represents, Jade inhabits a space which has been off-limits to women. She opens a new female territory in the outer limits of the West.

Jade "skips" from planet to planet via a mind link with her horse (named Hinx), a mental splice which transforms girl and animal into a living intergalactic vehicle. This arrangement coincides with the fantastic alternatives to mechanistic hardware which routinely appear in feminist SF. Jade further conforms to this routine when she learns that the "secret of freedom was to never make anything" (Piserchia, 98). This orphaned adolescent, a female Huck Finn, roams freely and rejects civilization's products and restrictions. She is a new combatant in the "literary gender war" (Tompkins, 374) between the female-authored novel and the Western. Her battle plan includes rebelling against the story about women's stationary domestic place and rewriting the rule that women cannot be Western heroes. As free and uncivilized as Huck Finn or any Western hero, Jade "never learned any culture" (Piserchia, 44). She specifically rejects earth civilization, observes that people on earth "tore up their world, made a smelly outhouse of it, and they saw to it that nobody could ever live on it again" (Piserchia, 32). Her most important agenda is to move through outer space, a wide-open space west of everything. Jade explains that "without Hinx I couldn't go anywhere, and if I couldn't travel I might as well have been dead" (Piserchia, 23).

Jade's best friend is her ultrahorsepowered horse. She adores him and enjoys a better relationship with him than with people. Jade and Hinx had "skipped all over the place, eaten when we'd felt like it, gone swimming in clear lakes, lain under blue suns. Hinx. My friend. We needed nothing and no one but each other" (Piserchia, 63). Piserchia provides a new version of the estranged relationship between female and male characters Fiedler describes in *Love and Death in the American Novel*. Jade loves her horse. She is a bona fide female hero of the Western, a full participant in a genre which privileges "the male realm of public power, physical ordeal, homosociality, and the rituals of the duel" (Tompkins, 374). Her presence questions this privilege and indicates that the Western's male story is exhausted. Jade replenishes the Western by "light[ing] out for the territory" (Fiedler, 26) with the Jaks (descendants of humans) who, in Jade's words, "kissed this galaxy good-bye and lit out" (Piserchia, 169). Piserchia's new story results from rewriting Leslie Fiedler in terms of Jane Tompkins, from imagining the Western hero as a female escapee from civilization who is born from the marriage between the Western and feminist SF.

In Piserchia's feminist Western, the hero is a girl and the schoolmarms are aliens called varks. *Star Rider* portrays the galaxy as "a one-room schoolhouse with everyone eager to break out. . . . Varks were given the job of watching over the children of men. We [varks] don't want the job anymore. It's too tedious" (Piserchia, 214). Varks explain that, like the Western, the story of women as domestic civilizing enforcers is exhausted. Rejecting their schoolmarm role, varks allow everyone to venture to the West: "The varks have decided to hold a marathon. You can skip, anyone can skip, to wherever you please, but we're holding you to doing it together. No one goes before the others" (Piserchia, 214). Although the varks' marathon recalls the settlers who lined up to enter the Oklahoma Territory, their version of homesteading functions counter to women's usual isolated place in the home. Their insistence that no one should receive a head start allows Jade to become part of a community. Her initial desire that she and Hinx travel "out of our galaxy and [reach] that other one way over there across a big ocean of black space" (Piserchia, 6) is attained by a cooperative community, not by her and Hinx alone: "Big Jak, Shaper and I skipped for dear life. For the very first time, maybe in history, Jakalowar cooperated and did a thing together" (Piserchia, 219).

Hence, *Star Rider* also recasts Arthur C. Clarke's *Childhood's*

End. In contrast to Clarke's characters, who are no longer *Homo sapiens* when humanity's childhood concludes, the Jakalowar, humanity's children, remain human. Liberated by the schoolmarm varks, Piserchia's protagonists learn to cooperate with each other. Jade and her male counterparts Big Jak and Shaper—who do not wish to wage literary gender war—transcend the gender roles Tompkins and Fiedler describe. The human race's future depends upon cooperating to pull "a wagon train, an endless stream of mounted jaks and independent varks" (Piserchia, 218) to a new galaxy. Any "drop out" will "kill the whole species" (Piserchia, 218). Jade leads a community of homesteaders who settle the space beyond patriarchal definitions. They line up to venture west of patriarchy, west of everything. They move off into the sunset of patriarchy while galloping toward utopian cooperation between women and men. Patriarchal stories become dust tracks on the Jakalowar's road, new imprints in outer space which, in the real world, continue to exist in a location beyond human perception. The patriarchal discourses obliterated by Hinx's hooves, Jade and Hinx merge to form an interplanetary flying machine, become narratives "under erasure" (McHale, 99–111).

Those who define the postmodern American novel would do well to emulate Jade's open mind, a point of view described as "a vastness that has no boundaries. Its perimeters extend to no terminals, but rather toward limitless space. . . . The other jaks who were tested had fences in their brains. Jade sees no end to reality" (Piserchia, 177). Opening postmodern fiction to female authors entails abolishing boundaries, taking down fences in critics' brains, and defining postmodernism as a limitless potential space for women as well as men. This recognition involves going the "farthest ever!" (Piserchia, 219)—going "west . . . as far west as you can go, west of everything" (Tompkins, 359). Although Tompkins explains that to go west of everything "is to die" (Tompkins, 359), this extreme directional mode is a constructive move for contemporary fiction. If literary postmodernism does not venture far beyond the territory of its male-centered orientation, it might—like the Western—exhaust itself.

In contrast to this potential moribundity, when Jade leads her wagon train west of everything to metaspace—outer space beyond outer space—she celebrates maturity and life development. Her presence in contemporary literature indicates that feminist meta-fiction vitalizes as well as rewrites patriarchal fiction. *Star Rider*, a postmodern SF Western about rewriting the Western, describes how the West was won for feminism. This novel indicates that, like the Western, postmodern literature is not restricted to one particular human type—men. It announces that limiting literary postmodern-ism to an enclosed space, the patriarchal corral, is not OK. Feminist fabulation answers male postmodernism. In the ongoing literary gender war, like the Western, postmodern literary space can be won by women.

Female characters can be Huck Finn too. When Jade empowers a wagon train that leaves misogynistic restriction in the dust, mother and sister texts about female Huck Finns pull with her: Charlotte Perkins Gilman's "Benigna Machiavelli," Susan Warner's *The Wide Wide World*, and Mona Simpson's *Anywhere but Here*. The story of Huck lighting out for the territory does not have to be exhausted by gender limitations. "Benigna Machiavelli" and *The Wide Wide World* engender *Star Rider* and *Anywhere but Here*: literary replen-ishment results from feminist textuality, from feminist texts inspir-ing other feminist texts. In my concluding section, I argue that tex-tual offspring born from maternal words vitalize literature.

How Not to Be "a Sucker": Feminist Textuality/Space/Postmodern Fiction

Feminist textuality frees feminist writing from the anxiety of patri-archal influence, allows feminist writing to engender new feminist writing. A particular image in *Star Rider*, Jade's tongue attached to a plant (called a sucker) resembling ice, represents the need for the liberating characteristics of feminist textuality. Jade is unable to free her tongue after she places it on the sucker. Lacking an alternative, she waits for the sucker to dehydrate her: "There was only so much twisting I could do without damaging my tongue, and before long I hunkered sore-mouthed and exhausted over the alien strip that held me prisoner. No matter what I did, I stayed fastened as securely as ever. . . . [Big Jak left] me with my tongue stuck solid, and no matter how I yammered he didn't come back to get me out of my fix. Nothing for me to do but crouch over the slab and wait for it to drain me of my body fluids" (Piserchia, 40, 42). Jade's experience reflects women's relationship to patriarchal stories.

Attracted by an alien substance—the patriarchal text—many women voluntarily attach their tongues (or voices) to it without sufficient investigation. Patriarchal texts entrap women's tongues— muddle and nullify their voices—drain their particular creative fluids by defining blood and milk as inappropriate ink. "Yelling," "yanking" (Piserchia, 40), expecting to be extricated by men, and all attempts to pull away from the encumbrance by speaking while fettered fail to alleviate the situation. These methods cause further pain without releasing captive female tongues. Like Jade, many silenced women become complacent. Jade, though, is open to learning something new while waiting to die: "Learned something when the sun went down. The blue slab was really called a sucker, and it would have been difficult to find a better name for the thing. Humans were a curious lot and a sucker was a human who relied on half his brain instead of the whole organ. Anyone who stuck his tongue on a blue chunk just because it looked like ice was a sucker" (Piserchia, 42). Jade learns that she must change language and stories; she must change the definition of "sucker." It is appropriate for Jade to define herself and the plant as something other than a sucker. The notion that "it is difficult to find a better name" for Jade and the plant is a fiction. Jade survives by changing this story—by rewriting, as feminist metafiction, the fiction about the plant's and her own characteristics.

The plant is not always a sucker. "The moment the sun dropped behind the horizon, the blue slab let me go. It was a plant and at sundown it quit its daily activities and went to sleep" (Piserchia, 42). The sucker releases its hold; Jade does not live with her brain attached to femininity's limitations. Jade and the plant function outside the language system which defines them as suckers. They unmask and oppose the fictionality of master narratives which define women and nature. When Jade and the plant redefine "sucker"— when they refuse to act like suckers—they suggest that an informatics of liberation is derived from feminist textuality, that feminist texts engender other feminist texts.

E. M. Broner's *Her Mothers* and Italo Calvino's *Cosmicomics* are pregnant texts which give birth—replenish literature—before readers' eyes. A dialogue between protagonist Beatrix Palmer and her mother is interspersed throughout *Her Mothers*. Their conversation, a text about a mother enforcing patriarchal rules in regard to her daughter and granddaughter, speaks to and creates the second text in Broner's novel—the story of establishing a new communicative paradigm between mothers and daughters. According to this new paradigm, mothers will no longer serve as patriarchal enforcers when interacting with their daughters. One text in Broner's novel, then, is born from its opposition to another text in the novel.

Beatrix, when she imagines that her unborn daughter, Lena, is fearless and sings in her womb, seems to predict that Lena will overcome the harm caused by mothers who articulate patriarchal texts to their daughters:

> "Mother, I'm pregnant with a baby girl."
> "What is she doing?"
> "She is singing."
> "Why is she singing?"
> "Because she's unafraid." (Broner, 241)

Lena's lack of fear implies that mothers who tell their daughters patriarchal stories contribute to the literature of exhaustion. Mothers might, instead, convey new, liberating stories.

Like Broner, Calvino contributes to the literature of replenishment by creating pregnant texts. The italicized epigraphs which precede each story in *Cosmicomics* give birth to the stories which follow them. (The stories emerge from the differing italicized texts.) Further, like Broner, Calvino imagines new stories emanating from a new maternal voice. In his "All at One Point," Mrs. Ph(i)NKo, a maternal entity confined in a single point with all other entities, articulates a desire which gives birth to the universe. She explains that she wishes to have enough room to make noodles:

> "Oh, if I only had some room, how I'd like to make some noodles for you boys!" And in that moment we all thought of the space that her round arms would occupy, moving backward and forward with the rolling pin over the dough, her bosom

leaning over the great mound of flour and eggs which cluttered the wide board while her arms kneaded and kneaded. . . . we thought of the space that the flour would occupy, and the wheat for the flour, and the fields to raise the wheat, and the mountains from which the water would flow to irrigate the fields, and the grazing lands for the herds of calves that would give their meat for the sauce; of the space it would take for the Sun to arrive with its rays, to ripen the wheat; of the space for the Sun to condense from the clouds of stellar gases and burn; of the quantities of stars and galaxies and galactic masses in flight through space which would be needed to hold suspended every galaxy, every nebula, every sun, every planet, and at the same time we thought of it, this space was inevitably being formed, at the same time that Mrs. Ph(i)NKo was uttering those words: ". . . ah, what noodles, boys" the point that contained her and all of us was expanding in a halo of distance in light-years and light-centuries and billions of light-millennia, and we were being hurled to the four corners of the universe . . . and she, dissolved into I don't know what kind of energy-light-heat, she, Mrs. Ph(i)NKo, she who in the midst of our closed, petty world had been capable of a generous impulse, "Boys, the noodles I would make for you!," a true burst of general love, initiating at the same moment the concept of space and, properly speaking, space itself, and time, and universal gravitation, and the gravitating universe, making possible billions and billions of suns, and of planets, and fields of wheat, and Mrs. Ph(i)NKos, scattered through the continents of the planets, kneading with floury, oil-shiny, generous arms, and she lost at that very moment, and we, mourning her loss. (Calvino, 46–47)

According to Calvino's imagery, space is invented by a woman's maternal language.[5]

A woman who speaks about generosity and nurturing locates the idea of space in the minds of the community which hears her. As opposed to patriarchal domination of women and nature, Calvino imagines a feminine voice acting as a catalyst for nature's existence. Outer space nourishes Calvino's woman-created world space; femininity, in turn, nourishes outer space. Woman's word, not the patriarchal god, creates the heaven and the earth. "Boys, the noodles I would make for you!" is a new, replenishing alternative to patriarchal master narratives. As creator, Mrs. Ph(i)NKo counters the literature of exhaustion by offering a generous new possibility for the closed, petty, patriarchal world.

Calvino imagines that discourse and space stem from an explosion caused by the word of a Mother who resembles a real-world woman. Jardine, on the other hand, describes the end of symbolization resulting from an implosion caused by the representation of nonmaternal, unreal Woman: ". . . without Images, without the Father and without the Mother, without Man or History. The discourses of philosophy, religion, and history all rejoin, and each echoes the other two when contemplating the ends of Man. And it is Woman and her 'obligatory connotations'; Woman as other than the Mother, who represents for the male theorists of modernity the *space* at the end point of Man's symbolization—utopia—or the Empty Temple of Judaic thought at our foundations" (Jardine, 87). Calvino describes a beginning in terms of a female creator; Jardine describes an ending in terms of Woman who has nothing to do with women. I am concerned with writing's relationship to real-world people who exist at the present postmodern moment, a time which might be the compromising middle space located between the extremes of start and finish discussed by Calvino and Jardine, respectively. Calvino's Woman as Mother is responsible for the beginning of symbolization; Jardine's unmotherly Woman is responsible for the end of symbolization. Who generates discourse during the postmodern present, the space between the beginning and the end? I would like to think that, as opposed to "male critics of modernity" (Jardine, 87) who exclude women, feminist critics of postmodernism would answer the question in terms of the real-world women and men who create feminist fabulation. Unlike Woman—who disappears when history begins, progresses, and ends—real women should have a strong and recognized presence within postmodern fiction.

Mrs. Ph(i)NKo, certainly no omnipotent creator, disappears within the space she makes possible. When she is reduced to "scattered" energy, she becomes as "lost" as Jardine's Woman. Feminists might appropriately mourn Mrs. Ph(i)NKo's loss, recognize that relatively undefined scattered female energy, nonetheless, exists. Feminists seek Mrs. Ph(i)NKo when they rediscover female energy and theorize its potential use. If their search is successful, Russ's "little daughter book" may yet "live merrily" (Russ, *Female Man*, 213) in a world acknowledged to have been created by a mother's voice.

A French feminist theorizes Calvino's vision of an Italian mother creating the world. Cixous describes an infinite, unselfish female body as an immense space in outer space, characterized by love and equality: "If there is a 'propriety of woman,' it is paradoxically her capacity to depropriate unselfishly, body without end, without appendage, without principal 'parts.' If she is a whole, it's a whole composed of parts that are wholes, not simple partial objects but a moving, limitlessly changing ensemble, a cosmos tirelessly traversed by Eros, an immense astral space not organized around any one sun that's any more of a star than the others" (Cixous, 259). Cixous and Calvino concur. Alternatives to patriarchal spaces and master narratives arise from the limitless dissemination of feminist stories about spaces where all people shine equally. These stories describe a world in which the generous gesture to cook noodles can sometimes create the universe and is always respected. Most of these stories are presently concentrated all at one point, lost within feminist SF. Feminist critics can relocate them; feminist critics' words, spoken in the manner of Mrs. Ph(i)NKo's utterance, can enable stories about feminist worlds to break out of their concentration in a ghetto within the SF ghetto. The feminist "energy-light-heat" which fuels imaginative alternatives to patriarchal reality is no longer lost in space, no longer marginalized and confined by being labeled as feminist science fiction.

Oh, if I only had some room, how I'd like to make some new feminist narratives available for you boys so that you would read stories about alternative worlds where men are not any more of a star than women. I do have room. *Feminist Fabulation* occupies space which can create other feminist spaces, engender other feminist texts. My words can help marginalized women's stories to break out of their confinement and expand into the literary postmodern canonical cosmos. A feminist critic is, after all, a descendant of Mrs. Ph(i)NKo; a feminist critic "is cosmic, just as her unconscious is worldwide. Her writing can only keep going, without ever inscribing or discerning contours . . . she goes on and passes into infinity" (Cixous, 259–260). I am a feminist critic who hopes to redefine inscribed canonical contours through observing that, in contrast to exhausted patriarchal stories, feminist writing can only keep going; it can continue to rewrite worldwide patriarchy in terms of feminist cosmic space. Feminist fabulation is our postmodern era's literature of replenishment.

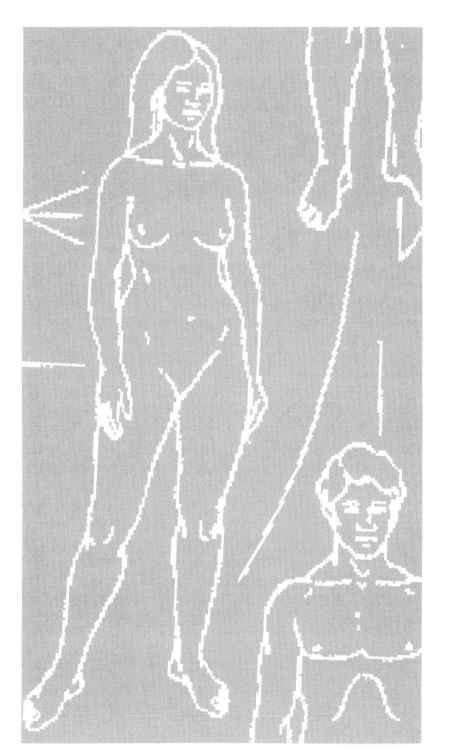

Werner van den Valckert, Three Lady Governors and the Matron of the Leper Asylum at Amsterdam, *1624. Rijksmuseum-Stichting, Amsterdam.*

Werner van den Valckert, Four Governors and the Master of the Leper Asylum at Amsterdam, *1624. Rijksmuseum-Stichting, Amsterdam.*

★ ○ ❯ ★ ○ ❯ ★ ○ ❯

Afterword: Back to the Future

Back to the preface: the *Pioneer* spacecraft's depiction of women and men retells a story Werner van den Valckert (c. 1585–1627) represents more equitably in his paintings *Three Lady Governors and the Matron of the Leper Asylum at Amsterdam* (1624) and *Four Governors and the Master of the Leper Asylum at Amsterdam* (1624).[1] Unlike the people *Pioneer* portrays, in van den Valckert's pictures of equally ranking females and males, women and men both make communicative gestures (they point to texts and write). Van den Valckert seems to represent my effort in *Feminist Fabulation* to narrow the schism between female and male literary communities and to raise the stature of marginalized contemporary feminist writers.

A real-world example of this schism and its impact upon women occurred when I heard two eminent individuals, Adrienne Rich and George Steiner, speak at New York University's Bobst Library within a week of each other.[2] While Steiner's mixed audience consisted of more men than women, few men were among those who packed the room to hear Rich. The makeup of these audiences reflects a perception that Steiner speaks in a universal voice while Rich does not. This perception, however, contradicts the manner in which the *MLA Newsletter* describes Rich's work. The *Newsletter* states, upon the occasion of Rich winning the 1991 Common Wealth Award in Literature, that in "considering Rich, the jurors noted that her deep moral sense and vision and her impeccable control of her craft have made her one of the preeminent writers in English today. Rich's explorations of personal experience speak about the self, but they also reveal universal themes that speak to the community. Her work is an outstanding example of writing as a private and public act" ("Adrienne Rich," 1). Many men, as the Bobst Library audience indicates, do not perceive Rich's work to be universal and do not want to hear this woman who is regarded as one of the preeminent writers in English today. A writer who—because of false impressions—does not engage both genders is, in truth, prevented from being universal. Male readers' lack of interest marginalizes both "high" and "low" women writers—Rich and little-known SF writers alike.

Van den Valckert seems to indicate that the term "separate but equal" does not appropriately describe literary communities. His ladies possess accoutrements of both public and private worlds: loose coins appear on the table and the matron holds a skein of cotton. Signs of economic and domestic environments surround these women, who do not write words which are as enduring as the words men write. The lady governor uses chalk and holds a chalkboard; her male counterpart uses ink and, like the male on the *Pioneer* craft, communicates with his hand. The lady governor, a more positive alternative to the silent woman drawn on *Pioneer*, might represent the tenuous nature of women's narrative; she writes in a manner which can be erased easily. Further, while the male governor writes words, the lady governor makes nonlinguistic marks. I would like to think that, in the manner of the fantastic textual modes I discuss in chapter 6, she writes outside patriarchal language and signals the possibility that nonpatriarchal language can become viable.

As the foregrounded female and male writers in the van den Valckert paintings seem to address possibilities for language change, the backgrounded scenes from the life of Lazarus might evoke the differing, unequal positions of numerous ostracized feminist fabulators and canonized male metafictionists. Of the two biblical characters named Lazarus, one is raised from the dead (John 11). The other, a beggar whom a rich man refuses to assist monetarily, enters heaven; the rich man who, unlike Lazarus, received good things in life does not enter heaven (Luke 19). These stories pertain to my attempts in *Feminist Fabulation* to resurrect important examples of contemporary women's fiction which patriarchal indifference buries. By advocating expanding the postmodern canon to include many types of feminist fiction, I try to ensure that more feminist texts will garner the good things the literary community offers. I call upon masculinist postmodernism to share its privileges with feminist fabulation so that the latter does not become analogous to a beggar who dies before receiving a just reward.

This recasting of feminist fabulation as a lady Lazarus, of course, brings one of Sylvia Plath's images to mind—the female voice which routinely and miraculously emerges from the grave of literary neglect. The voice announces,

> I have done it again.
> One year in every ten
> I manage it——
>
> A sort of walking miracle . . . (Plath, "Lady Lazarus")

Through addressing the literary system's burial of many contemporary women writers, *Feminist Fabulation* might make it possible for more of Plath's female descendants to avoid the need to be resurrected. As Plath emphasizes, reemerging female voices are strong:

> Out of the ash
> I rise with my red hair
> And I eat men like air. (Plath, "Lady Lazarus")

The feminist academic critical empire can strike back against the established forces which cause many women's voices to vanish into thin air.

I, however, prefer a less warlike approach in which men are not always positioned as what Plath calls "Herr Enemy." I would like to replace "Herr Enemy" with a real version of her "Herr Doktor" (a benign Herr Professor Doktor, to be exact) who, instead of deserving to have resurrected Woman eat him like air, chose to air a discussion about men in feminism while dressed in kitchen garb. At a 1988 MLA Convention panel called "The Future of Men with Feminism, the Future of Feminism with Men," Robert Scholes, expert on both "high" theory and "low" SF, while reading his paper attired in an apron, himself pictured the juxtaposition of the feminine, the masculine, and marginalized genre fiction. Through this act of "cognitive estrangement" (Darko Suvin's term), by presenting himself as "a strange newness, a *novum*" (Suvin, 4), in which he wore a garment no one had ever before worn to an MLA presentation, Scholes, in a manner pertinent to female experience, personified his definition of speculative fabulation as "the presence of at least one clear *representational* discontinuity with life as we know it" (Scholes, *Structural Fabulation*, 61–62). While publicly appearing tied within a domestic garment, Scholes represented the slash which at once separates and attaches communities of ostracized feminist fabulators and canonized male metafictionists. He embodied a juncture between the masculine public voice and the feminine private world. I have gone back to the Scholes presentation, the van den Valckert paintings, and the *Pioneer* drawing to imagine a future in which disappearing is not something that must be "done again" (Plath, "Lady Lazarus") by women writers.

I attempt to contribute to grounding this future by arguing for replacing women's separate and unequal relationship to postmodern canons with women's integration within postmodern canons. I cannot avoid framing this argument according to a method I will now directly address: I must act as a woman in patriarchy. Scholes can take off his apron after he finishes speaking about men in feminism. When discussing women in postmodernism (or any other scholarly topic), I cannot discard a particular truth: my past academic training and, hence, my predominant present voice—which is, in part, based upon this training—are tied to men. Elaine Showalter remarks that "although virtually all American feminist critics of the first wave were trained by men . . . none became a disciple of a particular male teacher. It might be said that like the women of the Amahagger tribe described by Rider Haggard in *She*, pioneering American feminist critics 'never pay attention to or even acknowledge any man as their father, even when their male parentage is perfectly well known'" (Showalter, 37). I am going to break from this tradition established by the feminist critics who came before me. As the author of *Feminist Fabulation*, a book which advocates emphasizing real-world women's experiences rather than Woman as catalyst to masculinist theory, I want to name the men who directly (and in one instance, in terms of the title I chose for this study, very obviously) influenced me; I want to acknowledge my male academic parentage. I studied with Leslie Fiedler, Norman N. Holland (the director of my dissertation), and Eric S. Rabkin, a student of Robert Scholes. I am comfortable being the descendant of mavericks. I cannot act as the rebellious daughter of a dissertation director who instructed me to write in my own voice. As the female scion of an academic family with many investments in SF, I feel no anxiety of influence.

Bonnie Zimmerman explains that in the "Bloomian battle between representational fathers and experimental sons, the daughter cried out, 'What do you mean, realism is dead. Whose reality? Not mine—I haven't had a chance yet to defend it!' For women's relationship to literary tradition has been that of an 'anxiety of authorship,' and the task of feminist fiction has been to create an authoritative voice, not to undermine an already existing one" (Zimmerman, 176). I am the daughter of experimental fathers. Having no need to undermine their existing work, I set about to use it as a tool to read contemporary feminist fiction as an authoritative voice which tries to undermine patriarchal master narratives. Since I was taught to ask "whose reality?," it comes as no surprise to me that realism is dead. Unlike those feminist critics who devote all of their attention to realistic literature, I investigate feminist fiction about alternatives to patriarchal reality. Fathers served as the models for my own maverick authoritative voice, my insistence upon reserving canonical space for feminist nonrealistic literature. Recognizing that, like myself, this literature has no academic mother, I attempt to assume a maternal role in relation to it. (As the editor of *Future Females*, the first critical anthology about women and SF, and the author of *Alien to Femininity*, the first book about speculative fiction and feminist theory, I "mothered" feminist SF.) In order to speak about women's literature, I look back to my pedagogical experiences with men and to "fabulation," a term generated by a man. I hope that feminist critics of the next generation will not have to act in kind. I hope that they will retell my retold theoretical tale by renaming feminist fabulation according to a feminist rubric. Hence, my pioneering gesture involves going back to the future so that ensuing feminist work on this book's subject can move forward.

I discuss the strange newness of an equal canonical space for both female and male postmodern writers. Feminist fabulation can transform the canon into a novum which will have "nunavit" in regard to containing virtually nothing other than patriarchal stories. May the term "feminist fabulation" set off "fabulatory fireworks" (Waugh, *Feminine Fictions*, 126) to celebrate the recognition that, contrary to what patriarchy and NASA advocate, launching images drawn from sexist stereotypes into outer space is no pioneering feat. The *Pioneer* craft tells outer space how to look at us; *Feminist Fabulation* tells us how to look at feminist space fiction as a literary craft appropriately located in canonical space.

How to Look at Space,[3] a cartoon created by Ad Reinhardt (1914–1967), the first important American artist to begin his career as an abstract painter and to remain one throughout his life, appears to speak to those who tell beings in outer space how to look at us. Reinhardt, a dissenter who used comics and cartoons to attack or subvert art activity, can address feminist fabulation's subverting of patriarchal representation. The text which is a part of *How to Look at Space* announces that "all through history a man's idea of what was 'real' depended mainly on how he felt and what he thought about 'space.' Each age developed its own ways of describing its space . . . A 'picture' was a one-sided representation of this space . . . YOU, SIR, ARE A SPACE, TOO." All through history, men constructed "real" women to fit changing patriarchal spaces.

Patriarchal pictures of women are one-sided, fictitious representations. Feminist fabulation unmasks and rewrites these fictions, talks back to Man, informs him that he, too, is a space. By articulat-

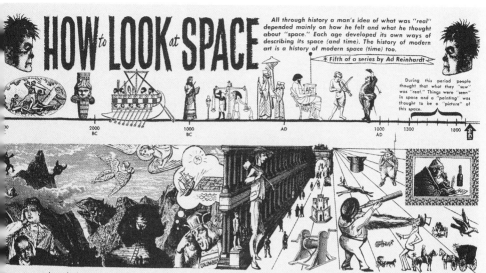

Ad Reinhardt, How to Look at Space, P.M., *April 28, 1946. Photograph by Bill Jacobson. The Pace Gallery, New York.*

ing feminist definitions of what constitutes reality, feminist fabulation tells "the other side" (Molly Hite's term) of the one-sided patriarchal story. Feminist fabulation is the postmodern age's idea of how
to retell, from a feminist viewpoint, the patriarchal stories which
construct the world. Postmodern canons should contain space for
feminist fabulators who inform the very human patriarchal "Herr
God" that he, the constructor of women's space, is a space too.

★　○　）　★　○　）　★　○　）

Notes

Preface: Having "Nunavit"

1. Carl Sagan believes that feminist critiques of the *Pioneer* drawing do not have merit:

The Pioneer 10 and 11 plaque, simple as it was, elicited a public reaction both amusing and amazing. . . . There were letters from outraged feminists protesting that the woman on the plaque appeared to be subservient to the man. Was she not in fact standing behind him, and why for heaven's sake was the man's hand raised and not hers? This all came as a shock to the artist, Linda Sagan, who felt herself to be a liberated woman. . . . After this barrage of criticism, we decided that most of these criticisms had no merit, and we felt that no great mistake had been made. (Sagan, 57, 59)

2. Hereafter, unless I indicate otherwise, "postmodern" refers to postmodern fiction. "Postmodern canon," depending on my context, refers either to one of the many contradictory postmodern canons—which all exclude important feminist fiction—or to my vision of an expanded postmodern canon.

3. For a study of feminist genre fiction, see Anne Cranny-Francis, *Feminist Fiction: Feminist Uses of Generic Fiction.*

4. Jardine defines gynesis as "the putting into discourse of 'woman' as that *process* diagnosed in France as intrinsic to the condition of modernity; indeed, the valorization of the feminine, woman, and her obligatory, that is, historical connotations, as somehow intrinsic to new and necessary modes of thinking, writing, speaking" (Jardine, 25).

5. My discussion (in chapter 1) of Linda Leith's review of Mona Knapp's *Doris Lessing* exemplifies a feminist theorist's discomfort with SF.

6. The Museum of Modern Art's exhibit "High & Low Modern Art and Popular Culture" appeared in New York City from October 7, 1990, to January 15, 1991.

7. See chapter 3, note 1, for information about the law which prohib-

ited women from flying combat missions. This law was changed in 1991.

8. Stuart Wrede comments that Ambasz's "projects such as the house at Cordoba, Spain; the house at Bierges, Belgium; the Schlumberger Research Laboratory in Austin, Texas; or the Botanical Gardens in San Antonio, simply cannot be separated from the landscape: they *are* the landscape. . . . Concerned about anchoring his projects to existing physical landscape features, . . . [Holl] has used the Erie Barge Canal in Rochester, or in Phoenix . . . the more obscure traces of the mysterious canals built long ago by the Hohokum Indians" (Wrede, 2–3).

9. Filler states that "Mr. Holl's radical notion is to . . . extend Frederick Law Olmsted's original design for Riverside Park southward to West 59th Street beyond its current boundary of West 72d Street. In a bold turnaround, he would build 10 sliver towers—the tallest 40 stories high—offshore in the Hudson River. Grouped into three megastructures, with towers connected by horizontal bridges containing lateral 'elevators,' the buildings would be reached via underwater passageways leading from the riverbank" (Filler, 28).

1. The Feminist Anglo-American Critical Empire Strikes Back

1. Throughout this study, I use "feminist speculative fiction" to include SF, fantasy, and utopian literature. I also use Doris Lessing's term "space fiction" as a synonym for SF.

2. I have been criticized for arguing that feminist speculative fiction can have an impact upon reality: "Throughout [*Alien to Femininity*], she insists that speculative fiction, when read in terms of feminist theory, 'can provide women with the insight, motivation, knowledge— and power—to change the world.' This statement might be admirably idealistic if it were about any subject other than the political power of art. . . . Art . . . is ineffectual, even irrelevant as a political act" (White, 565). I stand by my argument, which is echoed by other feminist theorists. For example, in *Re-making Love: The Feminization of Sex*, Barbara Ehrenreich, Elizabeth Harris, and Gloria Jacobs explain how the popular musical art of the 1960s (such as Beatles concerts) changed female sexuality. In addition, Chris Weedon states that feminist poststructuralist theory can be used "in the fight for change" (Weedon, 175). She brings "feminist futuristic novels" to bear upon this fight by indicating that these novels present new subject positions for women and challenge existing gender roles (Weedon, 40, 104).

3. See Robin Roberts, "Postmodernism and Feminist Science Fiction," for a reading of Sheila Finch's *Triad* in terms of postmodernism.

4. Scholes reacts in the manner of contemporary feminist theorists who find language's resonances of meaning to be inadequate and who confront the lack of terminology to discuss new female modes. In 1967, when he did not have appropriate terminology with which to describe a new literary mode, Scholes explained that "evaluation and appreciation depend helplessly on recognition of kind, and recognition requires appropriate linguistic categories. . . . My intention in introducing the term 'fabulation' is to provide a new name for these new literary artifacts. Once we can see them not as misfits which have failed to become proper novels or satires or whatever, we can begin to see them as themselves" (*Fabulators*, 13–14). "Fabulation" once provided a new name for new literary artifacts; "feminist fabulation" can presently accomplish the same objective. I hope that the proper term for a new category of feminist literature will eventually point the way toward formulating new terms for defining women according to female criteria, not as feminine misfits who fail to become proper humans.

5. Angela Carter implies that launching phallic machines into the sky might not be a fruitful undertaking: "Man lives in historicity; his phallic projectory takes him onwards and upwards—but to where? Where but to the barren sea of infertility, the craters of the moon!" (Carter, *Passion of New Eve*, 53).

6. When Miller remarks that women's literature is about literary plots and unsatisfactory, constructed reality, she implies that all women's literature is metafictional:

The plots of women's literature are not about "life" and solutions in any therapeutic sense, nor should they be. They are about the plots of literature itself, about the constraints the maxim places on rendering a female life in fiction. . . . The attack on female plots and plausibilities assumes that women writers cannot or will not obey the rules of fiction. . . . It does not see that the maxims that pass for the truth of human experience, and the encoding of that experience in literature, are organizations, when they are not fantasies, of the dominant culture. To read women's literature is to see and hear repeatedly a chafing against the "unsatisfactory reality" contained in the maxim. (Miller, "Emphasis," 356–357)

7. Lévy views power as a simultaneous "all and nothing" (Lévy, 16). He explains that if "the Prince has no throne and no definite place, he can never be reached and we can never attack the kernel of his authority

. . . precisely because he is not *one* thing, because he is a *nothing*, he thereby becomes *all*, all of reality and the entire world. . . . If authority has no roots, no location, and no density, then revolt cannot be radical, and there is no way it can come into existence" (Lévy, 14). There cannot be a radical, feminist revolt against the canon because, in Lévy's words, "mastery is the law of this world, and no proclamation, no earthquake, can ever succeed in overturning it" (Lévy, 15). Foucault explains that power figures in all human interactions and that power, rather than being negative, generates new knowledge and cannot be eliminated completely. Foucault states: "No body of knowledge can be formed without a system of communications, records, accumulation and displacement which is in itself a form of power and which is linked, in its existence and functioning, to the other forms of power" (Foucault, quoted in Sheridan, 131). The canon, like power, is an unavoidable system; some texts will always be chosen at the expense of other texts. New knowledge is generated by changing and expanding canons, not by the impossible wish of eradicating canons. Like Foucault and Lévy, Primo Levi also claims that power is pervasive and not necessarily harmful: "Power exists in all the varieties of the human social organization, more or less controlled, usurped, conferred from above or recognized from below, assigned by merit, corporate solidarity, blood or position. Probably a certain degree of man's domination over man is inscribed in our genetic patrimony as gregarious animals. There is no proof that power is intrinsically harmful to the collectivity" (Levi, 46). Similarly, the canon must be present in all varieties of professional literary activities. Different groups within the profession compete for the power to control the canon. This competition is not necessarily harmful.

8. Molly Hite also comments upon Anglo-American feminist critics' emphasis upon women's realistic fiction. She points out that associating women's fiction with realism and aesthetic conservatism leads to positioning women's fiction outside the canon:

The notion that women are . . . "natural" or "straight" writers, who manage to get reality . . . onto the page with a minimum of art or decision making, has informed a whole practice of feminist criticism, so that some of the most important examples of this criticism have fostered the association between women's writing and aesthetic conservatism. Many of the Anglo-American feminist critics who began with the intent of doing justice to women's fiction as a chronicle of female experience seem to have found themselves in the process purveying an exaggerated theory of mimesis, in which authors are simply mirrored in their own texts. . . . [Presumptions about women's "natural" or "straight" style] consign women to subordinate roles in literary culture inasmuch as they consign women writers to the conservation of past traditions. In any period of literary history, new and innovative writing tends to supersede writing that maintains and continues older practices: canonization is, among other things, a means of consolidating the emblematic forms with which the period comes to be identified. . . . the likely-to-be-canonized or "precanonized" works of the contemporary period are for the most part works of postmodernism. The writing perceived as the avant-garde at a particular moment tends to define that moment in literary history. (Hite, 13, 15-16)

Despite these comments, as I point out in my preface, Hite does not explore the relationship between feminist SF and female postmodern writers. As my second chapter explains, placing feminist SF under the rubric of feminist fabulation facilitates canonizing, rather than ostracizing, this nonrealistic, innovative literary form.

9. I discuss the relationship between Chodorow and Van Scyoc more fully in "Reproducing Reproduction, Manipulating Motherhood: Pregnancy and Power," the concluding chapter of *Alien to Femininity: Speculative Fiction and Feminist Theory*.

10. In "Why Are Americans Afraid of Dragons?," Ursula Le Guin observes that a fear of the fantastic is at the heart of American culture.

2. Canonizing the Monstrous

1. Jane Gallop states that "feminism is precisely the defense and valorization of such 'monsters,' the celebration of their beauty. Feminism has saved such monsters from the loneliness of their singularity and recognized them as members of the collective body of women" (Gallop, 23-24). Hélène Cixous views the monstrous Medusa as positive: "You only have to look at the Medusa straight on to see her. And she's not deadly. She's beautiful and she's laughing" (Cixous, 255).

2. Feminist literary critics who question the very notion of a canon would, of course, take issue with this chapter's title. I respond by articulating my belief in changing systems while positioned within systems. In my opinion, postmodern literature's male emphasis can be challenged most effectively by locating feminist fabulation within postmodern literary canons. See the comments about the canon in chapter 1, note 7.

3. See Richard Law, "Joanna Russ and the Literature of Exhaustion," for an article which reads Russ in terms of Laurence Sterne, Nabokov, Borges, and Barth. For Russ's comments on the need to associate "avant-garde" SF with mainstream literature, see "The Image of Women in Science Fiction." She describes women's avant-garde SF as "part of the recent rapprochement between the most experimental of the science fiction community and the most avant-garde of what is called 'the mainstream.' This takes us out of the field of science fiction altogether" (Russ, "Image," 88–89).

4. Russ states that "we come to the one occupation of a female protagonist in literature, the one thing she can do, and by God she does it and does it and does it over and over and over again. She is the protagonist of a Love Story" (Russ, "What Can a Heroine Do?," 9).

5. Sarah Webster Goodwin's 1987 MLA presentation, "Feminism: Implicit and Explicit Utopias," first acquainted me with the notion that "Babette's Feast" can be read as an implicit feminist utopia. This presentation has been published as "Knowing Better: Feminism and Utopian Discourse in *Pride and Prejudice*, *Villette*, and 'Babette's Feast.'"

6. Alma H. Bond casts Jody Scott's fantastic version of Virginia Woolf's death back into the realm of the real. Bond interprets Woolf's death in terms of duplicity: "It is my contention that the multiple motivations for her suicide were far more covert than is suspected, and that we deliberately have been kept from understanding the dynamics. . . . as a result of this widespread duplicity, despite the cascading proliferation of books and essays on her works and life we do not really understand Virginia Woolf" (Bond, 15).

7. Marguerite Duras's "The Crushed Nettle" portrays one such alternative to violent patriarchal stories. "The Crushed Nettle"—published in *The War: A Memoir*, a collection of linked tales which shares the structure of *Seven Worlds*—describes the transition from war to peace. The collection's last tale, "Aurelia Paris," a fairy tale rendition of a Jewish girl's plight during World War II, signals that war is a story. Duras seems to imply that humans, like Rogans, enliven themselves by continuing to act out war stories. Further, American culture, like Rogan culture, craves new material. Stories of the transition to peace, such as "The Crushed Nettle," can supply new, constructive alternatives to cultural artifacts which foster environments unconducive to peace.

8. Morgan's gesture toward peace is quite congruent with Susan Stanford Friedman's understanding of Sandra M. Gilbert and Susan Gubar's objectives in *The War of the Words*, volume 1 of *No Man's Land: The*

Place of the Woman Writer in the Twentieth Century. Friedman explains that Gilbert and Gubar "boldly confront the current of gynophobic violence that runs through the male literary tradition—violence which they refuse to excuse because of its packaging as 'high' art, theory, satire, or humor. They implicitly align themselves with feminists like Adrienne Rich and Audre Lorde, who argue that we ignore patriarchy's culture of violence at our peril: that violence in the streets, the bedrooms, the battlefields, the theatres and the books must be confronted, named and understood" (Friedman, 14). Caraker is another feminist who seeks to name and understand violence. Fighting to canonize feminist fabulation is yet another battle against violence inflicted upon women's texts. Such efforts will forever be stymied if feminist fabulation continues to lose the war of the words and remains in a non-canonical no-man's-land.

3. "A Dream of Flying"

1. United States Air Force Major Wayne E. Dillingham refers to this law and argues that it does not apply to spacecraft engaged in combat missions. He says the limitation on the authority of the Secretary of the Air Force to assign duties to members of the Air Force

> is set forth in 10 U.S.C. Sec. 8549 . . . as follows: "Female members of the Air Force . . . may not be engaged in combat missions." . . . the statute permits the Secretary to assign women to any ground duties desired—no matter how combat-related or hazardous those duties may be. . . . If the Secretary eventually should desire the assignment of Air Force Women to duty in *spacecraft* engaged in combat operations, would this same statutory prohibition apply? No. As previously discussed, the statute is narrowly drawn and sets forth no general prohibition against women in combat. (Dillingham, 14–15)

It is virtually certain that this law will be repealed. On August 1, 1991, Eric Schmitt reported in the *New York Times* as follows:

> The Senate voted overwhelmingly today [July 31] to overturn a 43-year-old law that bars women from flying warplanes in combat. The new measure, an amendment to the military budget bill for the 1992 fiscal year, would permit, but would not require, the Air Force, the Navy, the Army and the Marine Corps to allow women to fly

combat missions. Today's vote made enactment of the measure virtually certain. The House of Representatives approved similar legislation last month. . . . Supporters of the amendment to lift the ban on female combat aviators cast the existing law as an "archaic, antiquated, Neanderthal" statute that discriminated against women and undermined the national security by putting sex ahead of talent. (Schmitt, 1, 13)

2. Emily Toth states that "the new frontier in women's writing is not the sensitive man/career woman coupling—but the love and friendship between women" (Toth, 791).

3. This is how a young girl on Whileaway reacts to the idea of loving a man: "'Yuki,' [Janet, Yuki's parent] said, 'do you think you could fall in love with a man?' and she whooped derisively. 'With a ten-foot toad!' said my tactful child. But men are coming to Whileaway" (Russ, "When It Changed," 2268).

4. Ann describes her multiple selves: "The Anna who stayed in New York with her parents and grew up to room with Ilse Stein at Barnard; the Anna who went back to New York and lived with Carol Sommers; the Anna who lived on Stockton Street and attended San Francisco State; the Anna who remained in London and married Reuben; the Anna who adopted Leah and returned to the States. . . . Sometimes Anna felt that she was the composite of all those experiences and possibilities, more mature and complex for the variables faced and chosen. Sometimes she felt . . . that she would be better off as one of the other Annas" (Miner, 443).

5. See Jacqueline Cochran and Maryann Bucknum Brinley, *Jackie Cochran: An Autobiography*, New York: Bantam Books, 1987.

6. The point that *All Good Women* and *Gone to Soldiers* are positioned outside the canon was exemplified on December 7, 1991, the fiftieth anniversary of the Pearl Harbor attack. To mark this occasion, Joseph Heller, Samuel Hynes, Mary Lee Settle, Louis Simpson, and William Styron spoke at New York's Poetry Center of the 92nd Street Y as members of a panel called "World War II: Literature and Experience." A woman in the audience asked the panel for information about female authors who write novels about women's experience in the Second World War. Not one of the panelists could answer her question.

7. Here is how the *New York Times* reported preparations for launching the shuttle:

With the future of the nation's civilian space program hanging in the balance, the space shuttle Discovery was readied today to carry

American astronauts into orbit for the first time since the Challenger disaster 32 months ago. . . . [T]he pressure and tension of preparing for such a crucial launching led Frank Merlino, a test director of the Kennedy Space Center, to remark with a shake of the head, "It's not been a breeze. If trouble develops and it can be corrected in a hurry, the launching could be delayed as long as two and a half hours and still get off Thursday." . . . Officials of the National Aeronautics and Space Administration said tonight that preparations were proceeding smoothly and with rigorous caution. . . . Rear Adm. Richard H. Truly, the associate administrator for space flight, said: "The space shuttle is ready to fly. The payload is ready to fly. The U.S. is ready to go." (Wilford)

The next day the paper reported the successful launch:

Gathered anxiously in front of their television screens, millions of Americans watched the space shuttle Discovery thunder spectacularly into orbit yesterday morning amid applause and cheers but, most of all, amid an overwhelming sense of relief. The launching of the Discovery offered Americans more than renewed pride; it provided a kind of national exorcism, an opportunity to purge the doubts and uncertainty about the nation's *prowess* [italics mine] and technological ability that had lingered since the explosion of the shuttle Challenger in 1986. In Washington, a beaming President Reagan told an audience in the Rose Garden, "America is back in space." But he also confessed that during the launching, "I think I had my fingers crossed like everybody else." (Schmidt)

8. According to the *New York Times*, "Florence Griffith Joyner broke the world record in a semi final heat of the 200-meter dash with a time of 21.56 seconds, 15 hundredths of a second under the record held by Marita Koch of East Germany" (September 29, 1988).
9. Gena Corea describes the reproductive brothel: "Under the . . . brothel model, women are collected together and held, unable to come and go freely. Sold as sexual commodities to men, the women are interchangeable. They are not seen as human beings with individuality and spiritual worth. . . . This brothel model, which reduces woman to what she sells, is efficient. The women do not get out. They are controlled with force, degradation, drugs. . . . Not only could dead women be used in reproductive brothels. So could women who were never even born" (Corea, 39, 46)

4. Just What Is It That Makes Today's Homes So Different, So Appealing?

1. *Just What Is It That Makes Today's Homes So Different, So Appealing?*, as I explain in the preface, is British artist Richard Hamilton's collage on paper. The collage served as an exhibition poster for the "This Is Tomorrow" show held in London in 1956.

2. Xavière Gauthier defines witches as positive and equates suppressing witches with suppressing women's power: "If the figure of the witch appears wicked, it is because she poses a real danger to phallocratic society. We do constitute a danger for this society which is built on the exclusion—worse, on the repression—of female strength. If women were not dangerous for this society they would not have been gagged, imprisoned, repressed for centuries" (Gauthier, 203).

3. This point is discussed in Susie Orbach's *Fat Is a Feminist Issue: The Anti-Diet Guide to Permanent Weight Loss* and in Kim Chernin's *The Hungry Self: Women, Eating, and Identity.*

5. All You Need Is Love?

1. In addition to Chicago, Cleveland, Detroit, and Minneapolis are midwestern cities which contain skyscrapers. Since Cleveland and Detroit do not contain major universities within their borders, Benn does not reside in these cities. The University of Minnesota is located in Minneapolis, but whether or not Minneapolis contains one of the tallest skyscrapers in America is open to interpretation. Minneapolis's 57-story, 775-foot IDS Tower, which is not an exact counterpart to Bellow's 102-story Electronic Tower, is approximately half as tall as America's tallest building, Chicago's 110-story, 1,454-foot Sears Tower (*The 1990 Information Please Almanac*). Further, the Midwest itself conforms to the blurred realistic setting in *More Die of Heartbreak*. Real borders which can be located on a map are not the most important characteristics of the Midwest. According to *The New Encyclopaedia Britannica* (volume 8, 1989, 109), "The Middle West has become more an idea than a region, an area of immense diversity but somehow consciously representative of a national average."

2. As *More Die of Heartbreak* includes more than one story about nephews interacting with their uncles, *The Finishing School* includes more than one story about daughters engaging with other mothers. Ursula acts as a mother to Justin; Justin's cousin (Becky) would like Louise to mother her (Godwin, 261, 337).

3. For a discussion of feminist utopias written during the 1970s see Joanna Russ, "Recent Feminist Utópias."

4. See also Harry Brod's *The Making of Masculinities: The New Men's Studies* and Franklin Abbott's *New Men, New Minds: Breaking Male Tradition, How Today's Men Are Changing the Traditional Rules of Masculinity.*

5. For a discussion of Le Guin's focus upon the marriage of opposites, see James W. Bittner's *Approaches to the Fiction of Ursula K. Le Guin.*

6. John Updike's *S.* might be read as a portrayal of this transition. Its protagonist, Sarah Worth, a New Englander, rejects her Puritan heritage and patriarchal family structure when she journeys to Arizona to create a new world for herself as a member of a religious commune.

7. Lee Eisenberg, *Esquire's* editor-in-chief, states:

Name the issue: the environmental mess, the drug problem, the homeless, America's place in the world's political and economic order—you'd think that each of these outrages would have brought forth an angry young man or woman who could point us in a new, true, certain direction. Someone who could seize the stage and force us to listen and to *act*.

We were delivered, instead, Dan Quayle. We were told he was the face of the next generation. But what he is is a bummer of a baby boomer. As for his Vietnam record, he acted neither on orders nor on conscience. As a member of the most widely educated generation in the history of the world, he was throughout unmotivated or mediocre, or both. If he is possessed by any particular passion, that passion is *golf*. If anything makes him angry, it's his slice. (Eisenberg, 37)

8. I refer to the examples set by Geraldine Ferraro, Jesse Jackson, and Douglas Wilder. Although his candidacy did not prevail, Wilder, Virginia's first black governor, on November 9, 1990, declared his intention to seek his party's presidential nomination.

9. Carol Moseley Braun is one of these women. The March 22, 1992, *New York Times* reports that "Senator Alan J. Dixon's vote to confirm Supreme Court Justice Clarence Thomas last year upset many women, among them Carol Moseley Braun, the Cook County, Ill., Recorder of Deeds. On Tuesday Mrs. Braun defeated Mr. Dixon in the Illinois Primary. If she beats Richard S. Williamson, a Republican who's never held elective office, in the general election this fall, she will become the first black woman to serve in the United States Senate. . . . Braun said the Anita Hill–Clarence Thomas hearings shattered her view

of the Senate as 'a Vallhalla where decisions were made by serious men—instead we saw that they were just garden-variety politicians making bad speeches.'"

10. Russ describes feminist utopias as "classless, without government, ecologically minded, with a strong feeling for the natural world, [and] quasi-tribal in feeling" (Russ, "Utopias," 76). For an article about the powerful impact baby boomers have in relation to literary studies, see James Atlas, "The Battle of the Books."

11. In a passage I have already cited at the end of my preface, Jardine states that for Goux, "history has been the history of Man and men, but now we are entering a new historicity. The End of History, the Death of Man . . . as we move . . . toward a 'new access to the feminine.' This (re)union with the feminine is the end point of History—u-topia— where . . . the Phallus, as the ultimate metaphor in patriarchal culture, collapses. . . . In any case, it would seem to be the beginning of the end of patriarchal history" (Jardine, *Gynesis*, 33). Jardine refers to Jean-Joseph Goux's *Économie et symbolique* and *Les iconoclastes*.

6. Hesitation, Self-Experiment, Transformation— Women Mastering Female Narrative

1. Unlike Barth's Sherry (a protagonist in "Dunyazadiad," which I discuss in chapter 7) and Gilman's protagonist, who becomes a witch (in "When I Was a Witch," which I discuss in chapter 4), Atwood's, Johnson's, and Piercy's protagonists find the particular magic word which works for women—"myself."

2. Hesitation figures in two of Todorov's three conditions which make up his definition of the fantastic: "First, the text must oblige the reader to consider the world of the characters as a world of living persons and to hesitate between a natural and a supernatural explanation of the events described. Second, this hesitation may also be experienced by a character; thus the reader's role is so to speak entrusted to a character, and at the same time the hesitation is represented, it becomes one of the themes of the work" (Todorov, 33).

3. Lem criticizes Todorov's bibliography: "Now we can more readily understand the make-up of Todorov's bibliography, as to the names (Balzac, Poe, Gogol, Hoffmann, Kafka) and the works it includes. The theoretician has taken as his 'sample' that which could not involve him in difficulties, since it had already passed its cultural screening examina-

tion and by that token could give him no trouble. A therapist, if he were to proceed analogously, would take as patients only robust convalescents" (Lem, 231). Rabkin believes that Todorov's understanding of hesitation's relationship to the fantastic is limited: "Todorov radically limits not only Fantasy, but the fantastic to the realm of a single genre. . . . [hesitation] can give us an organizing principle for studies larger than those of Todorov's 'literary genre'" (Rabkin, 118).

4. It takes a full three paragraphs after the man throws the liquid for it to be identified as "the blue die, or ink, or whatever it was, trickl[ing] down her leg and into her shoe" (Johnson, 177).

5. This fortune also describes the discovery made by the female protagonist of Christa Wolf's "Self-Experiment." And, it could appropriately serve as a maxim for Beth Phail to write on her wall.

6. See note 4, page 273, for a definition of gynesis.

7. Baudrillard also describes signs which are not connected to pages and patriarchal narrative. He points out that rocks in the American desert contain signs which critique American culture in terms of nonhuman, geological language. He explains that the signs in the desert originated "long before man appeared, in a sort of pact of wear and erosion struck between the elements. Among this gigantic heap of signs— purely geological in essence—man will have had no significance. . . . And yet they *are* signs. . . . For the desert is simply that: an ecstatic critique of culture, an ecstatic disappearance" (Baudrillard, 3, 5).

8. Feminist SF protagonists meet different versions of themselves in Joanna Russ's *The Female Man* and Sheila Finch's *Infinity's Web*.

7. Gender and the Literature of Exhaustion

1. The following incident reported in the *New York Times* on February 17, 1991 ("Kicked Out," section 4), exemplifies my comment about racist and sexist humor becoming impossible within the academic community:

> In recent years a number of universities have enacted "hate speech" regulations, declaring it a violation of school policy to make harassing racial and ethnic slurs. While some civil libertarians have complained that the rules violate the First Amendment, university officials say they are needed to combat a rise in campus racism. Last week, Douglas Hann, a varsity football player at Brown University,

became what is thought to be the first person in the country expelled for violating one of the rules. . . . Mr. Hann stood in a dormitory courtyard shouting what witnesses later said were insults against blacks, homosexuals and Jews.

In a letter to the *New York Times*, Brown University president Vartan Gregorian defended the decision to expel Hann for using abusive and racist language.

2. I refer to caricature in the sense of John Houseman's portrayal of Professor Kingsfield in the television program "The Paper Chase." Kingsfield, a typical powerful white male academic, functions primarily as a parody of powerful male professors and only secondarily as a representation of that power. The audience's most lasting impression of Kingsfield centers upon humor, not power. Further, recent roles for male film stars (such as Harrison Ford in *Regarding Henry* and William Hurt in *The Doctor*) suggest that the omnipotent white male professional is becoming an exhausted image.

3. Wolf's "narrative network" resembles a text I discuss at the conclusion of chapter 6, Vonnegut's Tralfamadorian "clump of symbols" read "all at once, not one after the other" (Vonnegut, 88).

4. President George Bush devoted the week of June 12, 1989, to environmental issues, for example.

5. There is a real-world counterpart to Calvino's fictitious Italian mother who gives birth to the cosmos and makes noodles. Moshe Dayan's Jewish mother, Deborah Dayan, describes baking bread, transforming harvested grain into sustenance which supports and creates the kibbutz:

> "Bread for fifty people!" I say to myself, and alternately I swell up with pride and shrink with terror. How does a little creature like myself come to undertake this tremendous task, and face a gigantic oven full of loaves? . . . It seems to me that only yesterday I was a thing torn by doubts and hesitations . . . the question would suddenly confront me: Why are you doing these things? Who needs you? Can't they do without you and people like you? And in such moments a paralysing apathy would creep over me. . . . But now? My comrades are out in the field, mowing the harvest which we have sown. Close by I hear the mill grinding out grain. And the flour from the mill comes straight to me, and I bake the bread for all of us. Bread is surely needed. (Dayan, 27)

Mrs. Dayan's story about bread and nurturing, a woman's story, is as important to Israel's survival as her son's story of politics and war.

Afterword: Back to the Future

1. The Rijksmuseum, Amsterdam, owns these paintings. The male governors seated at the table are Siewerd Sem, Hendrick van Bronckhorst, Ernest Rocters, and Dirck Vlack. The female governors seated at the table are Tryntie ten Bergh, Anna Willekens, and Tryntie Weeline.

2. George Steiner spoke at New York University on April 22, 1991. Adrienne Rich spoke there on April 29, 1991.

3. *How to Look at Space* is the fifth in a series of thirty cartoons Reinhardt created between 1946 and 1956.

★ ○) ★ ○) ★ ○)

Bibliography

Abbey, Lynn. *The Guardians*. New York: Ace, 1982.

Abbott, Franklin, ed. *New Men, New Minds: Breaking Male Tradition, How Today's Men Are Changing the Traditional Rules of Masculinity*. Freedom, Calif.: Crossing Press, 1987.

"Adrienne Rich Wins 1991 Common Wealth Award." *MLA Newsletter* 23 (1991): 1.

Allen, Virginia, and Terry Paul. "Science and Fiction: Ways of Theorizing about Women." In *Erotic Universe: Sexuality and Fantastic Literature*, ed. Donald Palumbo, pp. 165–183. Westport, Conn.: Greenwood Press, 1986.

Anderson, Laurie. *United States*. New York: Harper and Row, 1984.

Arac, Jonathan. *Critical Genealogies: Historical Situations for Postmodern Literary Studies*. New York: Columbia University Press, 1987.

Ardener, Edwin. "Belief and the Problem of Women." In *Perceiving Women*, ed. Shirley Ardener, pp. 1–17. London: Malaby Press, 1975.

———. "The 'Problem' Revisited." In *Perceiving Women*, pp. 19–27.

Arendt, Hannah. *The Human Condition*. Chicago: University of Chicago Press, 1958.

Atlas, James. "The Battle of the Books." *New York Times Magazine*, June 5, 1988.

Atwood, Margaret. *The Handmaid's Tale*. Boston: Houghton Mifflin, 1986.

———. *Lady Oracle*. New York: Fawcett Crest, 1976.

Auerbach, Nina. *Communities of Women: An Idea in Fiction*. Cambridge: Harvard University Press, 1978.

———. *Woman and the Demon: The Life of a Victorian Myth*. Cambridge: Harvard University Press, 1982.

Bachelard, Gaston. *The Poetics of Space*. 1958. Reprint. Boston: Beacon Press, 1964.

Bainbridge, William Sims. "Women in Science Fiction." *Sex Roles* 8 (1982): 1081–1092.

Barr, Marleen S. *Alien to Femininity: Speculative Fiction and Feminist Theory*. Westport, Conn.: Greenwood Press, 1987.

————, ed. *Future Females: A Critical Anthology*. Bowling Green, Ohio: Popular Press, 1981.

————. Review of *Feminist Utopias*, by Francis Bartkowski. *Science-Fiction Studies* 17 (1990): 401–404.

Barth, John. *Chimera*. New York: Fawcett Crest, 1972.

————. "The Literature of Exhaustion." In *The Friday Book: Essays and Other Nonfiction*, pp. 62–76. New York: G. P. Putnam, 1984.

————. "The Literature of Replenishment." In *The Friday Book: Essays and Other Nonfiction*, pp. 193–206.

Barthelme, Donald. *Paradise*. New York: Penguin Books, 1986.

————. "Paraguay." In *Sixty Stories*, pp. 127–143. New York: G. P. Putnam, 1981.

Bartkowski, Francis. *Feminist Utopias*. Lincoln: University of Nebraska Press, 1989.

Baudrillard, Jean. *America*. 1986. Reprint. London and New York: Verso, 1990.

Bellow, Saul. *More Die of Heartbreak*. New York: William Morrow, 1987.

Berger, John. *Ways of Seeing*. London and New York: Penguin Books, 1973.

Berkley, Miriam. "Ursula K. Le Guin." *Publishers Weekly* (May 1986): 72.

Bittner, James W. *Approaches to the Fiction of Ursula K. Le Guin*. Ann Arbor: UMI Research Press, 1984.

Blonsky, Marshall. *On Signs*. Baltimore: Johns Hopkins University Press, 1985.

Bond, Alma Halbert. *Who Killed Virginia Woolf?: A Psychobiography*. New York: Human Sciences Press, 1989.

Borges, Jorge Luis. "The Babylon Lottery." In *Ficciones*, pp. 65–72. New York: Grove Press, 1962.

————. "The Circular Ruins." In *Ficciones*, pp. 57–63.

————. "The Library of Babel." In *Ficciones*, pp. 79–88.

————. "Tlön, Uqbar, Orbis Tertius." In *Ficciones*, pp. 17–35.

Bradley, Marion Zimmer. *The Inheritor*. New York: Tor, 1984.

————. *The Mists of Avalon*. New York: Knopf, 1983.

Brod, Harry, ed. *The Making of Masculinities: The New Men's Studies*. Boston: Allen and Unwin, 1987.

Broner, E. M. *Her Mothers*. Bloomington: Indiana University Press, 1975.

Brooke-Rose, Christine. *A Rhetoric of the Unreal: Studies in Narrative and Structure, Especially of the Fantastic.* Cambridge and New York: Cambridge University Press, 1981.

Brown, Terry. "Feminism and Psychoanalysis, a Family Affair?" In *Discontented Discourses: Feminism/Textual Intervention/Psychoanalysis*, ed. Marleen S. Barr and Richard Feldstein, pp. 29–40. Urbana: University of Illinois Press, 1989.

Butler, Octavia. *Dawn.* New York: Popular Library, 1987.

Calvino, Italo. "All at One Point." In *Cosmicomics*, pp. 43–47. New York: Harcourt Brace Jovanovich, 1968.

———. "Cybernetics and Ghosts." In *The Uses of Literature*, pp. 3–27. New York: Harcourt Brace Jovanovich, 1986.

Caraker, Mary. *Seven Worlds.* New York: Signet, 1986.

Carter, Angela. *Nights at the Circus.* New York: Viking Press, 1985.

———. *The Passion of New Eve.* London: Virago Press, 1977.

Charnas, Suzy McKee. *Walk to the End of the World.* London: Women's Press, 1989.

Chernin, Kim. *The Hungry Self: Women, Eating, and Identity.* New York: Harper and Row, 1986.

Chodorow, Nancy. *The Reproduction of Mothering: Psychoanalysis and the Sociology of Gender.* Berkeley: University of California Press, 1978.

Chopin, Kate. *The Awakening.* In *The Norton Anthology of American Literature*, ed. Nina Baym et al., vol. 2, pp. 508–599. New York: W. W. Norton, 1989.

———. "Her Letters." In *Haunted Women: The Best Supernatural Tales by American Women Writers*, ed. Alfred Bendixen, pp. 133–142. New York: Frederick Ungar, 1985.

Cixous, Hélène. "The Laugh of the Medusa." In *New French Feminisms: An Anthology*, ed. Elaine Marks and Isabelle de Courtivron, pp. 245–264. New York: Schocken Books, 1981.

Cixous, Hélène, and Catherine Clément. *The Newly Born Woman.* Minneapolis: University of Minnesota Press, 1986.

Clarke, Arthur C. *2001: A Space Odyssey.* New York: New American Library, 1968.

Cockburn, Cynthia. *Machinery of Dominance: Women, Men and Technical Know-how.* London: Pluto Press, 1985.

Corea, Gena. "The Reproductive Brothel." In *Man-Made Women: How New Reproductive Technologies Affect Women*, ed. Gena Corea et al., pp. 38–51. Bloomington: Indiana University Press, 1987.

Cranny-Francis, Anne. *Feminist Fiction: Feminist Uses of Generic Fiction.* Cambridge, U.K.: Basil Blackwell, 1990.

Daitch, Susan. *L.C.* San Diego: Harcourt Brace Jovanovich, 1987.

Davis, Natalie. *Society and Culture in Early Modern France.* Stanford: Stanford University Press, 1975.

Dayan, Deborah. "My Coming to Palestine." *Shdemot: Cultural Forum of the Kibbutz Movement* 24 (1985): 27.

de Beauvoir, Simone. *The Second Sex.* New York: Knopf, 1968.

de Lauretis, Teresa. "The Technology of Gender." In *Technologies of Gender: Essays on Theory, Film, and Fiction*, pp. 1–30. Bloomington: Indiana University Press, 1987.

del Rey, Lester. "Helen O'Loy." In *The Science Fiction Hall of Fame*, ed. Robert Silverberg, pp. 42–51. Garden City, N.Y.: Doubleday, 1970.

Derrida, Jacques. *Positions.* Trans. Alan Bass. London: Athlone Press, 1981.

Dillingham, Wayne E. "The Legal Status of United States Air Force Women in Front-Line Space Combat Operations." Nexus: Science and Science Fiction Conference. United States Air Force Academy. Colorado Springs, Col., May 1989.

Dinesen, Isak. "Babette's Feast." In *Anecdotes of Destiny*, pp. 23–68. New York: Random House, 1958.

———. "The Blank Page." In *Last Tales*, 1957, pp. 99–105. New York: Random House, 1975.

———. "The Cardinal's First Tale." In *Last Tales*, pp. 3–26.

———. "Copenhagen Season." In *Last Tales*, pp. 247–314.

———. "Echoes." In *Last Tales*, pp. 153–190.

———. "Night Walk." In *Last Tales*, pp. 45–51.

———. "Of Hidden Thoughts and of Heaven." In *Last Tales*, pp. 53–62.

———. "Tales of Two Old Gentlemen." In *Last Tales*, pp. 63–72.

Doane, Mary Ann. "Veiling over Desire: Close-ups of the Woman." In *Feminism and Psychoanalysis*, ed. Richard Feldstein and Judith Roof, pp. 105–141. Ithaca and London: Cornell University Press, 1989.

Doolittle, Hilda. *Tribute to Freud.* 1956. Reprint. Boston: D. R. Godine, 1974.

Duras, Marguerite. "Aurelia Paris." In *The War: A Memoir*, pp. 173–183. New York: Pantheon Books, 1986.

———. "The Crushed Nettle." In *The War: A Memoir*, pp. 160–172.

———. *Hiroshima, Mon Amour.* New York: Grove Press, 1961.

Ehrenreich, Barbara, Elizabeth Hess, and Gloria Jacobs. *Re-making Love: The Feminization of Sex.* Garden City, N.Y.: Doubleday, 1986.

Eisenberg, Lee. "Dan Quayle's Face." *Esquire* (December 1988): 37.

Elgin, Suzette Haden. *Native Tongue.* New York: DAW Books, 1984.

Fairbairns, Zoë. *Closing.* New York: E. P. Dutton, 1987.

Fiedler, Leslie A. *Love and Death in the American Novel.* New York: Stein and Day, 1966.

Filler, Martin. "A Once Modest Architect Lets Out the Stops." *New York Times,* May 26, 1991, section 2.

Finch, Sheila. *Infinity's Web.* New York: Bantam, 1985.

———. *Triad.* New York: Bantam, 1986.

Forte, Jeanie. "Women's Performance Art: Feminism and Postmodernism." *Theatre Journal* 40 (1988): 217–235.

Foucault, Michel. *The Order of Things: An Archeology of the Human Sciences.* New York: Pantheon Books, 1970.

———. "Theories et Institutions Penales." *Annuaire du Collège de France.* 1971–1972. Quoted in *Michel Foucault: The Will to Truth,* by Allan Sheridan. London and New York: Tavistock, 1980.

French, Marilyn. *The Women's Room.* New York: Summit Books, 1977.

Friedman, Susan Stanford. "Texts in the Trenches." Review of *No Man's Land: The Place of the Woman Writer in the Twentieth Century,* vol. 1, *The War of the Words,* by Sandra M. Gilbert and Susan Gubar. *Women's Review of Books* (July 1988): 14.

Fryer, Judith. "Women and Space: The Flowering of Desire." *Prospects* 9 (1984): 187–230.

Gallop, Jane. "The Monster in the Mirror: The Feminist Critic's Psychoanalysis." In *Feminism and Psychoanalysis,* ed. Richard Feldstein and Judith Roof, pp. 13–24. Ithaca and London: Cornell University Press, 1989.

Gauthier, Xavière. "Why Witches?" In *New French Feminisms: An Anthology,* ed. Elaine Marks and Isabelle de Courtivron, pp. 199–203. New York: Schocken Books, 1981.

Gearhart, Sally M. *The Wanderground.* Boston: Alyson Publications, 1984.

Gentle, Mary. *Golden Witchbreed.* New York: New American Library, 1985.

Gilbert, Sandra M., and Susan Gubar. *The Madwoman in the Attic: The Woman Writer and the Nineteenth-Century Literary Imagination.* New Haven: Yale University Press, 1979.

———. *No Man's Land: The Place of the Woman Writer in the Twentieth Century.* Vol. 1, *The War of the Words.* New Haven: Yale University Press, 1988.

Gillmore, Inez Haynes. *Angel Island.* New York: New American Library, 1988.

Gilman, Charlotte Perkins. "Benigna Machiavelli." In *The Charlotte Perkins Gilman Reader*, ed. Ann J. Lane, pp. 141–168. New York: Pantheon Books, 1980.

———. "The Cottagette." In *The Charlotte Perkins Gilman Reader*, pp. 47–56.

———. "If I Were a Man." In *The Charlotte Perkins Gilman Reader*, pp. 32–38.

———. "What Diantha Did." In *The Charlotte Perkins Gilman Reader*, pp. 123–140.

———. "When I Was a Witch." In *The Charlotte Perkins Gilman Reader*, pp. 21–31.

———. "The Yellow Wallpaper." In *The Norton Anthology of American Literature*, ed. Nina Baym et al., vol. 2, pp. 649–660. New York: W. W. Norton, 1989.

Godwin, Gail. *The Finishing School*. New York: Avon, 1984.

Goldstein, Lisa. *The Dream Years*. 1985. New York: Bantam, 1986.

Goodman, Nelson. *Ways of Worldmaking*. Indianapolis: Hackett Publishing Company, 1978.

Goodwin, Sarah Webster. "Knowing Better: Feminism and Utopian Discourse in *Pride and Prejudice, Villette*, and 'Babette's Feast.'" In *Feminism, Utopia, and Narrative*, ed. Libby Falk Jones and Sarah Webster Goodwin, pp. 1–20. Knoxville: University of Tennessee Press, 1990.

Goux, Jean-Joseph. *Économie et symbolique*. Paris: Editions du Seuil, 1973.

———. *Les iconoclastes*. Paris: Editions du Seuil, 1978.

Grass, Günter. *The Flounder*. New York: Harcourt Brace Jovanovich, 1978.

Green, Aaron G. "Organic Architecture: The Principles of Frank Lloyd Wright." In *Frank Lloyd Wright in the Realm of Ideas*, ed. Bruce Brooks Pfeiffer and Gerald Nordland, pp. 133–142. Carbondale and Edwardsville: Southern Illinois University Press, 1988.

Gregorian, Vartan. "Brown Expulsion Not about Free Speech." *New York Times*, February 21, 1991.

Gubar, Susan. "'The Blank Page' and the Issue of Female Creativity." In *Writing and Sexual Difference*, ed. Elizabeth Abel, pp. 73–93. Chicago: University of Chicago Press, 1982.

Hall, Sandi. *The Godmothers*. London: Women's Press, 1982.

Haraway, Donna. "A Manifesto for Cyborgs: Science, Technology, and Socialist Feminism in the 1980s." *Socialist Review* 15 (1985): 65–107.

Harding, Sandra. *The Science Question in Feminism*. Ithaca and London: Cornell University Press, 1986.

Hassan, Ihab. "The Literature of Silence." In *The Postmodern Turn: Essays in Postmodern Theory and Culture*, pp. 3–22. Columbus: Ohio State University Press, 1987.

———. "Pluralism in Postmodern Perspective." In *The Postmodern Turn: Essays in Postmodern Theory and Culture*, pp. 167–187.

Hays, H. R. *The Dangerous Sex*. New York: G. P. Putnam, 1964.

Heath, Stephen. "Male Feminism." In *Men in Feminism*, ed. Alice A. Jardine and Paul Smith, pp. 1–32. New York and London: Methuen, 1987.

———. "Men in Feminism: Men and Feminist Theory." In *Men in Feminism*, pp. 41–46.

Heilbrun, Carolyn G. *Writing a Woman's Life*. New York: Ballantine, 1988.

Higgins, Dick. *A Dialectic of Centuries: Notes towards a Theory of the New Arts*. New York and Barton, Vt.: Printed Editions, 1978.

Hill, Carol. *The Eleven Million Mile High Dancer*. New York: Holt, Rinehart, and Winston, 1985.

Hite, Molly. *The Other Side of the Story: Structures and Strategies of Contemporary Feminist Narrative*. Ithaca and London: Cornell University Press, 1989.

Holland, Norman N. "Postmodern Psychoanalysis." In *Innovation/Renovation: New Perspectives on the Humanities*, ed. Ihab Hassan and Sally Hassan, pp. 291–309. Madison: University of Wisconsin Press, 1983.

Hurston, Zora Neale. "The Gilded Six-Bits." In *Spunk: The Selected Stories of Zora Neale Hurston*, pp. 54–69. Berkeley, Calif.: Turtle Island Foundation, 1985.

———. "Isis." In *Spunk: The Selected Stories of Zora Neale Hurston*, pp. 9–18.

———. "Muttsy." In *Spunk: The Selected Stories of Zora Neale Hurston*, pp. 19–37.

———. "Spunk." In *Spunk: The Selected Stories of Zora Neale Hurston*, pp. 1–8.

———. "Sweat." In *Spunk: The Selected Stories of Zora Neale Hurston*, pp. 38–53.

Hutcheon, Linda. *A Poetics of Postmodernism: History, Theory, Fiction*. New York and London: Routledge, 1988.

Irigaray, Luce. *Éthique de la différence sexuelle*. Paris: Minuit, 1984.

Jameson, Fredric. "Postmodernism and Consumer Society." In *Postmodernism and Its Discontents: Theories, Practices*, ed. E. Ann Kaplan, pp. 13–29. London and New York: Verso, 1988.

———. "Postmodernism, or The Cultural Logic of Late Capitalism." *New Left Review* 146 (1984): 53–92.

Jardine, Alice A. *Gynesis: Configurations of Woman and Modernity*. Ithaca and London: Cornell University Press, 1985.

Jardine, Alice A., and Paul Smith, eds. *Men in Feminism*. New York and London: Methuen, 1987.

Johnson, Diane. *Persian Nights*. New York: Fawcett Crest, 1987.

Jong, Erica. *Any Woman's Blues: A Novel of Obsession*. New York: Harper and Row, 1990.

———. *Fear of Flying*. New York: Holt, Rinehart, and Winston, 1973.

———. *Serenissima: A Novel of Venice*. New York: Houghton Mifflin, 1987.

Kaplan, E. Ann. "Introduction." In *Postmodernism and Its Discontents: Theories, Practices*, ed. E. Ann Kaplan, pp. 1–9. London and New York: Verso, 1988.

Keil, Sally Van Wagenen. *Those Wonderful Women in Their Flying Machines: The Unknown Heroines of World War Two*. New York: Rawson, Wade, 1979.

Keller, Evelyn Fox. *Reflections on Gender and Science*. New Haven and London: Yale University Press, 1985.

Kidd, Virginia, ed. *Millennial Women*. New York: Delacorte, 1978.

King, Stephen (writing as Richard Bachman). *Thinner*. New York: New American Library, 1984.

Klein, Renate Duelli. "What's 'New' about the 'New' Reproductive Technologies?" In *Man-Made Women: How New Reproductive Technologies Affect Women*, ed. Gena Corea et al., pp. 64–73. Bloomington: Indiana University Press, 1987.

Knapp, Mona. *Doris Lessing*. New York: Frederick Ungar, 1984.

Kolodny, Annette. "Dancing between Left and Right: Feminism and the Academic Minefield in the 1980s." *Feminist Studies* 14 (1988): 453–466.

Kuhn, Thomas S. *The Structure of Scientific Revolutions*. Chicago: University of Chicago Press, 1970.

Landolfi, Tommaso. "A Woman's Breast." In *Words in Commotion and Other Stories*, ed. Kathrine Jason, pp. 113–124. New York: Penguin Books, 1986.

Lane, Ann J. "The Fictional World of Charlotte Perkins Gilman." In *The*

Charlotte Perkins Gilman Reader, ed. Ann J. Lane, pp. ix–xlii. New York: Pantheon Books, 1980.

Langbaum, Robert. *The Gayety of Vision: A Study of Isak Dinesen's Art.* New York: Random House, 1964.

Law, Richard. "Joanna Russ and the Literature of Exhaustion." *Extrapolation* 23 (1984): 146–156.

Lawrence, D. H. *Women in Love.* 1920. Reprint. New York: Penguin Books, 1985.

Le Guin, Ursula K. "Daddy's Big Girl." *Omni,* January 9, 1987.

———. *The Dispossessed: An Ambiguous Utopia.* New York: Harper and Row, 1974.

———. "Sur." In *The Norton Anthology of Literature by Women,* ed. Sandra M. Gilbert and Susan Gubar, pp. 2007–2022. New York: Norton, 1985.

———. "Why Are Americans Afraid of Dragons?" In *The Language of the Night: Essays on Fantasy and Science Fiction,* ed. Susan Wood, pp. 39–45. New York: G. P. Putnam, 1979.

Leith, Linda. "Canopus in Limbo." *Science-Fiction Studies.* (1986): 320–321.

Lem, Stanislaw. "Todorov's Fantastic Theory of Literature." In *Microworlds: Writings on Science Fiction and Fantasy,* ed. Franz Rottensteiner, pp. 209–232. San Diego: Harcourt Brace Jovanovich, 1984.

Lessing, Doris. *Documents Relating to the Sentimental Agents in the Volyen Empire.* New York: Knopf, 1983.

———. *The Making of the Representative for Planet 8.* New York: Knopf, 1982.

———. *The Marriages between Zones Three, Four, and Five.* New York: Random House, 1980.

———. *Memoirs of a Survivor.* New York: Knopf, 1975.

———. *Re: Colonised Planet 5, Shikasta.* New York: Knopf, 1979.

———. *The Sirian Experiments: The Report by Ambien II, of the Five.* New York: Knopf, 1980.

Levi, Primo. *The Drowned and the Saved.* New York: Random House, 1989.

Levin, Ira. *Rosemary's Baby.* New York: Dell, 1979.

Lévy, Bernard-Henri. *Barbarism with a Human Face.* 1977. New York: Harper and Row, 1979.

Lyotard, Jean-Françoise. "Answering the Question: What Is Postmodernism?" In *Innovation/Renovation: New Perspectives on the Humanities,* ed. Ihab Hassan and Sally Hassan, pp. 329–341. Madison: University of Wisconsin Press, 1983.

manities, ed. Ihab Hassan and Sally Hassan, pp. 329–341. Madison: University of Wisconsin Press, 1983.

————. *The Postmodern Condition: A Report on Knowledge.* Minneapolis: University of Minnesota Press, 1979.

Markham, Beryl. *West with the Night.* 1942. Reprint. San Francisco: North Point Press, 1987.

Masback, Craig A. "Siren of Speed." *Ms.* (October 1988): 34–35.

Masters, Hilary. *Cooper.* New York: St. Martin's Press, 1987.

McCaffery, Larry. *Postmodern Fiction: A Bio-Bibliographical Guide.* Westport, Conn.: Greenwood Press, 1986.

McHale, Brian. *Postmodernist Fiction.* New York and London: Methuen, 1987.

Merchant, Carolyn. *The Death of Nature: Women, Ecology, and the Scientific Revolution.* New York: Harper and Row, 1980.

Miller, Nancy K. "Emphasis Added: Plots and Plausibilities in Women's Fiction." In *The New Feminist Criticism: Essays on Women, Literature, and Theory,* ed. Elaine Showalter, pp. 339–360. New York: Pantheon Books, 1985.

————. *Subject to Change: Reading Feminist Writing.* New York: Columbia University Press, 1988.

Miner, Valerie. *All Good Women.* Freedom, Calif.: Crossing Press, 1987.

————. "Writing Fiction across Generations." *Sojourner: The Women's Forum* 13 (1988): 22–23.

Minow-Pinkney, Makiko. *Virginia Woolf and the Problem of the Subject.* New Brunswick, N.J.: Rutgers University Press, 1987.

Mitchison, Naomi Haldane. *Memoirs of a Spacewoman.* London: Women's Press, 1985.

Moi, Toril. *Sexual/Textual Politics.* London and New York: Methuen, 1986.

Morris, Meaghan. *The Pirate's Fiancée: Feminism, Reading, Postmodernism.* London and New York: Verso, 1988.

Ms. "The New Politician." (July/August 1990): 59.

Namjoshi, Suniti. *The Conversations of Cow.* London: Women's Press, 1985.

Orbach, Susie. *Fat Is a Feminist Issue: The Anti-Diet Guide to Permanent Weight Loss.* New York: Berkley, 1987.

Palmer, Jane. *The Planet Dweller.* London: Women's Press, 1985.

————. *The Watcher.* London: Women's Press, 1986.

Phelps, Elizabeth Stuart. "The True Story of Guenever." In *Haunted*

Women: The Best Supernatural Tales by American Women Writers, ed. Alfred Bendixen, pp. 66–79. New York: Frederick Ungar, 1985.

Piercy, Marge. *Gone to Soldiers.* New York: Summit Books, 1987.

———. *Small Changes.* New York: Fawcett Crest, 1972.

Piserchia, Doris. *Star Rider.* London: Women's Press, 1987.

Plath, Sylvia. "Lady Lazarus." In *The Norton Anthology of Modern Poetry,* ed. Richard Ellmann and Robert O'Clair, p. 1295. New York: W. W. Norton, 1973.

Pynchon, Thomas. *The Crying of Lot 49.* 1966. Reprint. New York: Bantam, 1982.

Rabkin, Eric S. *The Fantastic in Literature.* Princeton: Princeton University Press, 1976.

Reed, Ishmael. *Flight to Canada.* New York: Random House, 1976.

Roberts, Robin. "Postmodernism and Feminist Science Fiction." *Science-Fiction Studies* 17 (1990): 136–152.

Roth, Philip. "The Breast." In *A Philip Roth Reader,* pp. 445–483. New York: Farrar, Straus and Giroux, 1980.

Rowland, Robyn. "Motherhood, Patriarchal Power, Alienation, and the Issue of 'Choice' in Sex Preselection." In *Man-Made Women: How New Reproductive Technologies Affect Women,* ed. Gena Corea et al., pp. 74–87. Bloomington: Indiana University Press, 1987.

———. "Reproductive Technologies: The Final Solution to the Woman Question?" In *Test-Tube Women: What Future for Motherhood?,* ed. Rita Arditti, Renate Duelli Klein, and Shelley Minden, pp. 356–369. London: Pandora Press, 1985.

Russ, Joanna. *The Female Man.* 1975. Reprint. New York: Gregg Press, 1977.

———. "The Image of Women in Science Fiction." In *Images of Women in Fiction: Feminist Perspectives,* ed. Susan Koppelman Cornillon, pp. 79–94. Bowling Green, Ohio: Popular Press, 1972.

———. Letter to Marleen Barr, March 4, 1991.

———. *On Strike against God.* Trumansburg, N.Y.: Crossing Press, 1980.

———. "Recent Feminist Utopias." In *Future Females: A Critical Anthology,* ed. Marleen Barr, pp. 71–85. Bowling Green, Ohio: Popular Press, 1981.

———. "Reflections on Science Fiction: An Interview with Joanna Russ." *Quest: A Feminist Quarterly* 2 (1975): 40–49.

———. "What Can a Heroine Do? Or Why Women Can't Write." In *Images of Women in Fiction: Feminist Perspectives,* ed. Susan Koppelman Cornillon, pp. 3–20. Bowling Green, Ohio: Popular Press, 1972.

———. "When It Changed." In *The Norton Anthology of Literature by Women*, ed. Sandra M. Gilbert and Susan Gubar, pp. 2262–2269. New York: Norton, 1985.

Russo, Mary. "Female Grotesques: Carnival and Theory." In *Feminist Studies/Critical Studies*, ed. Teresa de Lauretis, pp. 213–229. Bloomington: Indiana University Press, 1986.

Sagan, Carl, et al. *Murmurs of Earth: The Voyager Interstellar Record.* New York: Random House, 1978.

Sargent, Pamela. *The Alien Upstairs.* 1983. Reprint. New York: Bantam, 1985.

———. *The Shore of Women.* New York: Crown, 1986.

Scarborough, Elizabeth Ann. "The Camelot Connection." In *Invitation to Camelot*, ed. Parke Godwin, pp. 47–82. New York: Ace Books, 1988.

Schmidt, William E. "Shouts, Tears and Applause amid a Vast Wave of Relief." *New York Times*, September 30, 1988.

Schmitt, Eric. "Senate Votes to Remove Ban on Women as Combat Pilots." *New York Times*, August 1, 1991.

Scholes, Robert. *Fabulation and Metafiction.* Urbana: University of Illinois Press, 1979.

———. *The Fabulators.* New York: Oxford University Press, 1967.

———. "Foreword." In *The Fantastic: A Structural Approach to a Literary Genre*, by Tzvetan Todorov, pp. v–xi. 1970. Reprint. Ithaca, N.Y.: Cornell University Press, 1975.

———. "The Roots of Science Fiction." In *Science Fiction: A Collection of Critical Essays*, ed. Mark Rose, pp. 46–56. Englewood Cliffs, N.J.: Prentice-Hall, 1976.

———. *Structural Fabulation: An Essay on the Fiction of the Future.* Notre Dame and London: Notre Dame University Press, 1975.

Schor, Naomi. "The Portrait of a Gentleman: Representing Men in (French) Women's Writing." *Representations* 20 (1987): 113–133.

Schwartz, Hillel. *Never Satisfied: A Cultural History of Diets, Fantasies and Fat.* New York: Free Press, 1986.

Scott, Jody. *I, Vampire.* London: Women's Press, 1986.

———. *Passing for Human.* London: Women's Press, 1986.

Showalter, Elaine. "Feminist Criticism in the Wilderness." In *The New Feminist Criticism: Essays on Women, Literature, and Theory*, ed. Elaine Showalter, pp. 243–270. New York: Pantheon Books, 1985.

———. "Women's Time, Women's Space: Writing the History of Feminist Criticism." *Tulsa Studies in Women's Literature* 3 (1984): 29–43.

Silk, Mark. "The Hot History Department." *New York Times Magazine*, April 19, 1987.

Simpson, Mona. *Anywhere But Here.* New York: Knopf, 1986.

Slonczewski, Joan. *A Door into Ocean.* New York: Avon, 1986.

Smith, Paul. "Men in Feminism: Men and Feminist Theory." In *Men in Feminism*, ed. Alice A. Jardine and Paul Smith, pp. 33–46. New York and London: Methuen, 1987.

Sobchack, Vivian. "The Virginity of Astronauts: Sex and the Science Fiction Film." In *Shadows of the Magic Lamp: Fantasy and Science Fiction in Film*, ed. Eric S. Rabkin and George Slusser, pp. 41–57. Carbondale: Southern Illinois University Press, 1985.

Staël, Madame de (Anne Louise Germaine). *Corinne, or Italy.* New Brunswick, N.J.: Rutgers University Press, 1987.

Steinbacher, Roberta. "Futuristic Implications of Sex Preselection." In *The Custom-made Child? Women-centred Perspectives*, ed. Helen B. Holmes, Betty B. Hoskins, and Michael Gross, pp. 187–191. Clifton, N.J.: Humana Press, 1981.

Stimpson, Catharine R. "Woolf's Room, Our Project: The Building of Feminist Criticism." In *The Future of Literary Theory*, ed. Ralph Cohen, pp. 129–143. New York and London: Routledge, 1989.

Suvin, Darko. *Metamorphoses of Science Fiction: On the Poetics and History of a Literary Genre.* New Haven and London: Yale University Press, 1979.

Tillman, Lynne. *Haunted Houses.* New York: Poseidon Press, 1987.

Tiptree, James, Jr. "Love Is the Plan, the Plan Is Death." In *Warm Worlds and Otherwise*, ed. Robert Silverberg, pp. 173–193. New York: Ballantine, 1975.

———. *Up the Walls of the World.* New York: Berkley, 1978.

———. "The Women Men Don't See." In *Warm Worlds and Otherwise*, ed. Robert Silverberg, pp. 131–164. New York: Ballantine, 1975.

Todorov, Tzvetan. *The Fantastic: A Structural Approach to a Literary Genre.* 1970. Reprint. Ithaca, N.Y.: Cornell University Press, 1975.

Tompkins, Jane. "West of Everything." *South Atlantic Quarterly* 86 (1987): 357–377.

Toth, Emily. "Female Wits." *Massachusetts Review* 22 (1981): 783–793.

Trask, Haunani-Kay. *Eros and Power: The Promise of Feminist Theory.* Philadelphia: University of Pennsylvania Press, 1986.

Updike, John. *S*. New York: Knopf, 1988.

Van Scyoc, Sydney J. *Star Mother*. New York: Berkley, 1976.

Varnedde, Kirk, and Adam Gopnik. *High & Low Modern Art and Popular Culture*. New York: Museum of Modern Art, 1990.

Vonnegut, Kurt. *Slaughterhouse Five*. 1966. Reprint. New York: Dell, 1968.

Walker, Alice. "In Search of Our Mothers' Gardens." In *The Norton Anthology of Literature by Women*, ed. Sandra M. Gilbert and Susan Gubar, pp. 2374–2382. New York: Norton, 1985.

Warner, Susan. *The Wide, Wide World*. 1878. Reprint. New York: Feminist Press, 1986.

Wasserman, Harvey. *America Born and Reborn*. New York: Macmillan, 1983.

Waugh, Patricia. *Feminine Fictions: Revisiting the Postmodern*. London and New York: Routledge, 1989.

———. *Metafiction: The Theory and Practice of Self-Conscious Fiction*. London and New York: Methuen, 1984.

Weedon, Chris. *Feminist Practice and Poststructuralist Theory*. Oxford: Basil Blackwell, 1987.

Weldon, Fay. *The Cloning of Joanna May*. New York: Viking Penguin, 1990.

———. *Darcy's Utopia*. New York: Viking Penguin, 1991.

White, Leslie. "Spreading the Word, Thin(ly): The Limits of Pop Feminism." *American Quarterly* 41 (1989): 563–567.

Wilford, John Noble. "Space Shuttle, after 32 Months, Makes Comeback Attempt Today." *New York Times*, September 29, 1988.

Wolf, Christa. *Cassandra*. In *Cassandra: A Novel and Four Essays*, pp. 3–138. New York: Farrar, Straus and Giroux, 1984.

———. "Conditions of a Narrative: Cassandra." In *Cassandra: A Novel and Four Essays*, pp. 141–305.

———. "Self-Experiment: Appendix to a Report." *New German Critique* 13 (1978): 109–131.

Woolf, Virginia. *Orlando*. 1928. Reprint. Orlando, Fla.: Harcourt Brace Jovanovich, 1956.

———. *To the Lighthouse*. New York: Harcourt, Brace, 1927.

Wrede, Stuart. "Introduction." In *Emilio Ambasz Steven Holl Architecture*, pp. 2–3. New York: Museum of Modern Art, 1989.

Wright, Frank Lloyd. *Buildings, Plans and Designs*. New York: Horizon Press, 1963.

———. *The Natural House*. New York: Horizon Press, 1954.

———. *A Testament.* New York: Horizon Press, 1957.

Yaeger, Patricia. *Honey-Mad Women: Emancipatory Strategies in Women's Writing.* New York: Columbia University Press, 1988.

Zimmerman, Bonnie. "Feminist Fiction and the Postmodern Challenge." In *Postmodern Fiction: A Bio-Bibliographical Guide,* ed. Larry McCaffery, pp. 175–188. Westport, Conn.: Greenwood Press, 1986.

★ ○ ☽ ★ ○ ☽ ★ ○ ☽

Index

Le Guin, Ursula, 6–7, 15, 158, 170–172, 223, 252
Leith, Linda, 16
Lem, Stanislaw, 200, 284
Lenin, Vladimir Ilyich, 70
Lessing, Doris, xiv, xix, xxiii, 12, 17, 22, 36–37, 134, 151–155, 158, 160–161, 163, 168–170, 175, 179
Levi, Primo, 10, 276
Lévy, Bernard-Henri, 10, 275–276
"The Library of Babel" (Borges), 24
Little Women (Alcott), 13
Love, Nancy, 69
"Love Is the Plan, the Plan Is Death" (Tiptree), 36
Low art stigma, xx–xxi
Lyotard, Jean-François, xviii, 154–155, 246, 248–250

McCaffery, Larry, xiii
McHale, Brian, xiii, xvi, xix–xx, xxviii, 64–66, 69–71, 80, 145, 202, 255
Machinery of dominance, 68
McIntyre, Vonda, 4, 9
Magritte, René, xxi, xxiv, 3, 227–228
Mailer, Norman, 44
The Making of the Representative for Planet 8 (Lessing), 36–37
Markham, Beryl, xxii, 52, 93
The Marriages between Zones Three, Four, and Five (Lessing), 134, 152, 156–159, 161
Marriott Marquis (hotel), xxv
Masters, Hilary, xxii, 52–57, 59, 89, 93
Memoirs of a Space Woman (Mitchison), 43
Memoirs of a Survivor (Lessing), 17
Merchant, Carolyn, 105
Miller, Nancy K., 3, 7, 186–189, 275

Miner, Valerie, xx, xxii, 52, 57–66, 70, 74–75, 85, 90, 92–93
Minow-Pinkney, Makiko, 148, 150, 173
The Mists of Avalon (Bradley), 22
Mitchison, Naomi Haldane, 43
Moby-Dick (Melville), 140
Moi, Toril, 12–14
Mommy Track, 197
Monroe, Marilyn, 122, 167, 170
Monster Rally (Addams), 139
More Die of Heartbreak (Bellow), 10, 133–141, 147, 150–152, 155, 157, 179
Morris, Meaghan, 185
Morrison, Toni, xii, xix, 39
Motherlines (Charnas), 170
"Muttsy" (Hurston), 27
My Fair Lady, 145–146
Myth of feminine evil, 161

Namjoshi, Suniti, 153, 155, 157
Native Tongue (Elgin), 14
Nights at the Circus (Carter), 52, 90–93
"Night Walk" (Dinesen), 24
Nixon, Richard, 70, 175

"Of Hidden Thoughts and of Heaven" (Dinesen), 24–25
Oldenburg, Claes, xxi–xxii, 23
"The Old Man and the Sea" (Hemingway), 140
On Strike against God (Russ), 114, 127
Orlando (Woolf), 35–39, 173

Paley, Grace, xix
Palmer, Jane, xii, xxii, 52, 89, 222
Paradigm shift, 5–7
Paradise (Barthelme), 99, 116, 126–131, 136
"Paraguay" (Barthelme), 202